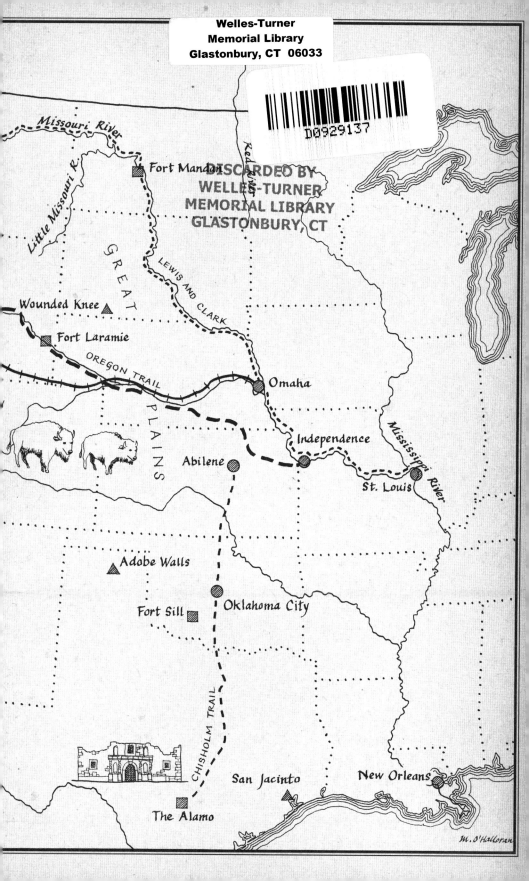

Missouri River

Little Missouri R.

Fort Mandan

Red River

GREAT

LEWIS AND CLARK

Wounded Knee

Fort Laramie

OREGON TRAIL

PLAINS

Omaha

Independence

Mississippi River

Abilene

St. Louis

Adobe Walls

Fort Sill

Oklahoma City

CHISHOLM TRAIL

San Jacinto

New Orleans

The Alamo

M. O'Halloran

DREAMS OF EL DORADO

ALSO BY H. W. BRANDS

Heirs of the Founders

The General vs. the President

Reagan

The Man Who Saved the Union

American Colossus

Traitor to His Class

Andrew Jackson

Lone Star Nation

The Age of Gold

The First American

TR

DREAMS OF EL DORADO

A HISTORY OF THE AMERICAN WEST

H. W. BRANDS

BASIC BOOKS

New York

Basic Books
Hachette Book Group
1290 Avenue of the Americas, New York, NY 10104
www.basicbooks.com

Printed in the United States of America

First Edition: September 2019

Published by Basic Books, an imprint of Perseus Books, LLC, a subsidiary of Hachette Book Group, Inc. The Basic Books name and logo is a trademark of the Hachette Book Group.

The Hachette Speakers Bureau provides a wide range of authors for speaking events. To find out more, go to www.hachettespeakersbureau.com or call (866) 376-6591.

The publisher is not responsible for websites (or their content) that are not owned by the publisher.

Images courtesy of the Library of Congress

Print book interior design by Trish Wilkinson

Library of Congress Cataloging-in-Publication Data

Names: Brands, H. W., author.
Title: Dreams of El Dorado : a history of the American West / H.W. Brands.
Description: New York : Basic Books, Hachette Book Group, 2019. | Includes
    bibliographical references and index.
Identifiers: LCCN 2018048887 (print) | LCCN 2018050581 (ebook) | ISBN
    9781541672536 (ebook) | ISBN 9781541672529 (hardcover)
Subjects: LCSH: West (U.S.)—Discovery and exploration. | West
    (U.S.)—History. | United States—Territorial expansion. | Frontier and
    pioneer life—United States.
Classification: LCC F591 (ebook) | LCC F591 .B814 2019 (print) | DDC
    978/.02—dc23
LC record available at https://lccn.loc.gov/2018048887

ISBNs: 978-1-5416-7252-9 (hardcover); 978-1-5416-7253-6 (ebook)

LSC-C

10 9 8 7 6 5 4 3 2 1

CONTENTS

PART IV: THE GREAT MIGRATION

PART V: THE WORLD IN A NUGGET OF GOLD

PART VI: STEEL RAILS AND SHARPS RIFLES

PART VII: THE MIDDLE BORDER

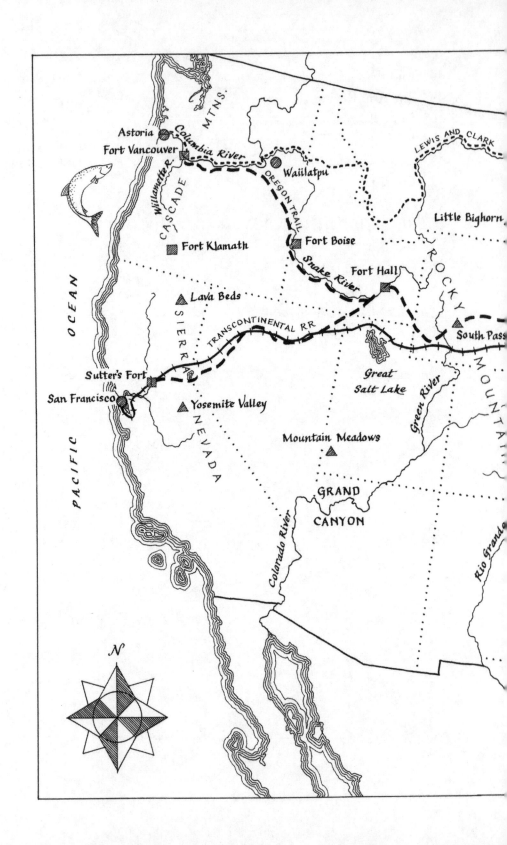

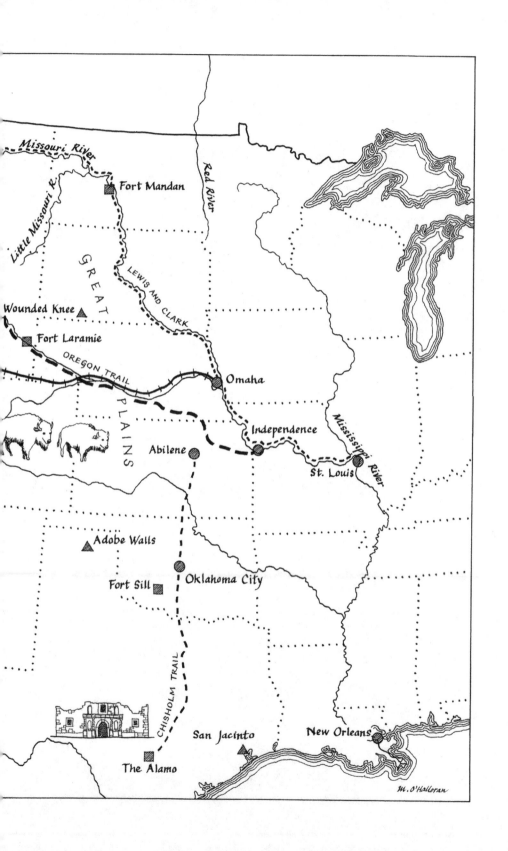

Missouri River

Little Missouri R.

Fort Mandan

Red River

G R E A T

LEWIS AND CLARK

Wounded Knee

Fort Laramie

OREGON TRAIL

P L A I N S

Omaha

Independence

Mississippi River

St. Louis

Abilene

Adobe Walls

Fort Sill

Oklahoma City

CHISHOLM TRAIL

San Jacinto

New Orleans

The Alamo

M. O'Halloran

PROLOGUE

F OR THEODORE ROOSEVELT IT WAS LOVE AT FIRST SIGHT.
Which was saying a lot, since Roosevelt's first sight of the
West didn't show the region to best effect. The young New Yorker,
plagued in boyhood by illness and a sense of physical insufficiency,
had long dreamed of the West. Its explorers, hunters, soldiers and
cowboys became his heroes, the models of the man he struggled to
be. On a break from a budding political career, he took a Western
vacation in 1883. He rode a train across the prairies west of Chicago and onto the high plains of Dakota Territory. In the middle
of the night the Northern Pacific conductor deposited him at the
scruffy hamlet of Little Missouri, where the rail line crossed the
river of that name. "It was bitterly cold," he wrote to his wife, Alice, though the calendar registered early September. "And it was
some time before, groping about among the four or five shanties
which formed the 'town,' I found the low, small building called the
'hotel.'" Roosevelt hammered on the door and eventually roused
the innkeeper, who cursed him for spoiling his sleep. The visitor
was shown to a barracks room, where he spent the rest of the night
amid snoring, snorting men the likes of which the silk-stocking
Manhattanite had rarely seen, let alone slumbered with.

Morning made him wonder what had brought him to this
locale. "It is a very desolate place," he wrote, "high, barren hills,
scantily clad with coarse grass, and here and there in sheltered

places a few stunted cottonwood trees; 'wash-outs,' deepening at times into great canyons, and steep cliffs of the most curious formation abounding everywhere." The scenery didn't improve on closer examination. Roosevelt enlisted a guide to show him the Badlands, as the crazily eroded terrain was called. They rode mustangs—horses as wild in appearance as the land—around and through the gullies, hoodoos, buttes and cliffs. It was "frightful ground," Roosevelt said. And utterly inhospitable. "There is very little water, and what there is, is so bitter as to be almost a poison, and nearly undrinkable."

The weather was as dismal as the scenery. The autumn rains commenced upon Roosevelt's arrival, and for days the leaden sky poured, drizzled and misted, turning ground that had been dusty days before into a sticky, bottomless gumbo. Roosevelt had come to Dakota to hunt buffalo; he had been told that some of the last remnants of the once uncountable herds had been seen on the Little Missouri. But his guide was reluctant to venture out into the slop. The buffalo knew enough to take shelter, he said; so should hunters. Yet Roosevelt insisted, and offered a bonus. Out they went. They got cold, soaked and muddy. And they found no buffalo. But Roosevelt, who equated tests of the body with tests of the soul, found the experience exhilarating. He had been slightly ailing before coming west. No longer. "I am now feeling very well, and am enjoying the life very much," he told Alice.

Eventually the weather broke. His guide located a buffalo—a feat the nearsighted Roosevelt could never have managed on his own. Roosevelt skirted downwind of the beast, which was even more myopic than he was, and crawled close enough to get a shot. He fired once, then twice more. The buffalo took off running. Roosevelt thought he might have missed entirely. But he and the guide gave chase, and after crossing a ridge they discovered the buffalo lying dead on its side. Roosevelt whooped for joy and did a victory dance. He pulled out a hundred-dollar bill and gave the guide a bonus.

The experience persuaded Roosevelt to plant a flag in the West. His difficulty finding a buffalo drove home the fact that the West was changing; the indigenous bovines were being replaced by introduced ones: cattle. Roosevelt scouted the opportunities for investment in the cattle industry, and before he left Dakota he designated two locals as his agents, with instructions to buy him a cattle ranch. Believing Westerners more honest than the swindlers he knew in the East, where his political enemies included the grafters of New York's Tammany Hall, Roosevelt wrote a check for fourteen thousand dollars and accepted no security beyond a handshake.

He got his ranch and became a cattleman. He struggled to master the arts of the cowboy. To Roosevelt, as to many of his generation in America, the cowboy was the embodiment of the West and of its spirit of rugged individualism. If Roosevelt could prove himself as hardy, as resourceful, as brave and strong as the cowboys who rode the Dakota range, he would have become the man he longed to be.

He made an odd figure for a cowboy. His laconic neighbors chuckled at the "Bully!" and "Deee*light*ed!" that burst from his mouth. His thick eyeglasses earned him the inevitable moniker "Four-eyes," which alternated with "the Dude." But his determination and stamina eventually won him the respect of his new comrades. He learned to ride like a cowboy, rope like a cowboy, herd cattle like a cowboy, stand up to thieves and other bad men like a cowboy.

He poured his inheritance into his Dakota ranch, and following the untimely death of his wife, he poured his heart into it. Alice had been his only true love, and he was devastated by her loss. He sought refuge on the ranch and in the solitude of the Badlands. He fell under the spell of the West. "I have been three weeks on the roundup and have worked as hard as any of the cowboys," he wrote from the range to an Eastern friend. "But I have enjoyed it greatly. Yesterday I was eighteen hours in the saddle—from 4 a.m.

to 10 p.m.—having a half hour each for dinner and tea. I can now do cowboy work pretty well."

He dreamed of becoming a cattle baron, a Western equivalent of the business tycoons of the East. Many others had made fortunes in the West; why couldn't he?

He learned soon enough. Winters in Dakota had been deceptively mild during the brief time since whites had begun settling there. The winter of 1886–1887 reverted to the mean, and then some. Rainfall had been scanter than usual that summer, and it didn't pick up in the fall. The cattle became thin, rather than packing on the weight needed to carry them through the winter. And winter came early. A typical winter on the plains featured brief storms that dropped a few to several inches of dry snow on the ground and then abated. The air might be cold, but the snow wasn't too deep for the cattle to paw aside, baring the cured grass beneath. This winter was different. The first storm came in November as a full-bore blizzard. It caught the cattle not only thin from the summer but lacking their winter coats. It dropped drifts of snow that defied the efforts of the hungry animals to dig through it. Where they did manage to penetrate to the bottom of the drifts, there wasn't any grass, due to the summer's drought.

This first storm was followed by another, and another. Temperatures plummeted far below zero. The cowboys, who normally thought nothing of risking their lives for the cattle, couldn't leave their cabins without themselves freezing in minutes. The cattle sought shelter in creek bottoms and wherever the wind slackened. But it was in precisely these places that the snow drifted deepest, burying the cows until they couldn't move or even breathe.

The winter went on and on. The cattlemen could only guess at the toll it was taking on the herds. When spring finally came, they got their answer. "In the latter part of March came the Chinook wind, harbinger of spring, releasing for the first time the iron grip that had been upon us," recalled a neighbor of Roosevelt on the Little Missouri. "At last, it seemed, the wrath of Nature had been appeased." The ice in the river broke apart, and the stream brought it down in big chunks. It soon brought something else, something the cattlemen could never have imagined. "For days on end, tearing down with the grinding ice cakes, went Death's cattle roundup of the upper Little Missouri country," Roosevelt's neighbor continued. "In countless valleys, gulches, washouts, and coulees, the animals had vainly sought shelter from the relentless 'Northern Furies' on their trail. Now their carcasses were being spewed forth in untold thousands by the rushing waters, to be carried away on the crest of the foaming, turgid flood rushing down the valley."

ROOSEVELT'S WESTERN DREAM DIDN'T SURVIVE THAT BRUTAL winter. He gradually retired from the West and returned to politics in the East. But he never lost his emotional connection to the West, nor his belief that the West, for all its ability to shatter dreams, was where the American spirit shone brightest and most true.

The evoking and shattering of dreams was one theme of Western history. A second touched Roosevelt less directly, but he benefited from it nonetheless. Roosevelt's Dakota ranch lay two hundred miles from the battlefield where Lakota warriors under Sitting Bull and Crazy Horse had annihilated a contingent of the U.S. 7th Cavalry led by George Custer a decade earlier. The victory had been a pyrrhic one for the Indians, for it prompted a federal response that broke the back of native resistance to white encroachment upon Indian lands. It was no accident that the demise of the Plains tribes coincided with the destruction of the buffalo, which had long been their sustenance. The violence against the Plains Indians and the buffalo was merely the latest, and, as it turned out, almost the last, manifestation of the persistent violence that had marked the West since before it became American.

Roosevelt was too sober-minded to appreciate a third theme of Western history. Irony is inherent in human endeavor and therefore human history, but in no area of American history has irony—in the form of paradox, contradiction and unintended consequence—been more central to the tale than in the West. The

West was often viewed as the last bastion of American individualism, but woven through its entire history was a strong thread—at times a cable—of collectivism. Western individualism sneered, even snarled, at federal power, but federal power was essential to the development of the West. The West was America's unspoiled Eden, but the spoilage of the West proceeded more rapidly than that of any other region. The West was the land of wide open spaces, but its residents were more concentrated in cities and towns than in most of the East. The West was where whites fought Indians, but they rarely went into battle without Indian allies, and their ranks included black soldiers. The West was where fortune beckoned, where riches would reward the miner's persistence, the cattleman's courage, the railroad man's enterprise, the bonanza farmer's audacity; but El Dorado was at least as elusive in the West as it ever was in the East.

Its elusiveness simply added to its allure. Dreams of El Dorado inspired one generation of Americans after another to head west. Not all sought immense wealth, but most expected a greater competence than they could find in the East. Their dreams drove them to feats of courage and perseverance that put their stay-at-home cousins to shame; their dreams also drove them to acts of violence against indigenous peoples, foreigners and one another that might have appalled them if they hadn't been so hell-bent on chasing the dreams.

Any work of history must have a beginning and an end. This one commences with the Louisiana Purchase at the start of the nineteenth century, when the United States first gained a foothold—a very large one—beyond the Mississippi. It ends in the early twentieth century, when the West had become enough like the East to make the Western experience most comprehensible as a piece of the American whole rather than as a thing apart. Western dreams didn't die; Hollywood and Silicon Valley would be built on such dreams. But the dreams were no longer as distinctively Western as they once had been.

I

NAPOLEON'S GIFT

1

THE RIVER AT
THE HEART OF AMERICA

AMERICA'S WEST ENTERED HUMAN HISTORY AS ASIA'S EAST
and Beringia's south. Except that Asia, in that archaic time,
didn't think of itself as Asia, and Beringia, the northern plain that
connected Asia and America when the oceans were low, didn't
think of itself as anything at all. It was cold, windy and barren, the
sort of place people transited rather than settled. The transit took
hunters from Asia to America, where they spread and multiplied.
The process consumed thousands of years, during which the earth's
climate warmed, glaciers melted, sea levels rose, Beringia was submerged, and the hunters, now Americans, were cut off from Asia
and its peoples.

They forgot where they had come from; most developed origin stories that fixed them in place from time immemorial. They
knew as little of the peoples beyond the Americas as those peoples
knew of them. At least once the two worlds met: when Norse-
men planted a colony on the Atlantic coast of what would become
Canada. But the colony didn't last, and knowledge of its existence,
which had never spread far inland, faded.

In a few places dense populations developed and, with them,
cities and elaborate systems of government. From the Valley of Mexico the Aztecs conquered an empire. The Mayas did

something similar in lowland Central America, and the Incas in the Andes Mountains of South America. But elsewhere populations were mostly thinner, and governments less complicated.

Different factors inhibited population growth in different regions. In what would become the American West, the critical constraint was lack of water. A coastal strip beside the Pacific caught clouds and rain, and mountains inland snagged snow in winter, feeding a few large rivers. But elsewhere—in the valleys and basins between the mountains, and on the great plains that would form the eastern zone of the West—aridity was the unrelenting theme. Agriculture was out of the question, for the most part; the inhabitants hunted, fished and gathered to support themselves. The optimal size of bands of hunters and gatherers is no more than a few hundred, and they require large amounts of land to sustain themselves. Even today, an air traveler crossing the West is struck by the barrenness of vast parts of it. The vegetation is sparse, and evidence of humans sparser still.

In select spots, however, nature and the cleverness of those humans combined to sustain larger communities. Along the Columbia River and its tributaries, the spawning salmon made the fishing peoples rich and powerful. A thousand miles to the southeast, where the Rio Grande descends from the Rocky Mountains en route to the southern desert, communities of farmers corralled the runoff from the mountains to irrigate crops of corn and beans and squash. They built small cities of stone and dried mud—nothing like the grand cities of Mexico and Peru, but notable for the American West. And on the Great Plains, enormous herds of bison, or buffalo, provided the same kind of concentrated food source that salmon did in the Northwest. The buffalo weren't as helpful as the salmon in gathering for their own slaughter; the peoples of the Great Plains had to chase the buffalo, much as their Siberian and Beringian ancestors had chased deer and woolly mammoths to America in the first place. The moving limited the size of the Plains bands and tribes, but the resource was reliable and their existence relatively secure.

But only *relatively* secure. The fat living of the favored peoples drew the attention of hungrier sorts. Competition developed for control of the hunting and fishing grounds and the corn and bean fields. Nothing like the wars of Europe and Asia—lasting years or decades and involving tens of thousands of soldiers—occurred in the American West; even the most favored tribes lacked the numbers and resources for such hostilities. But the wars of the West could be sharply violent. A tribe seeking to displace the possessor of a bountiful ground might wipe out an entire village and move in. Warring tribes carried off women and children to boost their own populations, sometimes enslaving the captives, sometimes incorporating them into the tribes.

Successful tribes grew stronger; unsuccessful ones diminished and occasionally disappeared. Fragments of failing tribes might band together to create a new tribe, or they might apply to join a successful one. The tribes of the West lacked writing, and such records as recalled the histories of tribes were generally oral, handed down from generation to generation. But in a few places physical remains told of earlier times and peoples. The Pueblo peoples of the upper Rio Grande lived among ruins left by predecessors they called the Anasazi, who had vanished for reasons unknown. The ghosts of the Anasazi whispered among the ruins, but what they said the Pueblos couldn't quite grasp.

AT THE HEART OF NORTH AMERICA WAS THE GREATEST RIVER of the continent, whose tributaries drained most of what would become the United States. The Mississippi took its name from an Ojibwa phrase for "great river," and it had three main branches. The Ohio River originated in the mountains of the East and flowed west. The Mississippi proper rose in the North and ran south. The Missouri began in the highlands of the West and flowed east. Especially in those days before convenient and cheap land travel—and long before air travel—the Mississippi held the key to the future of much of the continent.

The victory of the United States in the Revolutionary War delivered the eastern half of the Mississippi basin to the new nation. The western half, originally claimed by France, had been transferred to Spain to keep it out of British control. Until this point the name Louisiana had applied to the whole Mississippi watershed; henceforward it meant just the western half of the region. Yet this was still a mighty realm, larger than modern Mexico.

And now it was Spanish. Or rather, its title was Spanish: in nomenclature—*Louisiane* became *Luisiana*—and in international law. Its people were French, African and Native American. The French merchants and planters, the African and African American slaves, and the Native Americans belonging to scores of different tribes paid little attention to the change of management. Most likely a majority of the people who lived within the boundaries of Louisiana—the Mississippi in the east, the crest of the Rocky Mountains in the west, the Red River Valley of Texas in the south, the Milk River basin of Canada in the north—never knew their home had changed hands. French authority had been notional beyond New Orleans, the city near the mouth of the Mississippi, and in a few other populated spots. Spanish authority, stretched painfully thin in New Spain, was vaguer still.

Yet it was sufficient to rankle the Americans who depended on the Mississippi for their livelihood. In the days before canals and railroads, nearly everything grown, mined or manufactured in the Ohio and Mississippi valleys funneled down to New Orleans, where it was gathered and loaded onto ocean-going ships bound for the American East Coast, the West Indies and Europe. Whoever controlled New Orleans controlled the fate of all those American farmers, miners and manufacturers. In the negotiations at the end of the Revolutionary War, Benjamin Franklin insisted on the importance of the Mississippi to America's future. "I would rather agree with them to buy at a great price the whole of their right on the Mississippi than sell a drop of its waters," Franklin said, referring to the Spanish. "A neighbor might as well ask me to sell my street door."

Franklin and America got a partial right to the Mississippi. American territory included most of the eastern bank of the Mississippi, conferring navigation rights on that stretch of the river. But Spain kept Florida, whose panhandle then ran all the way to the Mississippi and Spanish Louisiana. Thus the Spanish controlled both banks of the river near its mouth, and hence the river itself. Franklin and other American diplomats negotiated for navigation rights on the lower river, and for the right of deposit at New Orleans—the right to use the docks and warehouses of the city without tariffs— but they were only inconsistently successful. In 1795 Spain signed a treaty with the United States securing the right of navigation and deposit to American shippers, but in 1798 the Spanish revoked the treaty and the right. Americans in the Ohio Valley hated the "dons," as they called the Spanish; more than a few spoke of dispossessing them forcibly of Florida, Louisiana and perhaps Mexico. At the very least, the American government must restore and guarantee the free passage of the Mississippi and the right of deposit at New Orleans.

The problem became Thomas Jefferson's in 1801, upon the Virginian's inauguration as president. Jefferson had been looking west for decades. He saw the country's population expanding, and he judged that America's territory must expand, too, lest America become as crowded and conflict-prone as Europe. Jefferson understood the dissatisfaction of the Ohioans and Kentuckians and Tennesseans; he didn't doubt that if the American government didn't resolve their Mississippi River concerns, they might take matters into their own aggressive hands.

Once in the White House, Jefferson started modestly, by seeking to purchase New Orleans. This would guarantee the right of deposit and navigation. He discovered that France, under Napoleon Bonaparte, had reacquired Louisiana from Spain, by a treaty that was supposed to be secret but didn't stay so for long. Jefferson sent envoys to Paris with authority to spend $10 million for New Orleans.

Napoleon answered with a breathtaking counterproposal. Would the Americans care to purchase *all* of Louisiana? Napoleon had dreamed of re-creating France's New World empire, but his dream had foundered in Haiti, where a slave revolt and yellow fever had exacted a frightful toll on French troops. Napoleon proposed to cut his losses and liquidate his western holdings: the Americans could have Louisiana for ready cash.

The offer flummoxed Jefferson. The president prided himself on his strict construction of the Constitution, and the Constitution said nothing about acquiring new territory. Where the charter was silent, Jefferson had always said, government mustn't venture. He had been willing to stretch his philosophy to accommodate the purchase of New Orleans. But the purchase of *all* of Louisiana? His philosophy would be in tatters.

Yet Napoleon was offering the deal of a lifetime. The acquisition of Louisiana would double the size of the United States, ensuring a handsome patrimony for generations of American farmers. And the mercurial Napoleon might change his mind. He might resurrect his plans for a French American empire, or return Louisiana to the Spanish, strengthening New Spain and forestalling future American expansion.

Jefferson couldn't say no. He swallowed his scruples and signed an agreement promising France $15 million for Louisiana. Jefferson's Federalist opponents in Congress, who had branded his small-government thinking naive when they were in power, had a moment's enjoyment at Jefferson's expense before falling into line. Not even for political benefit could they spurn the handsomest bargain their country was ever likely to see.

2

THE CORPS OF DISCOVERY

WHAT, EXACTLY, THE BARGAIN CONSISTED OF REMAINED to be determined. The purchase of Louisiana created the American West as it would be understood for the next century. America's earlier West, between the Appalachians and the Mississippi, was suddenly annexed to the East in the minds of forward-thinking Americans. To be sure, many Bostonians still considered Ohio to lie at the western edge of America, if not of the earth. Eastern provincialism would persist into the twenty-first century. But Jefferson's bargain, viewed broadly, established a new template for American geography. The country now had two halves, an East and a West, with the Mississippi providing both the line of division and the seam tying the halves together.

Only a comparative handful of Americans—traders working out of St. Louis, mostly—had penetrated much beyond the Mississippi into the new West. Otherwise Louisiana was terra incognita to nearly all but the Indians who called it home. Jefferson set about filling in the blank space on the map between the great river and the crest of the Rocky Mountains. In doing so he diverged still further from the small-government philosophy that had carried him to office, and established an enduring principle of Western history. Development of the trans-Mississippi West would be a top-down affair driven by the federal government. East of the Mississippi, individuals and states had taken the lead in promoting settlement and development. State claims to territories east of the Mississippi antedated the creation of the federal government, which subsequently gave its blessing to the creation of new states but otherwise kept to the rear. West of the river there were no states or state claims; all the land was federal land. The Louisiana Purchase provided Jefferson a tabula rasa on which to write the federal will. As he did so, and as subsequent presidents and Congresses followed suit, they dramatically expanded federal powers. The American West owed its existence—as an *American* West—to the federal government. And the federal government owed much of the legitimacy and authority it assumed during the nineteenth century to the American West.

As a first step toward promoting Western development— beyond the huge step of the Louisiana Purchase itself—Jefferson persuaded Congress to support expeditions of scientific and geographic discovery into the West. The precedent Jefferson established here, of putting the federal government in the business of sponsoring scientific research and exploration, would far transcend the West and long outlast the nineteenth century; at the two-thirds mark of the twentieth century it would transport Americans to the moon. Congress gave Jefferson money for four expeditions. One would ascend the Red River, another the Ouachita, a third the Arkansas and the last the Missouri. The Missouri was the largest of the tributaries to the Mississippi, and it deserved the biggest expedition.

The Missouri expedition would have an additional purpose. From the headwaters of the Missouri its members would cross the mountains to the Columbia River and trace that stream to the Pacific. The region the Columbia traversed, called Oregon after an old name for the river, wasn't part of Louisiana. The United States had no legal title to it. But an American merchant captain, Robert Gray, in 1792 had been the first non-Indian to recognize and enter the mouth of the river, which he named for his ship, the *Columbia Rediviva*. Gray's feat gave the United States at least as solid a claim to Oregon as those put forward by Britain and Spain, the pushiest rivals, and Jefferson intended to improve the American claim by an exploration of the Columbia from headwaters to mouth. Already the greatest expansionist in American history—a distinction he would never lose—the mild-mannered Virginian audaciously thrust his young republic into the game of empires.

For agent he chose a man he knew well. Meriwether Lewis was the son of two of Jefferson's neighbors in Albemarle County, Virginia. His father had died when Meriwether was a boy, and his mother and stepfather took him to Georgia, where he learned the ways of the woods and streams. He returned to Virginia to be educated and eventually joined the Virginia militia. He transferred to the U.S. army, ascending to the rank of captain. Jefferson tapped him for a presidential aide, and he came to live in the White House. He and the president shared a passion for science and natural history; Jefferson saw in Lewis a younger, more active version of himself. As important as Jefferson was to the history of the American West, he never personally ventured farther west than western Virginia. Lewis would go where Jefferson did not.

To aid Lewis, Jefferson selected William Clark, a much younger brother of Revolutionary War hero George Rogers Clark and himself a soldier. The choice was potentially problematic in that Lewis had served under Clark in the army; to minimize the awkwardness, Lewis treated Clark as co-commander, though Jefferson still accounted Lewis the leader and Congress insisted on paying Clark at a lower rate.

The president made clear what he wanted from Lewis. "The object of your mission is to explore the Missouri river, and such principal stream of it as by its course and communication with the waters of the Pacific ocean—whether the Columbia, Oregon, Colorado or any other river—may offer the most direct and practicable water communication across this continent for the purposes of commerce," he said. Getting more specific, Jefferson continued, "Beginning at the mouth of the Missouri, you will take observations of latitude and longitude at all remarkable points on the river, and especially at the mouth of rivers, at rapids, at islands,

Meriwether Lewis and William Clark. These portraits were painted after the explorers became famous.

and other places and objects distinguished by such natural marks and characters of a durable kind as that they may with certainty be recognized hereafter." Lewis and his corps should learn everything they could about the peoples of the West: "The names of the nations and their numbers; the extent and limits of their possessions; their relations with other tribes of nations; their language, traditions, monuments; their ordinary occupations in agriculture, fishing, hunting, war, arts and the implements for these; their food, clothing, and domestic accommodations; the diseases prevalent among them and the remedies they use; moral and physical circumstances which distinguish them from the tribes we know; peculiarities in their laws, customs and dispositions; and articles of commerce they may need or furnish and to what extent."

Jefferson admonished Lewis to be diplomatic toward the Indians. "Treat them in the most friendly and conciliatory manner which their own conduct will admit," he said. "Allay all jealousies as to the object of your journey, satisfy them of its innocence." The Americans came as explorers, not as colonizers; there should be no reason for the Indians to be hostile. Yet if they were, Lewis must be prepared. He should not shrink in the face of challenge. But neither should he endanger his men and the mission unduly. "We value too much the lives of citizens to offer them to probable destruction." If proceeding became too dangerous, the expedition should turn back.

Jefferson instructed Lewis that he should convey to the Indians that though the Americans came in peace, they also came of right. Louisiana was America's by right of purchase, while Oregon would be America's by right of first discovery. Jefferson supplied Lewis with several dozen silver medals showing the president in profile on the front and two hands clasped in friendship on the back. Lewis was to distribute these medals to the chiefs of the tribes he met, explaining that the United States was the sovereign of the West and the president the "great father."

Jefferson hoped for the best for Lewis but told him to prepare for the worst. "To provide, on the accident of your death, against anarchy, dispersion, and the consequent danger to your party, and total failure of the enterprise, you are hereby authorized, by any instrument signed and written in your own hand, to name the person among them who shall succeed to the command on your decease," Jefferson wrote.

THE THREE DOZEN MEN OF THE CORPS OF DISCOVERY, AS THE Lewis and Clark expedition was formally styled, left St. Louis in May 1804. The going at first was slow; the expedition's three boats—a large keelboat and two flat-bottomed pirogues—battled the current of the Missouri for six hundred miles to the mouth of the Platte. Sometimes the wind favored their course and they raised sails to catch it; the rest of the time they paddled, rowed, pulled and pushed against the muddy flow. Lewis often walked the banks collecting specimens; with the boats averaging less than a mile per hour, he didn't worry about being left behind.

Yet he did worry about not seeing any Indians. An important purpose of the expedition was to cultivate the native peoples, but the native peoples kept their distance, and Lewis didn't know why. He saw evidence of Indian encampments and, hoping to make contact, sent scouts to track the Indians down and invite them to the corps' camp. But he got no response. Only at sunset on August 2, near the mouth of the Platte, did a delegation of Otoes and Missouris arrive. "Captain Lewis and myself met those Indians and informed them we were glad to see them, and would speak to them tomorrow," Clark wrote in the expedition journal. "Sent them some roasted meat, pork flour and meal. In return they sent us water melons. Every man on his guard and ready for anything."

Lewis and Clark inferred that these were chiefs of some sort but not the principal ones. "Made up a small present for those people in proportion to their consequence," Clark wrote. The Indians accepted the gift in a friendly manner. Speeches were exchanged, through an interpreter. Lewis closed the parley with more gifts and a display of weaponry. "We gave them a canister of powder and a bottle of whiskey and delivered a few presents to the whole, after giving them a breech cloth, some paint, gartering and a medal to those we made chiefs, after Captain Lewis's shooting the air gun"—a novel rifle of Austrian design—"which astonished those natives."

Lewis eventually learned the source of the Indians' standoffishness. Smallpox had afflicted the region recently and decimated the population. Diseases exotic to America had been the scourge of Eastern tribes since first contact with Europeans in the sixteenth century; the wave of destruction moved inland as the line of contact advanced. Smallpox reached the Missouri by the late eighteenth century, and it left the tribes there vulnerable to enemies and skittish. Those on Lewis and Clark's route weren't sure whether the Americans came in war or peace and so approached them diffidently.

Illness carried off one of the Americans two weeks later. "Sergeant Floyd is taken very bad all at once with a bilious colic," Clark wrote on August 19. "We attempt to relieve him, without success as yet. He gets worse and we are much alarmed at his situation." The illness intensified. "Sergeant Floyd much weaker," Clark wrote the next day. The corps made a start on the day's journey, with Floyd suffering in one of the boats. "Sergeant Floyd as bad as he can be. No pulse, and nothing will stay a moment on his stomach or bowels." A short while later Floyd breathed his last. "Sergeant Floyd died with a great deal of composure," Clark wrote. "We buried him on the top of the bluff ½ mile below a small river to which we gave his name."

Floyd's death—likely from a ruptured appendix—reminded all concerned how capricious existence could be in the wilderness. It also underscored the sobering fact that any change in the numbers of the corps would be by subtraction; a man lost could not be replaced.

This fact inclined Lewis to be lenient in a case of desertion. Moses Reed tired of the hard toil up the river and concocted a story that he had forgotten a knife at a previous campground. Lewis gave him permission to retrieve it but soon realized his mistake. "The man who went back after his knife has not yet come up," Clark wrote. "We have some reasons to believe he has deserted." The captains allowed Reed another day to make good, and when he still failed to appear, they sent a party in search of him—"with order if he did not give up peaceably to put him to death."

Catching Reed took ten days, but eventually he was brought in. Lewis conducted a trial in which Reed confessed to desertion and theft of a rifle and ammunition. He threw himself on the mercy of the captains, requesting that they be as forgiving as they could be consistent with their oaths of office. "Which we were and only sentenced him to run the gauntlet four times through the party and that each man with 9 switches should punish him and for him not to be considered in future as one of the party," Clark wrote.

THE EXPEDITION ENTERED THE GREAT PLAINS AND ENCOUN-tered large herds of buffalo. Lewis looked for the most storied of the northern tribes that lived on these large animals—the Lakotas, or western Sioux. Thomas Jefferson had read of the Sioux in the journals of French traders, and he thought they held the key to American control of the upper Missouri. "On that nation we wish most particularly to make a friendly impression, because of their immense power, and because we learn they are very desirous of being on the most friendly terms with us," Jefferson told Lewis. Events proved the president too optimistic about the desire of the Sioux to cultivate the Americans, but his assessment of their power was accurate.

At first the Sioux kept away, hunting buffalo and raiding their neighbors. But eventually they made contact. Lewis and Clark learned that a Sioux village was nearby. "We prepared some clothes and a few medals for the chiefs of the Tetons bands of Sioux which we expect to see today at the next river," Clark wrote on September 24. And so they did. "We soon after met 5 Indians and anchored out some distance and spoke to them, informed them we were friends and wished to continue so but were not afraid of any Indians."

They got no closer until the following day. "Raised a flag staff and made an awning or shade on a sandbar in the mouth of the Teton River, for the purpose of speaking with the Indians under," Clark recorded. The five Indians they had seen the evening before approached. "The 1st and 2nd chief came. We gave them some of our provisions to eat. They gave us great quantities of meat, some of which was spoiled. We feel much at a loss for the want of an interpreter; the one we have can speak but little." They smoked a peace pipe. Lewis started to give a speech but cut it short when he realized his words weren't getting through.

The chiefs were invited to board the keelboat. They examined various trade items Lewis laid out. He offered them whiskey and almost immediately wished he hadn't. "We gave them ¼ a glass of whiskey which they appeared to be very fond of," Clark wrote. "Sucked the bottle after it was out and soon began to be troublesome, one, the 2nd chief, assuming drunkenness as a cloak for his rascally intentions."

Lewis ordered the chiefs off the boat. They departed angrily, causing Clark to follow them in the pirogue in hope of assuaging injured feelings. This made matters worse. "As soon as I landed the pirogue three of their young men seized the cable," Clark wrote. "The chief's soldier hugged the mast, and the 2nd chief was very insolent both in words and gestures, declaring I should not go on, stating he had not received presents sufficient from us. His gestures were of such a personal nature I felt myself compelled to draw my sword. At this motion Capt. Lewis ordered all under arms in the boat."

A standoff ensued, with both sides glaring. "I felt myself warm and spoke in very positive terms," Clark recounted. Patrick Gass, one of Clark's men, recalled, "He told them his soldiers were good, and that he had more medicine aboard his boat than would kill twenty such nations in a day."

The Tetons probably didn't get the details of Clark's boast, which was unclear anyway. He might have been talking about bullets. Or he might have been suggesting that he would unleash an epidemic. The latter threat would have been extremely imprudent, as the experience of others who made such threats would show.

But the Tetons definitely caught Clark's angry drift, and the confrontation escalated. "Most of the warriors appeared to have their bows strung and took out their arrows from the quiver," Clark recorded. The Indians wouldn't let him return to the keelboat, yet he managed to get a message back to Lewis, who dispatched reinforcements. "The pirogue soon returned with about 12 of our determined men ready for any event."

The Tetons took stock of the situation. They decided not to test the Americans' resolve and, after some final glares, withdrew. Clark and the others got back safely to the keelboat, which was anchored near a small island. "I call this island Bad Humored Island as we were in a bad humor," he closed the journal entry for the day.

HUMAN NATURE BEING WHAT IT IS, THE AMERICANS IMPUTED evil motives to the Teton Sioux. "These are the vilest miscreants of the savage race, and must ever remain the pirates of the Missouri until such measures are pursued by our government as will make them feel a dependence on its will for their supply of merchandise," Clark recorded.

At the same time, he acknowledged a logic in the actions of the Indians, who were protecting their monopoly of trade on the upper Missouri. "Relying on a regular supply of merchandise through the channel of the river St. Peters"—connecting the upper Mississippi with British Canada—"they view with contempt the merchants of the Missouri, whom they never fail to plunder, when in their power." The St. Louis traders preferred to pay extortion rather than challenge the Tetons, which encouraged the Indians to persist in their racket. "A prevalent idea among them, and one which they make the rule of their conduct, is, that the more illy they treat the traders the greater quantity of merchandise they will bring them, and that they will thus obtain the articles they wish on better terms."

The immediate question for the Tetons, as for every other tribe that dealt with interlopers like these Americans, was whether their interests would be served better by tolerating the invaders or by attacking them. The Tetons outnumbered the Americans and could have crushed them, though not without suffering casualties of their own. But if this group of Americans was simply the spearhead of a larger force, killing them might be counterproductive. The Sioux had heard enough about the Americans to know that there were very many of them. Perhaps they couldn't all be killed.

Complicating the matter for the Tetons was a contest within the tribe for political control. Three chiefs—Black Buffalo, Buffalo Medicine and the Partisan—struggled for preeminence. The struggle, which became apparent to the Americans only gradually, caused the Tetons' attitude toward the Americans to swing between confrontation and accommodation.

Black Buffalo allowed Lewis to approach the Teton village, where a hundred tepees and their several hundred inhabitants attested to the force the Indians could bring to bear against the

Americans. But then Black Buffalo and the other chiefs invited the Americans to a grand feast, at which they plied the intruders with great quantities of roasted buffalo meat, delicate cuts of dog, and platters of pemmican and prairie turnips. Male drummers beat a rhythm for female dancers, who waved the scalps of slain enemies in a salute to the martial power of the Sioux, another reminder that the tribe must not be trifled with. The culmination of the evening was an offer of female companionship to the American chiefs. Lewis and Clark declined the offer, to the puzzlement of the Tetons.

Tension suddenly escalated again the next day when Black Buffalo alerted his people that an attack by hostile Omahas was imminent. Two hundred warriors leaped to the ready, armed and eager to fight. But no Omahas appeared. Lewis and Clark considered the matter, then concluded that they had witnessed a manufactured display of force. They didn't let on. "We shewed but little sign of a knowledge of their intentions," Clark wrote. Just in case, they conspicuously put their own men on armed alert.

Captains and men kept vigilant till they got past the Teton territory. Lewis and Clark were pleased at having broken through the Sioux barrier. Yet they didn't fool themselves into thinking they had accomplished Jefferson's goal of establishing good relations with the most powerful of the upper Missouri peoples.

3

WEST BY NORTHWEST

THE WEATHER CONTINUED FAIR, BUT THE NIGHTS GREW longer and colder. By mid-October, morning ice greeted the Americans, and Lewis and Clark began looking for a place to winter. They reached the villages of the Mandans at month's end and determined to build a fort nearby. The warmth of the Mandans toward the Americans contrasted sharply with the chill of the Sioux, yet it had the same origin: the prospect that the Americans would break the Sioux blockade of the Missouri River. The Mandans, and their neighbors the Hidatsas, were famous traders; the great bend in the Missouri became a lively market in the late summer and autumn of each year as tribes of the northern plains and Rockies gathered with British and French Canadian merchants of the North West Company, coming from Canada, and intrepid American traders from St. Louis. Yet the Americans and their goods arrived less freely and therefore more expensively than the Mandans desired, on account of the Sioux blockade. And the lack of American competition allowed the North West Company to raise its prices. The advent of Lewis and Clark, with the message that the American government intended to open the Missouri to commerce, was the best thing that had happened to the Mandans in decades, and they did all they could to accommodate the explorers.

The Mandan chiefs helped Lewis and Clark locate a favorable spot for building Fort Mandan, as the Americans called their winter quarters, near modern Bismarck, North Dakota. Mandan hunters and women brought supplies of buffalo, corn and beans. Mandans and Hidatsas wandered in and out of the fort almost at will. Many of the Americans, though apparently not Lewis and Clark, consorted with women of the two tribes.

On New Year's Day 1805, the Americans celebrated with their Indian hosts. The festivities began with a salute of arms. "Two shots were fired from the swivel"—a light cannon mounted on the keelboat—"followed by a round of small arms, to welcome the New Year," Patrick Gass recorded. "Captain Lewis then gave each a glass of good old whiskey; and a short time after another was given by Captain Clark." Charles Ordway, another corpsman who kept a journal, related the next phase of the fun: "Fifteen of the party went up to the first village of Mandans to dance, as it had been their request. Carried with us a fiddle and a tambourine and a sounding horn. As we arrived at the entrance of the village, we fired one round, then the music played. Loaded again, then marched to the center of the village, fired again. Then commenced dancing. A Frenchman"—a boatman hired by Lewis at St. Louis—"danced on his head and all danced round him for a short time, then went in to a lodge and danced a while, which pleased them very much. They then brought victuals from different lodges and of different kinds of diet. They brought us also a quantity of corn and some buffalo robes which they made us a present of. So we danced in different lodges until late in the afternoon."

The Mandans were intrigued to watch the whites cavorting, but they were amazed at the actions of the one black man in the expeditionary corps, Clark's slave York. Many of the Mandans had seen white faces, but none had seen a black face, and most didn't know what to make of this one. Some thought the blackness came from paint like that with which they painted their own skins at times, and tried to rub it off. York's curly hair reminded them of buffalo fur. He was a big man, yet agile, and Clark directed him to join the fun. "I ordered my black servant to dance, which amused

the crowd very much and somewhat astonished them, that so large
a man should be active," Clark wrote.

DURING THEIR MANDAN WINTER, LEWIS AND CLARK ENLISTED
the services of two people who proved essential to the success of
the American expedition. Toussaint Charbonneau was a French
Canadian trader who had lived among the Hidatsas for some
years. One of his wives was a young Shoshone woman captured
during a raid by the Hidatsas and then sold to Charbonneau; her
name was Sacagawea. Charbonneau's knowledge of the region and
its peoples appealed to Lewis and Clark, who hired him for the
journey west. Sacagawea enhanced Charbonneau's appeal, being
from a tribe whose territory they would be crossing. She knew the
landscape and presumably the trails, and she knew the language.
This was not quite the blessing it might have been, as the chain of
translation would be awkwardly long: from Lewis or Clark in English to François Labiche, a private in the expedition, who would
speak in French to Charbonneau, who would address Sacagawea
in Hidatsa, who would communicate in Shoshone to the message's
ultimate recipients. By the time the reply returned through the
chain of speakers, only the gist of the message, if that, might remain. But it was better than nothing, and preferable to the hand
signs on which the expedition had relied with the Sioux.

Sacagawea brought a bonus. As a woman, she cast a peaceful
glow upon the American contingent. The two-score armed men
otherwise looked like a war party; her presence offered reassurance that the intruders came in peace. Moreover, she was several
months pregnant; when the baby arrived, the peace signal would
be all the stronger.

THE WINTER ON THE UPPER MISSOURI WAS THE COLDEST ANY
of the Americans had ever endured. The thermometer fell far
below zero; whatever was exposed for more than a few seconds
risked freezing. This included fingers, noses, ears and body parts
bared when the men answered the call of nature. Lewis and Clark

served as the expedition's doctors, treating frostbite, sometimes by amputation; the cuts and bruises inflicted by sharp ice and frozen ground; dog bites; digestive ailments; and assorted maladies resulting from the unbalanced, heavily carnivorous diet that carried the men through the winter. They also treated venereal diseases, which seemed unavoidable and accordingly inconsequential. "All the party in high spirits," Clark wrote as the end of winter approached. "They pass but few nights without amusing themselves dancing, possessing perfect harmony and good understanding towards each other. Generally healthy except venereal complaints which is very common amongst the natives and the men catch it from them."

Patrick Gass said more on the subject. "It may be observed generally that chastity is not very highly esteemed by these people, and that the severe and loathsome effects *of certain French principles* are not uncommon among them," Gass wrote in the edited version of his journal. Americans of Gass's day, following long English practice, blamed the French for spreading venereal disease. "The fact is," Gass continued, "that the women are generally considered an article of traffic and *indulgencies* are sold at a very moderate price. As a proof of this I will just mention, that for an old tobacco box, one of our men was granted the honour of passing a night with the daughter of the headchief of the Mandan nation."

The men's spirits rose further as the ice on the Missouri began to break up and they made ready to resume the journey. Lewis and Clark sent the keelboat back to St. Louis, since the channel of the river had shallowed sufficiently to make the big vessel more trouble than it was worth. The men fashioned canoes out of trees growing near the river, hollowing the logs with adzes and fire and rounding the ends till the crafts floated high enough to keep the water out and maneuvered well enough to make travel upstream possible, if not easy.

The melting Missouri carried great chunks of ice. The Mandans conducted the oddest hunt—of buffalo—that any of the Americans had ever seen. "I observed the extraordinary dexterity of the Indians in jumping from one cake of ice to another, for the purpose of catching the buffalo as they float down," Clark wrote. The buffalo in question had frozen upstream during the winter and their carcasses remained fresh and edible. Adding to the strangeness of the scene, pillars of flame and smoke arose beside the icy stream, evidence of the time-tested practices of the Indians in managing their environment. "The Plains are on fire on both sides of the river," Clark noted. "It is common for the Indians to set those Plains on fire near their village for the advantage of the early grass for the horse and as an inducement to the buffalo to visit them."

4

TO THE PACIFIC

THE CORPS GOT AWAY FROM FORT MANDAN IN EARLY
April. Lewis swelled with pride as they embarked into the
unknown. To this point they had covered territory white men before them had seen; from here west, they would traverse territory
unknown to all but the natives. He grandly but understandably lik-
ened himself to other great explorers. "Our vessels consisted of six
small canoes and two large pirogues," he wrote in his journal. "This
little fleet although not quite so respectable as those of Columbus
or Capt. Cook were still viewed by us with as much pleasure as
those deservedly famed adventurers ever beheld theirs; and I dare
say with quite as much anxiety for their safety and preservation.
We were now about to penetrate a country at least two thousand
miles in width, on which the foot of civilized man had never trod-
den; the good or evil it had in store for us was for experiment yet to
determine, and these little vessels contained every article by which
we were to expect to subsist or defend ourselves." Lewis understood that peril and testing lay ahead. Yet he was thrilled. "Enter-
taining as I do, the most confident hope of succeeding in a voyage
which had formed a darling project of mine for the last ten years, I
could but esteem this moment of our departure as among the most
happy of my life."

Their immediate goal was the Rocky Mountains, the western
boundary of Louisiana and the gateway to Oregon. Virginians

Jefferson and Lewis, envisioning mountains like the Alleghenies, supposed that but a modest distance separated the headwaters of the Missouri from the tributaries of the Columbia. The corps would ascend the Missouri until the canoes could go no farther; then they would carry the boats and their cargoes across the ridge, place them into a westering stream, and proceed rapidly to the Pacific.

But the Rockies proved frustratingly elusive. The Missouri had completed its upstream westward bend, giving the Americans the satisfaction of knowing they were finally headed straight toward the mountains, yet week after week the landscape through which they toiled remained wide and almost level. They saw buffalo by the many thousands, and elk and antelope in lesser numbers. They found plenty of beaver, whose fur—the object of the trade Jefferson sought to wrest from the British and Canadians—Lewis pronounced to be of the finest quality. They doubted the stories the Indians told of terrible grizzly bears, until some of the party encountered the beasts and almost didn't live to relate the meetings.

During the winter with the Mandans, Lewis had inquired about the rivers that entered the Missouri; one, the Yellowstone, was described to him in terms that caused him to think of it as central to American policy for the entire region. "We are informed that there is a sufficiency of timber near the mouth of this river for the purpose of erecting a fortification, and the necessary buildings," Lewis wrote, for Jefferson's eyes. "In point of position, we have no hesitation in declaring our belief of its being one of the most eligible and necessary that can be chosen on the Missouri, as well in a governmental point of view as that of affording to our citizens the benefit of a most lucrative fur trade. This establishment might be made to hold in check the views of the British North West Company on the fur-trade of the upper part of the Missouri." Lewis had heard that the North West Company was aiming to establish a trading post in the region, and he warned about the consequences. "If this powerful and ambitious company are suffered uninterruptedly to prosecute their trade with the nations inhabiting the upper portion of the Missouri, and thus acquire an influence with those people, it is not difficult to conceive the obstructions which they might hereafter, through the medium of that influence, oppose to the will of our government or the navigation of the Missouri."

Consequently, Lewis was delighted on reaching the Yellowstone and discovering that it matched his vision. "This morning I walked through the point formed by the junction of the rivers," he wrote in the journal entry for April 27. "The woodland extends about a mile, when the rivers approach each other within less than half a mile; here a beautiful level low plain commences and extends up both rivers for many miles, widening as the rivers recede from each other, and extending back half a mile to a plain about 12 feet higher than itself." He located a promising spot for the fort he projected. "On the Missouri about 2½ miles from the entrance of the Yellowstone river, and between this high and low plain, a small lake is situated about 200 yards wide extending along the edge of the high plain parallel with the Missouri about one mile. On the point of the high plain at the lower extremity of this lake I think would be the most eligible site for an establishment."

The good news made him more eager than ever to reach the Rockies. But still the great dividing range continued to elude him. Physics and geography decreed that it must exist; a height of land of one sort or another separated Atlantic-bound waters from those destined for the Pacific. White traders and travelers had glimpsed the range from a distance, with its unforested peaks giving rise to the name Stony or Rocky Mountains. Yet for maddening months it refused to reveal itself to Lewis and Clark.

Finally the moment came. At the end of May, while Clark and the men in the boats struggled wearily against the Missouri's current, Lewis sought a vantage above the stream. "On arriving to the summit of one of the highest points in the neighbourhood I thought myself well repaid for any labour, as from this point I beheld the Rocky Mountains for the first time," he wrote in the journal. He could see only the highest peaks, but there was no mis-taking their identity. "These points of the Rocky Mountains were covered with snow and the sun shone on it in such manner as to give me the most plain and satisfactory view."

Lewis was torn by conflicting emotions. "While I viewed these mountains I felt a secret pleasure in finding myself so near the head of the heretofore conceived boundless Missouri; but when I reflected on the difficulties which this snowy barrier would most probably throw in my way to the Pacific, and the sufferings and hardships of myself and party in them, it in some measure coun-terbalanced the joy I had felt in the first moments in which I gazed on them." He determined to focus on the positive. "As I have al-ways held it a crime to anticipate evils, I will believe it a good com-fortable road until I am compelled to believe differently."

COMPULSION CAME SOON. LEWIS STILL IMAGINED AN EASY portage from the headwaters of the Missouri to those of the Co-lumbia, even after hearing from the Indians downstream about a great falls of the Missouri. He knew the Great Falls of the Ohio, a river of comparable size to the Missouri, and knew that the Ohio falls were really but rapids, which disappeared when the Ohio was in flood and otherwise dictated a portage of mere hun-dreds of yards.

Lewis discovered that the falls of the Missouri were something quite different. He and one of the men had set out ahead of the boats on the morning of June 13, cutting across a neck of land. "I had proceeded on this course about two miles with Goodrich at some distance behind me when my ears were saluted with the agreeable sound of a fall of water, and advancing a little further I saw the spray arise above the plain like a column of smoke," he wrote. The sound grew louder as they approached the top of a ridge, from which he saw the falls. "I hurried down the hill which was about 200 feet high and difficult of access, to gaze on this sublimely grand spectacle. I took my position on the top of some rocks about 20 feet high opposite the center of the falls. This chain of rocks appear once to have formed a part of those over which the waters tumbled, but in the course of time has been separated from it to the distance of 150 yards lying parallel to it and forming an abutment against which the water after falling over the precipice beats with great fury." The smooth sheet of water at the top of the falls became a howling maelstrom at the bottom. "The irregular and somewhat projecting rock below receives the water in its passage down and breaks it into a perfect white foam which assumes a thousand forms in a moment. . . . The water after descending strikes against the abutment before mentioned or that on which I stand and seems to reverberate, and being met by the more impetuous current they roll and swell into half-formed billows of great height which rise and again disappear in an instant."

Lewis now realized that these falls posed a challenge of a different order than the falls of the Ohio; what he did *not* realize was that he was looking at but one of five leaps the Missouri made from the mountains to the plains. Surmounting the series of falls eventually consumed a month of the most arduous work the corps had done on the journey so far. Long before the boats and the last of the cargo had cleared the final rise, the men's feet were bloody and torn from the rocks and cactus they had trod over in worn-out moccasins.

With the Rockies still towering in the distance, the portage thoroughly disabused Lewis of the notion of a convenient water route across the continent. His own corps would soon have to abandon the boats for horses, if horses could be found; future travelers would have to make similar accommodations. Though Thomas Jefferson wouldn't realize it for many months, on this June morning in 1805 the president's vision of an easy route to the Pacific wafted away on the mists Lewis saw rising from the falls of the Missouri.

LEWIS HAD BEEN TOLD THE SHOSHONES WERE A HORSE PEOPLE who frequented the territory between the falls and the Rockies; now that he knew their horses were essential, the search for them grew intense. But the Shoshones could not be found. Sacagawea started to recognize landmarks from her youth, before she had been stolen by the Hidatsas, so Lewis and the others knew they were in the right place. "The Indian woman recognized the point of a high plain to our right, which she informed us was not very distant from the summer retreat of her nation on a river beyond the mountains which runs to the west," Lewis wrote in the journal for August 8. "This hill she says her nation calls the Beaver's Head from a conceived resemblance of its figure to the head of that animal. She assures us that we shall either find her people on this river or on the river immediately west of its source, which from its present size cannot be very distant."

Lewis took a few men and went ahead of the main party, determined to find the Shoshones and their horses. On August 13 they made contact, first with some women and then with a mounted war party. The warriors were distrustful, never having seen white men, but Lewis conspicuously put down his rifle and advanced alone. He had given some modest gifts to the women, who told the warriors of his largesse. Their leaders considered the matter for a moment, then decided that the white men could be friends—or at least suppliers of weapons and other useful items. "Both parties now advanced and we were all caressed and besmeared with their grease and paint till I was heartily tired of the national hug," Lewis remarked.

When the rest of the corps joined Lewis, a most remarkable thing happened. Sacagawea discovered that the leader of this Shoshone band was her long-lost brother, Cameahwait—or, rather, she was his long-lost sister. She ran to him and threw her arms around him, weeping tears of joy. He responded with the reserve becoming a chief, but the warmth of the reunion convinced Lewis and Clark that the Shoshones would be friends indeed.

Yet they were also canny traders. From their ample herds they supplied the Americans more than two dozen horses, but the price in trade goods of the horses rose as the Shoshones discovered how desperately the explorers needed the animals. Lewis grumbled, yet paid the price, judging the horses absolutely essential to the success of the mission.

HE DIDN'T KNOW HOW RIGHT HE WAS. AT THE BEGINNING OF September the corps tackled the Bitterroot Mountains, a wild stretch of the Rockies avoided even by the locals. Lewis enlisted a Shoshone guide, but the trail he traced was steep, rugged, and in places treacherous for man and beast. It grew so faint that the guide lost the trail and they had to backtrack. Game animals shunned the region as much as the Indians did; soon the men were marching on short rations. Early snows—it was only September—chilled the men; rain soaked them when the snow abated. Dysentery spread among the corps, weakening and discouraging the men further. Lewis began wondering if they would have to give up and try an entirely different route, but by this time he didn't know if they had the strength to get out of the mountains by the way they had come. He decided to press forward.

Out of food, they began killing the horses to eat them. The men staggered on, counting the horses and estimating the number of days these new rations might last. "I have been wet and as cold in every part as I ever was in my life," Clark wrote on one grueling day in mid-September. "Indeed I was at one time fearful my feet would freeze in the thin moccasins which I wore."

At length they broke out of the mountains and emerged into a level, park-like patch. In the distance they saw a village of Indians the guide identified as Nez Perce. This was most welcome, as the Nez Perce were a people of the western slope of the mountains. The Indians offered the starving wanderers dried salmon, which they ate greedily. They soon regretted doing so, for after weeks of hunger, the rich flesh of the salmon wreaked havoc on their bowels, leaving them groaning in agony.

But as their distress diminished, they realized for the first time that their goal was within reach. The journey had been uphill and upstream the entire way from St. Louis; gravity had been their constant foe. From this point forward, the route was downhill and downstream; gravity was their friend. They made canoes out of pine trees and on October 7 set off down the swift-flowing Clearwater River.

Three days carried them to the Snake River; another week brought them to the Columbia. The miles flew past: three days more yielded sight of the Cascade Mountains. "I ascended a high cliff about 200 feet above the water, from the top of which is a level plain extending up the river and off for a great extent," Clark wrote on October 19. "At this place the country becomes low on each side of the river, and affords a prospect of the river and country below for great extent both to the right and left. From this place I discovered a high mountain of immense height covered with snow. This must be one of the mountains laid down by Vancouver, as seen from the mouth of the Columbia River. From the course which it bears, which is west, I take it to be Mt. St. Helens." Clark was almost right: the mountain was Mount Adams, the nearer and taller neighbor of Mount St. Helens. Both had been named by the British naval commander George Vancouver, who had seen them from the lower Columbia a decade earlier. But either way, Clark and the others realized that they were within two sightlines of the ocean. At their present pace of travel, the Pacific was just days away.

Yet they couldn't keep it up. Lewis had reckoned, even before reaching the Continental Divide, that the Columbia and its tributaries must be swifter and more turbulent than the Missouri. From the elevation of the divide to sea level took the Missouri and then the Mississippi four thousand miles to accomplish; the Columbia achieved the same descent in a quarter of that distance. The current in the Clearwater and Snake was thrillingly rapid in some places, frighteningly so elsewhere, but the expedition passed the rough spots without serious incident.

The cataracts of the Columbia were a different beast. During the eons in which the Cascade Mountains had been rising, driven upward by the crumpling pressure of tectonic plates, the Columbia had been carving a channel through them. The Columbia Gorge remained a work in progress, with the heavy labor commencing at Celilo Falls. "The country on both sides of the river here is high, and the bluffs rocky," Patrick Gass wrote. "For three miles down, the river is so confined by rocks (being not more than 70 yards wide) that it cannot discharge the water as fast as it comes over the falls, until what is deficient in breadth is made up in depth. About the great pitch the appearance of the place is terrifying, with vast rocks, and the river below the pitch, foaming through different channels." The expedition portaged around the falls, carrying cargo and canoes past the cataract and reloading at the base.

They had company in making the passage—more company than they wanted. The falls and rapids of the Columbia were the epicenter of the salmon fishery of the region, drawing Indians from far and near to trade for the dried fish. The Americans arrived after the height of the spawn, but the rotting carcasses and the general debris of the seasonal market gave an indication of the extent of the commerce. Hundreds of Indians remained on the banks of the river,

Salmon fishing at Celilo Falls. This photograph is from the twentieth century, but the Indians' practice of catching salmon as they struggled past the choke point on the Columbia River hadn't changed for a thousand years.

observing with curiosity and humor the labors of the white men in getting their boats and goods past the falls. Some helped, and helped themselves to whatever the Americans didn't guard zealously. "The natives are very troublesome about our camp," Charles Ordway remarked in his journal.

Lewis dealt even more carefully with the Columbia Indians than he had with the tribes on the Missouri. He was acutely aware that ever since crossing the Rockies he and the corps had been in an international no-man's-land, where British traders had as much right to operate as Americans. That they had indeed been operating in the region was evident from the manufactured goods the Indians along the river possessed: copper bracelets, iron kettles, a blue sailor's jacket. In time the United States might win title to the lands along the Columbia and then be able to impose its will on the natives of the region, but for now, persuasion, rather than coercion, was required. Lewis gave presents to the chiefs and swallowed his annoyance at the spate of petty thefts.

Below Celilo Falls were the Dalles, a narrow chute into which the wide stream was violently constricted, and the Cascades, a long stretch of rapids. In some places the Americans lowered the canoes by ropes through the furious waters; in others they took their lives in their hands and went through in the boats. Men and cargo were frequently soaked; days were spent drying both.

But by early November they had cleared the Columbia Gorge and reached tidewater. "Great joy in camp," Clark wrote on November 7. "We are in view of the ocean, this great Pacific Ocean which we have been so long anxious to see. And the roaring or noise made by the waves breaking on the rocky shores (as I suppose) may be heard distinctly."

In fact they were not in view of the Pacific Ocean, but of the estuary of the Columbia; the roar they heard was not of the surf, some twenty miles distant, but of the wind. And the wind never stopped roaring for the next three weeks, making the final twenty miles as vexing as any stretch of comparable length during the whole journey. The gales raised canoe-swamping waves, pinning the explorers to the north bank of the river; they also delivered a constant, cold, drenching rain that had them all within a few degrees of hypothermia.

But finally, after two thousand miles in boats and on horses, Lewis and Clark scrambled the last mile on foot. On December 3, they climbed a cape that jutted into the stormy Pacific. Each carved his name on a tree. Clark added: "By land from the U. States in 1804 & 1805."

II

A SKIN FOR A SKIN

5

ASTORIA

A S PROUD AS THEY WERE ON REACHING THE PACIFIC, Lewis and Clark were disappointed at not meeting any trading vessels near the mouth of the Columbia. American or European witnesses to their feat would have made it more satisfying and lent the accomplishment greater weight in the balance of the international competition for control of Oregon. In later decades, sympathizers with the plight of the Native Americans would imagine an alternative history in which the Indians had been left to enjoy their lands in peace. Leaving aside that the different Indian tribes regularly battled against one another, this was never a plausible option. If the United States had failed to advance its claim to Oregon, that region would have been snapped up by an international competitor: Britain, Spain, or Russia. The nineteenth century was the great age of empire, with European powers and the United States scrambling to seize parts of the world unable to defend themselves against the imperialists' technology. In North America, the scramble had been going on since the sixteenth century, and it was reaching its climax about the time Lewis and Clark carved their names on the cape overlooking the Pacific.

A ship, moreover, would have spared some of the expedition's members the toil of retracing their steps across the continent. Jefferson had provided Lewis letters of credit to purchase passage home. The president had also directed Lewis to send by ship a copy of the expedition's journals, lest, having survived the outbound hazards of Indians, cataracts, portages, hunger, accident and illness, the priceless documents be lost in a reprise of the perils.

But no ship was seen, and the expedition spent a dismal winter on the gray Oregon coast. In nearly four months, rain fell on all but twelve days. Come spring they reversed their course, this time with the advantage of knowing where they were going. They made much better time than they had heading west, and despite engaging some Blackfeet in a skirmish in which two of the Indians were killed, losing half their horses to Crow rustlers, and having to float a gauntlet of angry Tetons, they reached St. Louis in September 1806.

"I received, my dear sir, with unspeakable joy your letter of Sep. 23 announcing the return of yourself, Capt. Clarke & your party in good health to St. Louis," Jefferson wrote Lewis by way of congratulation. "The unknown scenes in which you were engaged, & the length of time without hearing of you had begun to be felt awfully." Indeed, many of those who knew of the expedition had given its members up for dead, and their seemingly miraculous return was celebrated as a triumph of American courage and acumen. Publishers clamored for rights to the official journals of the expedition and to the diaries Patrick Gass and others had kept. Word of mouth told of the rich resources of the region beyond the Missouri.

Yet there was disappointment within the triumph, at least for Jefferson, the founding father of America's westward expansion. The length of time the Lewis and Clark journey took had hinted to the president that the West would be a harder nut to crack than he had thought. The journals confirmed those hints. Lewis and Clark had broken *through* the Sioux blockade of the upper Missouri, but they hadn't *broken* it. Jefferson's attitude toward trade in the West was the diametrical opposite of his approach to trade generally. For a decade the British and French had been preying on America's Atlantic commerce, but Jefferson did little to defend that commerce. Indeed, not long after the return of Lewis and Clark, Jefferson essentially surrendered the commerce, persuading Congress to embargo all American overseas trade. Yet he was determined to promote American trade in the West, by force against the Sioux if necessary. Not for the last time, dreams of the West warped the views and even the principles of a person who could be reasonable on most other subjects. Jefferson had turned one political somersault to justify purchasing Louisiana, another to launch the federal government on a career of supporting scientific research; in this third cartwheel he reversed his course on trade to become its most aggressive advocate. Yet his agents, Lewis and Clark, had made no observable headway.

Another result of the Lewis and Clark expedition was perhaps more disappointing. Jefferson had known, in rough geographical terms, how far Oregon was from the American East, but until he read the journals he hadn't appreciated how hard it was in *human* terms to reach it. There would be no water link between the Mississippi basin and Oregon; from what Lewis and Clark reported, even building a road fit for wagons might be a daunting task. This meant that Oregon would never—or at least not in Jefferson's lifetime—become an organic part of the United States. The force of gravity, acting on water, had turned Jefferson's attention to New Orleans and Louisiana in the first place; that same force, Jefferson now realized, would pull Oregon away from the United States. In an earlier decade Jefferson had wondered if nature might have destined America's trans-Appalachian region to spin off the United States and form a Mississippi Valley republic; now he had to take seriously the possibility that nature had destined Oregon— and perhaps Spanish California—to form a Pacific republic. As president of the United States, Jefferson wasn't about to relinquish America's claim to Oregon, but as a scientist he had to acknowledge that any president's powers might fail against those of nature.

The disappointments attached to the Lewis and Clark expedition set the pattern for many disappointments to follow. Time and again Americans would project their dreams onto the West and be disappointed. Jefferson dreamed of a water route to the Pacific and of America capturing the trade of the upper Missouri; other Americans would dream of opportunities and riches of different sorts. A few would realize their dreams, but many more would endure danger and hardship only to come up short. Yet so broad was the West, and so great its promise, that there were always others with dreams as yet undashed.

JOHN JACOB ASTOR READ THE LEWIS AND CLARK JOURNALS and drew his own conclusions. Astor might have become a butcher had his father made more of the meat trade in the German town of Walldorf, where Astor was born, but the family business struggled, and Astor decided to try his chances in America. He landed in New York just after the Revolutionary War, when commercial relations between the fledgling United States and British Canada were resuming. Astor heard that Canadian furs commanded high prices in New York, so he set off up the Hudson River to find out for himself.

He discovered that the fur trade was not for the frail or timid. He endured sub-Arctic winter weather, hostile Indians and cutthroat—literally, in some cases—competitors. But he also learned that a man of hardy ambition might make a fortune catering to the taste of New York's upper and striving classes for headgear made from the processed fur of beavers. He bought beaver pelts from Indian and French Canadian trappers, carried them to New York and tallied his profits.

Astor's ambition grew, and he sought fresh opportunities. He met merchants who brought tea and silk from China, and he supposed he could do the same. He reckoned that the fur trade and the tea trade might complement each other. He bought a share in a ship carrying thirty thousand pelts from New York to Canton; these were swapped for tea and other luxury items, and when the ship arrived back in New York, the profits inspired Astor to put all his capital into this new version of his business.

He was sketching a plan when Lewis and Clark returned from the dead, as it seemed. Their successful crossing of the continent inspired Astor to focus on Oregon and the untapped fur resources it was said to contain. He plotted an invasion of Oregon from two directions at once: by land from the Mississippi Valley and by sea from the Pacific. He would dispatch a party of trappers and traders who would cross the Rockies and establish connections with the Indian tribes on the western slope. The Indians and Astor's men would gather furs for transport down the Columbia to its mouth, where Astor's seaborne contingent would establish a command post near Lewis and Clark's wintering spot.

For the marine arm Astor built the *Tonquin*, a three-masted bark capable of carrying nearly three hundred tons of cargo. The ship had a crew of twenty, commanded by Lieutenant Jonathan Thorn, on leave from the U.S. navy, and it mounted ten guns. Astor filled the vessel with trading goods to tempt the natives of Oregon, as well as materials for the construction and provisioning of the fort at the mouth of the Columbia. Also aboard were four subordinate partners of Astor's, who would direct the commercial affairs of the enterprise from the fort and such additional posts as they saw fit to establish in the interior. These men would be remunerated by shares of the profits. A dozen salaried clerks, several craftsmen and thirteen French Canadian *voyageurs*, veterans of the Canadian fur trade, completed the ship's roster.

Astor doubted the loyalty of the voyageurs, several of whom had lately worked for the North West Company, whose business Astor was trying to undercut. But he couldn't find Americans with the talents and experience the Canadians possessed, and so he took the chance. He *should* have doubted the loyalty of the four partners, especially the two of Scots descent who, unbeknownst to Astor, apprised the British minister in America, then visiting New York, of Astor's project, which was supposed to be a secret. The intelligence was timely, as Britain and the United States were on the verge of war on account of Britain's continued seizure of American merchant ships and their crews. The British might have seized the *Tonquin* if Astor hadn't arranged its escort out of harbor and out to sea by the most storied ship in the American navy, the frigate *Constitution*. The *Tonquin* departed New York on September 8, 1810; on Christmas Day it rounded Cape Horn and entered the Pacific. Seven weeks later it dropped anchor in Hawaii, a regular reprovisioning spot for ships in that part of the world. Finally, in March 1811, the *Tonquin* reached the mouth of the Columbia.

Meanwhile, Astor's overland party struggled up the Missouri River. Wilson Price Hunt, another share partner, led four other partners and fifty voyageurs up the Missouri from St. Louis on the same route Lewis and Clark had followed, with an interpreter who was the son of Lewis and Clark's interpreter. But, learning from their predecessors, the Astor party bypassed the domain of the Blackfeet and turned west well before the Missouri did. They encountered flocks of passenger pigeons that filled the sky from horizon to horizon, and herds of buffalo that covered the prairie. Their southerly route enabled them to avoid the Bitterroot Mountains, which had taxed the men of Lewis and Clark so sorely. They met the Snake River where it comes out of the Rockies, and they judged that it would carry them to the Columbia. But the Snake proved too turbulent, and after the drowning death of one man they abandoned their canoes and struck out overland on horses bought from the Shoshones. Winter caught them in the Blue Mountains, which served as a near substitute for the Bitterroots in terms of hardship inflicted on travelers. Not until February 1812 did they reach the mouth of the Columbia.

BUT THE *TONQUIN* WAS NOT THERE, AND NEITHER WERE ITS captain and crew. Seeing no sign of the overlanders, who were still hundreds of miles away, Jonathan Thorn had hesitated to cross the Columbia's stormy bar, where the powerful current of the river slams into the tides of the Pacific. Instead he dispatched a boat with five men to sound the channel. The first mate, chosen to command the boat, was no more eager than Thorn to risk destruction, not least since the boat's crew consisted of voyageurs familiar with inland rivers but unacquainted with oceans and surf. Moreover, the mate's uncle had drowned on this very spot a few years before. Yet Thorn closed his ears to the mate's misgivings and ordered him to go. The mate took his case to the partners. "I am sent off without seamen to man my boat, in boisterous weather, and on the most dangerous part of the northwest coast," he said. "My uncle was lost a few years ago on this same bar, and now I am going to lay my bones along side of his."

The partners interceded with Thorn, but the captain would not relent. He called the mate's forebodings cowardice and demanded that the boat be off. The voyageurs pulled on the oars and the craft approached the bar. All hands crowded the rail to observe the progress of the boat, which rose and fell on the surging waves, bobbing in and out of sight. The boat grew smaller and smaller with distance before it suddenly disappeared. Observers from the ship couldn't tell whether it had gone behind the waves or beneath them.

Minutes passed, with no reappearance of the boat. Minutes became hours, and still no boat. Daylight waned and night fell. Nothing was seen or heard from the boat.

The next day dawned, with still no sign. The captain ordered another boat launched to seek the first boat. But the seas were almost as high as on the previous day, and the second boat returned before it discovered anything.

The captain sent out a third boat. This one all but foundered in the waves and made it back to the ship moments before it would have sunk.

Yet again the captain ordered men into a boat. This time they were to seek the channel, and the ship would follow close behind. The operation succeeded well enough for the *Tonquin* to cross the bar, but the crash of current against tide nearly swamped the boat. The crew lost control and the boat was swept past the ship to sea, with the crew shouting in vain for help. The *Tonquin* ran aground and came within a nasty wave or two of breaking up. Before the ship had escaped the shoal and reached a semblance of safety inside the bar, the boat was out of sight and darkness was falling.

The next morning Captain Thorn sent parties ashore, hoping that at least some of the men from the missing boats had made it to land. The searchers found one of the members of the last boat's crew staggering disorientedly and clothed in tatters. He told a grim tale, saying that the boat, after being carried to sea, had been battered by huge waves that had washed the crew overboard and filled the craft with water. Two men were lost at once and seen no more. Three others clung to the sides of the boat and bailed out enough of the water to keep it afloat. They clambered back in.

All three were hypothermic from the cold water and the wind. One expired in the boat, but the other two managed to row through the surf to shore. One of these collapsed, barely alive, upon reaching solid ground; the other was the man the ship's men found, in shock. He was just able to lead them to his surviving partner.

The other missing boat was never discovered, nor any of its crew. Eight men had been lost in the last mile of the *Tonquin*'s eight-thousand-mile voyage.

YET WORSE WAS TO COME. THE CHIEF OF THE CHINOOK TRIBE that inhabited the lower Columbia was named Comcomly, and he appeared pleased to learn from the Americans on the *Tonquin* that they intended to establish a trading post. He had dealt with itinerant traders whose ships touched this part of the coast irregularly, and he concluded that having traders always at hand would be a great convenience. He assisted the Astorians; when two of the partners, after a visit to Comcomly's lodge, ignored his warning that the waves in the estuary had grown too high for them to return safely to the *Tonquin*, he followed their boat in his own canoe and fished them out of the water when their craft capsized. While laborers from the ship erected the fort, which they called Astoria, Comcomly and his people brought beaver and otter pelts for barter with the partners.

The partners were happy for the business, but Captain Thorn was annoyed by the "Indian ragamuffins," as he called them, swarming about his ship. Thorn was eager to get away and cruise up the coast seeking other trading spots, as his instructions from Astor and his own profit interests directed him to do. Besides, during the long voyage from New York he had fallen into bickering with the partners and wished to be rid of them. Eventually he made his departure, crossing the bar on a fine June day and heading north.

Thorn sailed the *Tonquin* to Vancouver Island, where he anchored in a cove near the northern tip. The Indians there were accustomed to trade with visiting vessels, and the *Tonquin* was surrounded by canoes. Astor had cautioned Thorn against allowing Indians onto the ship, but Thorn thought he knew better. He laid his trade goods upon the decks and let the Indians aboard. They proved harder bargainers than he had expected, and he grew exasperated at their demands for high prices for their otter pelts. His temper got the better of him, and he confronted their chief, shouting in English. The chief didn't understand, provoking Thorn the more. In his fury, Thorn snatched a pelt from the chief and slapped him in the face with it. He kicked and thrashed at the other pelts the Indians had brought aboard, and in further gestures he made clear he thought the Indians thieves and savages. He ordered them off the ship, punctuating his words with shoves and more kicks.

The chief was incensed by this treatment, but he ordered the Indians away from the vessel. They took their pelts, climbed into their canoes and paddled to shore. Thorn cursed in satisfaction and declared that the Indians would be back soon and ready to accept his price. But the one partner who had accompanied him told him he must weigh anchor and leave the spot, for he had mortally offended the chief's pride. Thorn dismissed the caution with a sneer. He pointed to the guns the *Tonquin* carried and said that if the natives made trouble he'd blow them to pieces.

The next morning brought evidence that Thorn was right to think the Indians would relent. The canoes returned, and the Indians seemed chastened and willing to trade on Thorn's terms. The captain let them aboard. But a local interpreter who had been en-listed by Thorn noticed that several of the Indians seemed to be hiding things under their shirts. The interpreter warned the part-ner, who in turn alerted Thorn. The captain scoffed but nonethe-less ordered the crew to weigh anchor and make sail, both as a precaution and as a bargaining tactic. If the Indians thought Thorn was about to leave, he thought, they would be even more willing to trade.

Trade wasn't what they had in mind this day. At a shout from one of them, the Indians pulled knives and clubs from beneath their shirts and viciously assaulted the whites aboard the *Tonquin*. The ship's clerk went down first, stabbed in the back. The part-ner suffered a grievous blow from one of the Indian clubs; he fell over the rail into the water, where he was quickly killed by Indian women in the canoes. Thorn fought back as best he could, but such was the surprise that he was armed only with a folding knife. He stabbed a leader of the Indians in the heart, killing him at once. But he was then overwhelmed by several other Indians, whose blows knocked him to the deck. The Indians leaped upon him and stabbed him to death. His body was tossed overboard.

The remaining members of the crew fought desperately for their lives. With clasp knives and marlin spikes they wounded several of the Indians. But the Indians were better armed and too numerous, and one by one the crew members fell in their own blood.

Yet a few managed to retreat to the ship's cabin, where they barricaded themselves behind its locked door. They seized some muskets in the cabin and, smashing holes in the cabin wall, fired at the Indians on deck. This changed the balance in the fight, and the Indians leaped off the deck into the water to escape the bul-lets. They climbed into the canoes and backed away from the ship. Heartened, the surviving crew members emerged from the cabin and manned the ship's cannons, which they trained on the ca-noes. Several volleys wreaked mayhem on the attackers, who fled for safety.

The bay fell quiet. Even the wind died. The sails of the ship went slack. For several hours the vessel showed no signs of life. The Indians couldn't tell if the whites had all succumbed of their wounds or were simply lying low. Night fell.

At dawn the next day the *Tonquin* remained where she had been. The Indians grew curious and cautiously approached, hoping to seize its cargo. As they drew near, the ship's clerk, who had survived his stab wound, appeared on deck. In gestures that betokened surrender, he invited them to come aboard. They did so—a few at first, then dozens and scores, each eager for his share of the booty. In their haste they failed to notice that the clerk had gone below.

Suddenly a huge explosion blew the ship to pieces. Bodies of the Indians were hurled far into the air; severed arms and legs littered the surface of the water. Many were killed outright; others died of their wounds shortly or after lingering in pain.

The explosion shocked and mystified the Indians who survived the carnage. But they recovered sufficiently to take their vengeance on four members of the crew who had slipped away from the ship during the night in a boat, hoping to make their way south to Astoria. The wind had been against them, and they had been forced ashore. Exhausted by their efforts and by the events of the day, they fell into a deep sleep. Before they awoke they were discovered by the Indians and taken captive. They were brought to the Indians' village, where they lived long enough to tell their story to the Indian interpreter. They explained that during the night they had weighed their chances of escape. The clerk wanted them all to take the ship to sea and sail to Astoria. But the four crew members pointed out that the wind was in the wrong direction; it would simply drive them to shore. The four proposed escaping in the boat; the clerk, weakened from his wound, said they would have to go without him. In any event, he had plans for vengeance against the Indians. The four did leave, and the next day the clerk had his vengeance. After luring the Indians on board, he descended to the powder magazine. He touched a spark to the powder, killing himself and several score Indians.

The surviving four didn't live much longer—they were tortured and killed. Eventually the Indian interpreter carried the gruesome tale of the *Tonquin* and its spectacular demise to Astoria, where the remaining Astorians heard it and shuddered.

6

COMCOMLY'S DISMAY

THE DESTRUCTION OF THE *TONQUIN* DEALT A HEAVY BLOW to the Astor project; it also revealed the simple but ineluctable theme of violence in the history of the American West: of humans killing one another in the struggle for control of Western resources. As time would prove, violence would be the *defining* characteristic of the West. When the violence diminished to the background level of the rest of the country, the West would no longer be the West but simply another part of America.

At the moment, the loss of the *Tonquin* deprived the Astorians of transport for the furs they would acquire, and the loss of its cargo left them short of the wherewithal to pay for the furs. The grisly deaths of Thorn and the others spooked the survivors, causing them to eye Comcomly with grave distrust. At one point one of the partners at Astoria resorted to a stratagem whose consequences would haunt Americans in Oregon for generations. He summoned Comcomly and the other Chinook chiefs and told them he was of vengeful mind on account of the evil fate that had befallen the *Tonquin*. He warned them not to cross him and showed them a bottle. In the bottle, he said, was smallpox. The Indians knew about the disease: a smallpox epidemic had ravaged the coastal tribes a few years before, following a visit by another trading ship. If he uncorked the bottle, the partner said, smallpox would escape and devastate the Indians again. His hand was restrained for the

51

moment, but if the Indians did the whites any harm, the smallpox would be unleashed.

The Indian leaders swore their friendship. They would never harm the whites, they said. The bottle must never be uncorked.

The partner nodded severely. The smallpox would remain in the bottle, but only so long as the Indians behaved themselves.

DUNCAN MCDOUGALL HAD ANOTHER PLAN FOR DEALING with the Chinooks. McDougall was one of the Scots partners, and he thought to preach love rather than vengeance. Specifically, he asked Comcomly for the hand of his daughter in marriage. Perhaps McDougall really loved the girl; he would hardly be the first or last white man to take an Indian wife in the West, and some of the unions evinced great tenderness and durability. But practicality likely inspired the idea. Comcomly was a vital supplier of salmon, smelt and sturgeon to the fort, and whatever helped keep the fish coming would aid the enterprise.

Comcomly, for his part, thought the plan a splendid one. A family connection to the Astorians and their supplies of trade goods would reinforce his position as the dominant chief of the Chinooks. The Americans eventually called Comcomly the "King of the Chinooks," and like many another king he was pleased to employ matrimony in the service of his realm.

The arrangements were made through emissaries. Comcomly, ever the shrewd bargainer, insisted on suitable compensation for delivering his beloved daughter. A deal was struck, and the great day dawned. Comcomly and the royal family crossed the Columbia from the Chinook village on the north bank to Astoria on the south in a fleet of canoes bedecked for the occasion. He wore a blue blanket and a red breech cloth; special paint accentuated his features and feathers adorned his head. The bride, too, was painted, according to Chinook marital custom, and anointed with oil; a beautiful pony awaited her at the landing of the canoes and carried her to the fort, where the bridegroom received her with appropriate gratitude and honor.

The ceremony was followed by a honeymoon on the premises of the fort, as there was nowhere better for the newlyweds to go. Whether or not there was a meeting of hearts, the union served its commercial and political purpose. Comcomly became a regular presence at Astoria, visiting his daughter and advising his son-in-law on relations with the Chinooks and other tribes, on practical matters of supply, and on additional questions important to the survival of the Astor enterprise. Comcomly particularly favored the blacksmith's shop, and his requests for knives and axes caused the smith to set aside his current work to fill the chief's order. Comcomly appreciated the consideration and became even more supportive of his son-in-law.

YET THE UNDERLYING PROBLEMS OF ASTORIA PERSISTED. THE expected war between the United States and Britain broke out in June 1812, and the British promptly imposed a blockade on the American coast. The blockade prevented the timely dispatch of ships to replace the *Tonquin* and develop the Pacific trade. After one Astor vessel, the *Lark*, did get through the British cordon on the East Coast, it sank off Hawaii on the way to Oregon.

The decline of Astoria's fortunes, compounded by the onset of war, prompted Duncan McDougall to reassess his partnership with John Jacob Astor. McDougall had previously worked for the North West Company, and he concluded he might do so again. Indeed, in the denouement of what transpired, friends of Astor alleged that McDougall had plotted defection all along. Whether or not this was true, McDougall surreptitiously communicated with agents of the North West Company and hinted that he might be willing to deliver Astoria to them for a modest price, including a partnership for him in their company. McDougall's interpretation of his contract with Astor allowed him to do this in case the Astor enterprise failed. McDougall now judged that failure was nigh. He rationalized that the sale of Astoria and its inventory to the North West Company would salvage for Astor as much as was possible under the circumstances.

News from the war forced his hand. The North West men alerted him that a British warship was bound for the Columbia, with the goal of seizing Astoria for the British crown. McDougall reckoned that a sale at any price was better than a seizure, and he made the final arrangements with the Northwesters.

The British warship arrived in due course. The officers and men expected to win a handsome prize of furs, which might be converted to cash and shared among them, according to the rules of warfare at the time. They were greatly annoyed to discover that there was no booty to seize, as the American goods now belonged to British subjects.

More annoyed than the British crew was Comcomly. The old chief knew about the war between the Americans and the British, but he didn't know about the sale of Astoria to the Northwesters. When the British warship arrived, Comcomly grew excited at the prospect of fighting the invaders at the side of his son-in-law. He explained how his warriors would kill the British. His men would conceal themselves in the woods that ran down to the shore, and when the British boats landed, the warriors would attack. The King George men would die before they could mount any resistance. It would be a glorious victory.

McDougall explained that this could not be. The British must be treated as friends. There would be no resistance.

Comcomly was mystified and disappointed. He returned to his longhouse convinced that he had erred in selecting a son-in-law. To all who would listen, he complained that he had thought his daughter was getting a brave chief for a husband, but instead she got an old woman.

7

THE WHITE-HEADED EAGLE

I F JOHN JACOB ASTOR WAS NOT TO BE THE LORD OF THE
Western fur trade, perhaps John McLoughlin would be. Astor
later disputed the sale of Astoria, after the War of 1812 ended in
the 1815 Treaty of Ghent, which stipulated a return to the *status
quo ante bellum*. Astor reasonably contended that the transfer of
Astoria to the North West Company was a forced sale, a de facto
seizure. Yet he lost the argument, and the business. The ground
beneath Astoria indeed reverted to American control, but the sale
of the inventory and equipment was treated as a commercial trans-
action. More important, the suspension of the activities of Astor's
company allowed the North West Company to entrench itself all
along the Columbia. Rooting the Northwesters out would have required a commercial and political war Astor might have been willing to wage if he had received the support of the U.S. government.
But the government at that time was less solicitous of the welfare
of American enterprise than the British government was of British
enterprise, and when the administrations of James Madison and
James Monroe ignored Astor's requests for help, he dropped the
project, leaving Oregon to the North West Company.

The Northwesters had their own problems, starting with a nasty
struggle with the Hudson's Bay Company. The latter had deep
roots in the history of British North America, dating from 1670,
and powerful friends in the British government. The North West

Company had been founded in 1779 to compete with the Hudson's Bay Company, and during the next four decades the two companies battled for control of the fur trade of western Canada and the Oregon country. Tactics ranged from stealing equipment and bribing Indians to trapping out a region—creating a fur desert—and instigating physical violence. The violence at times rose to the level of irregular war. In 1816, in Canada's Red River Colony, near where Winnipeg would grow up, Métis—mixed-race—employees and associates of the North West Company responded with outrage to a decision by the governor to ban the export of pemmican, a vital foodstuff in the fur trade. The decision was seen as a gift to the Hudson's Bay Company and a heavy blow to the North West Company. A band of Métis seized an inventory of Hudson's Bay pemmican, claiming that the Hudson's Bay Company had stolen it from them. As they carried it off, they were challenged by a group of Bay Company men led by the colony's new governor, the successor to the pemmican hoarder. Someone fired; then everyone fired. Within minutes, twenty-two people were dead, including the governor. The great majority of the dead were Bay Company men.

John McLoughlin missed the Battle of Seven Oaks, as the affair was called. McLoughlin had worked for the North West Company for more than a decade, and he was on his way to Red River when he learned of the impending trouble. He slowed his pace long enough to avoid the bloodletting. But the episode convinced him, as it did many others on both sides of the fur-trade war, that things were getting out of control. The British government pressured the two companies to cease fire. The result was a shotgun marriage, effected in 1821, that retired the name North West Company and left the augmented Hudson's Bay Company in sole command of the fur trade of western Canada and Oregon. The company's Latin motto, *Pro Pelle Cutem*, translated as "A skin for a skin," seemed apter than ever.

THE MERGER MADE MCLOUGHLIN A PARTNER IN THE HUDSON'S Bay Company, and the company's head, George Simpson, made

McLoughlin the chief factor—director—for the Columbia district, which was to say Oregon. McLoughlin and Simpson traveled together down the Columbia to Astoria, where the North West Company continued to operate a trading post. But they decided that Astoria was the wrong place for the regional command post the company required. It was too far from the richest beaver streams of the upper Columbia, tempting Indians and trappers to sell their pelts to Americans coming across the Rockies from St. Louis. It lacked sufficient arable land to make the district self-supporting in foodstuffs, as the cost-cutting Simpson insisted and the empire-building McLoughlin desired.

And it was on the wrong side of the Columbia River. By the early 1820s the only countries actively competing for title to Oregon were Britain and the United States. The Spanish had relinquished their claim in an 1819 treaty with the United States. Russia talked about expanding south from settlements in Alaska, but James Monroe in 1823 issued a statement warning all the European countries against planting new settlements or colonies in the Americas. Only later would Monroe's statement be called the Monroe Doctrine, and its contemporary effect on Russian thinking is unclear. The Russians were stretched in America already; Monroe's warning might have been superfluous. In any case, Russia never subsequently pressed a claim to Oregon.

This left Britain and America. In the wake of their recent war, neither side sought a confrontation over Oregon, and so in 1818 they agreed to defer a decision. For ten years, nationals of both countries could conduct trade and other activities in Oregon without prejudice to the interests of either country. In 1828 the matter would be revisited.

Neither John McLoughlin nor George Simpson—nor anyone else, for that matter—required much imagination to suppose that Oregon would one day be divided between Britain and the United States. The obvious geographical marker was the Columbia River, and the likely outcome was that Britain would get the north bank of the river and the United States the south. If this did occur, the

Hudson's Bay Company would lose whatever investment it made in a command post at Astoria.

Consequently McLoughlin and Simpson chose a new site for the regional headquarters a hundred miles up the Columbia from Astoria. "From what I had seen of the country," McLoughlin recalled later, "I formed the conclusion, from the mildness and salubrity of the climate, that this was the finest portion of North America that I had seen, for the residence of civilized man." Fort Vancouver, named for George Vancouver, arose on the Columbia's north bank a few miles above the point where the Willamette River enters the Columbia from the south. The site had magnificent vistas: the broad Columbia immediately in front, the Coast Range to the west, the Cascades to the east, with snow-covered Mount Hood towering five thousand feet above the ridgeline of the Cascades, themselves reaching six thousand feet.

The new fort was erected on a plain above the river—at first not far enough above: it had to be relocated after some early flooding. As it matured it evolved into a small village, with some forty buildings surrounded by a wooden stockade twenty feet high, in the shape of a rectangle 750 feet long by 450 feet wide. The buildings included storage sheds, workshops, houses and barracks, a chapel, a school and other structures. Surrounding the fort were vegetable gardens, fields planted in wheat and potatoes, orchards and pastures. A dairy provided milk, a sawmill boards, a tannery leather, a shipyard boats. As the population based at the fort grew, additional housing was constructed outside the stockade.

Fort Vancouver became the largest community of non-Indians west of the Rockies. Its residents consisted primarily of the Hudson's Bay Company "servants," or salaried employees. These were French Canadians and Métis, as well as a sizable group of Hawaiians, called Kanakas. Iroquois and Cree Indians from Canada joined the assemblage, as did varying numbers of Englishmen, Scots and Irish. In addition to the employees, local Indians from several tribes frequented the vicinity of the fort. The languages spoken reflected the diversity of the residents: French among the

Fort Vancouver. This drawing dates from a few years after the Hudson's Bay Company post was handed over to the U.S. army, but the location and layout were established by the Bay Company's John McLoughlin. The Columbia River rolls by just to the south (right, in the picture), and Mount Hood guards the eastern horizon.

French Canadians and Métis, Hawaiian among the Kanakas, several Indian tongues, and English, the language of official company business. A regional pidgin called Chinook Jargon facilitated trade among the polyglot group.

PRESIDING OVER IT ALL WAS JOHN MCLOUGHLIN. TALL, POWERfully built, with white hair that fell to his shoulders, and piercing eyes, McLoughlin was called the White-Headed Eagle by the Indians around the fort. He had trained to be a physician and been licensed to practice in his native Quebec at the tender age of eighteen. But a mysterious incident involving an army officer and McLoughlin's fiery temper prompted him to flee Quebec for the west. He signed on with the North West Company as a physician, yet soon displayed a knack for commerce and administration. By the time of the merger of the North West and Hudson's Bay companies, he was an obvious choice to manage the Columbia district.

Yet he was far more than a manager of a trading company. The treaty of joint occupation of Oregon created no institutions of government for the country, either British or American. McLoughlin filled the void by making himself the de facto czar of the region. His power flowed from his command of the resources of the Hudson's Bay Company, but it was shaped by a stern code of morality, and it encompassed both the servants and the associates of the company and the native peoples. McLoughlin encouraged peace among the Indians, and he enforced peace between the Indians and the whites.

Ships' captains visiting the Columbia never mastered the treacherous bar; one ship, the *William and Ann*, carrying a cargo for the Hudson's Bay Company, ran aground in the crossing and all persons aboard were lost. McLoughlin wasn't surprised at the grounding, but the loss of the entire crew appeared suspicious. He guessed that Indians had killed the crew and dumped the bodies in the water, in order to steal the goods the ship held. He had no proof of this, though, and consequently wasn't prepared to punish anyone for murder. He confined himself to sending a message to the chiefs of the Indians he suspected, demanding the return of the cargo. They refused. He then sent a boat with a swivel gun downriver to make his point more clearly. The Indians fired on the boat, whose crew returned fire with the boat's gun. The Indians scattered into the forest, and the crew went ashore, where they discovered some of the ship's cargo. One of the Indian chiefs, approaching from behind the trees, cocked his musket to shoot at the company men. One of the men heard the cock and quickly fired, killing the chief.

The killing, combined with the power of the swivel gun, convinced the Indians that the Bay Company was not to be meddled with. Most of the cargo of the *William and Ann* was never recovered, but the lesson stuck. Two years later another ship ran aground. The crew got ashore and made their way upriver to Fort Vancouver. McLoughlin sent a boat down to the mouth and found the ship's cargo untouched.

On another occasion an American, Jedediah Smith, aiming to break the Hudson's Bay monopoly of the Oregon fur trade, led a party of trappers from St. Louis across the Rockies into Oregon via the Snake River. They wandered west and south, reaching San Francisco Bay. From there they ventured north back into Oregon. They managed to avoid serious trouble with Indians until they arrived at the Umpqua River in southern Oregon. There the large quantity of furs they carried proved too tempting for a local tribe. The Indians at first greeted the Americans in a friendly manner, but the next morning, after the party had split up, with Smith and another man seeking a ford across the stream, the Indians attacked. Fifteen of the nineteen Americans were killed. Smith and his companion heard the shooting and, judging there was nothing they could do for the others, fled across the river and away to the north. Two other men, after desperate hand-to-hand fighting, also escaped. They, too, worked their way north, and the four Americans eventually reached Fort Vancouver, starved and exhausted.

McLoughlin recognized them at once as competitors but also as fellow white men and presumptive Christians. He extended the full welcome of the fort. He acknowledged that he couldn't return Smith's dead comrades to life, but he offered to help him retrieve the stolen furs.

Smith declined the offer. "It is of no use," he said. The furs were gone forever.

McLoughlin refused to accept this. He sought justice for the Americans, but he also insisted on order in his realm. "I will manage it," he told Smith. Stepping to the veranda of his house, he shouted, "Mr. McKay! Thomas McKay! Where the devil is McKay?" Thomas McKay was the mixed-race son of one of the Astorians killed in the *Tonquin* explosion; when his widowed mother married John McLoughlin, McKay became the stepson of the most powerful man in the Oregon country. McLoughlin made McKay his assistant, and as McLoughlin's assistant McKay leaped to answer the chief factor's command. "Tom, this American has been robbed, his party massacred," McLoughlin said. "Take fifty men. Have the horses driven in. Where is La Framboise, Michel, Baptiste, Jacques? Where are all the men? Take twenty pack horses; those who have no saddles ride on blankets, two blankets to each man. Go light. Take some salmon, peas, grease, potatoes. Now be off. Cross the river tonight, and if there be one of you here at sunset I will tie him to the twelve pounder and give him a dozen." McKay did as ordered. When the group was leaving the fort, McLoughlin handed him an envelope. "Be off; read it on the way!"

"I divulged my plan to none," McLoughlin recalled later, "but gave written instructions to the officer"—McKay—"to be opened only when he got to the Umpqua, because if known before they got there, the officers would talk of it among themselves, the men would hear it and from them it would go to their Indian wives, who were spies on us, and my plan would be defeated. The plan was that the officer was, as usual, to invite the Indians to bring their furs to trade, just as if nothing had happened. Count the furs, but because the American trappers mark all their skins, keep these separate, give them to Mr. Smith and not pay the Indians for them, telling them that they belonged to him; that they got them by murdering Smith's people."

Thomas McKay followed the plan. The Indians denied that they had killed the Americans, although they admitted having purchased the furs from the actual murderers. McKay told them to look to the murderers for payment. McLoughlin learned secondhand what happened when they did so. "As the murderers would not restore the property they had received, a war was kindled among them, and the murderers were punished more severely than we could have done," he observed.

McLoughlin was pleased with the outcome. "We recovered property for Mr. Smith to the amount of three thousand two hundred dollars, without any expense to him, which was done from a principle of Christian duty, and as a lesson to the Indians to show them they could not wrong the whites with impunity."

8

MOUNTAIN MAN

Joseph Meek didn't grow up intending to enter the fur trade. Nor, when he ran away from home in Virginia at the age of seventeen, did he think he would wind up in Oregon. But those who knew him saw traits characteristic of many Americans who found their way west. He chafed under the expectations of family and society. And he was willing to take a gamble on his future.

Meek's mother had died when he was a boy. His father remarried, and Meek and his stepmother didn't get along. His father sided with his new wife. As soon as Meek thought he could manage on his own, he took off, without wishing his parents goodbye. "They did not grieve," he said later.

A neighbor heading west gave him a ride to Kentucky, and Meek's momentum carried him to St. Louis, where in the spring of 1829 he met William Sublette, a partner in the Rocky Mountain Fur Company. The company was the brainchild of William Ashley, who in 1822 had issued a call for a hundred enterprising young men to join him at St. Louis for the adventure of their lives. The men would be trained in the ways of the mountains, the Indians and the beaver, and they would attack the monopoly of the Hudson's Bay Company in the name of American patriotism and personal profit. Those who answered Ashley's call became the pioneering class of American mountain men; they included Jedediah

Joseph Meek. He dressed differently in the mountains.

Smith, Jim Bridger, Hugh Glass and William Sublette. By 1829 Sublette had become a partner, and in that capacity he visited St. Louis seeking provisions and new recruits.

Joe Meek was tall, rangy and full of the confidence of the naive. He said he wanted to sign up.

"How old are you?" demanded Sublette.

"A little past eighteen," Meek replied.

"And you want to go to the Rocky Mountains?"

"Yes."

"You don't know what you are talking about, boy. You'll be killed before you get halfway there."

"If I do, I reckon I can die!" said Meek, unabashed.

"That's the game spirit," Sublette said, satisfied. "I think you'll do, after all. Only be prudent, and keep your wits about you."

"Where else should they be?" said Meek, most pleased with himself.

Sublette's party set off. They crossed the Missouri River and angled northwest to the Platte, which they followed to the Sweetwater and then the Wind River. The spring weather drenched and chilled them; the traverse of the plains bored them. One moment of excitement was more thrilling than even veterans like Sublette preferred, involving a band of a thousand armed Indians who rode toward the sixty trappers like a whirlwind, shrieking ferociously as they came. Sublette later owned that he thought he had seen his last dawn. But at the final moment, the leader of the Indians pulled his pony to a halt. He gestured to Sublette that he wanted to talk rather than fight. Sublette was willing, and the parley resulted in the Indians receiving a generous gift and the trappers departing with their lives. Joe Meek learned a lesson, interpreted by Sublette and the other old-timers, who explained that the Indians could have killed them and seized their entire stock of goods, but would have lost some men in doing so, since the trappers wouldn't yield without a fight. The chief decided to settle for the gift, at no cost.

The first goal of the march was the annual rendezvous of traders, trappers and Indians. The rendezvous was an invention of the Rocky Mountain Fur Company, which employed a different business model than the Hudson's Bay Company. Instead of gathering furs at permanent trading posts, the Rocky Mountain men each summer arranged a meeting of the various parties to the fur business at a convenient spot in the mountains. The traders brought goods the trappers and Indians couldn't procure on their own: lead, powder, traps, tobacco, coffee, salt, liquor. The trappers and Indians brought furs, and the parties swapped.

But the rendezvous became much more than a swap meet. During the several weeks when each rendezvous took place, it was the largest community west of St. Louis, with hundreds of traders and trappers from one or more companies, and at least as many Indians. The site of the rendezvous was chosen with care, for it had to be extensive enough to accommodate all the people and their horses, and it had to have access to wild game to feed the group.

The rendezvous served important social functions. At the rendezvous, trappers found Indian wives, who made life in the mountains less lonely, in the way marriages everywhere do, and safer, by linking the trappers to the tribes of their spouses. For the wives, the tie to the trappers could bring distinction and comparative wealth, beyond the companionship of the unions. The unions—which were often informal, like common-law marriages—produced children, who played at the rendezvous with other children. Husbands bought presents at the rendezvous for their wives, displaying their success by the lavishness of the gifts. The men gambled and raced horses; they told stories about their adventures in the mountains; they got into fistfights, knife fights and gunfights; they drank a year's worth of liquor in a few weeks. Indians took measure of the whites, and vice versa. Life in the mountains was hard, as the trappers battled cold and want and daily risk of death; the rendezvous, held during soft summer—when the furs on the beaver were thin and not worth hunting—provided a respite and release. A trapper might spend a year's earnings and walk away from the rendezvous broke, and consider the experience worth every penny, even after sobering up. Besides, with no access to banks, the trappers had few ways to save money even if they wanted to.

Joe Meek's first rendezvous took place on the Popo Agie, a tributary of the Bighorn River, and it opened his eyes to the ways of the mountain men. He talked with veterans who were hardly older than himself; their tales both daunted and challenged him. He observed Indians in their daily activities and began to distinguish between one tribe and another. He watched the trading and gambling and fighting, and occasionally took part. He soaked up the beauty of the mountains and felt their allure. And he decided, by the end of the rendezvous, that this was the life for him.

He followed Sublette to the headwaters of the Snake River. Sublette and the Rocky Mountain Company were taking dead aim at the Hudson's Bay Company, which had hitherto controlled the Snake region. The Sublette party passed the distinctive peaks of the Three Tetons and sojourned in Pierre's Hole, awaiting the cold weather that caused the beaver furs to thicken.

They also awaited Jedediah Smith, not knowing that Smith's party had been nearly annihilated on the Umpqua River. Smith arrived late and explained his tardiness, noting the considerate treatment of John McLoughlin toward him. Smith said that, under the circumstances, he didn't have the heart to take on McLoughlin's company this season.

Sublette agreed, although less from respect for McLoughlin than from the shorthandedness caused by the Smith party's misfortune. Surviving in the mountains required strength of numbers. Indians who had no hesitation about killing intruders in small groups thought twice about challenging substantial bodies of armed men. Sublette reluctantly decided to return to the Wind River and set up winter quarters. The serious trapping wouldn't happen till the following spring, when they might have reinforcements.

THE DELAY GAVE JOE MEEK A CHANCE TO LEARN THE ART OF the beaver trapper, which required learning something about the beaver, the unlikely object of the commercial lust of the small armies of trappers and traders who chased the critter across the wilds of North America. *Castor canadensis* is a large rodent with protruding orange teeth, beady eyes, coarse fur, a flat, scaly tail, and an odor that only other beavers can love. Its saving grace, for humans, is a soft underfur that can be tailored into warm coats and stoles, or, for the fashionable gents of Europe and the Eastern states in the nineteenth century, pounded into felt for stylish top hats. As the species name suggests, the North American beaver was first noticed, by whites, in Canada—hence the head start gained by the Hudson's Bay and North West companies in the beaver business. But the animal's range extended deep into the American West, wherever trees grew beside rivers and creeks. The green tissue of the trees provided food to the beaver; the woody branches and trunks were used to dam the streams and build lodges in the ponds behind the dams. Beavers are nocturnal, with weak

The beaver. This shy animal was the basis of a global commerce.

eyesight but acute senses of smell and hearing. They are champion swimmers and can remain submerged for a quarter of an hour at a time. Growing to more than fifty pounds, they can live past twenty years of age.

Unless they encounter the like of Joe Meek and his traps. The standard trap in Meek's day was a steel device weighing some five pounds and consisting of a pair of spring-loaded jaws, a flat plate that acted as a tripping device, and a steel chain. The trap was placed in a stream where beavers had been at work building their dams and lodges. The jaws and the plate were submerged several inches below the surface of the water and covered with leaves or other debris for concealment. The chain, perhaps five feet long, was stretched out into the water, with its end secured by a stake driven into the bottom of the stream. The trap was baited with beaver scent, taken from the glands of a previously killed animal. Beavers are aggressively territorial, and the scent drew other beavers to confront the presumed intruder. When all went as planned, an unlucky beaver's foot hit the plate and sprang the jaws, which clamped on the beaver's leg. The secured chain prevented the animal from swimming away with the trap; heavily encumbered, the beaver became exhausted and drowned. The trapper, returning after a day or two, retrieved his prize and the trap.

Under the best of circumstances the work of the trapper was arduous. The weight of the traps wore on the muscles, and the clambering in and out of cold streams chilled the trapper to the bone. If the trap was not secured adequately, the trapper might have to take a swim to retrieve it and the beaver. In areas not previously trapped, the beavers didn't know to avoid the traps and trappers, but with experience the animals became warier. The trapper had to hide his tracks and mask his own scent, and even then his traps might remain empty. It was no wonder William Sublette and the other fur-company partners had to travel to St. Louis each year to recruit newcomers like Joe Meek; the attrition from drowning, death by pneumonia and other ailments, and simple exhaustion depleted the ranks.

9

COLTER'S RUN

A ND THEN THERE WERE THE INDIANS. BEFORE THE Sublette party left the Snake River, Joe Meek had his first encounter with the Blackfeet. Perhaps the Blackfeet were still angry about their tribesman killed by the Lewis and Clark expedition; perhaps they nursed new grievances against whites; perhaps—as most of the whites and many of the other Indians believed—they were simply violent and vicious. In any event, they were the scourge of the Rockies and the adjacent valleys and plains. When possible the trappers steered clear of the Blackfeet; when they couldn't avoid them they tried to travel in large groups. Woe to the trapper who found himself alone or in small company when the Blackfeet appeared.

Meek's first scrape with the Blackfeet had a comparatively happy ending. A small raiding party descended on the Sublette camp early one morning with the design of stampeding the horses and mules. But their timing was off, and the attackers arrived, shouting and firing rifles, before most of the animals had been turned out for their breakfast graze.

The men in the camp leaped to arms and onto horseback to repel the raid. A sharp firefight ensued, with the Indians being driven back. Sublette's men determined to punish the attackers, and they chased the Blackfeet into a ravine. A standoff developed, lasting several hours. Casualties were incurred on both sides, though none of the Sublette party were killed. Finally the Indians slipped away and were seen no more.

The incident prompted Sublette to redouble the guards posted at night. Joe Meek took his turn along with a veteran named Reese. The night was calm and cold; the combination caused both men, wrapped in their blankets, to become drowsy. They nodded off. Sublette, who periodically checked on the guards by calling to them, heard no response from Reese and Meek. Aware of the danger to life and property that lurked in the dark, he grew angry and sallied forth to investigate. "Sublette came round the horse-pen swearing and snorting," Meek recalled. "He was powerful mad. Before he got to where Reese was, he made so much noise that he waked him; and Reese, in a loud whisper, called to him, 'Down, Billy! Indians!' Sublette got down on his belly might quick. 'Where? Where?' he asked. 'They were right there when you hollered so,' said Reese. 'Where is Meek?' whispered Sublette. 'He is trying to shoot one,' answered Reese, still in a whisper. Reese then crawled over to where I was, and told me what had been said, and informed me what to do. In a few minutes I crawled over to Reese's post, when Sublette asked me how many Indians had been there, and I told him I couldn't make out their number. In the morning a pair of Indian moccasins were found where Reese *saw the Indians*, which I had *taken care to leave there*; and thus confirmed, our story got us the credit of vigilance, instead of our receiving our just dues for neglect of duty."

Vigilance, real or feigned, didn't prevent another attack by the Blackfeet. This one occurred almost at the crest of the Continental Divide and resulted in the death of two of the trappers and Meek's separation from the main body of the Sublette party. He had only his mule, his blanket, his gun and his wits. The last told him not to use his gun lest he alert the Blackfeet to his presence. He climbed a ridge to get his bearings and map his strategy. To the west, the Snake River rolled toward the Columbia and the Pacific. To the north, the Missouri began its long journey to the Mississippi and the Gulf of Mexico. To the east, the Yellowstone sliced toward its intersection with the Missouri. In all that space he saw no sign of humans, neither Sublette and his comrades nor, thankfully, Blackfeet. He knew that off to the south lay the land of the Crows, who were friendlier to whites than the Blackfeet. Toward them he determined to travel.

Meek spent a cold night in the forest—winter's first snows had fallen. He did without a fire lest its smoke draw unwelcome attention. The next day he headed toward the Crow country. He soon felt the drag of hunger. His mule did, too, and showed less determination than Meek to survive. Meek left the mule behind.

Two more days carried him fifty miles closer to the Crows, but also closer to starvation. Then good luck brought a band of mountain sheep within rifle range. Risking detection, Meek shot and killed one. Taking a further risk, he lit a small fire and cooked the wild mutton. He ate hastily, looking over his shoulder for signs of Indian approach, his rifle at the ready.

Three more days of walking brought him to the brink of a broad valley. As Meek caught his breath and looked ahead, he couldn't make out, and then couldn't believe, what his eyes were seeing. The valley appeared to be on fire, with smoke pouring from gashes in the ground. The wind carried the smell of brimstone. "I have been told the sun would be blown out and the earth burnt up," he said to himself, referring to the words of his family's minister back home. "If this infernal wind keeps up, I shouldn't be surprised if the sun were blown out. If the earth is *not* burning up over there, then it is that place the old Methodist preacher used to threaten me with."

He descended to investigate. He found hot springs bubbling and geysers blasting steam and water into the air. He had been constantly cold, and the singular heat took the edge off his chill. "If it were hell," he recalled thinking, "it were a more agreeable climate than I had been in for some time."

Joe Meek had heard of "Colter's Hell," named for John Colter, one of the members of the Lewis and Clark expedition. Colter had a greater aversion to civilized life than most other members of the

Corps of Discovery, and on the return trip, while they were growing misty-eyed at the thought of seeing St. Louis again, he asked
and received permission from Lewis to join a group of trappers
heading the other way, back up the Missouri. That winter he wandered about the region Joe Meek later entered, and he became the
first white person to see the geothermal wonders of the Yellowstone region. His fellow mountain men weren't sure they believed
his stories, and they jestingly labeled the quarter Colter's Hell. Joe
Meek discovered that it was real, and hellish indeed.

Meek knew something else about Colter: that he had run an
epic race for his life after capture by the Blackfeet. Colter and
a trapper named Potts were paddling two canoes up the Jefferson Fork of the Missouri River when a band of several hundred
Blackfeet appeared on the shore. Their chief demanded that the
two men bring their boats ashore. Colter realized that successful
resistance was impossible. Hoping he would be merely robbed, he
stealthily dropped his traps into the water on the side of the canoe
away from the Indians, that he might retrieve them later, but otherwise conspicuously complied with the chief's demand. When he
reached the shore he was seized and stripped naked.

Potts didn't like the looks of this and stayed in his canoe. One
of the Indians fired and hit him. Potts fired back, killing one of the
Blackfeet. Thereupon a hundred bullets rained upon and through
Potts, killing him in seconds. Several Indians splashed into the
stream and dragged the canoe ashore. Potts's body was hauled
out and slashed to pieces with knives and hatchets. His heart and
other internal organs were cut out and thrust into Colter's face.
Relatives of the dead Indian demanded that Colter receive similar
treatment, and Colter braced himself for a gory end.

But a council of the leaders of the band, convened on the spot,
decreed a different fate. One of the chiefs gestured to the wide
prairie that stretched away from the river, and in the Crow language, which Colter understood, said, "Go! Go away!"

Colter supposed they were planning to shoot him and only
wanted him to get clear of the crowd of Indians before doing so.

Not sure he wished to play along, he nonetheless walked slowly in the direction the chief had pointed. An old Indian walked beside him, urging him to move faster. Yet Colter kept walking. The old Indian shouted and gesticulated, trying to get him to hurry. Finally Colter looked back and saw the younger Blackfeet taking off their leggings, as if preparing for an athletic contest. He now grasped his situation: there was to be a race—for his life.

He started running, and as he did so he heard whoops from his pursuers, who took up the chase with a will. For each of them, Colter's scalp was a prize that would bring honor and rank. He looked over his shoulder and saw their spears flashing in the sun, each sharp point intended for his heart.

He knew that the Madison Fork lay five miles ahead, and he headed in that direction. But the ground was rough and the rocks tore his feet. Yet he mustn't slow, and fear for his life made him run faster than he had ever thought he could. Halfway to the Madison he burst a blood vessel in his lungs or nose and began spewing blood from his nostrils. He felt faint and stopped to avoid passing out.

He saw that he had distanced all of his pursuers but one, who was closing upon him with a spear in his right hand and a blanket over his left shoulder. The Indian dropped the blanket, took the spear in both hands, and hurled himself on the naked, bleeding, apparently defenseless Colter.

Colter somehow dodged the blade and seized its shaft. The Indian, propelled by his own momentum, stumbled to the ground, and his weight and Colter's remaining strength broke the spear shaft. Colter swiftly grasped the blade end and stabbed the fallen Indian.

Withdrawing the blade, he snatched up the Indian's blanket. The other Blackfeet were now approaching, and, inflamed by the death of their fellow, they redoubled their efforts to catch and kill Colter. The new danger gave his legs fresh life, and he tore off again.

A line of willows marked the banks of the Madison, and Colter flew toward them. Reaching the trees, he briefly cut himself off from the view of the Blackfeet. His eye scanned the stream for a hiding place, and it lit on an old beaver lodge. He dove under the water and, holding his breath, managed to find the entrance. He wriggled through and into the lodge itself, which stood above the waterline.

He shivered from the cold of the water and from his continuing fear of imminent death, but he made no sound as the Blackfeet searched for him. He heard and felt the footsteps of one Indian who mounted the outside of the beaver lodge for a better view up and down the river. He was certain the Indians would tear open the lodge or set it afire, but the possibility that he was inside apparently didn't occur to them. Their voices gradually died away as they moved on.

Colter stayed where he was, recouping his strength and pondering his next move. In an hour or two he heard the Indians again, evidently returning to the Jefferson Fork after concluding that they had lost their quarry. Again the voices died away.

Colter remained quiet. He waited several hours more, till full night had fallen. Still hearing nothing, he crawled and swam out of the lodge and broke the surface of the river. He looked carefully around and, seeing no sign of the Blackfeet, clambered out onto the far bank and began walking. He avoided trails and passes the Indians might frequent, instead climbing one mountain ridge by a nearly impossible route. He descended from the mountain onto a broad plain that stretched to the east. During the next eleven days he traveled three hundred miles across the plain, subsisting on roots and tree bark. He finally arrived at Manuel's Fort on the Bighorn River, exhausted, emaciated and dirty, but alive.

He told his story to the men at the fort, who knew him but didn't at first recognize him. They told his story to others; in time, "Colter's Run" became a part of the lore of the mountains.

10

URSUS HORRIBILIS

J OE MEEK HAD HEARD THE STORY, AND AS HE WANDERED alone about Colter's Hell, knowing there were Blackfeet nearby, he wondered if he might have to recapitulate Colter's Run. The sudden sound of two gunshots heightened his concern. He crouched and sought the source of the fire, priming his own weapon to return it.

But then a voice called out, "It *is* old Joe!" Meek recognized the speaker as one of the Sublette company, come with a comrade to look for him. The three shook hands on their reunion and set out after the main party, which was trudging through the snow toward the wintering ground.

Winter was the harshest time of the year for the mountain men, but it was also the easiest. The cold was bitter; temperatures far below zero were common. Deep snow made moving around difficult and travel all but impossible. The horses and mules had to be fed, as the grass was buried beneath the drifts. Yet experience had schooled the mountain men in surviving. They fed the animals on the bark of cottonwoods, which they peeled from the trees with their large knives. The task was laborious but the fodder nutritious, and despite the brutal temperatures the animals grew fat.

The trappers grew fat, too. The cottonwoods attracted buffalo, which became easy prey for the hunters of the party. The men ate a lot, and what they didn't eat, they dried. The buffalo skins were cured and fashioned into moccasins, leggings and shirts. Sometimes the men did the work; those with Indian wives turned it over to their spouses. Even for the men without spouses, the workload didn't fill the available hours, and the remainder was devoted to card-playing, story-telling and other pastimes.

Joe Meek spent much of the winter remedying a deficiency he had felt since his rebellious school days: he learned to read. The library of the camp wasn't large, consisting of a Bible and a one-volume Shakespeare. But under the tutelage of a trapper named Green, Meek found his way through those volumes and began looking for more.

The fat time of winter gave way to the working time of spring. The trappers set out as soon as the ice began breaking in the streams and the beavers came out of their lodges. This season was distinctively dangerous, for other animals came out as well. Joe Meek and two partners one day were trapping and enjoying good luck, which included a buffalo they shot and dined on. Lest small varmints steal the leftovers, they cut the choicest steaks from the carcass and placed them under their blankets for the night. Weary from their labors and with full stomachs, they slept soundly. Only at dawn was Meek disturbed by the snuffling and snorting, then pawing and trampling, of something large and nosy, which turned out to be a grizzly bear.

"You may be sure that I kept very quiet, while that bear helped himself to some of my buffalo meat and went off a little way to eat it," Meek related afterward. But one of his partners wasn't so circumspect, sitting up and inadvertently attracting the attention of the bear. "Back came the bear," Meek said. "Down went our heads under the blankets, and I kept mine covered pretty snug while the beast took another walk over the bed." The bear went off to finish its breakfast.

The third member of the group whispered to Meek that he wanted to shoot the bear. Meek answered, "No, no, hold on, or the brute will kill us, sure." The bear heard the voices and again came back to investigate, once more walking over the recumbent men. "I'd have been happy to have felt myself sinking ten feet in the ground while that bear promenaded over and around us," Meek recalled. But the animal couldn't figure out what made the lumps in the blankets, and it eventually wandered away.

When Meek decided that the coast was clear, he arose and grabbed his rifle. "Wanting to be revenged for his impudence, I went after him, and seeing a good chance, shot him dead. Then I took my turn at running over him awhile!"

Spring also brought encounters with the Indians. The Crows could be as troublesome as the Blackfeet, and one night a band divested Meek's company of three hundred horses. Without the horses the trappers were helpless; retrieving them was a matter of life and death. The trappers decided to go after the rustlers on foot, lest they risk losing the few horses that remained. Meek and sixty or seventy others trailed the Crows for two hundred miles, hardly stopping to eat and not stopping to sleep. The Crows, thinking they had left the hapless whites behind, did allow themselves repose. Consequently they were sound asleep when Meek and the others slipped up on them.

Two of the trappers got to the horses, untied them and started to drive them off. Noise from the animals awoke the Crows, who jumped up to pursue them. Meek and the mountaineers were ready, and they fired a rifle volley into the ranks of the Indians. Meek later learned that seven were killed in the initial blast. The Crows recoiled, and as they did, the trappers leaped onto the horses and, riding them bareback, set the whole herd galloping on the trail back to their camp. They didn't hear from that band of Crows again, though they took greater precautions with the horses at night.

Joe Meek, dodging grizzly bears and battling Indians, had scant opportunity to reflect on the larger forces at work in the fur trade. He didn't appreciate what was distinctive about that trade as it related to American history. Although the high country of the Rockies was as remote as any place in what would become the United States, it was intimately entangled in the affairs of the broader world. Not for several generations would the word *globalization* be used to describe supply chains that spanned oceans and continents, but it applied to the nineteenth-century fur trade and the work of Meek and his comrades. Joe Meek had a job because gentlemen in London liked beaver hats. American farmers in that era generally produced for regional markets; coopers, blacksmiths and mechanics of a dozen other descriptions catered to markets more local still. But Meek was a man of the world. Invisible threads tied him to customers six thousand miles away. A twinge on those threads—a simple change in taste in England—could undo the business model that sustained the annual rendezvous, that made allies of some Indian tribes and enemies of others, and that forced Bill Sublette to recruit new men each year to replace trappers killed in the mountains. Joe Meek had only the vaguest notion of the complex linkages involved, yet the fur trade was the instrument by which the world economy penetrated the deepest recesses of the American West.

There was another term economists would coin that applied to the fur trade. The pelts the trappers hunted belonged to no one until they were caught. The fur companies—the Hudson's Bay Company and the various American companies—had every incentive to catch as many as possible as quickly as possible, lest other companies get there first. To conserve the resource was economically foolish. The companies found themselves caught in a *tragedy of the commons*, where the unavoidable outcome was the exhaustion of the resource. The harder Joe Meek and his comrades worked, the more certain was the collapse of their industry. They raced the clock, but the clock was sure to win.

As THE COMPETITION INCREASED, THE TRAPPERS VENTURED into areas previously considered unpromising. In the summer of 1832 Meek joined a band headed by Milton Sublette, William

Sublette's brother, that crossed the northern part of the Great Basin, the large region west of the Rockies and south of the Snake
River from which no rivers exit to the sea. The basin is arid, yet
its higher elevations catch rainfall and so were thought to contain
beaver. This proved true, but the region didn't contain much game,
at least not that summer, and Meek and his comrades grew hungry, then ravenous.

They tried eating beaver, which was barely palatable in the best
of circumstances but downright poisonous in these, as the beavers
had been grazing on wild parsnip, whose toxins passed through
the beavers to the trappers. Several men became badly ill. They
all grew hungrier than ever, until they were reduced to culinary
items and methods they had never before imagined. "I have held
my hands in an ant-hill until they were covered with the ants, then
greedily licked them off," Joe Meek remembered. "I have taken the
soles off my moccasins, crisped them in the fire, and eaten them.
In our extremity, the large black crickets which are found in this
country were considered game. We used to take a kettle of hot water, catch the crickets and throw them in, and when they stopped
kicking, eat them. That was not what we called *cant tickup ko hanch*
(good meat, my friend), but it kept us alive."

The Indians of this part of the Great Basin were the poorest
Meek or most other visitors had ever seen. The whites contemp-
tuously called them Diggers for the amount of time they spent
scratching grubs and insects out of the ground for food. The contempt went beyond nomenclature. Milton Sublette's party joined
forces with a band led by New Englander Nathaniel Wyeth; the
groups were working together when Joe Meek discovered one of
the Diggers lurking around a stream where Meek had set out some
traps. Meek shot him dead.

"Why did you shoot him?" Wyeth asked when Meek related
the incident.

"To keep him from stealing my traps," Meek replied.

"Had he stolen any?"

"No, but he looked as if he was going to," Meek said.

Meek didn't mention it, but he never would have taken such unprovoked action against a member of a more formidable tribe. The murder of one of the Blackfeet or Crows or Snakes would have triggered reprisal, leading to a hard battle and likely loss of life. A Digger could be killed with impunity.

Yet Wyeth didn't object to Meek's reasoning. And Meek didn't apologize for his action. Both men judged, from experience, that the Diggers would have killed Meek for his traps if they caught him alone and off guard.

This thinking inspired one of the bloodiest encounters between mountain men and any of the Indian tribes. A group of trappers led by one Jo Walker was working a tributary of the Humboldt River, and their progress attracted a growing crowd of Diggers. The Indians loitered about the camp during the day; at night they stole what they could lay hands on. Eventually the Indians greatly outnumbered the trappers, who became nervous and exasperated. Angry gestures and warnings did nothing to dissuade or disperse the Diggers. Finally Walker declared, "We must kill a lot of them, boys. It will never do to let that crowd get into camp." The trappers, assenting, drew up in a line, and when the Indians again refused to disperse, Walker gave the order to fire. The trappers unleashed a deadly volley that ripped through the crowd of Indians. Three or four score were killed, and the rest finally scattered.

OBSERVERS OF THE FUR TRADE OFTEN REMARKED THAT THE American trappers seemed at constant war with the Indians, while the Hudson's Bay Company dealt with the natives peaceably. This observation overstated the matter, as the Americans had Indian allies as well as Indian enemies, but it did identify a central truth. And this truth turned less on the belligerence in the American character, pronounced though that was, especially in the West at this time, than on the policies of the British and American governments toward the fur companies.

The Hudson's Bay Company operated as a monopoly in those territories it occupied, with exclusive privileges dating from a seventeenth-century charter not dissimilar to the charter of the same era's Virginia Company, which settled Jamestown. The Bay Company's monopoly secured it the financial wherewithal to build networks of trading posts that doubled as forts, secure from Indian attack, from which company officers like John McLoughlin imposed peace in the company's zone. Indians who caused trouble were frozen out of the trade by the Bay monopoly and were thereby denied access to firearms and other manufactured articles on which they had become dependent.

The Americans, by contrast, operated in a Hobbesian world of all against all. America's nascent democracy didn't believe in government-sponsored monopolies, and no company gained a monopoly on its own. As a result, none of the companies could afford to build and maintain fort systems like those of the Bay Company. The alternative to forts was the rendezvous system, which served the same business purpose of facilitating exchange between the parties to the fur trade, but offered no similar security. The competition among the American companies, moreover, caused the Indians to realize that an attack on one party of Americans would *not* foreclose trade with another party, which would be more than happy to seize the attacked party's market share. The Indians were constantly making and breaking alliances with the trappers, who were doing the same to them. The Indians learned that small groups of whites could be robbed or killed with impunity, as there was no law beyond the Missouri and no private group that had the power to act as a quasi-government the way the Hudson's Bay Company did in its territory.

In time the American federal government would impose order in the American West in the way the Bay Company had long done in what would become the Canadian West. Meanwhile, the competitive chaos in the American West left men like Joe Meek at chronic risk. When Meek and his fellow trappers discovered, through repeated experience, that any Indians they encountered would take their scalps and their furs if given a chance, they tended to shoot first.

OCCASIONALLY A SENSE OF HONOR SURFACED AMONG THE warring parties. Meek was traveling in a party led by Thomas Fitzpatrick in September 1834 when a band of Crows approached. The Crow chief evinced a desire to parley with Fitzpatrick, who doubted the bona fides of the chief but, not wishing to insult him, kept his doubts to himself and paid the chief a visit. While he and the chief were sharing a peace pipe, a group of warriors from the chief's camp slipped away and attacked Fitzpatrick's camp, driving off all the horses and stealing much else besides. Fitzpatrick, unaware, ended his visit with the chief and was returning to his own camp when he was met by the Crow warriors with their booty, who derided him for his folly and, to emphasize their point, robbed him, too, compelling him to walk the rest of the way to camp, unarmed and nearly naked.

Fitzpatrick felt badly used by the Crow chief and, returning to the Crow camp the next day, told him so. The chief pleaded inability to control his young men, who, he said, had acted impulsively as young men often do. He said he would try to make things right. He spoke to the young braves and by a combination of promise and threat persuaded them to restore most of the Americans' possessions.

Fitzpatrick accepted the explanation and the goods, and returned to camp. But he ordered his men to move the camp as quickly as possible, for he supposed that the chief's sense of honor applied to that sole instance and that the young Crows, having robbed the Americans successfully once, might try to do so again. And in fact they did, even as the Americans were departing the neighborhood, but with less success the second time around.

YET SUCH CASES WERE THE EXCEPTION. THE RULE OF LIFE IN the mountains was eternal vigilance, and the price of distraction was often death. One day Joe Meek was working a creek above Pierre's Hole with a trapper named Allen when they were surprised by a party of Blackfeet. The two made for a willow thicket on the far side of the creek. Meek, in the lead, got there first and went into hiding. Allen slipped while crossing the creek and got his rifle wet. He continued across and found his own hiding place. The Blackfeet had seen him, but not Meek, and they approached the thicket with care, not wishing to be shot. Allen, hoping to dry the gun, snapped its firing mechanism to clear the water. The Blackfeet, hearing the sound, went straight toward the defenseless trapper and quickly seized him. They dragged him out of the thicket to an open place beside the creek. While Meek watched helplessly from the willows, they cut Allen to pieces with their knives, extending his agony and celebrating his pain, until he finally expired.

Meek moved not a muscle, remaining hidden until nightfall, long after the Crows had left. He was not a man to dwell on trying moments, but by his own later testimony he could never rid his memory of what he saw that dreadful day.

III

GONE TO TEXAS

11

MOSES AUSTIN'S DYING WISH

JOE MEEK'S VIRGINIA BIRTHPLACE WAS A DAY'S RIDE UP THE Shenandoah Valley from a hamlet the locals called Austinville, after its leading family. If Meek knew any of the Austins, he didn't record the acquaintance for posterity. But one branch of the family shared Meek's wandering spirit, and two members of that branch followed a winding trail to the American Southwest while Meek was tramping about the Northwest.

Like Joe Meek, Moses Austin made a career out of commercializing natural resources. Meek extracted furs from the mountains; Moses Austin extracted ore from mines beneath mountains. He entered the mining business in Virginia but moved to the Louisiana territory, into what would become Missouri, while it was still Spanish. Austin developed lead mines and earned a fortune digging and refining that humble but handy metal. In the early nineteenth century, lead was used to make bullets and shot, plumbing pipe, paint, ceramics, printer's type, tableware, window glazing, medications and many other products. It was known to be toxic, but people who worked around lead learned how to avoid its worst effects. And in any event, its benefits seemed to outweigh its costs.

Moses Austin's business benefited from the transfer of Louisiana to the United States, and by 1810 he was one of the wealthiest men in the American West. Yet ambition drove him to expand his operations further. He did so with borrowed money, and when the British blockade in the War of 1812 cut him off from his markets in the East—lead being too heavy to transport economically overland—he found himself buried in debt. His creditors had him thrown in prison, to ponder the error of his ways and perhaps devise a plan for repayment.

What he came up with was a land scheme centered on Texas. Moses Austin was a geologist, by practice if not formal education, yet he might not have appreciated the way geology had shaped the history of New Spain's northern frontier province. Like much of what would become the American West, Texas had lain for eons beneath the sea, with a steady shower of shells and other detritus of marine creatures gathering on the ocean floor. The material accumulated and compressed, sometimes producing fossil-laced limestone, sometimes oil-bearing sandstone and shale. Tectonic forces eventually pushed the sea floor upward, but where in other parts of the West—the Rocky Mountains, the Sierra Nevada and the Cascades—the violent upthrust formed jagged ranges, in Texas the process was gentle, amounting to little more than a modest tilting that left Texas almost flat while sloping gradually downward from northwest to southeast.

Because of this, Texas developed a river system unique in the West and rare anywhere. The state has a dozen rivers of roughly equal size that run almost parallel on their way to the Gulf of Mexico. In other places, small streams converge into bigger ones until a single river—like the Mississippi and the Columbia, to cite America's most prominent examples—ends up draining a broad area. Such great rivers attract explorers and conquerors, for by seizing the mouth the conquerors can hope to control a vast interior. No such prize drew explorers to Texas. The Spanish happened upon Texas by accident, when the remnant of a sixteenth-century expedition to Florida shipwrecked on the Texas coast. The survivors, including a soldier named Álvar Núñez Cabeza de Vaca, wandered for several years, enduring hunger, cold, sun, slavery and celebrity—a lucky cure caused them to be treated by their Indian

captors as powerful healers—before reaching the Spanish settlements of northern Mexico. Cabeza de Vaca's account of their
experience was mostly the stuff of hardship and survival, but one
sentence set Spanish hearts aquiver: "We saw many signs of gold."
Coming two decades after the Spanish conquests of gold-laden
Mexico and Peru, this intelligence inspired visions of a new El
Dorado in what would become the American Southwest. Francisco Vázquez de Coronado led an expeditionary army that sighted
the Grand Canyon of the Colorado River in Arizona, crossed the
Llano Estacado of Texas, and brutalized the Pueblo peoples of
New Mexico. But Coronado found no gold, and after executing
an Indian guide for leading him astray, he returned to Mexico in
disgust. During the next two centuries, the Spanish established a
presence on the upper Rio Grande in New Mexico, but they left
Texas largely alone. A handful of missions planted in the eighteenth century never thrived; as late as the early nineteenth century, the whole of Texas had fewer non-indigenous inhabitants
than a single neighborhood of Madrid.

Yet if the rivers of Texas attracted little outsider attention, they
accomplished something else. Precisely because they were small
and their gradient slight, they kept the sediment they washed
down from the northwest. The Missouri River was called the Big
Muddy for the soil it stole from Montana and delivered to the
delta of the Mississippi. The Brazos River, the largest of the Texas
streams, deposited its silt along its own banks, forming bottom-
lands of deep black soil that most farmers only dreamed of.

Moses Austin might or might not have known much of this. But
he did know that Texas was underpopulated, from the perspective
of New Spain, and he knew it might attract land-hungry farmers.
He meanwhile observed that Mexico was in turmoil. Nationalists
had raised the flag of Mexican independence and were battling
Spanish troops. The northern frontier of New Spain, more than a
thousand miles from Mexico City, had never been secure, and now
it was more precarious than ever. The Comanches, invading Texas

from the vicinity of the southern Rocky Mountains, were on the verge of pushing the Spanish out of Texas entirely.

Austin's scheme was to offer the Spanish a solution to their Texas problem. He would bring American settlers to Texas, where they would form a barrier against the Comanches. The Spanish would compensate the settlers for their services by granting them tracts of that luscious land. For his part in the deal, Austin would get a finder's fee, which would enable him to fend off his creditors and stay out of prison.

He trekked to San Antonio and presented his plan to the Spanish governor of Texas. The governor listened—in French, the language the two men shared. The governor liked the plan enough to forward it to his superiors in Mexico City.

Moses Austin knew that an answer would take months, so he headed back to Missouri. En route his horse and provisions were stolen by a traveling companion, and he was left to complete the winter journey on foot. By the time he staggered into his home he was sorely ill. His wife put him to bed.

He was beneath covers, shivering, when word arrived that the Spanish government had approved his plan. The news lifted his spirits; he could finally see his way out from under his debts.

But the news came too late. The fever wouldn't let him go. He died a short while later.

With his final breath he whispered to his wife: "Tell dear Stephen that it is his dying father's last request to prosecute the enterprise that he had commenced."

THIS WAS NOT WHAT STEPHEN AUSTIN WANTED TO HEAR. Stephen had observed his father's rise and fall, taking particular note of the latter. Their temperaments could hardly have been more different. Stephen was cautious where Moses was a gambler, studious where Moses learned from life, modest in ambition where Moses always sought more and better. Stephen Austin had heard his father talk about Texas, and had determined to have nothing to do with Moses's brainstorm.

He was apprenticing to an attorney in New Orleans when his mother relayed his father's dying wish. Filial piety alone might not have diverted Stephen from the law; a son had to make his own choices. But he had to consider the family debt, which now hung over his head. Prison wasn't out of the question. The Texas venture seemed the only escape.

Reluctantly Stephen Austin put down his law books. In July 1821 he crossed the Sabine River from American Louisiana to Spanish Texas. "The first 4 miles fine timber and poor land," he wrote in a journal of his trip. "We then suddenly came to an open rolling country thinly timbered, soil about the color of Spanish brown, and in some places redder. This land is very productive and is covered with the most luxuriant growth of grass I ever beheld in any country; almost any of it would produce as much hay as the best meadows. The country so far is well watered."

Austin's impression of Texas only improved the farther into it he got. "The general face of the country from within 5 miles of the Sabine to Nacogdoches is gently rolling," he observed. "The grass is more abundant and of a ranker and more luxuriant growth than I have ever seen before in any country and is indicative of a strong rich soil. . . . The creeks are numerous and water very pure and limpid."

Austin found himself thinking his father might not have been so crazy after all. If the goal was to entice American settlers, Texas seemed to have a lot going for it. "Large rich bottoms on the banks and good pasturage on the upland," he wrote west of Nacogdoches. After two weeks he reached the Brazos River. "Very good: rolling prairie, black soil." The Colorado—a separate stream from that which carved the Grand Canyon of Arizona—ran through a verdant valley. "Grapes in immense quantities on low vines, red, large and well flavored, good for red wine," he noted. The San Marcos River was smaller but no less promising: "Country beautifully rolling, soil very black and rich." The Guadalupe River was even more appealing. "Country the most beautiful I ever saw—rolling prairies, soil very black and deep."

AUSTIN'S IMMEDIATE OBJECTIVE WAS TO SEE IF THE ACCEP-
tance tendered by the government of New Spain to Moses Austin
applied to him as well. He prepared the arguments he would make
to the Spanish governor in San Antonio. But before he reached
the town he learned that the Spanish no longer governed Texas.
Mexico's war of independence had finally succeeded; Mexico now
governed itself.

If Stephen Austin had been looking for an excuse to drop the
Texas project, this was it. There was no assurance the new government of independent Mexico would see Texas as the Spanish had.
Nor was it clear who constituted the new government of Mexico.
The aftermath of revolution is often uncertain. Austin could reflect that the United States had swapped one national government
for another within just a few years of victory in its own war of
independence.

Yet by this time Austin was *not* looking for an excuse to go back
to his law studies. His father's debt still loomed, for one thing.
For another, something of the family ambition had taken hold of
him. As he rode across Texas, he imagined himself becoming a
great man, the founder of a colony. And what a colony it might be!
Texas was lush and sprawling; a whole country might be made of
it. He, Stephen Fuller Austin, could be its founding father.

He proceeded to San Antonio, where the governor who had
negotiated with his father remained in place. The governor initially
encouraged Austin to believe that the deal was still on, but as news
of political turmoil in Mexico City arrived, he waffled. He told
Austin that the only way to be confident in moving forward was
for Austin to go to Mexico City himself.

Austin's spirits sagged. He had come seven hundred miles already; another nine hundred to Mexico City was enough to dismay anyone. But concluding he had no choice, he set out, teaching
himself Spanish from a language primer along the way.

Just south of the Nueces River he encountered the Indians he
had heard much about. "Fifty Comanches charged upon us a little
before sunrise," he wrote in his diary. Austin was traveling with

two other men, but the pair were retrieving the horses from an overnight graze. The Comanches were upon him before he could react. "They surrounded me in an instant and took possession of every article we had." A few moments later his companions returned—as prisoners of other Comanches.

Austin's Texas project might have ended at that point, with his death. But he wouldn't die without a fight, or rather an argument. "I then expostulated with them for treating their friends the Americans in such a manner," Austin recorded. He knew that the Comanches had encountered Americans primarily as traders— suppliers of guns, knives and other items useful against the Spanish. And they had indeed treated the Americans as friends. These Comanches had mistaken Austin and his companions for Spaniards. "When they found there were no Spaniards with me, they gave us back our saddle bags, saddles, and everything else except four blankets, a bridle, my grammar and several other little things and all our provisions." Even so, Austin didn't count on the next band of Comanches to make the same distinction. He sought safety in larger numbers. "I have waited for the company that is going on tomorrow."

He eventually reached the capital city of the new country, whose leaders couldn't decide whether to create an independent monarchy or a republic. Their indecision postponed any decision on Austin's project; not until nearly a year had elapsed did he receive the necessary approvals. Even then he wasn't sure how long they would last. "The revolution is complete," he wrote. "All is quiet." But perhaps only for the moment. "I will not vouch for its being permanent," he said of the calm.

12

TEXAS WILL BE LOST

WILLIAM DEWEES WAS ONE OF AUSTIN'S FIRST TEXAS colonists. A financial panic in 1819 had sent waves of foreclosures rolling across America, displacing many thousands of farmers, mechanics and others who now hoped for better luck in the West. Dewees left Tennessee for Arkansas, where he contracted malaria and alternately sweated and shivered for six months. He joined a band of buffalo hunters on the southern plains, where he was nearly killed by Osage Indians, then by cold and finally by rotgut liquor. Multiple informants told him that Texas was the coming thing for a young man like himself, and he decided to give it a try. He had already crossed the international frontier when he learned of the colony Stephen Austin was planting. He went directly there.

"I have just had the pleasure of spending a few days in the company of Stephen F. Austin," Dewees wrote in his journal. "He was on this river"—the Colorado—"with a surveyor, having lots laid off from a tract of land that he had just located for the purpose of building a town, about eight miles above the crossing of the old Atascocito road. But he has since abandoned it, and located his town, which he calls San Felipe de Austin, on the Brazos River."

Dewees took up one of Austin's Colorado River tracts. The living was hard at first. "There have been a great many new settlers come on this fall," Dewees wrote in December 1823, "and those who have not been accustomed to hunting in the woods for support are obliged to suffer. Were it not for a few of us boys who have no families, their wives and children would suffer much more than they now do; in fact I fear some of them would starve."

Things got worse as winter arrived. "Game is now so scarce that we often hunt all day for a deer or a turkey, and return at night empty handed," Dewees wrote. "It would make your heart sick, to see the poor little half-naked children, who have eaten nothing during the day, watch for the return of the hunters at night. As soon as they catch the first glimpse of them, they eagerly run to meet them, and learn if they have been successful in their hunt. If the hunters return with a deer or a turkey, the children are almost wild with delight, while on the other hand, they suddenly stop in their course, their countenances fall, the deep bitter tears well up in their eyes and roll down their pale cheeks."

Hunger drove some of the settlers back to the United States. Those who remained had to manage another peril. Austin's deal with the Mexican government made no provision for Indian approval of the new colony, and in fact the tribes in the vicinity took sharp exception to the whole project. Like most other tribes, they had tolerated, even encouraged, outsiders to come to their land as traders: transients who brought useful goods and left. Settlers were a different matter. They came in much larger numbers than the traders, and they occupied land the Indians considered their own. Moreover, precisely because of their larger numbers and their designs on the land, they were harder to intimidate.

The Karankawas, the dominant group on the Colorado and Brazos, certainly tried. "They are an exceedingly fierce and warlike tribe, and also perfect cannibals," Dewees remarked of the Karankawas. "Their weapons are bows and arrows; each man carries a bow of precisely his own height, and so very strong that scarcely any American can bend it. They can shoot with their bows and arrows one hundred yards with as great accuracy as an American can with his rifle, and with an equally deadly aim."

Dewees got his first taste of battle after a settler named Brotherton staggered into one of the cabins with a Karankawa arrow in his back, and told of an attack that had killed two settlers and wounded one other. "We immediately raised a force of fourteen men," Dewees recalled. "At midnight we arrived at the place where Brotherton had been wounded. We there dismounted, and five of us went to search out the encampment of the Indians." They found it in a canebrake, gathered the others and crept forward. "As silently as possible, we crawled into a thicket about ten steps behind the camps, placing ourselves about four or five steps apart, in a sort of half-circle, and completely cutting off their retreat from the swamp." They waited till dawn. "When the light was sufficient for us to see clear, we could not see anything of the Indians. We now commenced talking, in order to draw them from their wigwams; in this we succeeded. They rushed out as if greatly alarmed. We fired upon them and killed nine upon the spot. The rest attempted to escape, but having no way to run, except into the open prairie, we rushed upon them, and killed all but two, who had made their escape, though wounded, after the first fire. The number killed, nineteen."

Dewees's battle wasn't over. "Moved somewhat by a spirit of retaliation, I concluded I would take the scalp of an Indian home as a trophy." He discovered that scalping was an art, and rather than slicing the head skin neatly, he was reduced to sawing it. His courage failed. "The skin of his head was so thick, and the sight so ghastly, that the very thought of it almost makes the blood curdle in my veins," he said decades later.

AUSTIN'S COLONY SURVIVED THE HUNGER AND THE INDIAN attacks. The settlers' crops took hold, the Karankawas were kept at bay, and more settlers followed Dewees and the first arrivals to the banks of the Brazos and Colorado rivers. Within a few years a prosperous community emerged.

Austin and his colonists, and settlers who joined other Texas colonies on terms similar to Austin's, owed their prosperity to the government of Mexico, as most of them acknowledged. The Mexican government had given them land—far more land than most of them would ever have acquired in the United States. At a time when a farm in Tennessee might encompass a quarter-section, or 160 acres, the standard grant in Austin's colony was a league, or more than 4,000 acres. A common concern of farmers in America was that their children, upon reaching adulthood, would have to move away to find farms of their own. Lack of land was one of the principal forces driving America's westward movement. In Texas, a patriarch had land enough for all his children and *their* children. Mexican law made princes of many who might have been paupers in the United States.

But not all the Americans who came to Texas did so under the auspices of Mexican law. By handfuls at first, then by scores, then by hundreds and thousands, illegal immigrants poured into Texas. They seized whatever land parcels weren't occupied and made them their homes. Mexican officials were few in Texas, and they were distracted by the turbulence that continued to roil Mexican politics. The squatters could be in place for months or years before the government took notice. By then the squatters thought of the land as their own, and they didn't hesitate to defend it with deadly force.

Within several years of Austin's arrival in Texas, the situation in Texas was spinning out of Mexico's control. The government appointed a commission to examine the Texas question; at its head was Manuel de Mier y Terán, a general in the Mexican army, a former government minister and member of the Mexican congress, an engineer and a scientist. Terán reached Texas in the spring of 1828 and spent the next several months traveling about the settled regions. He visited San Antonio, which remained thoroughly Mexican. But farther east the American influence took hold. His party crossed the Guadalupe River. "On the eastern bank of this river there are six wooden cabins, whose construction shows that those who live in them are not Mexicans," Terán wrote. "Though the house is a single piece, it has two rooms, a high one and a low one. In the latter is found the storeroom and kitchen, whose chimney sticks up on the outside, and in the higher part are the bedroom and living room."

The Americans at first seemed standoffish. "I approached a cabin in hopes that its owner might offer me shelter, but it was in vain," Terán wrote. "I learned later that the North Americans are not used to making such invitations. One arrives quite naturally, sure of being well received. But if one stops at the door, no one encourages him to come inside."

Certain other Americans were as pleasant as could be. Terán's party crossed the Colorado River on a ferry owned by an American named Beeson. "He is quite urbane, his family very honorable," Terán noted. "Their services were very helpful to us." Beeson's wife had learned enough Spanish to explain how well Texas suited them. They had built a cabin and expanded their herd of cattle. "Madame says they have 1,200 pesos in savings. They have been on this land for five years, and they speak with great satisfaction of its fertility and good climate. In a word, they seem happy."

Terán got to Austin's colony in late April. He was highly impressed with the energy and productivity of the immigrants, reckoning the colony's annual corn crop at 64,000 bushels and the cotton crop at 240,000 pounds. Most of the former and essentially all of the latter were exported, as were mules that the Americans raised for sale in the West Indies. Terán had expected to see self-sufficient farms; what he found instead was a hive of commercial enterprise.

Terán asked the Americans what had brought them to Texas. Many mentioned the Texas climate. "To the north the freezing temperatures and snows create obstacles to their work for several months and force them to labor harder. In Texas they work year-round and therefore in greater moderation. In winter they clear and prepare the land that they will plant in the spring." Others referred to the Mexican markets for the crops they raised. "In the north"—of Mexico—"agricultural production outstrips demand, and the prices are exceedingly low. The colonists hope for greater appreciation in the ports and on the coast of Mexico." The Americans had big goals. "They hope to take over the supply of flour, grains, and meats in the ports."

The residents of Austin's colony had the makings of solid Mexican citizens, Terán allowed, even if they clung to their American ways. He couldn't say the same about the Americans he encountered farther east. Nacogdoches marked the beginning of a kind of no-man's-land that stretched to the Sabine River and American territory. The inhabitants put even Terán's party of soldiers on guard. "A great number of the foreigners who have entered the frontier are vicious and wild men with evil ways," Terán wrote. "Some of them are fugitive criminals from the neighboring republic; within our borders they create disturbances and even criminal acts." The United States and Mexico had not worked out border enforcement and extradition rules. "The inhabitants take advantage of their friends and companions to attack and to defend themselves and cross from one side to the other in order to escape punishment."

At Nacogdoches Terán reflected on what he had seen. "As one travels from Béxar"—San Antonio—"to this town, Mexican influence diminishes, so much so that it becomes clear that in this town that influence is almost nonexistent," he wrote. "But where could such influence come from? Not from the population, because the ratio of the Mexican population to the foreign is one to ten; nor from its quality, because the population is precisely the contrary: the Mexicans of this town consist of what people everywhere call the abject class, the poorest and most ignorant." The Americans in Nacogdoches operated an English-language school for their children. "The poor Mexicans neither have the resources to create schools, nor is there anyone to think about improving their institutions and their abject condition." As a result, English had become the language of the region, and American influence appeared to be its future.

So what was to be done with the American immigrants? How to stem the invasion? Terán saw no easy answers. "Nature tells them that the land is theirs," Terán wrote, "because, in effect, everyone can appropriate what does not belong to anyone or what is not claimed by anyone. When the occasion arises, they will claim the irrefutable rights of first possession." Terán acknowledged that the legal immigrants of Austin's colony were a different sort than the illegals of the border region. But he wasn't sure that this made the future of Mexican Texas any more secure. "I must say in all frankness that everyone I have talked to here who is aware of the state of the country and devoted to its preservation is convinced, and has convinced me, that these colonies, whose industriousness and economy receive such praise, will be the cause for the Mexican federation to lose Texas unless measures are taken soon."

What kind of measures? First, a stronger military presence. "On the frontier there are intrigues," Terán wrote. And lest the intrigues become rebellions, Mexico needed more soldiers in Texas. Second, immigration should be suspended until it could be controlled. The border must be policed and illegal immigrants deported. Third, and most important, Mexico needed to make Texas truly Mexican, before the Americans made it irretrievably American. "The land of Texas, or at least its eastern part where its principal rivers begin to be navigable, should be reserved for Mexican settlers," Terán declared. He didn't advocate removing legal immigrants like those in Austin's colony, but any new settlers must come from Mexico, not from the United States. Terán proposed that the government provide incentives to attract five thousand Mexicans to the Trinity River, to act as a bulwark against the Americans.

His plan would be expensive, Terán conceded. But he saw no other choice. If current trends persisted, Texas would be lost.

13

RUIN AND REDEMPTION

S AM HOUSTON DID HIS BEST TO ENSURE THAT TEXAS *WOULD* be lost. Houston made it his life's work to separate Texas from Mexico. At least he did so after his other life's work failed. Born in Virginia, like Stephen Austin (and Joe Meek and Meriwether Lewis and William Clark: there was something in Virginia's soil that propelled her sons in a westerly direction), Houston moved to Tennessee with his mother and eight siblings after his father's death. Houston was fourteen. A tattered copy of the *Iliad* fell into his hands, inspiring romantic notions of great deeds. When romance collided with the reality of life behind a plow, Houston ran away from home and took up with a band of Cherokees. The leader of the band became his surrogate father; the Cherokee word for Raven became his adopted name.

After a few years he returned to white society. America was going to war against Britain, and the country needed soldiers. Houston, a strapping fellow with a head and mane like a lion's, answered the call, albeit as much for the pay, to retire some debts, as from patriotism. Yet he served with conspicuous courage, especially in the 1814 battle of Horseshoe Bend, where an army under Andrew Jackson defeated a faction of Creek Indians that had lately massacred hundreds of whites, including women and children, at Fort Mims in Mississippi Territory. Houston led a charge over a well-defended Creek rampart and was so badly wounded that the medics gave him up for dead and left him lying on the battlefield. Yet he survived, and crawled into camp the next day, to the amazement and chagrin of the medics. Andrew Jackson was impressed.

Houston was recuperating when Jackson defeated a British army at the 1815 Battle of New Orleans. The British, propelled by the momentum of having sacked Washington, D.C., and burned the Capitol and the White House, aimed to drive up the Mississippi River and split America's West from its East. The former—essentially the Louisiana Purchase—would be taken by Britain directly or made into a Britain-friendly Indian territory. In either event, America's westward expansion would be blocked and its future cast into serious doubt.

Jackson's astonishing victory—his army inflicted losses of more than two thousand on the British while itself suffering fewer than one hundred—thwarted the British plan. News of the feat reached Washington and New York just ahead of word that a peace agreement had been reached in Ghent, in modern Belgium, two weeks ahead of the battle. Whether the agreement would have nullified a British victory at New Orleans, few Americans much cared to debate; the overwhelming interpretation was that Jackson had saved the West and thereby America. At once he was hailed as the reincarnation of George Washington, with New Orleans called the counterpart to Yorktown. And just as Washington had been rewarded with the presidency, so should Jackson, in due course.

Sam Houston watched all this and concluded that it was Jackson, in fact, who was the second father he had been looking for. Jackson, meanwhile, lacking a natural son and recalling Houston's heroics at Horseshoe Bend, began thinking of Houston as a surrogate son. Houston followed Jackson into the practice of law in Nashville; with Jackson's help he was elected to Congress, where he became a driving force in a campaign to draft Jackson for the presidency.

By the time Jackson was elected in 1828, Houston, again with Jackson's help, had become governor of Tennessee. In his early thirties, he seemed a likely successor to Jackson in the White House—Young Hickory to Old Hickory.

But Houston's résumé lacked a crucial entry: a wife. Voters then, as later, liked their candidates married: marriage showed an ability to make and sustain commitments of the kind crucial to the lives of most Americans. Houston decided to remedy his lack. He let out that his bachelor days were over; he was looking for a wife.

Many of Tennessee's maidens showed interest; their parents showed even more. Houston was handsome, brave, successful. Who *wouldn't* want to marry him, or want him to marry their daughter?

Eliza Allen, a nineteen-year-old beauty, caught Houston's eye and won his heart. Their wedding was the event of the social season in central Tennessee; the gaze of their family, friends and admirers turned discreetly aside as the couple embarked on their honeymoon.

And then something happened that changed the course of history. No one at the time besides Houston and Eliza knew for sure what that something was. No one afterward definitively figured it out. But the marriage fell apart, suddenly and spectacularly. Eliza went home to her parents and never returned to Houston's house. Tongues wagged, tracing the troubles to the wedding night. Houston's allies blamed Eliza, whispering that perhaps she had come to his bed less than a virgin. Eliza's friends suggested that Houston, on account of his battle wounds, was unable to perform his husbandly duties.

Houston ignored the libels against him and vowed to punish those against Eliza. As he left Nashville in mortification, having resigned the governorship, he made a grim promise: "If any wretch ever dares to utter a word against the purity of Mrs. Houston I will come back and write the libel in his heart's blood."

Years later a friend of Houston's claimed to have heard the true story of the ill-fated wedding night from Houston himself. "About one o'clock in the morning I was waiting and smoking as he staggered into the room," the friend said. "His face was rigid. His eyes had a strange stare. He looked like some magnificent ruin. He sat upright in his chair finally, and running his fingers through his hair said, 'It was so infamous, so cruel, so vile. . . . Cursed be the human fiends who force a woman to live with a man whom she does not love. Just think of it, the unending torture. . . . She has never loved me; her parents forced her to marry me. She loved another from the first.'"

HEARTSICK AND HUMILIATED, SUDDENLY WITHOUT A FUTURE, Houston sought refuge among his Cherokee friends, who had moved under duress to the Indian Territory in what would become Arkansas and Oklahoma. He drowned his sorrows in alcohol, to the point that the Cherokees retired his old name, Raven, and replaced it with Big Drunk. The import of liquor for resale was forbidden in the Indian Territory; Houston, caught with nine barrels in his possession, beat the rap by explaining, convincingly, that the stock was for his personal consumption.

Houston's admirers wondered what had become of him. "I have this moment heard a rumor of poor Houston's disgrace," Andrew Jackson wrote when the news reached Washington. "My God, is the man *mad*?"

He often seemed mad, not least when he began to ramble about a project that would regain for him the reputation he had lost. Houston had never been to Texas, but he knew that many Tennesseans were going there. Some went honestly, intending to become loyal citizens of Mexico like Stephen Austin. But increasing numbers went illegally and with the idea that Texas should become American. Houston determined to take the lead of this group and do something no American had ever done before: conquer territory to add to the American domain.

He thought Andrew Jackson would approve. Jackson was known to covet Texas, and Houston proposed to deliver it. But

Jackson at first wanted nothing to do with someone who had so badly lost his bearings. Besides, Jackson just then was trying to purchase Texas from Mexico, and anything like what Houston proposed would blow up the negotiations. Jackson froze Houston in his tracks. "It has been communicated to me that you had the illegal enterprise in view of conquering Texas," Jackson wrote Houston. "I must really have thought you deranged to have believed you had so wild a scheme in contemplation." Jackson insisted that Houston pledge to do no such thing.

Houston gave the pledge, but he didn't give up the idea. Jackson's effort to acquire Texas by peaceful means went nowhere. Mexican officials had read the report of General Terán, and his warning that Mexico was losing Texas to illegal American immigrants made them loath to legitimize the operation by sale.

Houston approached Jackson again. During the summer of 1832 he visited the president at the Hermitage, Jackson's home outside Nashville. The meeting was private, and neither man ever related what was said. But shortly thereafter Houston obtained a passport from U.S. army officers in Arkansas authorizing his travel as a federal agent investigating relations with various Indian tribes. Some of the tribes Houston could meet on American soil, in the Indian Territory, but others would require him to go to Texas.

With this diplomatic cover, Houston entered Texas from the north, across the Red River. He traveled throughout the eastern half of Texas, where the Americans lived. He asked about the Indians, per his job description. At San Antonio he even met some Comanches, from a band that was momentarily friendly. But he spent most of his time surreptitiously measuring the support of the Americans in Texas for the breakaway he had in mind.

They told him what he wanted to hear. Or so he portrayed their response in his report to Jackson. The vast majority—"nineteen twentieths of the population"—wanted to see Texas detached from Mexico and annexed to the United States, Houston said. They were sick and tired of Mexican misrule. "They are now without laws to govern or protect them." The rights of the Americans were repeatedly trampled. "The government is essentially despotic and must be so for years to come."

HOUSTON'S LETTER EXAGGERATED THE PROPORTION OF AMER-icans wishing to exchange Mexican rule for American. And his de-scription of their complaints was misleading. What the Americans in Texas feared was not the failure of Mexican officials to enforce the law, but the possibility that they *would* enforce the law—in particular that portion of Mexican law forbidding slavery.

Slavery had been part of the American experience in Texas from the start. It was built into Stephen Austin's business model. Americans would come to his Texas colony to establish home-steads, but those homesteads would also be commercial farms. The eastern part of Texas was an extension of the Gulf Coast Plain on which cotton culture was booming. Austin intended his colony to be part of the boom. Especially in the difficult early days of his col-ony, Austin looked to cotton for deliverance. "The primary prod-uct that will elevate us from poverty is cotton," he declared. As on the America side of the border, cultivating cotton required bound labor. "We cannot do this without the help of slaves," Austin said.

The settlers came, and they brought their slaves. But while they were doing so, the Mexican government was taking measures to abolish slavery, which grated on the republican conscience of the newly independent country. Loopholes and lax enforcement al-lowed the Texans to continue the practice, sometimes disguised as indentured servitude. But above the heads of the Texas planters always loomed the possibility that their slaves would be taken from them. As much as anything else, this was what caused the restive-ness of the Texas Americans that Houston misleadingly described.

Whatever its source, Houston determined to exploit the Amer-icans' dissatisfaction. He moved to Texas, nominally to start a law practice, but in fact to foment an uprising against Mexico. And he ran squarely into Stephen Austin. More than a decade after his arrival in Texas, Austin was the indispensable man in his adopted home. The Americans in Texas needed Austin to manage their affairs with the Mexican government. It was Austin who arranged the loopholes and the laxness that let slavery flourish in a corner of a country where it was nominally banned. For its part, the Mexican government needed Austin to keep the Americans in line. So long as Texas remained part of Mexico, Austin would continue to be the indispensable man. But if Sam Houston led Texas out of Mexico, *he* would become the hero. He would be the George Washington of Texas. Stephen Austin would be forgotten, if not trampled.

Each man had his supporters. Austin's were the old settlers, the legal immigrants who owed their land titles to him and to the existing network of Mexican laws. Houston's were the recent arrivals, often illegal, who had no stake in Mexican law and were temperamentally inclined to give the status quo a violent shaking.

The balance tipped in Houston's favor when Antonio López de Santa Anna, a charismatic soldier and politician, nullified the Mexican constitution and established himself as an autocrat. His actions alienated Mexicans in several parts of the country. Republicans in the state of Zacatecas raised arms to resist the dictator, and were promptly crushed. Santa Anna let his troops loot the city of Zacatecas as warning to anyone else considering resistance.

Americans in Texas took the warning, but not as Santa Anna intended. They decided they needed to make their break before he got stronger. Even Austin reluctantly agreed, concluding that Santa Anna's usurpation had shattered any hope of a happy, prosperous Texas within Mexico. Suddenly Houston, the latecomer to Texas, was the man of the hour.

14

VICTORY OR DEATH

THE REVOLT BEGAN WITH A SKIRMISH AT GONZALES, seventy miles east of San Antonio, in the autumn of 1835. Unrest in the area had prompted the Mexican army to try to retrieve a small cannon loaned to the town as defense against Indians. A group of Texans perceived in the effort a design against their liberties and refused to hand it over. They fired on the Mexicans, who returned the fire. The engagement lasted only minutes, and the casualties were few. The Mexican commander pulled back, having no orders to start a war.

The Texans, who *did* want a war, proclaimed a great victory. "It was our Lexington," one of the Texans declared. Like the famous American battle of 1775, the skirmish at Gonzales transformed a political contest into a military one. The Texans adopted the language and procedures of the American Revolution to justify their decision to seek independence from Mexico. The various communities of Americans in Texas selected delegates who gathered at a hamlet they called Washington-on-the-Brazos to draft a declaration of Texas independence. Their litany of grievances echoed that of Thomas Jefferson's declaration; Santa Anna stood in for George III as the villain of the piece. The Texas declaration, like the American, concluded with a rousing affirmation of a new political entity: "We, therefore, the delegates with plenary powers of the people of Texas, in solemn convention assembled, appealing to a candid world for the necessities of our condition, do hereby resolve and declare that our political connection with the Mexican nation has forever ended, and that the people of Texas do now constitute a FREE, SOVEREIGN, and INDEPENDENT REPUBLIC."

THE DECLARATION CAME TOO LATE FOR WILLIAM TRAVIS AND the garrison of the Alamo. Travis was a South Carolinian whose family moved to Alabama, where at the age of twenty he married. The marriage lasted but two years before Travis abandoned his wife, their son and an unborn child his wife was carrying. The neighbors whispered that Travis had been cuckolded—the unborn child was not his—and that he had killed the man responsible. The first part of the whispered stories explained Travis's abrupt departure; the second suffered from lack of a corpse. In any event, Travis headed to Texas, where he joined Stephen Austin's colony and listed his marital status as single.

There was no category on the enrollment form for hothead, but if there had been Travis should have marked it. He immediately joined the party agitating for war against Mexico. After the fight at Gonzales, he leaped to the front of those boasting they could whip ten times their number of Mexicans. He cited previous service in the Alabama militia and was given, at the age of twenty-six, command of a small force sent to San Antonio, which had been captured by the Texas rebels after a sharp battle.

At San Antonio Travis quarreled with James Bowie, who brought his own company of fighters. Bowie's background was even more checkered than Travis's. His trail to Texas was littered with land fraud, illegal slave-running, and deadly knife fights that caused blacksmiths throughout the lower Mississippi Valley to get requests for a monstrous blade like Bowie's. Bowie was a dozen years older than Travis and more experienced in the ways of Texas, and he saw no reason to defer to him. The quarrel threatened to split the San Antonio garrison, until Bowie fell ill and was confined to his sickbed.

The Alamo. This is the chapel, where the defenders made their last stand.

At just this time a large Mexican army appeared on the southern horizon. The Texans retreated into the Alamo, an abandoned mission with walls that offered shelter. At the head of the Mexican army was Santa Anna, come to Texas to crush the rebellion as he had crushed the revolt in Zacatecas.

The Mexicans surrounded and besieged the Texans. The siege wasn't airtight: Travis managed to send out letters calling for help. One in particular stirred the souls of those who read it even many decades later:

To the People of Texas and all Americans in the world:

Fellow Citizens and Compatriots—I am besieged by a thousand or more of the Mexicans under Santa Anna. I have sustained a continual bombardment and cannonade for 24 hours and have not lost a man. The enemy has demanded surrender at discretion; otherwise, the garrison are to be put to the sword, if the fort is taken. I have answered the demand with a cannon shot, and our flag still waves proudly from the walls. *I shall never surrender or retreat.*

Then, I call on you in the name of Liberty, of patriotism and every thing dear to the American character, to come to our aid with all dispatch. The enemy is receiving reinforcements daily and will no doubt increase to three or four thousand in four or five days. If this call is neglected, I am determined to sustain myself as possible and die like a soldier who never forgets what is due his own honor and that of his country. VICTORY or DEATH.

Unfortunately for Travis, his plea didn't stir enough souls in the days after it was sent. Sam Houston, named commander of the Texas army on the strength of his U.S. army service under Andrew Jackson, wanted nothing to do with the defense of the Alamo. He judged it too far from the center of the American communities in Texas, and indefensible against the force Santa Anna could bring against it. Indeed, he had ordered Travis to evacuate the Alamo and return to the rest of the army, but Travis had ignored the order. Houston refused to send reinforcements, believing they would be killed with Travis's garrison, victims of Travis's folly.

Travis did get support from a few dozen rebels who, on their own initiative, slipped past the Mexican siege lines at night. But he remained overwhelmingly outnumbered, with some two hundred fighters against Santa Anna's nearly two thousand.

The siege lasted thirteen days. Finally, in the predawn hours of March 6, 1836, Santa Anna launched the attack. "The moon was up," recounted José Enrique de la Peña, an officer in the Mexican army. "But the density of the clouds that covered it allowed only an opaque light in our direction, seeming thus to contribute to our designs. This half-light, the silence we kept, hardly interrupted by soft murmurs, the coolness of the morning air, the great quietude that seemed to prolong the hours, and the dangers we would soon have to face: all of this rendered our situation grave. We were still breathing and able to communicate; within a few moments many of us would be unable to answer questions addressed to us, having already returned to the nothingness whence we had come." The soldiers felt the fear of all who enter battle. But they felt patriotism too. "An insult to our arms had to be avenged, as well as the blood of our friends spilled three months before within these same walls we were about to attack."

Four Mexican columns approached the Alamo. The Texan sentries, exhausted by the siege, were dozing. Suddenly the Mexican bugles sounded, calling the charge.

The Mexican troops stormed the walls with ladders and began to climb. The Texans emptied their rifles down upon the Mexicans but not fast enough to keep them from coming over the top. The fighting was hand to hand—sword and bayonet, knife and pistol, rifle butt and fist—as the eastern sky lightened. The bravest of the Mexicans battled past the defenders on the ramparts and into the fort itself, then fought their way to the gates, which they threw open to their comrades. Hundreds of additional Mexican troops poured inside.

The fighting grew even more intense. Santa Anna had decreed that no prisoners were to be taken. The rebels were pirates trying to steal Mexican land, he said. Their lives were forfeit. The battle was to the death.

And it was utterly chaotic. "Our soldiers, some stimulated by courage and others by fury, burst into the quarters where the enemy had entrenched themselves, from which issued an infernal fire," de la Peña recorded. "Behind these came others who, nearing the doors and blind with fury and smoke, fired their shots against friends and enemies alike, and in this way our losses were most grievous. On the other hand, they turned the enemy's own cannon to bring down the doors to the rooms or the rooms themselves; a horrible carnage took place, and some were trampled to death. The tumult was great, the disorder frightful; it seemed as if the furies had descended upon us; different groups of soldiers were firing in all directions, on their comrades and on their officers, so that one was as likely to die by a friendly hand as by an enemy's."

The slaughter continued until the last Texans were cornered in the chapel. The Mexicans turned the rebels' cannons against the heavy structure, but its stone walls absorbed the blows intact. The cannoneers targeted the thick oak doors of the chapel. These finally gave way. The attackers stormed the building and didn't stop killing until the last Texan was dead.

OR PERHAPS NOT QUITE. DE LA PEÑA TOLD OF A HANDFUL of Texans who had been taken prisoner in the battle. "Among them was one of great stature, well proportioned, with regular features, in whose face there was the imprint of adversity, but in whom one also noticed a degree of resignation and nobility that did him honor. He was the naturalist David Crockett."

David Crockett was the most famous of the Alamo defenders. Indeed he was one of the most famous Americans of his generation. A Tennessee frontiersman with a knack for self-promotion, Crockett had been elected to Congress not long after Andrew Jackson became president. Jackson's foes lavished attention on Crockett, hoping to establish him as a foil to the Tennessean in the White House. Crockett played their game, humoring authors who wrote his biography and playwrights who put his life into dramatic form. Eventually Jackson's allies mounted a counteroffensive and contested Crockett's reelection. Crockett campaigned on a simple platform. "I told the people of my district that if they saw fit to reelect me, I would serve them as faithfully as I had done before," he said afterward. "But if not, *they might go to hell, and I would go to Texas.*"

He lost, and arrived amid the Texas revolution. Crockett had fought Indians and the British; he saw no reason he shouldn't fight Mexicans. Hearing that William Travis needed reinforcements in San Antonio, he traveled there, arriving not long before Santa Anna and the Mexican army.

Crockett became a favorite with the garrison during the siege, and he fought beside them during the climactic battle. If de la

Peña's account is accurate, he survived the battle and, with several others, was brought before Santa Anna afterward. A Mexican officer named Castrillón, sickened by the carnage of the morning, asked that Crockett and the others be spared. Crockett, he pointed out, was a foreigner, a late arrival to Texas.

The general refused. "Santa Anna answered Castrillón's intervention in Crockett's behalf with a gesture of indignation and, addressing himself to the sappers, the troops closest to him, ordered his execution," de la Peña related. "The commanders and officers were outraged at this action and did not support the order, hoping that once the fury of the moment had blown over, these men would be spared. But several officers who were around the president and who, perhaps, had not been present during the moment of danger, became noteworthy by an infamous deed, surpassing the soldiers in cruelty. They thrust themselves forward, in order to flatter their commander, and with swords in hand, fell upon these unfortunate, defenseless men just as a tiger leaps upon his prey. Though tortured before they were killed, these unfortunates died without complaining and without humiliating themselves before their torturers."

15

BLOODY PALM SUNDAY

I N THE AFTERMATH OF HIS VICTORY, SANTA ANNA SUMMONED
Susanna Dickinson, the wife—now widow—of one of the slain
defenders of the Alamo. She stepped forward, clinging to her infant daughter. Susanna Dickinson and several other women who
had come to the Alamo with their husbands had taken shelter with
their children in the chapel as the storm of battle raged. Though
terrified by the cannon blasts and the wholesale slaughter, they
survived and were spared by the Mexican soldiers.

Santa Anna gave each of the women two silver dollars, a blanket
and their freedom to go. Susanna Dickinson received, in addition,
an escort to the lines of Sam Houston's army. She was to convey
the news of the destruction of the Alamo and Santa Anna's warning
that a similar fate would befall any who continued to oppose him.

JAMES FANNIN GOT THE GRIM NEWS AT GOLIAD, NINETY MILES
southeast of San Antonio. Fannin commanded a rebel force of
some four hundred, of whom the great majority weren't Texans, but new recruits to the Texas cause. Upon the outbreak of
fighting the rebels had advertised in newspapers in Louisiana and
elsewhere for volunteers to defend liberty in Texas. In exchange
for their services the volunteers would each receive eight hundred
acres of land. The bargain seemed a good one before the fall of the
Alamo, and hundreds of volunteers had found their way to Goliad.

Fannin valued the reinforcements, but it galled him that the fate of Texas depended on these foreigners. "I have but three citizens in the ranks," he grumbled. "Though I have called on them for six weeks, not one yet arrived, and no assistance in bringing me provisions." Fannin considered himself badly used by his compatriots. "I feel too indignant to say more about them. If I was honorably out of their service, I would never re-enter it."

Yet here he was. And Santa Anna was approaching. Fannin received an order from Houston to evacuate Goliad and retreat to the east. The loss of the Alamo's garrison dealt the rebel cause a grievous blow; Houston couldn't afford the loss of Fannin's men too. "The immediate advance of the enemy may be confidently expected," Houston wrote. "Prompt movements are therefore highly important."

Fannin hesitated. At Goliad he could fight from behind walls. In the open he and his men would be more vulnerable. For days he couldn't decide.

He finally chose to follow Houston's order. He and his men burned the town and headed into an ominous quiet. "The country around us seemed entirely deserted," Herman Ehrenberg, one of the soldiers, recollected. "Even the usual spies had stopped prowling around." The evacuation did not go well. "A large number of wagons laden with foodstuffs and ammunition encumbered and slowed up our march, for, unwilling at first to lose all our belongings, we had taken with us much heavy baggage." Fannin, constantly looking over his shoulder in the direction from which the Mexican army would come, jettisoned a large part of the baggage. This measure helped some, but not enough. "Several wagons were broken up or merely abandoned, and their teams hitched to the remaining carts," Ehrenberg continued. Even this left the pace of the march too slow. Fannin ordered the rest of the vehicles left behind.

He didn't act soon enough. Mexican horsemen caught Fannin's column on the prairie that afternoon. He ordered his troops to form a hollow square, with cannons and rifles aiming out. As the Mexican cavalry charged, the Texans unleashed a raking fire that killed riders and horses alike. The Mexicans fell back. But, regrouping, they charged again. And again. Each time, they were driven back, but each time they inflicted more casualties on the rebels.

As the main force of the Mexicans reached the scene, Fannin realized his position was untenable. Low on ammunition, suffering from lack of water, outnumbered soon if not already, the Texans could hold out for a few hours, perhaps longer. But they could not prevail. And they could not escape.

Fannin delayed a decision overnight, on the thin chance reinforcements might appear. They didn't. Instead Mexican artillery was moved into position to obliterate the Texans. Fannin, after consulting his lieutenants, decided to raise a white flag and ask for surrender terms.

The answer he received became a matter of subsequent dispute. The Mexican commander, knowing Santa Anna permitted no quarter, said he could accept nothing but unconditional surrender. The Texans heard something different: that they would be treated as prisoners of war.

Both sides were happy to avert a massacre then and there. But Santa Anna was not. When he learned that Fannin and his men had been taken prisoner, he flew into a rage. His entire policy toward the rebels depended on swift and certain punishment of those who took up arms against his government. He ordered that the prisoners be executed at once. His subordinates reluctantly prepared to comply.

"GREY CLOUDS HUNG OVER THE HORIZON, AND THE AIR WAS hot and sultry," Herman Ehrenberg recalled of Sunday, March 27, 1836. The Texans had been marched back to Goliad and imprisoned there. Now they were ordered to march forth again. "Mexican soldiers met us on either side as we came out of the main entrance," Ehrenberg wrote. "They were drawn up in two lines, one man behind the other, so that we were closely guarded on both sides when we marched forward." Some of the prisoners thought they were being moved to a more secure location. Their guards offered no clue. "The Mexican soldiers, who were as a rule very talkative, were unbearably silent; our men were grave; the atmosphere hot and close," Ehrenberg said.

Half a mile from the fort the prisoners were ordered off the main road. "On our left there stood a row of mesquite trees, five or six feet high, stretching in a straight line as far as the bank of the San Antonio River, which lay some way off," Ehrenberg remembered. "The river flowed between banks thirty or forty feet high, which on our side rose almost perpendicularly from the water. We followed the hedge towards the river, wondering why we were being taken in this direction."

They learned soon enough. "A command to halt, given in Spanish, struck our ears like the voice of doom, for at that very moment we heard the distant rattle of a volley of musketry," Ehrenberg said. An officer ordered Ehrenberg and those around him to kneel. The Mexican soldiers leveled the muzzles of their guns at the prisoners.

Ehrenberg hoped the Mexicans were bluffing, perhaps to frighten the Texans into giving up their rebellion and joining the Mexican side. The Mexicans were deadly serious. "A second volley of musketry came to our ears from another direction; this time a wail of distress followed it." The soldiers at hand opened fire. "Thick clouds of smoke rolled slowly towards the river. The blood of my lieutenant spurted on my clothes, and around me the last convulsions of agony shook the bodies of my friends."

Somehow Ehrenberg survived the execution volley. Amazed he wasn't dead, he dove to the ground and scrambled away, providentially hidden by the smoke of the fire that had killed nearly all his comrades. He reached the river and threw himself in. Mexican soldiers fired at him, but between the obscuring effect of the smoke and the cover of the water, their bullets missed.

He swam to the other side, crawled out on the bank, and hid in some brush. He looked back. The Mexicans were still shooting and yelling. Amid the clamor Ehrenberg could just hear the groans of his dying comrades.

16

LAYING THERE YET

MORE THAN THREE HUNDRED TEXANS WERE KILLED AT Goliad, half again as many as at the Alamo. Yet fate had further blows for the Texans. The aim of Santa Anna's no-quarter strategy became clear in the weeks after the Goliad massacre. The Mexican leader, taking to heart General Terán's warning about the out-of-control Americans in Mexico's border province, determined to solve his American problem by removing all the Americans. "I am firmly convinced that we ought not to risk allowing either Anglo-American or European colonists to remain on the frontier," he told his war secretary. Legal immigrants who swore loyalty to Mexico should be relocated to the interior. As for the illegal immigrants: "They should be immediately expelled from Mexican territory."

Santa Anna realized that this amounted to an expulsion policy for *all* the Americans. Most of the legal immigrants would go back to the United States before they would accept forced relocation to the Mexican interior. Nor, after the killing of the Goliad prisoners, would the Americans have any confidence in Mexican promises.

The Americans didn't wait to be uprooted by the Mexican army. They uprooted themselves and fled before Santa Anna's approach. In what they would laconically call the "Runaway Scrape," thousands of Texans evacuated their homes and headed for the American border. Creed Taylor, a teenage soldier in the Texan army

119

who returned to his family's farm to help with the evacuation, re-called the fright that seized the populace on learning that Santa Anna was approaching. "The first law of nature, self-preservation, was uppermost in the minds of the settlers," Taylor wrote. "And thus the great exodus began."

The Taylor family had a single cart, with heavy wheels cut from a log. Taylor's mother wanted to load the family possessions onto the cart. Creed and his brother pointed out that they would never outrun the Mexicans in such a slow vehicle. They talked her into leaving most of their belongings behind and packing the rest on a horse, which could move faster.

Creed took a final look at the place where he had grown up. "There was a little corn left in the crib, a large supply of nicely cured bacon in the smokehouse, and the yard was full of chick-ens, turkeys, geese and ducks, besides a good stock of hogs," he recounted. "All of these we left to the invaders." Mrs. Taylor was stoic. "If mother shed a tear, I never knew it, though there was an unusual huskiness in her voice that day. Mother was brave and resolute, and I heard her say to a lady while crossing the Brazos, under great difficulties, that she was going to teach her boys never to let up on the Mexicans until they got full revenge for all this trouble."

On the main road east, they ran into many other families in flight. "People were trudging along in every kind of conveyance, some on foot carrying heavy packs," Creed Taylor said. "I saw every kind of conveyance ever used in that region, except a wheel-barrow, but hand-barrows, sleds, carts, wagons, some drawn by oxen, horses, and burros. Old men, frail women, and little chil-dren, all trudging along."

Taylor would live to see other hard times, but the Texans' flight before Santa Anna stuck in his memory. "I have never witnessed such scenes of distress and human suffering. True, there was no clash of arms, no slaughter of men and horses, as on the field of battle; but here the suffering was confined to decrepit old men, frail women, and little children"—the men of fighting age being mostly with the army. "Delicate women trudged alongside their pack horses, carts, or sleds, from day to day until their shoes were literally worn out, then continued the journey with bare feet, lacerated and bleeding at almost every step. Their clothes were scant, and with no means of shelter from the frequent drenching rains and bitter winds, they traveled on through the long days in wet and bedraggled apparel, finding even at night little relief from their suffering, since the wet earth and angry sky offered no relief."

Moments of hope glimmered through the darkness. A widow with four children, whose husband had died at the Alamo just weeks before, brought a fifth child into the world, with the help of strangers. "A family having a rickety open wagon drawn by two lean ponies gave the helpless mother bed and transportation by throwing part of their belongings from the wagon to make room for a woman they had never seen before," Taylor said. "During rains, by day or night, willing hands held blankets over the mother and babe to protect them from the downpours and chilling storms."

The trials of the weakest were the most heart-wrenching. "It was no uncommon sight to see women and children without shoes, and otherwise thinly clad, wading in mud and chilling water almost to their knees," Taylor recalled. "When a cart or wagon became mired, which was an hourly occurrence east of the Brazos, there was no dearth of helping hands. But in proportion the men were few, and so the women and children were forced to perform most of the labor. Thus these half-clad, mud-besmeared fugitives, looking like veritable savages, trudged along."

SAM HOUSTON RETREATED TOO. IN FACT IT WAS HIS RETREAT that triggered the flight of the civilians, who reckoned that if Houston was leaving there would be no one to protect them from Santa Anna. Many roundly cursed Houston for cowardice; those who lost loved ones to disease and exhaustion on the exodus never forgave him.

But Houston knew two things those who cursed him didn't. The first was that his army was no match for Santa Anna's. The

Mexican troops were trained and well armed; their officers understood discipline and tactics. They outnumbered the rebels badly. For Houston to stand and fight risked a third debacle, after the Alamo and Goliad, that would annihilate the army and snuff out the infant republic. Retreat was his only option.

The second thing Houston knew was that help awaited in his rear. The boundary between American Louisiana and Mexican Texas was the Sabine River. But there was some dispute as to which branch of the Sabine counted. Houston knew that Andrew Jackson took the western branch—which most people called the Neches River—as the boundary. Houston also knew that Santa Anna deemed the eastern branch the true boundary. If anything was certain about Andrew Jackson, it was that Old Hickory would defend every inch of what he considered American territory. Houston supposed something similar about Santa Anna: that he would defend all the territory he thought belonged to Mexico.

Houston judged that the future of Texas would be decided not by Texans alone, but by the United States and Mexico. If he could lure Santa Anna east, into a clash with U.S. forces, the future of Texas would be secure. Houston's aim all along had been to make Texas American; now it would have to become American by force of American arms, because of Texan arms there weren't enough.

And so he retreated. His men complained. They called Houston a coward. They hadn't joined his army to retreat, they said, but to fight. If Houston wouldn't fight, they would fight without him. The civil officials of the Texas republic echoed the troops. David Burnet, the provisional president of the republic, sent Houston a blunt note: "Sir: The enemy are laughing you to scorn. You must fight them. You must retreat no farther. The country expects you to fight. The salvation of the country depends on you doing so."

Houston continued to disagree, albeit silently. The salvation of the country depended on his *not* standing and fighting—and seeing his army destroyed. He continued to be outnumbered and outgunned. Salvation lay not on the Colorado or the Brazos, but on the Neches, in the arms of Andrew Jackson and the United States.

Houston's men grew more mutinous by the day. The crisis came at a fork in the road the army was traveling. The left branch continued toward the Trinity River, Houston's next goal. The right branch veered toward Harrisburg, where, according to recent intelligence, Santa Anna was headed with a flying column, hoping to capture the Texas government.

At the fork the men ignored Houston and went to the right.

Had Houston been Andrew Jackson, he would have shot the leaders of the mutiny. But he wasn't Jackson, and Texas in 1836 wasn't New Orleans in 1815. Discipline in the Texas army was nonexistent; the men did what they wanted, fought when they wanted, went home when they wanted.

Now they insisted on fighting, and Houston chose to make the best of it. Spurring his horse, he rode to the front of the column and led the men in the direction they had already decided to go.

They caught up with Santa Anna near the confluence of the San Jacinto River and Buffalo Bayou. Santa Anna, as scornful of the Americans as ever, let them come. He would complete his annihilation of the rebel army, and then proceed with the cleansing of Texas of all the Americans.

The two armies approached to within a mile of each other. Santa Anna, awaiting the arrival of an auxiliary column, let his men rest after an arduous march. Houston, sensing a lowering of the Mexican guard, ordered an afternoon assault.

The Texans slipped toward the Mexican camp, initially hidden by tall grass and a slight rise in the field between the two armies. At four hundred yards Houston gave the order to attack. His cannons blasted the Mexican position with shrapnel, and the men charged forward shouting, "Remember the Alamo! Remember Goliad!"

The Mexicans were nonplussed by the sudden assault. "I was in a deep sleep when I was awakened by the firing and noise," Santa Anna acknowledged later. "I immediately perceived we were attacked, and had fallen into frightful disorder." Pedro Delgado, one of Santa Anna's lieutenants, remembered trying to control the men. "The utmost confusion prevailed," Delgado said. "I saw our men flying in small groups, terrified, and sheltering themselves be-hind large trees. I endeavored to force some of them to fight, but all efforts were in vain—the evil was beyond remedy: they were a bewildered and panic-stricken herd."

The Texans fought like furies, seeking vengeance for their fallen comrades. The Mexican panic grew worse. "On the left, and about a musket-shot distance from our camp, was a small grove, on the bay shore," Delgado wrote. "Our disbanded herd rushed for it, to obtain shelter from the horrid slaughter carried on all over the prairie by the blood-thirsty usurpers." The bank of the bayou be-came a killing ground. "The men, on reaching it, would helplessly crowd together, and were shot down by the enemy, who was close enough not to miss his aim. It was there that the greatest carnage took place."

The Texans shot and clubbed and stabbed the pinned enemy. "It was nothing but a slaughter," one of the Texans remembered. "They at first attempted to swim the bayou but they were sur-rounded by our men and they shot every one that attempted to swim the bayou as soon as he took to the water, and them that re-mained they killed as fast as they could load and shoot them until they surrendered."

The slaughter didn't end with surrender. Still shouting about the Alamo and Goliad, the Texans exacted their revenge. Houston tried to get them to stop, but they again ignored him. Houston had led the charge and been wounded. "I observed Gen. Houston on a bay pony, with his leg over the pommel of the saddle," Nicholas Labadie, a medic, recalled. "'Doctor,' said he, 'I am glad to see you; are you hurt?' 'Not at all,' said I. 'Well,' he rejoined, 'I have had two horses shot under me, and have received a ball in my ankle, but am not badly hurt.' 'Do you wish to have it dressed?' said I. 'Oh, no, not now, but I will when I get back to the camp. I can stand it well enough till then.' He then faces his horse about, and orders the drum to beat a retreat. But the men, paying no attention to the order, shouted with expressions of exultation over the glorious vic-tory, and it was difficult to hear anything distinctly." Houston tried again. "While I was within ten feet of him, he cries out, as loud as he could raise his voice: 'Parade, men, parade!'" recounted Labadie. "But the shouts and halloing were too long and loud; and Houston, seeing he could not restore order, cries at the top of his voice: 'Gentlemen! Gentlemen! Gentlemen! (a momentary stillness ensues) Gentlemen! I applaud your bravery but damn your manners.'"

Robert Hunter, another soldier, was standing close by. "General Houston gave orders not to kill any more but to take prisoners," Hunter remembered. "Capt. Easlen said, 'Boys, take prisoners—you know how to take prisoners. Take them with the butt of your guns, club guns,' and said, 'Remember the Alamo, remember La Bahía'"—Goliad—"'and club guns, right and left, and knock their brains out.'" Hunter continued, "The Mexicans would fall down on their knees and say, 'Me no Alamo, me no La Bahía.'" But the Texans gave no quarter. The Mexicans ran for a lagoon beyond the battlefield. "Man and horse went in head and ears to the bottom," Hunter said. "That lagoon was full of men and horses for about twenty or thirty feet up and down it, and none of them ever got out. I think their bones are laying there yet."

IV

THE GREAT
MIGRATION

17

THE FOUR WISE MEN

TEXANS MISUNDERSTOOD THE MEANING OF THEIR VICTORY at San Jacinto, and nearly two centuries later, most still do. A monument erected above the battlefield declares, "San Jacinto was one of the decisive battles of the world." Even allowing for Texan pride, this grossly exaggerates the consequences of that bloody day. San Jacinto decided nothing important at all. Santa Anna's defeat didn't end the Texas war of independence, though the Texans soon told themselves it did. They captured the Mexican leader trying to escape the battlefield and compelled him to sign away his country's claim on Texas. But the government in Mexico City deposed Santa Anna, disavowed his disclaimer and continued to assert possession. During the next decade Mexican armies reinvaded Texas and twice reoccupied San Antonio.

They were able to do so because Sam Houston's dream of delivering Texas as a gift to Andrew Jackson stalled on the opposition of Northern members of Congress to the admission of Texas to the Union as a slave state. The antislavery elements weren't a majority, but a treaty of annexation required the approval of two-thirds of the Senate, which slavery's foes were able to deny the annexationists.

The result was that the Texas republic, envisioned as a swiftly transitional step to American statehood, acquired an unexpected permanence. Texans of later generations would wax nostalgic about their state's experience as an independent republic. A few Texans at the time warmed to the idea, imagining Texas expanding far to the west and becoming a great nation of its own. But most Texans, facing an empty treasury, a worthless currency, harrowing raids by Comanches, and embarrassing vulnerability to the Mexican army, still longed for attachment to the country from which the great majority of them had come. Texans would eventually profess to disdain the power of the American federal government, but in the dicey decade after San Jacinto that power seemed a comforting embrace they could only wish for.

Houston was shrewd enough, following his victory in a battle his men had forced him to fight, not to air his belief that the question of Texas wouldn't be settled until the United States went to war with Mexico. He had intended for this to happen in 1836, but his men's mutiny prevented it. San Jacinto, far from resolving the Texas question, left any resolution pending, awaiting that war.

WEEKS BEFORE THE OUTBREAK OF THE TEXAS REVOLUTION, the annual fur-trading rendezvous took place on the Green River in modern Wyoming. Joe Meek attended, as usual, and met two men who were *un*usual for the mountain fair. The rendezvous had acquired a colorful reputation that drew artists, scientists, writers and even tourists, but Marcus Whitman and his partner Samuel Parker were travelers of a different sort. They came west to scout the feasibility of travel to Oregon for the purpose of founding a religious mission.

They were answering a call by the native peoples of the Far West for education in the Christian gospel. Such, at any rate, was how Whitman and Parker and much of Protestant America interpreted an extraordinary tale recounted two years earlier in the *Christian Advocate and Journal and Zion's Herald* and reprinted in numerous papers afterward. An article about the relocation of the Wyandot Indians from their Ohio homeland to Indian Territory west of the Mississippi contained a letter from one of the Wyandots, a Christian convert named William Walker, to an Ohio

friend. Walker was surveying the territory for his tribe and report-
ing on its suitability as a new tribal home. As an aside he mentioned a visit to William Clark, Meriwether Lewis's old partner.
"Immediately after we landed in St. Louis on our way to the west,"
Walker wrote, "I proceeded to General Clarke's, superintendent
of Indian affairs, to present our letters of introduction from the
secretary of war, and to receive the same from him to the different
Indian agents in the upper country. While in his office and trans-
acting business with him, he informed me that three chiefs from
the Flat-Head nation were in his house and were quite sick, and
that one (the fourth) had died a few days ago. They were from the
west of the Rocky Mountains."

Walker asked to see the guests. Clark granted permission.
Walker had heard of the Flatheads but had never encountered any
in person. "I had always supposed from their being called 'Flat-
Heads' that the head was actually flat on top; but this is not the
case. The head is flattened thus"—he appended a sketch, which the
author of the article, or perhaps the editor, improved. Walker went
on explain the method of flattening the skull, by means of a board
pressed against an infant's forehead.

Then he got to the part of the story that sent shivers of holy joy
up the spines of the readers of the *Christian Advocate*. "The distance they had travelled on foot was nearly three thousand miles
to see Gen. Clarke, their great father, as they called him, he being
the first American officer they ever became acquainted with, and
having much confidence in him, they had come to consult him as
they said, upon very important matters. Gen. C. related to me the
object of their mission, and, my dear friend, it is impossible for me
to describe to you my feelings while listening to his narrative. I will
here relate it as briefly as I well can. It appeared that some white
man had penetrated into their country, and happened to be a spec-
tator at one of their religious ceremonies, which they scrupulously
perform at stated periods. He informed them that their mode of
worshipping the supreme Being was radically wrong, and instead
of being acceptable and pleasing, it was displeasing to him; he also

informed them that the white people away toward the rising of the sun had been put in possession of the true mode of worshipping the great Spirit. They had a book containing directions how to conduct themselves in order to enjoy his favor and hold converse with him; and with this guide, no one need go astray, but every one that would follow the directions laid down there could enjoy, in this life, his favor, and after death would be received into the country where the great Spirit resides, and live forever with him."

The Indians had called a council to consider this information. "Some said, if this be true, it is certainly high time we were put in possession of this mode, and if our mode of worshipping be wrong and displeasing to the great Spirit, it is time we had laid it aside. We must know something more about this; it is a matter that cannot be put off; the sooner we know about it the better. They accordingly deputed four of their chiefs to proceed to St. Louis to see their great father, Gen. Clarke, to inquire of him, having no doubt but he would tell them the whole truth about it."

The four chiefs had done just that. Clark, surprised at their appearance in St. Louis and sobered by the responsibility suddenly placed on his shoulders, proceeded—according to Walker's account—to confirm the truth of what the lone white man had said and to instruct the chiefs succinctly in the message of the Old and New Testaments.

"Poor fellows," Walker went on, "they were not all permitted to return home to their people with the intelligence. Two died in St. Louis, and the remaining two, though somewhat indisposed, set out for their native land. Whether they reached home or not is not known. The change of climate and diet operated very severely upon their health. Their diet when at home is chiefly vegetables and fish. If they died on their way home, peace be to their manes! They died inquirers after the truth."

THE AVERAGE READER OF THE *CHRISTIAN ADVOCATE* WAS IN NO position to question certain aspects of Walker's letter, starting with the fact that the visit to St. Louis he described took place in 1831 but he didn't get around to revealing it until 1833. Then there was the matter of the identity of the Indians. Independent evidence suggested that the visitors to William Clark were Nez Perce Indians rather than Flatheads, although one might have been half Flathead. Consequently the illustration of the flattened head was almost certainly an artistic flourish, since, in any event, the Flatheads didn't actually flatten heads; it was the Chinook and their kin who made the pointed heads, by contrast with which the Salish people known as Flatheads had ordinary, or flat, heads.

Yet these minor matters paled beside the astonishing essence of the story: that four enlightened heathens—soon dubbed the "Wise Men of the West"—had come east in search of the proper way to worship the Great Spirit. What made the story more astonishing still, and on that account perhaps more suspect, was that it reached the American East just as the Second Great Awakening was approaching its height of evangelizing fervor. This Christian revival movement—called the Second Awakening to distinguish it from an eighteenth-century forerunner—rejected the often-elitist rationalism of the Enlightenment in favor of a populist emotionalism. Baptists and Methodists benefited most from the surging demand for a religion a believer could *feel*, but the desire for a faith that transformed one's life touched Presbyterians and Congregationalists too.

Nowhere was the Awakening stronger than in western New York, called the "burnt-over district" for the revivals that swept across it, consuming the fuel of unbelief. Marcus Whitman was living in the village of Wheeler, in the heart of the burnt-over district, in the autumn of 1834, when the Reverend Samuel Parker came through summoning support for a mission to the Oregon country. The revivalists weren't content to save souls in the civilized regions of America; their zeal burned to share the gospel with heathens in distant lands. Some missionaries went out to the East Indies, others to the islands of the South Pacific. Parker, having read of the appeal of the Wise Men of the West, aimed for Oregon.

Marcus Whitman was a struggling doctor with a stingy practice and chronic aches from riding too many miles to see patients amid the harsh winters of western New York. He had been "saved," in the meaning of the revivalists, but he had never acted on his faith in the way many others in the movement did. His conscience nagged him to do so. He had scarcely heard of Oregon, but when Samuel Parker related the miraculous story of the Wise Men of the West, Whitman perceived the answer to his professional, physical and existential problems. He decided at once to give up his medical practice, move away from New York and devote his life to saving lost souls.

Four months later he was in St. Louis with Parker, heading west under the sponsorship of the American Board of Commissioners for Foreign Missions. The two men visited the offices of the American Fur Company and secured permission to travel with the company's annual caravan to the summer rendezvous. For Parker and Whitman the journey was a reconnaissance. They would not go all the way to the Columbia River, their eventual goal; rather, they would assay the prospects for taking women and wagons to Oregon. The former were crucial to the mission board's evangelizing strategy; experience had shown that unmarried men, even those of the cloth, were too often tempted beyond their strength by heathen women. Christian wives kept their husbands' passions in check. The wagons were important for the women, who would want to carry more west than could fit on the back of a mule, and for the general provisioning of the missions. Goods might be shipped west by sailing vessel, but the American Mission Board was aware that the Hudson's Bay Company controlled the lower Columbia, and the board didn't want its missions dependent on the goodwill of a British company. An overland connection to the United States would be far preferable to running the Hudson's Bay gauntlet.

By this time steamboats serviced the Missouri River as far as Liberty, Missouri, just east of the northward bend in the river. Parker and Whitman dipped into the funds the mission board had appropriated for their journey and purchased tickets. At Liberty their western experience really began. Friction developed at once between the God-fearing missionaries and the frequently God-damning mountain men to whom they attached themselves. The members of the caravan hadn't been consulted about being saddled with the Bible-thumping greenhorns, and they didn't like it. Parker asked the caravan leader if he and Whitman could put some of their provisions in the fur company's wagons. The caravan leader said they could not; the added weight would burden the horses. Anyway, in the West each man hauled his own provisions. The rank and file of the caravan were even less friendly toward the missionaries, who cramped the mountaineers' style and slowed the progress of the caravan. The missionaries refused to travel on the Sabbath, and though the caravan didn't wait for them, the overall pace was inevitably slowed as the missionaries struggled to catch up on the following days. Parker and Whitman felt the hostility, with Parker fearing at times for his and Whitman's lives.

Things got worse before they got better. The caravan had reached Sioux country when several of the travelers came down with cholera. This virulent disease had been unknown in North America, even among whites, before the 1830s. But during the first years of that decade it leapt the Atlantic and swept from Canada down the Atlantic seaboard and over the Appalachians into the Mississippi Valley. The outbreak the American Fur Company caravan encountered was likely a remnant of the initial epidemic, and it hit the caravan hard. "The weather was very warm, and there were showers from day to day," Parker observed by way of noting circumstances in which the disease commonly spread. Other contributors were the fault of the caravan crew themselves. "The intemperate habits of the men, and their manner of living, probably had a tendency to induce the disease." Three men died and several others were at death's door.

But heaven, and Marcus Whitman, came to the rescue, Parker explained. The sick men survived "through the blessing of God upon the assiduous attentions of Doct. Whitman, my associate,

and the free use of powerful medicines." The cholera outbreak, and
the way it ended, might well have spared Parker and Whitman an
evil fate. "This afflictive scourge, so far as respected Dr. W. and
myself, was providential," Parker said. "The assistance we rendered
the sick, and the medical skill of the Doctor, converted those into
permanent friends who had so disliked the restraints which our
presence imposed upon them that, as they afterwards confessed,
they had plotted our death and intended on the first convenient
occasion to put their purpose in execution."

Hardly had the caravan survived the cholera when several of its
members did something that made Parker wonder who were the
civilized and who the savages. "A man by the name of Garrio, a
half blood Indian chief of the Arickara nation, was shot under very
aggravated circumstances," Parker wrote. "Garrio and his family
were residing in a log cabin on the Papillon River. Six or seven
men, half intoxicated, went down to his house in the night, called
him up, took him away a half mile, and shot him with six balls,
scalped him, and left him unburied. The reason they assigned for
doing so was that he was a bad man and had killed white men."

Parker didn't know if this was true, but the presumption of the
vigilantes appalled him. "If he was guilty, who authorized them to
take his life?" The incident would surely spawn more violence. "The
Arickara nation will remember this and probably take revenge on
some innocent persons. This, I apprehend, is the way Indian wars
are often produced. While we charge the Indians with inveterate
ferociousness and inhuman brutality, we forget the too numerous
wrongs and outrages committed upon them, which incite them to
revenge."

THE CARAVAN ASCENDED THE PLATTE AND THEN THE
Sweetwater. August brought them to the Continental Divide and
the beginning of the Oregon country. They benefited, at two-
decades' remove, from the signal accomplishment of the Astor
project, the one great success amid the multiple disappointments
and ultimate failure of the grand design. A party of Astorians

returning east in 1812 was struggling toward the crest of the Rockies when a Shoshone told them of a better route over the Rockies
than those followed by Lewis and Clark and the Astorians themselves when heading west. "Learning that this Indian is perfectly
acquainted with the route," wrote Robert Stuart, the leader of the
Astor group, "I without loss of time offered him a pistol, a blanket of blue cloth, an axe, a knife, an awl, a fathom of blue beads,
a looking glass and a little powder and ball if he would guide us
to the other side, which he immediately accepted." The Shoshone
evidently changed his mind, for two days later he absconded, taking Stuart's horse with him.

Yet the hint of an easy pass prompted Stuart and the others to
look for it, and with effort they found it. Upon reaching the settlements on the Missouri they shared what they had learned with
others, and thereafter the South Pass route became the standard
for parties bound for Oregon.

To most travelers the South Pass seemed scarcely a pass at all.
"The passage through these mountains is in a valley so gradual in
the ascent and descent that I should not have known we were approaching them had it not been that as we advanced the atmosphere gradually became cooler," Samuel Parker wrote. The valley
varied in width from two to fifteen miles. "Though there are some
elevations and depressions in this valley, yet comparatively speaking it is level; and the summit, where the waters divide which flow
into the Atlantic and into the Pacific, is about six thousand feet
above the level of the ocean." Parker was mistaken about the elevation, which is closer to 7,500 feet, but he wasn't wrong in noting
that the South Pass made crossing the great range of the American
West easier than crossing much smaller ranges in the East.

Two days later they reached the rendezvous, where
Marcus Whitman won additional respect from the mountain men
by turning surgeon. He removed an iron arrowhead, three inches
long, from the back of Jim Bridger, where it had lodged in a fight
with the Blackfeet three years earlier. The extraction was tricky, as

the tip of the arrow had bent upon hitting a large bone, and the bent tip acted like a barb, holding the arrow in place. Moreover, cartilage had grown around the arrow. But Bridger wanted it out, and Whitman obliged. "The Doctor pursued the operation with great self-possession and perseverance," Parker recorded, "and his patient manifested equal firmness. The Indians looked on meanwhile with countenances indicating wonder, and in their own peculiar manner expressed great astonishment when it was extracted." Whitman's medical skills would prove both a boon and a bane in his subsequent work with Indians, for now they seemed marvelous. The mountaineers certainly thought so. A second trapper asked to have an arrow removed from his shoulder, and Whitman obliged. Many others queued up for minor surgeries and for medicines for assorted ailments.

At the rendezvous, Parker and Whitman met Nez Perce and Flathead Indians. The two missionaries referred to the Flathead (or Nez Perce) delegation to St. Louis described in the *Christian Advocate*, and they said their present journey was a response to the plea of that delegation to learn about the gospel. They asked whether the Indians indeed wished them to come to Oregon and teach them the ways of God. "The oldest chief of the Flatheads arose," Parker recorded, "and said, 'he was old, and did not expect to know much more; he was deaf and could not hear, but his heart was made glad, very glad, to see what he had never seen before, a man near to God (meaning a minister of the gospel).'" The principal chief of the Nez Perce spoke in a similar vein. "He had heard from white men a little about God, which had only gone into his ears; he wished to know enough to have it go down into his heart, to influence his life, and teach his people."

Parker drew the crucial, and welcome, conclusion: "The Nez Perces and Flathead Indians present a promising field for missionary labor, white for the harvest, and the indications of divine providence in regard to it are made plain by their anxiety to obtain Christian knowledge." Parker and Whitman decided that their first mission in Oregon must be among these peoples.

So encouraged were the two missionaries that they decided that Whitman should return east at once and gather associates and supplies for a full-fledged expedition to Oregon the following year. Leaving Parker to continue the reconnaissance, Whitman again joined the fur company caravan when, having exchanged its provisions for furs, it retraced the route over South Pass and down the Missouri to St. Louis. The caravan reached that city in early November. Whitman continued east to New York, arriving home in December.

18

FEMALES WANTED

MORE THAN EAGERNESS TO SAVE SOULS HASTENED
Marcus Whitman on his return. Love provided an equal
spur, for he was about to be married. Narcissa Prentiss, his fi-
ancée, was living in Amity, New York, not far from Whitman's
Wheeler. Unmarried at twenty-six, Narcissa was almost a spin-
ster by the standards of her day. Yet she was not without suitors,
including one Henry Spalding, whose proposal of marriage she
rejected. Spalding, a proud man, took the rejection hard, to Narcissa's dismay.

She decided Whitman was more to her liking. He was also
essential to some life plans she was just then formulating. Narcissa had attended a talk by Samuel Parker similar to that in which
Parker had won Whitman to the cause of an Oregon mission.
Parker's effect on Narcissa was almost identical. She had been
"saved" but was seeking an outlet for her energy and devotion. She
had taught school but was weary of the classroom. She desired
something more. "Is there a place for an unmarried female in my
Lord's vineyard?" she asked Parker after the lecture.

Parker said he didn't know but would check. "Are females
wanted?" he wrote the American Mission Board. "A Miss Narcissa
Prentiss of Amity is very anxious to go to the heathen. Her education is good—piety conspicuous—her influence is good. She will
offer herself if needed."

The board replied that unmarried women were *not* wanted. Married women, yes; unmarried women, no. Married couples were the model missionaries, and the board would stick with the model.

If Narcissa was discouraged by the reply, she didn't stay discouraged long. Instead she addressed her deficiency by becoming engaged to Marcus Whitman, six years her elder. Whitman visited friends in Amity in 1835 prior to his western reconnaissance with Parker. The friends knew Narcissa and were aware of her interest in missionary work, and introductions were made. Before Whitman's visit ended, he and Narcissa had reached an understanding that they would become the model couple the mission board wanted.

They might well have concluded that it was a match made in heaven. They were, after all, embarking on heaven's work. Was it also a meeting of the hearts? Not at first. "We had to make love somewhat abruptly and must do our courtship now we are married," Narcissa wrote to Parker's wife not long after she and Whitman were wed. But in an age when the practicalities of marriage were often considered as important as its romantic elements, this ordering was not unusual. They were married; they would learn to love each other.

AND THEY WOULD DO SO IN THE FACE OF CHALLENGES NOT confronting most newlyweds. Narcissa and Marcus Whitman traveled by steamboat to Cincinnati, where they were joined by Henry and Eliza Spalding. Henry had rebounded from Narcissa's spurning sufficiently to find a wife. Like Marcus and Narcissa, Henry and Eliza were fired by zeal to convert the Indians of Oregon. The mission board judged that two couples would do better than one on the western frontier and sent them out together. The board didn't know the background between Henry Spalding and Narcissa, and neither, apparently, did Marcus Whitman or Eliza Spalding. Henry Spalding and Narcissa Whitman seem not to have spoken of it, and Narcissa's letters and journal suggest she thought the ill feelings were in the past.

They continued by steamboat to Liberty, Missouri, where they prepared for the overland journey. Like Marcus Whitman the previous year, the foursome would join the annual caravan of the American Fur Company. But this time they would go all the way to Oregon, and they purchased provisions accordingly. They bought flour, salt and other foodstuffs they couldn't procure by hunting, fishing or trading along the way; trade goods for bartering with the Indians; seeds and equipment for starting a farm in Oregon; tools of various sorts; medical supplies; furniture and bedding; clothing and shoes; books and writing materials; guns, powder and lead. They bought the all-important wagons, a heavy one and a lighter one, which would carry the supplies and the women. They bought horses and mules to ride and to pull the wagons, and four saddles. The women's were side-saddles, considered appropriate for the demure sex when they chose to ride. They bought seventeen cattle, including four dairy cows, to stock the Oregon farm.

Marcus Whitman had known he would pay a frontier premium for all this, but the total bill shocked him. "Our expenses here have been much worse than I expected," he wrote to the mission board. "Horses and cattle cost over $1,000.00." But prices would only get higher—much higher for some items—farther west, and so he paid what the sellers demanded.

At Liberty the Whitmans and Spaldings were joined by another New Yorker, William Gray. The mission board had appointed him as a "secular agent": an all-purpose laborer and craftsman who would do or oversee much of the physical work of building houses, barns, fences, coops and sties when the missionaries got to Oregon. Whitman himself secured the services of two men to help with the animals and the setting up and breaking down of camp on the trail. Also traveling with the group were a pair of Nez Perce boys who had accompanied Whitman east the previous year to learn English and see how the white people lived. Their fathers had let them go after receiving Whitman's assurance that he would return them the following year, as he was now doing. A third Nez

Perce, who had traveled east on his own and wanted to return to his home country, completed the entourage.

THE GREEN RIVER WAS AGAIN THE SITE OF THE ANNUAL REN-dezvous. William Gray marveled at what he saw. "We will pass through this city of about fifteen hundred inhabitants—composed of all classes and conditions of men, and on this occasion two classes of women—starting from a square log pen 18 by 18, with no doors, except two logs that had been cut so as to leave a space about feet from the ground two feet wide and six feet long, de-signed for an entrance, as also a place to hand out goods and take in furs," Gray wrote. "It was covered with poles, brush on top of the poles; in case of rain, which we had twice during our stay at the rendezvous, the goods were covered with canvas, or tents thrown over them. Lumber being scarce in that vicinity, floors, doors, as well as sash and glass, were dispensed with. The spaces between the logs were sufficient to admit all the light requisite to do business in this primitive store." The trading hut stood a modest distance from the Green River, and the tents, saddles and paraphernalia of the fur company and its men formed two lines that ran down to the river. The lines of the tents, together with the river and the hut, set the boundaries of an area into which the company's horses and mules might be driven and be defended in case of Indian attack.

West of the fur company's camp was the camp of the hunters and trappers who came to the rendezvous to renew their supplies and acquaintances. East of the company's camp was the camp of the missionary group. A mile away, up Horse Creek, which en-tered the Green River just below the fur company camp, began the camps of various Indian tribes: Bannocks, Snakes, Flatheads and Nez Perces. These camps were similarly designed for defense, for though the tribes were at peace at the time of the rendezvous, none let down their guard. "The whole city was a military camp," Gray wrote. "Every little camp had its own guards to protect its occu-pants and property from being stolen by its neighbor. The arrow or the ball decided any dispute that might occur. The only law known for horse-stealing was death to the thief, if the owner or the guard could kill him in the act. If he succeeded in escaping, the only remedy for the man who lost his horse was to buy, or steal another and take his chances in escaping the arrow or ball of the owner or guard. It was quite fashionable in this city for all to go well armed, as the best and quickest shot gained the case in dispute."

The rendezvous began in earnest with the arrival of the fur company caravan, which was the raison d'être of the gathering. The Indians celebrated the arrival with a dramatic procession through the temporary city. "The Nez Perces and Flatheads, passing from their camps down the Horse Creek, joined the Snake and Bannock warriors, all dressed and painted in their gayest uniforms, each having a company of warriors in war garb, that is, naked, except a single cloth, and painted, carrying their war weapons, bearing their war emblems and Indian implements of music, such as skins drawn over hoops with rattles and trinkets to make a noise," Gray recalled. He and the Whitmans and Spaldings were alarmed. "When the cavalcade, amounting to full five (some said six) hundred Indian warriors (though I noticed quite a number of native belles covered with beads), commenced coming up through the plain in sight of our camps, those of us who were not informed as to the object or design of this demonstration began to look at our weapons and calculate on a desperate fight." They drove their horses, mules and cows into an area they thought they could defend and turned their guns outward. But veterans of the rendezvous laughingly explained that this was just for show. Gray adduced evidence on his own: "From the fact that no scalps were borne in the procession, I concluded this must be entirely a peace performance, and gotten up for the occasion."

The performance was especially spirited on the part of the Nez Perce, who had learned that the fur company caravan was accompanied by the missionaries, including the two women. The Nez Perce were delighted by this response to their entreaties and were fascinated by the white women, who looked out on the procession from the door of their tent. "The Indians would pass and repass the tent, to get a sight of the two women belonging to the white men," Gray recorded. In short order the Nez Perce became particularly enamored of Eliza Spalding, who learned their language with surprising speed. Narcissa Whitman was less adept with languages and made less effort.

NARCISSA WAS DISTRACTED BY FREQUENT CALLERS FROM THE camp of the mountain men. "Among these veteran Rocky Mountain hunters was a tall man, with long black hair, smooth face, dark eyes (inclining to turn his head a little to one side, as much as to say, 'I can tell you all about it'), a harum-scarum, don't-care sort of a man, full of 'life and fun in the mountains,' as he expressed it," Gray wrote. Gray didn't know this man, but it was Joe Meek. "He came and paid his respects to the ladies, and said he had been in the mountains several years; he had not seen a white woman for so long he had almost forgotten how they looked." Narcissa discovered Meek's penchant for telling stories. "Mrs. Whitman asked him if he ever had any difficulty or fights with the Indians," Gray recounted. "'That we did,' said he. 'One time I was with Bridger's camp; we were traveling along that day, and the Blackfeet came upon us. I was riding an old mule. The Indians were discovered some distance off, so all the party put whip to their horses and started to get to a place where we could defend ourselves. My old mule was determined not to move, with all the beating I could give her, so I sung out to the boys to stop and fight the Indians where we were; they kept on, however. Soon, my old mule got sight of the Blackfeet coming; she pricked up her ears, and on she went like a streak, passed the boys, and away we went. I sung out to the boys, as I passed, "Come on, boys, there is no use to stop and fight the Indians here."'"

Gray observed that Meek was accompanied by a small child and an Indian woman. The woman was a Nez Perce, and her name was Umentucken. Meek had met her in the mountains and fallen in love. "She was the most beautiful Indian woman I ever saw,"

Gray remembered. They were married, after the mountain fashion, and they had a child.

Gray saw Meek giving the little boy instruction in speaking English. "The father seemed, on my first noticing him, to be teaching this son of his to say, 'God d—n you,' doubtless considering this prayer the most important one to teach his son to repeat, in the midst of the wild scenes with which he was surrounded."

AT THE RENDEZVOUS THE WHITMAN PARTY LOST ITS ESCORT and had to find a new one. The American Fur Company caravan would go no farther; it had to return with its furs to St. Louis. The band of Nez Perce sought to persuade the missionaries to travel west with them. Whitman appreciated the offer, partly because it reconfirmed the tribe's desire to have a mission planted among them. But the Indians traveled swiftly and light, and he wasn't sure his party could keep up.

Fortunately, there arrived at the rendezvous a group from the Hudson's Bay Company. The appearance of the Bay men was no accident; the British company was patrolling the eastern frontier of its Oregon domain. John McLeod was the leader of the group; he was assisted by Thomas McKay, the stepson and assistant of John McLoughlin. The two Bay men wanted to make sure the American Fur Company didn't get ideas about penetrating farther west. The Bay Company had recently blocked a sally by an American named Nathaniel Wyeth, who had established a trading post on the Snake River, called Fort Hall, by buying Wyeth out. McLeod and McKay were escorting Wyeth to the rendezvous to ensure that he left the Oregon country. They themselves would be heading back to Fort Vancouver, and they offered to let the Whitman party go with them.

Had they been less focused on their rivals in the fur trade, they might not have been so helpful. To be sure, the Whitmans and the Spaldings weren't trappers or traders and so posed no immediate threat to the Bay Company's monopoly. But the missionaries represented a more distant threat: the settlement of Oregon by

Americans. Where wagons and women could go, families could follow. And where American families went, American governance would eventually follow. The Bay Company operated profitably on soil controlled formally by Britain or informally by its own agents, men like John McLoughlin, but it would not be able to do so on territory controlled by the United States.

Yet under the Anglo-American treaty of joint occupation for Oregon, neither side could hinder or molest the nationals of the other. The Hudson's Bay Company was willing to test the treaty in the rough-and-tumble world of the mountain men, squeezing and extorting its competitors wherever it could. But the Bay men, starting with John McLeod and Thomas McKay, appreciated that troubling women and missionaries would never do. Better to offer help, and thereby perhaps influence where the missionaries went and what they did.

"Dearest Mother," Narcissa wrote. "We commenced our journey to Walla Walla July 18, 1836, under the protection of Mr. McLeod and his company." Walla Walla was a Hudson's Bay Company post on the river of that name, near its confluence with the Columbia some two hundred miles above Fort Vancouver. It lay in the country of the Nez Perce and seemed to Marcus Whitman a likely place to start looking for a mission site. "The Flat Head and Nez Perce Indians and some lodges of the Snake tribe accompany us to Fort Hall," Narcissa continued. "While they are with us, we shall make but one camp a day."

Because John McLeod chose to travel with the Indians to Fort Hall, the missionaries did too. But the Indians were going to take a northern route from that point on the Snake River, to accommodate the Flatheads, while the Bay Company party would head more directly west toward Walla Walla. Until the parting, the missionaries felt obliged to accommodate the Indians' rapid pace, and they learned to dispense with their noontime camp.

The missionaries labored under a special handicap: their wagons. The route from the Green River to the Columbia was no road; in spots it was barely a trail. But the missionaries had their orders—to get the wagons through—and Marcus Whitman took them very seriously. The rocks and narrows eventually forced him to abandon one of the vehicles, but he clung to the other more zealously than ever. The traders and the Indians urged him to unload it and pack its contents on horses and mules. They hated the delay. The Hudson's Bay Company men seconded the advice, for a different reason: They wanted to prove that wagons could *not* get through. They hoped to keep as much of Oregon to themselves as possible.

Even Narcissa Whitman wished he would give it up. "Husband has had a tedious time with the wagon today," she wrote on July 25. "Got set in the creek this morning while crossing, was obliged to wade considerably in getting it out. After that in going between two mountains, on the side of one so steep that it was difficult for horses to pass, the wagon was upset twice. Did not wonder at this at all. It was a greater wonder that it was not turning a somerset continually." She feared for her husband. "It is not very grateful to my feelings to see him wear out with such excessive fatigue," she observed. "All the most difficult part of the way he has walked in his laborious attempt to take the wagon over."

Thirty hard miles farther she thought he would have to give it up. "One of the axle trees of the wagon broke today. Was a little rejoiced, for we were in hopes they would leave it and have no more trouble with it." But still he would not admit defeat. "Our rejoicing was in vain," she wrote.

They reached Fort Hall, where they received the hospitality of the Hudson's Bay Company. The Whitmans and Spaldings slept indoors for the first time since crossing the Missouri River. They also bade good-bye to the Indians. The Nez Perce again attempted to persuade the missionaries to join them. "The whole tribe are exceedingly anxious to have us go with them, use every argument they can invent to prevail on us to do so," Narcissa observed. Whitman and the others declined. "We all think it not best. We are very much fatigued and wish to get through as soon as possible."

John McLeod and the other Hudson's Bay men told Whitman that the route from Fort Hall to the Columbia was even rougher than that which they had covered. He must surely give up the wagon now.

He considered the matter once more and arrived at a compromise. Reasoning that two wheels, if not as good as four, would be better than none, he cut the wagon in half, making a cart of the front and loading the rear wheels and axle aboard. If he could get the cart through, he could rebuild the wagon bed and reconstitute the four-wheeler. And he could still claim that a wheeled vehicle had made it to Oregon.

The broad Snake River Valley vexed the travelers as no part of the trail had done so far. In some places it was a burning desert, in others a boggy wetland. Mosquitoes drove the travelers and the stock nearly mad. "We were so swarmed with mosquitoes as to be scarcely able to see," Narcissa wrote.

They forded the Snake River above Fort Boise. Whitman's cart barely survived. "Husband had considerable difficulty in crossing the cart," Narcissa wrote. "Both the cart and mules turned upside down in the river, entangled in the harness. The mules would have drowned, but for a desperate struggle to get them ashore. Then after putting two of the strongest horses before the cart and two men swimming behind to steady it, they succeeded in getting it over."

Fort Boise marked the beginning of the last leg of the journey to the Columbia. The Snake River turned north into the impassable Hell's Canyon, forcing travelers to strike out over the slightly less daunting Blue Mountains. At last Marcus Whitman conceded that his wagon, now a cart, wasn't going to make it all the way. He left it at Fort Boise, on the understanding that he might send for it later.

Struggling up the steep ridges of the Blue Mountains tested the weary muscles and bones of the travelers, but picking a way down tested their nerves. "Before noon we began to descend one of the most terrible mountains for steepness and length I have yet seen," Narcissa wrote on August 29. "It was like winding stairs in its descent and in some places almost perpendicular. We were a long time descending it. The horses appeared to dread the hill as much as we did. They would turn and wind in a zigzag manner all the way down. The men usually walked but I could not get permission to, neither did I desire it much. . . . Our ride this afternoon exceeded everything we have had yet."

But the day ended in triumph. They were still searching for a suitable camping site when they crested a final ridge that looked to the north and west. "We had a view of the valley of the Columbia River," Narcissa wrote. They stopped, caught their breath, and gazed at the goal toward which they had struggled so long. "It was beautiful," she said.

19

TRAPPED OUT

Life was getting harder for Joe Meek. This surprised him, for the opposite should have been true. In 1840 he had been nearly a decade in the mountains, and he had mastered their ways. He knew the rivers and streams of the regions like the back of his leathery hand; the mountains and passes were as familiar to him as the streets of Manhattan to a resident of that city. He could sense trouble—grizzly bears, Blackfeet, sudden storms—before trouble sensed him. He had learned to live on thin rations when he had to, and to fatten up when game was plenty. From a combination of good luck and perspicacity, he had suffered no serious injuries; no beaver trap had taken a finger, no bullet or arrowhead had lodged in his ribs or shoulder, no fall had broken a leg or an arm. In his late twenties, he was at the height of a man's physical strength: tall, sinewy, able to run for hours and walk forever, to hoist bales of furs and carry them for miles, to scamper up cliffs and over rocks like a mountain goat, to climb trees like a cat and swim rivers like a fish. Life should have been good for Joe Meek.

But it wasn't. The competition for furs that had brought him to the mountains in the first place had never been stemmed. Companies merged—the Rocky Mountain Company with the American—but new firms entered the field, and their trapping made beaver ever more scarce. A man like Meek had to work harder and longer to gather enough pelts to trade for the necessities of life. The annual rendezvous, once a carnival of commerce and the apex of social life in the mountains, attracted fewer merchants with less to sell, and fewer trappers with skins to trade, until it finally seemed like the circus grounds after the circus had moved on.

What Meek and the other mountain men, far removed from the civilized places of the earth, could apprehend only indirectly, if at all, was that changes in those civilized places were making their way of life—and making *them*—anachronistic. The beavers were fewer, to be sure, but scarcity often drives prices up, not down. What doomed Meek was that gentlemen in London no longer wanted beaver hats. A whole industry had been erected upon the tastes in haberdashery of persons who had not the slightest idea of where the raw materials that made their toppers came from. Fashions change, and the gents now wanted silk hats. The gears of commerce and technology adjusted; a new industry emerged, with new links of production, transport and distribution. New fortunes were made. The belts and wheels of the old industry slackened and slowed. No caravans of trade goods went out to the mountains; the rendezvous became a memory; the few remaining beavers were left to build their dams and lodges in peace. And Joe Meek, at twenty-eight, was out of work.

He consulted with others in the same fix. Some were for returning east whence they had come. They remembered farms they had left and families they still cherished. Meek had another idea. He recalled Narcissa Whitman and the way her eyes shone as she spoke of the new life she was about to begin in Oregon. He had heard the Hudson's Bay men talk of the Willamette Valley and how former trappers had settled on farms there. He wasn't sure he could become a farmer, fixed to one plot of ground. His decade in the mountains had made him a nomad, like the Indians who had been wandering for millennia. But at least he could take a look. He'd never been that far west, and he'd been told it was grand country.

Meek's friend and sometime partner Robert Newell had a similar thought. "Come," said Newell, "we are done with this life in the mountains—done with wading in beaver-dams, and freezing or starving alternately—done with Indian trading and Indian fighting. The fur trade is dead in the Rocky Mountains, and it is no place for us now, if it ever was. We are young yet, and have life before us. We cannot waste it here; we cannot or will not return to the States. Let us go down to the Willamette and take farms." Newell supposed that the grip of the Hudson's Bay Company on Oregon was loosening, with the arrival of missionaries and a scattering of settlers, and he was eager to be part of breaking that grip. "What do you say, Meek? Shall we turn American settlers?"

The conversation took place at Fort Hall on the Snake River, the post the Hudson's Bay Company had extorted from Nathaniel Wyeth. With the demise of the rendezvous, Meek and Newell had been reduced to selling their pelts to the Bay men. Neither liked doing so. "I'll be damned if I'll hang 'round a post of the Hudson's Bay Company," Newell said, by way of augmenting his case for Oregon.

Meek nodded.

"So you'll go?" asked Newell.

"I reckon I will," said Meek.

Newell had thought this out. He knew that Marcus Whitman had left his wagons on the Snake River when traveling to Oregon in 1836. Newell proposed completing what Whitman had begun. He and Meek would restore Whitman's wagons to working condition, buy horses and mules, and be the first to blaze a wagon trail all the way to the Willamette Valley. "You can drive one of the wagons, and take your family and traps along," Newell said. "Nicholas will drive the other, and I'll play leader and look after the train. Craig will go also, so we shall be quite a party, with what strays we are sure to pick up." Nicholas and Craig were mountain men as adrift as Meek and Newell.

Meek assented and the expedition was set in motion. Meek's first wife, Umentucken, had been killed in a raid by Bannock Indians. Their son seems to have gone back to her people. A second wife had left him. Meek's third wife, a Nez Perce woman, and their children—they eventually had at least eight—joined him for the trek to Oregon. Some of the other men brought families as well. Newell's prediction about picking up strays was borne out as a mild case of Oregon fever spread among the discouraged trappers loitering about Fort Hall. The trail west hadn't gotten easier since Marcus Whitman abandoned his wheeled vehicle, but this crew was fresh, not having already covered a thousand miles of plains and mountains, and the men were tougher, stronger and more resourceful than the missionaries. Not least important, they didn't have Hudson's Bay men telling them to abandon the wagons.

The journey was difficult. The party crossed lava beds and sage-strewn desert, rushing streams and rugged mountains. But they pressed forward. When the mules faltered, the men bent to help them. When the wagons tipped, the men righted them. They cut down trees and removed boulders that blocked the way. In due course, without fanfare or drama, they reached Waiilatpu, the site near the upper Columbia where Marcus and Narcissa Whitman had established their mission.

The Whitmans greeted them with pleasure. Marcus Whitman was gratified that his vision of a wagon route to the Columbia had been realized; Narcissa recalled her humorous conversations with the loquacious Meek from the rendezvous of 1836. Amid the mountains, Meek's wife had grown homesick for her own people, and left him and their daughter. Helen was the girl's name, and judging that he wasn't suited to raising her without a woman's help, and that she deserved a better education than he could give her, he placed her in the care of Narcissa Whitman at the small mission school.

He and Newell and the others set out for the Willamette. The autumn rains had come to the Cascade Mountains, causing Newell to leave the wagons at nearby Fort Walla Walla, with the idea of returning for them the next summer. The men transferred the wagons' cargo onto mules and proceeded west.

They stuck to the south bank of the Columbia past the Dalles, but on entering the Columbia Gorge they decided to cross to the north bank to avoid impassable cliffs that plunged directly into the stream. The Indians they hired to ferry them over stole some of the travelers' ropes; Meek and the others objected and nearly traded fire with the thieves. But recognizing how badly they were outnumbered, they contented themselves with remonstrance and moved on. They recrossed the Columbia above Fort Vancouver, which they deliberately avoided, not wishing to appear beholden to their old rival, though they could have used a square meal and dry clothes. They continued to a spot on the east bank of the Willamette below the falls of that river, where a few Americans had settled. The Americans had no more than a peck of potatoes they were willing to part with. This lasted Meek's party less than a day. Newell grudgingly backtracked to Fort Vancouver and bought dried salmon, hardtack, tea and sugar from John McLoughlin. Joe Meek remarked that pride came more easily on a full stomach than an empty one.

The weather was as wet and cold as Decembers can be in the Willamette Valley. Meek and the others needed shelter, and to find it they sought land they could claim for farms. They journeyed the short distance to Willamette Falls, where they found another associate from the mountains, a man named Doughty. The group crossed the river and set up a temporary camp on the west bank, plotting their next move. Word apparently got out that they were there, for shortly two more veterans of the mountains joined them. Together the trappers considered how to become farmers and where to commence the process.

Newell took the lead, being the best-educated of the bunch and the most experienced in the land business. Besides, it was Newell's money that had bought the horses and mules and provisions for the journey from the Snake River, and he retained financial primacy over the others. Newell proposed that they head twenty-five miles northwest to some open, rolling land along the Tualatin

River, where Doughty had built a cabin and where a scattering of farms had been established by a handful of those who had found their way to the Willamette.

Meek and the others assented, and they reached the Tualatin Plains on the dreariest Christmas Day most of them had ever experienced. The Rocky Mountains were cold in winter, but the sun often shone and the air was dry. In the Willamette Valley, the thermometer might show forty degrees warmer than on the Green River, but the rain soaked everything and made hypothermia a constant threat. Worse, the eating on the Willamette was poorer than in the mountains. There the trappers had feasted on buffalo meat; here there were no buffalo and precious few other game animals, at least that Meek and his companions could find. Food was fuel to outdoorsmen, and when the fuel consisted of paltry rations of boiled wheat kernels, the engines of activity slowed dramatically. Spirits sank in comparable measure.

Meek bore the wet and cold and hunger as long as he could, but finally determined to better his state, if only marginally. He crossed the ridge that separated the Tualatin from the Willamette and sought food from a retired Hudson's Bay man and his wife who lived on a large island where the Willamette meets the Columbia. The man was still eligible to buy provisions from Fort Vancouver, just several miles up the Columbia. Meek could have gone to the fort himself and bought provisions on credit, but he was too stubborn to accept John McLoughlin's help. He traded his skills as a hunter—of waterfowl, in this case—for dried salmon and hardtack, and both he and the island couple ate better that winter than either would have eaten apart.

The winter rains eased with the coming of spring. Meek and the others staked claims to promising parcels of land and, with seed grain and tools acquired from Fort Vancouver—there was no alternative—they sowed their first crop.

In that moment Joe Meek was transformed. For a decade he had been a nomad, a chaser after animals for his means of subsistence. Now he was a farmer, a tiller of the soil. Ownership had been a hindrance to a man on the move; ownership was now the foundation of his life. His nationality had hardly mattered in the mountains, for government—British or American—touched his life only rarely and in passing. Nationality meant much now, for government—American or British—would honor his land claim or deny it. Rootless since fleeing his Virginia home, Meek put down roots in Oregon.

20

WAIILATPU

Mission life was hard on Narcissa Whitman. She and Marcus, with the help of William Gray, had built the physical structures of their mission, but building the community of believers they envisioned was more difficult. The Whitmans and the Spaldings had split up, the better to proselytize the Nez Perce and their neighbors, the Cayuse Indians. Partly because of Whitman's stubbornness—no challenge daunted him—he and Narcissa got the Cayuse, who were indeed the greater challenge. They were slow to come to the mission, and the tribe's leaders didn't disguise their distrust of the whites. *They* hadn't requested any missionaries from the East, they reminded the Whitmans.

Marcus busied himself with the labors of the mission, which were endless. Narcissa's chores were myriad, too, and included the care of a young daughter, Alice—the first child born to an American woman in the Oregon country. Alice was the pride of her mother and father, their hope for an American future in the West. "She is a large, healthy and strong child," Narcissa wrote a week after Alice's second birthday. "She talks both Nez Perces and English quite fluently, and is much inclined to read her book with the children of the family, and sings all our Nez Perces hymns and several in English." Alice flitted about the mission house, charming the whites and Indians alike.

And then she vanished.

"Last Sabbath, blooming in health, cheerful and happy in herself and in the society of her much loved parents, yet in one moment she disappeared, went to the river with two cups to get some water for the table, fell in and was drowned," Narcissa wrote her sister two months later, still in shock. "Mysterious event! We can in no way account for the circumstances connected with it, otherwise than that the Lord meant it should be so. Husband and I were both engaged in reading. She had just a few minutes before been reading to her father; had got down out of his lap, and as my impression, was amusing herself by the door in the yard. After a few moments, not hearing her voice, I sent Margaret to search for her. She did not find her readily, and instead of coming to me to tell me that she had not found her, she went to the garden to get some radishes for supper. On seeing her pass to the water to wash them, I looked to see if Alice was with her, but saw that she was not. That moment I began to be alarmed, for Mungo had just been in and said there were two cups in the river. We immediately inquired for her, but no one had seen her. We then concluded she must be in the river. We searched down the river, and up and down again in wild dismay, but could not find her for a long time. Several were in the river searching far down. By this time we gave her up for dead. At last an old Indian got into the river where she fell in and looked along by the shore and found her a short distance below. But it was too late; she was dead."

Narcissa blamed herself. She had been inattentive. Her own memories accused her. "It came to my recollection that I had a glimpse of her entering the house and saying, with her usual glee, 'ha, ha, supper is most ready' (for the table had just been set), 'let Alice get some water,' at the same time taking two cups from the table and disappearing. Being absorbed in reading I did not see her or think anything about her—which way she went to get her water. I had never known her to go to the river or to appear at all venturesome until within a week past. Previous to this she has been much afraid to go near the water anywhere, for her father had once put her in, which so effectually frightened her that we had lost that feeling of anxiety for her in a measure on its account. But she had gone." And she would never return.

Narcissa's theology provided her both solace and punishment. "My Saviour would have it so. He saw it necessary to afflict us, and has taken her away. Now we see how much we loved her, and you know the blessed Saviour will not have His children bestow an undue attachment upon creature objects without reminding us of His own superior claim upon our affections."

THE LOSS OF HER DAUGHTER COLORED NARCISSA'S ATTITUDE toward everything around her. She found life on the edge of civilization more difficult than ever. The Indians wouldn't come to services at the mission, but she couldn't keep them out of her house. "The greatest trial to a woman's feelings is to have her cooking and eating room always filled with four or five more Indians—men—especially at meal time," Narcissa wrote her mother. "They are so filthy they make a great deal of cleaning necessary wherever they go, and this wears out a woman very fast."

She tried to keep them away, saying her house was off limits. The Cayuse reacted as though they had been horribly insulted. They accused the missionaries of stealing their land. Nor did the missionaries feed them well, which was the least they should do as uninvited guests. And now they tried to bar them from the house.

Narcissa couldn't stand it. "They are an exceedingly proud, haughty and insolent people, and keep us constantly upon the stretch after patience and forbearance," she wrote indignantly. "We feed them far more than any of our associates to their people, yet they will not be satisfied."

Her uneasiness grew. Catholic missionaries arrived in the region, causing the Methodist Whitmans to fear for the souls of those deluded by the rival dogma, and to fear for themselves as their own doctrine found fewer adherents among the Cayuse and neighboring tribes. The efforts of her husband to minister to the illnesses of the Indians put him at risk when those efforts failed, as they inevitably did at times. "These men are all firm believers in the *te-wats*, or medicine men," Narcissa said of the Cayuse. "This is a crying sin among them. They believe that the *te-wat* can kill or make alive at his pleasure."

A recent event made plain how her husband was at risk. A young Nez Perce had died of an illness while under the care of a *te-wat*, and his brother and friends had blamed the medicine man for the death. They said they would exact vengeance unless they were compensated in horses and other property. Marcus Whitman, on hearing of this, had berated the brother and his friends, saying they were bad men to attempt extortion. "They did not like such plain talk," Narcissa wrote. They said that anyone who could speak to them in such a way was evil and should be punished. "One of them, more daring than the others, gathered twelve or fourteen of his friends and came in the forenoon to frighten us. One had a bow and arrows with iron points; another had a rope and another had the war club. When they first made their appearance these things were concealed under their blankets. The head man commenced the talk by saying that he was always good and that husband"—Marcus Whitman—"was bad and was always talking bad to them; that he had brought in his friends that were very powerful. This he said to frighten us and excite his allies."

Marcus Whitman told him to stop. He refused. "After a little, one of them took down a hair rope that was hanging near, and threw it down near the doctor; one of them that stood near put his foot on it. I began to be suspicious of that movement and thought they were intending to tie him." Meanwhile two of the others moved forward menacingly. "A tall Indian advanced as the conversation increased in spirit; under his blanket I saw another rope and one behind him had a bow and arrows. I asked husband if I had not better call help; he said no, he was not afraid." But Narcissa was. "I had not yet discovered the war club, but I had seen enough to excite my fears greatly."

In this case the Indians were simply trying to scare Whitman. They broke off without doing him or Narcissa physical harm. "The aim, doubtless, was to frighten us," Narcissa commented. They had succeeded, certainly with her.

21

FOR GOD AND COUNTRY

IN THE AUTUMN OF 1842 MARCUS WHITMAN MADE A DIFFI-
cult decision. He resolved to travel back east in search of reinforcements. The trip itself, in the teeth of the approaching winter,
would be perilous; not even experienced mountain men crossed
the Rockies in winter if they didn't absolutely have to. Leaving
Narcissa, basically defenseless, was hardly easier. But Whitman's
faith let him believe no ill would befall her, or himself, that heaven
didn't ordain.

Even so, he wouldn't have set out had he not believed the work
of the last six years was in dire jeopardy. The dismal pace of con-
versions and the continuing expense of supporting the missions
had prompted the mission board to propose closing the Waiilatpu
mission and sending Marcus and Narcissa to another mission.
Marcus thought this a terrible idea and believed that he alone, in
person, could change the minds of the board members. He would
travel to Boston to do so.

In making his argument to the board, he would cite the growing
threat from Roman Catholic priests who had arrived in Oregon in
the last couple of years. Whitman knew that nothing fired the zeal
of Protestants like Catholic competition, and the reason he knew
this was that he felt the zeal himself. He and most of his fellow
Protestants considered the Catholics heretics and a greater danger
to the eternal welfare of Indians than their native paganism. For

the mission board to retrench would be to surrender ground and souls to the papists; this must not happen.

Patriotism entered Whitman's reckoning as well, allied to his Protestantism. The priests in Oregon ministered to the French Canadians associated with the Hudson's Bay Company, which itself operated in the interests of the British government. The future of Oregon remained diplomatically unresolved between Britain and the United States, and Whitman feared that the arrival of the priests portended an influx of Canadians, whose presence would bolster the British claim to Oregon, which in turn would secure the future of the Catholics there. In the 1840s American nationalism was scarcely distinguishable from militant Protestantism; the emerging ideology of Manifest Destiny portrayed Columbia, the spirit of America, advancing west with the flag in one hand and the Protestant Bible in the other.

So Marcus Whitman set his face to the East. He would rally his coreligionists in Boston and his compatriots in Washington. He would save Oregon for Protestant Christianity and American republicanism.

THE JOURNEY WAS AS ARDUOUS AS WHITMAN IMAGINED. HE left the mission in early October with a single companion. They reached Fort Hall on the Snake River in eleven days, intending to proceed to South Pass. But the Hudson's Bay head there told them that the Snake Indians were on the warpath and would make quick work of a party of two whites. Whitman opted to skirt south, toward Taos and the Santa Fe Trail to St. Louis. By doing so he and his partner avoided the Indians but not the winter. They hit deep snow and lost their way. Whitman nearly drowned crossing an ice-clogged river. They killed some of their mules for food. But after five grueling months, they staggered into St. Louis.

Whitman continued east by steamboat. He got to Washington, where he buttonholed as many government officials as he could, stressing the need for haste in making Oregon securely American. He spoke with President John Tyler, whose interest in Oregon was tempered by the deepening sectional rift, which made acqui-sition of any new territory problematic for its effect on the bal-ance between free and slave states. Oregon was the hobby of a few members of Congress, notably Thomas Hart Benton and Lewis Linn, the two senators from Missouri, the state that would benefit the most from any new traffic across the plains and mountains to Oregon. Most other lawmakers were apathetic at best.

Whitman received a warmer, or at least more curious, welcome in New York, his stopping point en route to Boston. "We were most agreeably surprised yesterday by a call from Doctor Whitman from Oregon, a member of the American Presbyterian Mission in that country," wrote Horace Greeley, the editor of the *New York Daily Tribune*. "A slight glance at him when he entered our office would convince any one that he had seen all the hardships of life in the wilderness. He was dressed in an old fur cap that appeared to have seen some ten years' service, faded, and nearly destitute of fur; a vest whose natural color had long since faded, and a shirt—we could not see that he had any—an overcoat, every thread of which could be easily seen, buckskin pants, etc.—the roughest man we have seen this many a day—too poor, in fact, to get any better wardrobe." Whitman's unprepossessing attire made his character the more im-pressive to Greeley. "A noble pioneer we judge him to be, a man fit-ted to be chief in rearing a moral empire among the wild men of the wilderness. We did not learn what success the worthy man had in leading the Indians to embrace the Christian faith"—Whitman had kept silent on this sensitive point—"but he very modestly remarked that many of them had begun to cultivate the earth and raise cattle."

Boston counted souls more closely than cattle. Whitman pre-sented himself to the members of the mission board, who imme-diately asked why he had left his station and incurred the costs of this unauthorized journey. Yet in the next moment the treasurer of the board slipped him several dollars and muttered, "Go get some decent clothes."

When Whitman returned, he convinced the board that the prospects in Oregon were better than they had been led to believe.

He exaggerated in saying that three hundred Indians regularly attended the services at the mission; he doubtless judged that God would forgive a fib if it helped save Cayuse souls—even if the Cayuse didn't yet realize they needed saving. The board members likely discounted his exaggeration; these hard-headed Bostonians hadn't learned to manage their sprawling mission empire by believing every word their missionaries said. Almost certainly Whitman's presence, more than his argument, was what won them over. A crossing of the Rocky Mountains in the dead of winter was a feat that manifested moral courage of the first order; the board, for all its fiscal rectitude, couldn't let down such a man as Whitman. They told him to return to Oregon and continue his good work.

"My Dear Husband," Narcissa Whitman wrote on October 7, 1842, just days after Marcus had left for the East. "I got dreadfully frightened last night. About midnight I was awakened by some one trying to open my bedroom door. At first I did not know what to understand by it. I raised my head and listened awhile and then lay down again. Soon the latch was raised and the door opened a little. I sprang from the bed in a moment and closed the door again, but the ruffian pushed and pushed and tried to unlatch it, but could not succeed; finally he gained upon me until he opened the door again." Narcissa had been screaming for help; at the last minute her calls frightened the intruder and he ran from the house. "Had the ruffian persisted I do not know what I should have done," she told Whitman. "I did not think of the war club, but I thought of the poker."

The assault shook Narcissa deeply. Though her sense of duty made her reluctant to abandon her post, she was quietly relieved when Archibald McKinley, the Hudson's Bay Company chief at Fort Walla Walla, insisted that she take refuge there. McKinley personally came to Waiilatpu with a wagon and carried her away.

Some of the Indians expressed regret at her departure, but others exploited it. The effort to scare away the missionaries escalated. The grain mill at the mission, which provided the staff of life to the Whitmans and all associated with them, was set ablaze. "Probably there was more than two hundred bushels of wheat and corn burnt and some flour," Narcissa wrote to her parents. "The mill bolt and threshing mill, even to part of the wheel, was burnt." She wondered if it was her fault for leaving her station. "I think, sometimes, if I had not left perhaps it would not have been burnt." She struggled to see God's message in this latest trial. "The sensible part of the Cayuses feel the loss deeply, and they will feel it still more when they want their wheat ground next fall. We hope it will be a good lesson to them and be one of making them a better people."

22

THE WAY WEST

MARCUS WHITMAN LEARNED OF THE ASSAULT ON Narcissa and the burning of the mill only months after the fact. But the knowledge that his wife was in peril every moment he was gone, and that the mission that had become his life's work could be destroyed in a moment of Indian rage, compelled him to leave Boston as soon as the board gave him its blessing. He stopped briefly in western New York to see members of his family, then proceeded as swiftly as he could to the Missouri.

En route he heard that a large group of emigrants was preparing to leave for Oregon. During the 1830s about the only traffic to the Columbia, aside from fur traders and the odd adventurer, had consisted of missionaries like the Whitmans, but in the early 1840s prospective settlers began to join the flow. Knowing that Whitman had guided women to Oregon made them think the journey was feasible for ordinary folks, and the combined success of Whitman, Joe Meek and Robert Newell in getting wagons to the Columbia caused them to conclude that whole households might be relocated. A handful of emigrants reached the Willamette in 1841; several dozen arrived in 1842.

The news that no great disasters had befallen the emigrants prompted still more to line up for departure in the spring of 1843. By now the mystery of the trek had been largely dispelled; the key points of the route were understood, the difficult passages plotted, the places where the danger of Indians dictated special precautions identified. The journey was still no stroll in the park; the emigrants would be at the mercy of the weather, sleeping roofless for months, chilled at times, broiling at others. Axles would break and oxen grow weary; children would fall under wagons or be kicked by mules; guns would discharge accidentally; women would die in childbirth. But the emigrants knew where they were going and how long the journey might take. Equally important, they knew that others no stronger, braver or more resourceful than they had survived the trek. So could they.

Whitman changed boats in St. Louis, where he visited Thomas Hart Benton. Besides being Missouri's senior senator and an ardent advocate of America's westward expansion, Benton was the father-in-law of John C. Frémont, a U.S. army officer who had already made a name in western exploration and who was about to embark on an expedition to Oregon. The three men brought different perspectives to the Oregon question: Whitman that of the missionary, Benton of the statesman, Frémont of the soldier. Their simultaneous presence in St. Louis in 1843 embodied the surge of interest in Oregon. Whitman shared his knowledge of Oregon with the others; Benton told of his political plans for binding Oregon to America; Frémont traced on a map the route he hoped to traverse. They agreed that America's western future had never been brighter.

PETER BURNETT LATER REMEMBERED WHAT HAD PROMPTED him to set out for Oregon with the 1843 wave of emigrants. Burnett was a Tennessean by birth and a Missourian since boyhood. He was a self-educated lawyer who had made himself unpopular with his neighbors by defending Joseph Smith and other Mormons charged with treason and lesser crimes. He was a merchant drowning in debts he saw no prospect of repaying. And he was a family man who at thirty-five couldn't figure out how to support his family in anything like the style he wished for them.

"There was a bill pending in Congress, introduced in the Senate by Dr. Linn, one of the Senators from Missouri, which proposed to donate to each immigrant six hundred and forty acres of land for himself, and one hundred and sixty acres for each child," Burnett recalled. "I had a wife and six children, and would therefore be entitled to sixteen hundred acres." The Linn bill had not yet passed, and it was no sure thing, as the brazenness of the land grab it proposed gave pause to many in Congress. The United States had no title to the land Linn sought to bestow. The joint occupation agreement with Britain was still in force, and the British had as much claim on Oregon as the Americans did. Employees of the Hudson's Bay Company, various missionaries and a modest number of settlers had established farms on parcels of land in the Willamette Valley, but no government had graced their squatting with legal authority. Moreover, the United States government had never given away land before. It had *sold* land from the public domain, but gifts were another matter. The recipients would be happy for the gifts, of course, but many of the potential donors, the taxpayers of America, expected the government to be a better steward of the nation's resources.

Yet the possibility of the gift, under the prospective aegis of American federal power, was enough to set Peter Burnett and several hundred other emigrants on the trail to Oregon in the spring of 1843. "I saw that a great American community would grow up, in the space of a few years, upon the shores of the distant Pacific; and I felt an ardent desire to aid in this most important enterprise," Burnett wrote. He was aware that the British had by no means abandoned their claim to Oregon, but he thought the emigrants could force them to. "If we could show, by a *practical* test, that American emigrants could safely make their way across the continent to Oregon with their wagons, teams, cattle, and families, then the solution of the question of title to the country was discovered. Of course, Britain would not covet a colony settled by American citizens."

In the bargain, Oregon would give Burnett a second chance. His creditors at first sought to prevent his fleeing Missouri, but he made a case that flight was in *their* best interest. "I said that if Dr. Linn's bill should pass, the land would ultimately enable me to pay up. There was at least a chance. In staying where I was, I saw no reasonable probability of ever being able to pay my debts." The creditors reluctantly accepted Burnett's reasoning—much as the creditors of Moses and Stephen Austin had accepted *their* reasoning about Texas. Burnett's creditors wished him well and joined the ranks of those rooting for passage of the Linn bill.

Burnett sold what he hadn't already lost, and purchased three wagons, four yoke of oxen, two mules and provisions for the journey. He traveled around Missouri to find others to join him on the journey west. "I visited the surrounding counties, making speeches wherever I could find a sufficient audience, and succeeded even beyond my own expectations."

In the same way that the trappers and merchants had arranged their rendezvous in the mountains each summer, the emigrants of 1843 arranged a rendezvous on the prairie that spring. Burnett and his party reached the appointed spot, a dozen miles west of Independence, Missouri, on May 17. A look at the crowd made him reassess the challenge of the journey. "It was not that the trip was beset with very great perils, for we had no war with the Indians," Burnett recalled. Rather, it was little things that would test the travelers. "At one time an ox would be missing, at another time a mule, and then a struggle for the best encampment, and for a supply of wood and water; and in these struggles, the worst traits of human nature were displayed, and there was no remedy but patient endurance. At the beginning of the journey there were several fisticuff fights in camp; but the emigrants soon abandoned that practice, and thereafter confined themselves to abuse in words only. The man with a black eye and battered face could not well hunt up his cattle or drive his team."

The emigrants might have found their way to verbal abuse unaided, but they wouldn't have found their way to Oregon, and so they were thrilled when Marcus Whitman, on his way back to Oregon, appeared at the rendezvous. Peter Burnett and the others took comfort from the knowledge that they would travel with one so experienced.

Whitman had his own impression of the emigrants. "They appear very willing, and I have no doubt are generally of an enterprising character," he wrote his brother-in-law. "There are over two hundred men, besides women and children, as it is said. No one can well tell, until we are all on the road and get together, how many there are."

As things happened, no one ever did figure out how many emigrants there were that year. Estimates varied from eight hundred to twelve hundred. No government authority gave them leave to depart and none greeted them on arrival in Oregon. No one kept a tally. But beyond doubt they were many more settlers than had ever ventured to the American West at once. Descriptions of the westering army caught the American imagination: a mighty people was on the march. They were the American dream in motion. Even many Americans who were content to stay in the East thrilled at what this great migration said about the energy of their country and its bright future.

Whitman was encouraged by what he saw. "The immigrants who are going out will be a good acquisition," he predicted. Oregon would benefit. "My expectations are high for that country. I believe it must become one of the best of countries very soon."

"IT IS FOUR O'CLOCK A.M.," JESSE APPLEGATE WROTE, DESCRIBing a day on the trail that season. Applegate would win a reputation, albeit checkered and controversial, as a trailblazer to Oregon, but in the spring of 1843 he took his pedestrian turn with the cow column on the emigrant march up the Platte. The news from Oregon had indicated that cattle were scarce there and expensive, and many of the emigrants brought stock with them. The cattle were gathered into a large herd for a longer drive than any Americans had ever attempted.

"The sentinels on duty have discharged their rifles—the signal that the hours of sleep are over—and every wagon and tent is pouring forth its night tenants, and slow-kindling smokes begin largely to rise and float away in the morning air," Applegate continued. "Sixty men start from the corral, spreading as they make through the vast herd of cattle and horses that make a semicircle around the encampment, the most distant perhaps two miles away." Each night the cattle and horses were turned loose to graze, guarded by sentinels to keep Indians from poaching. The guard was never fully secure, and so each morning the herders examined the grass at the edge of the grazing ground for signs that animals had been driven off. If they had, a retrieval party was organized and dispatched. Sometimes the animals were recovered from the Indians, often by ransom; sometimes they were written off as a loss.

This dawn there were no signs of disturbance, and the day shift commenced its work. "By 5 o'clock the herders begin to contract the great, moving circle, and the well-trained animals move slowly towards camp, clipping here and there a thistle or a tempting bunch of grass on the way. In about an hour five thousand animals are close up to the encampment, and the teamsters are busy selecting their teams and driving them inside the corral to be yoked." The corral was a circle of wagons, some hundred yards in diameter, with the tongue of each wagon chained to the rear of the wagon ahead of it on the perimeter. The corral served the second purpose of a stockade in the event of Indian attack. To the gratification of the emigrants of 1843, this purpose was never utilized.

"From 6 to 7 o'clock is a busy time; breakfast is to be eaten, the tents struck, the wagons loaded and the teams yoked and brought up in readiness to be attached to their respective wagons," Applegate explained. "All know when, at 7 o'clock, the signal to march sounds, that those not ready to take their proper places in the line of march must fall into the dusty rear for the day." Otherwise there was a strict rotation on the march. One day's lead wagon became the trailer the next day, moving stepwise toward the front on each successive day.

"It is on the stroke of seven; the rush to and fro, the cracking of whips, the loud command to oxen, and what seemed to be the

inextricable confusion of the last ten minutes has ceased. Fortunately every one has been found and every teamster is at his post.
The clear notes of a trumpet sound at the front; the pilot and his
guards mount their horses; the leading divisions of the wagons
move out of the encampment and take up the line of march; the
rest fall into their places with the precision of clock work, until the
spot so lately full of life sinks back into that solitude that seems to
reign over the broad plain and rushing river as the caravan draws
its lazy length towards the distant El Dorado."

On this morning Applegate accompanied the hunters, a band
of young men on horses who ranged to the side of the column in
search of buffalo and antelope. They rode for an hour to the bluffs
that here marked the edge of the Platte Valley. Applegate stopped
to take in the view. "To those who have not been on the Platte,"
he wrote, "my powers of description are wholly inadequate to convey an idea of the vast extent and grandeur of the picture, and the
rare beauty and distinctness of the detail. No haze or fog obscures
objects in the pure and transparent atmosphere of this lofty region.
To those accustomed only to the murky air of the seaboard, no
correct judgment of distance can be formed by sight, and objects
which they think they can reach in a two hours' walk may be a
day's travel away." The expanse swallowed sounds; the report of a
rifle carried mere furlongs. Yet the puff of smoke from the barrel
could be seen for miles.

Applegate looked back toward the Platte. "The broad river
glowing under the morning sun like a sheet of silver, and the
broader emerald valley that borders it, stretch away in the distance
until they narrow at almost two points in the horizon, and when
first seen, the vast pile of the Wind River Mountains, though hundreds of miles away, looks clear and distinct as a white cottage on
the plain."

From his vantage, Applegate could see the past, present and
future of the march. The camp of the previous night had been left
behind; the wagons rumbled forward; the scouts ranged ahead

seeking the best path. "Near the bank of the shining river is a company of horsemen," Applegate wrote, recognizing the scouts. "They seem to have found an obstruction, for the main body has halted while three or four ride rapidly along the bank of the creek or slough. They are hunting a favorable crossing for the wagons. While we look, they have succeeded; it has apparently required no work to make it passable, for all but one of the party have passed on, and he has raised a flag, no doubt a signal to the wagons to steer their course to where he stands. The leading teamster sees him, though he is yet two miles off, and steers his course directly towards him, all the wagons following in his track."

The train was a linear village. "They (the wagons) form a line three-quarters of a mile in length; some of the teamsters ride upon the front of their wagons, some march beside their teams; scattered along the line companies of women are taking exercise on foot; they gather bouquets of rare and beautiful flowers that line the way; near them stalks a stately greyhound, or an Irish wolf dog, apparently proud of keep watch and ward over his master's wife and children. Next comes a band of horses; two or three men or boys follow them, the docile and sagacious animals scarce needing this attention, for they have learned to follow in the rear of the wagons, and know that at noon they will be allowed to graze and rest. Their knowledge of time seems as accurate as of the place they are to occupy in the line, and even a full-blown thistle will scarce tempt them to straggle or halt until the dinner hour has arrived."

The cattle, bringing up the rear, were a different story. "Lazy, selfish and unsocial, it has been a task to get them in motion, the strong always ready to domineer over the weak, halt in the front and forbid the weak to pass them," Applegate observed. "They seem to move only in the fear of the driver's whip; though in the morning, full to repletion, they have not been driven an hour before their hunger and thirst seem to indicate a fast of days' duration. Through all the long day their greed is never satisfied, nor their thirst quenched, nor is there a moment of relaxation of the tedious and vexatious labors of their drivers, although to all others the march furnishes some season of relaxation and enjoyment. For the cow-drivers there is none."

Applegate decided that his sightseeing must end for the day. He rode back to the column in time for the nooning, the midday break. The pilot had selected the spot as having grass and water; the scouts improved the water supply by scooping shallow wells by the bank of the Platte that served as watering troughs for the animals. The oxen were not unyoked but merely let loose from the wagons; they grazed in pairs. The wagons were drawn up in columns rather than circled. The men, women and children ate without fuss or extensive preparation.

The business of the train was conducted at the noontime halt. On this day the business was judicial, with the elected council of the train seated as a court. One of the emigrants had hired a younger man to help with the work of the journey in exchange for bed and board. A dispute had arisen between the two, and the council was convened to resolve it. Each party was questioned; other members of the train were summoned as witnesses. The council rendered its decision, which was enforced by the cooperation of the train as a whole. The process permitted no appeal.

"It is now one o'clock," Applegate wrote. "The bugle has sounded and the caravan has resumed its westward journey." The warmth of the afternoon, the demands of digestion and the repetitiveness of the undertaking gradually took their toll. "A drowsiness has fallen apparently on man and beast; teamsters drop asleep on their perches and even when walking by their teams, and the words of command are now addressed to the slowly creeping oxen in the soft tenor of women or the piping treble of children, while the snores of the teamsters make a droning accompaniment."

An unexpected occurrence broke the spell, at least for those close at hand. "An emigrant's wife, whose state of health has caused Doctor Whitman to travel near the wagon for the day, is now taken with violent illness. The Doctor has had the wagon driven out of the line, a tent pitched and a fire kindled. Many conjectures are hazarded in regard to this mysterious proceeding, and as to why this lone wagon is to be left behind." But left behind it had to be, for the train had many miles to go, with the threat of winter always looming between the emigrants and their final destination.

The sun sank low in the west. The first wagons reached the place where the pilot waited, and where he directed the forming of the nighttime circle. Everyone knew the routine by now. "The leading wagons follow him so nearly around the circle that but a wagon length separates them. Each wagon follows its track, the rear closing on the front, until its tongue and ox-chains will perfectly reach from one to the other, and so accurate the measure and perfect the practice that the hindmost wagon of the train always precisely closes the gateway, as each wagon is brought into position." The circling took but ten minutes.

Dinner fires were kindled. Families settled in for the night. But as the sun touched the horizon many eyes looked back along the trail for the wagon left behind. In the waning light it appeared. "The absent wagon rolls into camp, the bright, speaking face and cheery look of the doctor, who rides in advance, declare without words that all is well, and both mother and child"—the latter, newborn, the cause of the halt—"are comfortable."

The evening routine unfolded. Dinner completed, the men gathered to smoke their pipes, the women to talk of the child born that day, the children to play inside the circle of the wagons. "Before a tent near the river a violin makes lively music, and some youths and maidens have improvised a dance upon the green; in another quarter a flute gives its mellow and melancholy notes to the still night air, which, as they float away over the quiet river, seem a lament for the past rather than a hope for the future." The day has been a good one: twenty miles traveled, and a life added to this moving village.

"Time passes; the watch is set for the night; the council of old men has been broken up and each has returned to his own quarter; the flute has whispered its last lament to the deepening night; the violin is silent, and the dancers have dispersed; enamored youth

Camp on the Oregon Trail. This is a stylized version of part of the daily routine. The women and children must be elsewhere.

have whispered a tender good-night in the ear of blushing maidens." The last fires were banked, and the firefly glow of the pipes winked out. Silence settled upon the weary travelers.

IN MID-JULY THE TRAIN REACHED FORT LARAMIE. SOME OF the members reprovisioned, at a steep cost. Coffee sold for $1.50 a pint, and brown sugar the same. Rough flour ran 25 cents a pound and lead 75 cents. Complaints at the high prices were greeted with shrugs and a warning that prices would only mount the farther the emigrants got from civilization.

The party met a band of Cheyennes at Fort Laramie, headed by an impressive chief. "He was a tall, trim, noble-looking Indian, aged about thirty," Peter Burnett remarked. "He went alone very freely among our people, and I happened to meet him at one of our camps, where there was a foolish, rash young man, who wantonly insulted the chief. Though the chief did not understand the insulting words, he clearly comprehended the insulting tone and gestures." Burnett watched him carefully, fearing the worst. "He made no reply in words, but walked away slowly, and when some twenty feet from the man who had insulted him, he turned around and solemnly and slowly shook the forefinger of his right hand at the young man several times, as much as to say, 'I will attend to your case.'"

Burnett would prove to be an able politician when he reached the West; now he showed some of the skills that would serve him then. "I saw there was trouble coming, and I followed the chief, and by kind earnest gestures made him understand at last that this young man was considered by us all as a half-witted fool, unworthy of the notice of any sensible man; and that we never paid attention to what he said, as we hardly considered him responsible for his language." Burnett was relieved to discover that his diplomacy was working. "The moment the chief comprehended my meaning I saw a change come over his countenance, and he went away perfectly satisfied. He was a clear-headed man; and, though unlettered, he understood human nature."

Other Indians occasioned worry. A party of several dozen Kansas and Osage warriors looked fearsome. "They were all mounted on horses, had their faces painted red, and had with them one Pawnee scalp, with the ears to it, and with the wampum in them." They also looked hungry. The party's paid guide, John Gantt, counseled the emigrants to give the Indians some provisions as a gesture of goodwill. Otherwise they would steal the cattle they wanted. Burnett and the others accepted the recommendation. "We deemed this not only good advice but good humanity, and furnished the starving warriors with enough provisions to satisfy their hunger."

For the most part the Indians were content to keep their distance from the train. "They must have been impressed with a due sense of our power," Burnett wrote. "Our long line of wagons, teams, cattle, and men, on the smooth plains and under the clear skies of the Platte, made a most grand appearance. They had never before seen any spectacle like it."

THEY GOT TO FORT HALL IN LATE AUGUST. BURNETT BEGAN to wonder that anyone had ever thought the journey to Oregon difficult. "Up to this point the route over which we passed was perhaps the finest natural road, of the same length, to be found anywhere in the world," he wrote.

He was assured that things would change. Marcus Whitman had been traveling with the group but not leading it; at Fort Hall he assumed charge from John Gantt, who hadn't intended to proceed farther. Whitman informed the emigrants that the road grew more difficult to the west.

They took the lesson almost too much to heart. "We had many misgivings as to our ultimate success in making our way with our wagons, teams, and families," Burnett recalled. "We had yet to accomplish the untried and most difficult portion of our long and exhaustive journey. We could not anticipate at what moment we might be compelled to abandon our wagons in the mountains, pack our scant supplies upon our poor oxen, and make our way on foot through this terribly rough country as best we could."

Whitman now bucked them up. "Dr. Whitman assured us that we could succeed, and encouraged and aided us with every means in his power." Burnett sought a second opinion. He asked Richard Grant, the Hudson's Bay Company trader at Fort Hall, what he thought. Could wagons get through to the Columbia?

Grant was circumspectly discouraging. "He replied that, while he would not say it was impossible for us Americans to make the trip with our wagons, he could not himself see how it could be done. He had only traveled the pack-trail, and certainly no wagon could follow that route; but there might be a practical road found by leaving the trail at certain points."

Some of the party, young men without families, preemptively ditched their wagons in favor of pack animals and forged ahead of the main group. Burnett and the rest lightened the loads in their own wagons and pressed on. "The road was rocky and rough," Burnett recalled of the track across the Snake Valley. Where it wasn't rocky it was covered with thickets of sage or wormwood, three feet high and a nuisance for the lead wagons to get through. The lead wagons beat down the sage bushes but also pulverized the soil. "It was very soft on the surface and easily worked up into a most disagreeable dust, as fine as ashes or flour." Fortunately the dry climate rendered the sage less sturdy than bushes that grew in the East. "Had the sage been as stout and hard as other shrubbery of the same size, we should have been compelled to cut our wagonway through it and could never have passed over it as we did, crushing it beneath the feet of our oxen and the wheels of our wagons."

THEY REACHED FORT BOISE ON SEPTEMBER 20. THE SEASON was late and they didn't tarry. They forded the Snake River where the water was worrisomely deep but not swift; they got over without mishap. An incident on the Powder River, at a place called Lone Pine, oddly deflated Burnett. "This noble tree stood in the center of a most lovely valley, about ten miles from any other timber," he wrote. "It could be seen at the distance of many miles, rearing its majestic form above the surrounding plain, and constituted a beautiful landmark for the guidance of the traveler. Many teams had passed on before me; and at intervals, as I drove along, I would raise my head and look at that beautiful green pine." Burnett drove farther, his mind wandering. Then he looked again toward the tree and had a shock. "The tree was gone. I was perplexed for the moment to know whether I was going in the right direction." The wagon tracks said he was, and he kept on until he discovered the cause of the disappearance. "That brave old pine, which had withstood the storms and snows of centuries, had fallen at last by vandal hands of men. Some of our inconsiderate people had cut it down for fuel." But the wood was too green to burn, and the vandals availed nothing by their crime. "It was a useless and most unfortunate act."

The Blue Mountains were a trial that contained a treasure. "On October 1st we came into and through the Grande Ronde, one of the most beautiful valleys in the world," Burnett wrote. "It was

generally rich prairie, covered with luxuriant grass and having numerous beautiful streams passing through it, most of which rise
from springs at the foot of the mountains bordering the valley."
The Nez Perce gathered camas root in the valley, and they were
willing to share. "We purchased some from them, and found it
quite palatable to our keen appetites."

The last leg to the Columbia, descending the Blue Mountains,
was the most difficult. "These hills were terrible," Burnett recalled.
A snowstorm on October 5 made the bad situation worse. "We had
great difficulty in finding our cattle, and the road was very rough."
Again the natives helped out. "From the Indians were purchased
Indian corn, peas, and Irish potatoes in any desired quantity. I
have never tasted a greater luxury than the potatoes we ate on this
occasion." Burnett didn't comment on the fact that the potatoes he
so enjoyed weren't part of the Indians' traditional cuisine; rather,
they and the corn and peas were products of the agricultural techniques learned from Whitman and his fellow missionaries. But the
Nez Perce had long been traders, and they had integrated the new
goods into their stock-in-trade. Burnett was glad they did. "We
gave the Indians, in exchange, some articles of clothing, which
they were most anxious to purchase. When two parties are both as
anxious to barter as were the Indians and ourselves, it is very easy
to strike a bargain."

They reached Waiilatpu on October 10 weary and still hungry
but whole. Burnett remembered with embarrassment that some of
his party did not behave well toward their recent guide and current host. "The exhausting tedium of such a trip and the attendant
vexations have a great effect upon the majority of men, especially
upon those of weak minds. Men, under such circumstances, become childish, petulant, and obstinate. I remember that while we
were at the mission of Dr. Whitman, who had performed much
hard labor for us and was deserving of our warmest gratitude, he
was most ungenerously accused by some of our people of selfish
motives in conducting us past his establishment, where we could
procure fresh supplies of flour and potatoes. This foolish, false, and

ungrateful charge was based upon the fact that he asked us a dollar a bushel for wheat and forty cents for potatoes." The emigrants, before leaving home, had been used to receiving half that for their produce. "They thought the prices demanded by the Doctor amounted to something like extortion, not reflecting that he had to pay at least twice as much for his own supplies of merchandise and could not afford to sell his produce as low as they did theirs at home." Burnett felt personally the cost of his fellow travelers' outrage. "So obstinate were some of our people that they would not purchase of the Doctor. I remember one case particularly, where an intimate friend of mine, whose supplies were nearly exhausted, refused to purchase, though urged to do so by me, until the wheat was all sold. The consequence was that I had to divide provisions with him before we reached the end of our journey."

23

THE BUSINESS OF THE TRAIL

O F THE CAUSES PROPELLING EMIGRANTS TO OREGON, THE most commonly mentioned was the desire to regain lost health. The Mississippi Valley, the source of the bulk of the emigration, was notorious for the toll it took on the health of the men and women who lived there. Winters were often cold and snowy, and for farmers, whose work required them to spend hours outdoors every day, the cold triggered or aggravated ailments of the lungs, joints and muscles. Summers were worse, with sweltering heat, oppressive humidity, and malaria, cholera, typhoid fever and other diseases transmitted by insects or carried by water. In an era of medical ignorance and misinformation, doctors could do little besides alleviate symptoms and often couldn't do that. People of means traveled to spas, which afforded temporary relief to the few. Oregon, by contrast, promised relief to the many. To be sure, getting to Oregon was a challenge, but once there, the health-seekers hoped, the equable climate, the salubrious winds off the Pacific and the dearth of endemic diseases would do what nostrums and medical men couldn't.

"The health of Mrs. Thornton and myself caused us to determine upon a residence in Oregon, with the hope that its pure and invigorating climate would restore this inestimable blessing we had long lost," Quinn Thornton wrote of their decision to strike west. "Having completed the necessary preparations, we departed from Quincy, Illinois, April 18, 1846. In due time we arrived at Independence, Missouri, the place of rendezvous." Thornton was a lawyer and erstwhile editor who knew Thomas Benton, the Missouri champion of Oregon. Benton had set Thornton thinking about Oregon, and when Thornton and his wife, Nancy, couldn't shake the ailments that nagged them in Quincy, they headed west.

By 1846, Independence, Missouri, had become the departure point for the westward journey, and it furnished a sight for curious eyes. "The town of Independence was at this time a great Babel upon the border of the wilderness," Thornton remarked. "Here might be seen the African slave with his shining black face, driving his six-horse team of blood-red bays, and swaying from side to side as he sat upon the saddle and listened to the incessant tinkling of the bells. . . . Here might be seen the indolent dark-skinned Spaniard smoking a cigar as he leans against the sunny side of a house. He wears a sharp conical hat with a red band, a blue round-about, with little brass buttons; his duck pantaloons are open at the side as high as the knee, exhibiting his white cotton drawers between his knee and the top of his low half-boots." Independence was a crossroads of commerce, with traders and their vehicles coming and going. Lumbering Spanish-style wagons rolled in from Santa Fe carrying as much as seven thousand pounds of cargo; their great height and the canvas covers that peaked in the front and rear made them look like ships of the prairie. The merchants of Independence bought from the Santa Fe traders and sold to the Oregon emigrants, at a markup that shocked the emigrants until they experienced prices farther west.

The adventure of westering had become an efficient business by now, and the outfitters of Independence knew what to sell to those with the means to buy. Thornton tallied the vital statistics of the train to which he and his wife attached themselves: "Wagons, 72; men, 130; women, 65; children, 125; breadstuff, 69,420 lbs.; bacon, 40,200 lbs.; powder, 1100 lbs.; lead, 2672 lbs.; guns, mostly rifles, 155; pistols, 104; cattle and horses, estimated at 710."

Their train looked fit for the enterprise. "The wagons were generally new, strong, and well-painted," Thornton wrote. "They were all covered with strong linen or cotton drilling; some of them being painted, so as more effectually to repel the rain." Not everyone was going to Oregon; a minority were bound for California. The latter, including a party headed by a man named Donner, would veer southwest on the far side of the Rockies. "Some of the wagons had 'California' painted on the cover; some of them displayed 'Oregon'; some added, in large letters, 'The whole or none'; some '54-40.'" The last two slogans referred to the demand that the United States claim all of the Oregon country, leaving none for Britain.

The anticipation of danger had largely disappeared from the westward trek by this time. Thornton noted, instead, a festive feeling. "All persons were remarkably cheerful and happy. Many were almost boisterous in their mirth. We were nearly all strangers, and there was manifestly an effort on the part of each to make the most favorable impression he could upon every other."

THE JOURNEY UP THE PLATTE WAS NOW PREDICTABLE, BUT it brought experiences new to the individual emigrants. Quinn Thornton and his train endured thunderstorms like none they had ever seen. "The early part of the day had been clear and warm, but about 12 o'clock the clouds began to gather and lower in the west," he wrote on May 21. "In a short time, peals of thunder were heard in the distance, the intervals between them gradually diminishing and the sound as gradually becoming louder. The clouds continued to roll toward the zenith, with green edges, but dark and murky in the main body, and to sweep upward like a vast body of smoke ascending from a smoldering volcano. In a brief period the sun was obscured. A green haziness began to fill the atmosphere and the whole distance between the moving clouds and the earth, and to throw a sort of dull green disastrous twilight upon all below. The lightning, followed by sharp peals of thunder, was observed at length to leap from cloud to cloud, like the advance columns of approaching armies engaging in a sharp conflict. A murmuring sound of a somewhat extraordinary nature was heard in the west, which became each moment more distinct, as of marshaling hosts rapidly preparing for dreadful conflict. In a very few minutes, a blasting flash of lightning, and a deafening crash of thunder, seemed to give the signal for a general and terrible engagement. The wind blew a tremendous blast, which laid the weeds and grass prostrate to the earth, and immediately the air was filled with flying leaves and twigs, swept before the advancing tempest. The winds passed on, and heaven's artillery seemed at once to open from every cloud, and immediately the earth was deluged with torrents of rain. Flash followed flash in rapid succession, casting a lurid glare upon every object; and thunder warred upon thunder, in a manner that awed every faculty and hushed every emotion and feeling but that of the sublime."

The train met a small band of Indians; the experienced captain convinced the travelers to pay a toll—a bribe—lest the Indians steal the train's cattle. A second, larger band got no bribe but an armed display of determination by the men of the train; the captain reckoned that *their* price would have been too high. The Indians suddenly acted friendly. "Indians are generally cowards," Thornton wrote dismissively. "They will seldom fight without a decided advantage in numbers, weapons, or position."

Thornton witnessed a wedding of two young lovers among the emigrants. He heard the moans of a woman in childbirth and the first cries of the newborn. He assisted in the amputation of the gangrenous leg of a young man who scarcely flinched while the amateur surgeon hacked at flesh and bone with a butcher knife. He helped bury the brave lad when the loss of blood carried him off.

Just west of South Pass, he bade farewell to the Donners and the rest of their California-bound party. The party had heard from a man named Hastings about a shortcut that would speed their journey and get them across the Sierra Nevada before the winter's snow set in. Most were delighted at the news, but George Donner's wife had misgivings. "She was gloomy, sad, and dispirited, in view of the fact her husband and others could think for a moment of leaving the old road and confide in the statement of a man of whom they knew nothing, but who was probably some selfish adventurer," Thornton observed. Yet Mrs. Donner's doubts were overruled, and the Donners marched off to the southwest.

Few of the emigrants were wholly immune to the allure of faster, surer routes to their destination. By 1846 the most difficult stretch of the trail to Oregon—the section of the journey that broke the most hearts and claimed the most lives—was the final two hundred miles. Getting wagons to the Columbia was by now almost mundane, if still wearisome; but getting wagons *down* the Columbia was as dangerous as ever. Some of the emigrants didn't even try, instead leaving their wagons above the Dalles and packing their goods on boats that risked the falls and rapids. Some removed the wheels from their wagons and placed the wagon boxes aboard rafts that tried the descent. The emigrants themselves typically walked around the biggest drops, but many rode partway through the swift water, and a dismaying number drowned in the attempt.

Quinn Thornton had heard about the perils of the Columbia, and consequently he listened to Jesse Applegate describe a route that circumvented the river. Applegate had reached the Willamette Valley with the emigrants of 1843 and become a leader among the small but growing community there. Most recalled with shudders their experience of the Columbia and asked how others might be spared. Most, too, wished to ensure that the new emigrants reach the Willamette Valley and bolster the community there, enhancing business opportunities, raising property values and generally rewarding the first settlers for their pioneering efforts. American nationalism entered the reckoning as well. Many of the settlers resented the continuing influence of John McLoughlin and the Hudson's Bay Company; by diverting new emigrants from the Columbia River and hence Fort Vancouver, the settlers could keep the emigrants out of McLoughlin's clutches.

Prompted by such motives, the Willamette men sent Jesse Applegate and several comrades to blaze a new trail to the Willamette Valley. Applegate and the others proceeded backward—that is, they started in the Willamette Valley and worked toward the Oregon Trail east of its intersection with the Columbia. The Applegate party headed south, up the Willamette, before crossing the Cascade Mountains and eventually striking Ogden's River, as the modern Humboldt River was often called. They ascended Ogden's River in a northeasterly direction and then crossed into the watershed of the Snake River. In early August 1846 they reached Fort Hall, where they met the Thornton train.

Applegate pitched his route as an appealing alternative to the Columbia River. "Applegate affirmed the following things, among others," Thornton recorded. "1. That the distance to Oregon, via the Dalles Mission, was from 800 to 850 miles. 2. That the distance by his cut-off was estimated by him to be at least 200 miles less than that route. 3. That the party who had explored the new route with him estimated it at even 300 miles nearer. 4. That the whole distance was better supplied with water and grass than the old road. 5. That it was not more than 190 or 200 miles to the point at which his cut-off left Ogden's River. 6. That the road was generally smooth and, with the exception of a dry drive of thirty miles, well-supplied with an abundance of good water, grass, and fuel."

Thornton had doubts, starting with the military titles Applegate and the others had conferred upon themselves. "The affair had an altogether too warlike aspect; here was Colonel Ford and Major Goff, and Major Harris, and Captain Applegate, and Captain Scott, in addition to majors, captains, and colonels that I may have forgotten." And there was something about Applegate himself. "I know not how it was, but, without being able to assign a very definite reason for my opinion, beyond having its origin in the expression of the man's countenance, I did not confide in his statements. I suspected that he was influenced by some motive purely selfish."

Yet others in the train found Applegate persuasive, and the thought of avoiding the Columbia, while saving hundreds of miles in the bargain, was more than they could resist. They voted to take the Applegate cutoff, and Thornton acceded to the group's decision.

"We resumed our journey, the most of our party being greatly elated with the prospect of good roads, fine grass, excellent water, and of having a road at least 200 miles shorter than the old one," Thornton wrote. Again and again he heard his fellow emigrants express thanks for their good luck in meeting Applegate and being able to benefit from his selfless enterprise.

ALL WENT WELL AT FIRST. "WATER AND GRASS GOOD; DRY willows sufficiently abundant for fuel," Thornton wrote on August 12. One of the travelers died the next day, but the death did little to detract from the hopefulness of the train.

The days grew hotter and the vegetation thinner. Sage and cactus supplanted less hardy flora. Some of the travelers had second thoughts and reverted to the main trail. "We were thus reduced to seven wagons," Thornton wrote. The route, dusty and smooth till now, was filled with boulders. "We passed over a portion of road so rocky and rough that I did not believe it possible to get the wagons over without dashing them to pieces."

Another man died, leaving a wife and three children. The death inspired reflections in Thornton he hadn't experienced at previous deaths. "This man had been my fellow-traveler upon the road," he observed. "And it was with an unusual interest that I now halted my team and pondered the question as to whether he had safely and prosperously terminated his weary pilgrimage." Thornton couldn't say, and he soon drove on.

The Indians along Ogden's River were the same Paiutes, or Diggers, who had evoked Joe Meek's lethal scorn. Thornton thought no better of them. "The Indians along the whole length of this river are very troublesome," he recorded. "They steal the cattle and conceal themselves behind the rocks and bushes, from which they assail the emigrant and his stock with their poisoned arrows." A clash occurred in which a number of the Indians were killed and several emigrants wounded. Thornton watched one of the latter die most painfully as the poison of an arrow worked through his system.

The route by Ogden's River stretched farther than Applegate had promised. Applegate himself was nowhere to be seen, having ridden ahead to clear the road. Thornton and others of the party thought they must have missed a northward turn. Yet they pressed on, reluctant to retreat and yield ground they had already traversed. After a few more days one of Applegate's comrades, David Goff, appeared from the west and said they were on the right course and he would guide them the rest of the way. The relief of Thornton and the others at this news was tempered by the knowledge that they had already gone much farther than the two hundred miles Applegate had said was the distance from Fort Hall to the turn. Thornton wondered what else Applegate had misrepresented.

He soon found out. Applegate had spoken of a thirty-mile desert just north of the turnoff and said this was the only dry march they would encounter. Thornton and the others filled their water kegs at the river and headed across the barren stretch. They traveled all one long day over a landscape more forbidding than anything Thornton had ever seen. "The earth appeared to be as destitute of moisture as if a drop of rain or dew had never fallen upon it from the brazen heavens above." The hours ticked painfully by, with humans and animals growing ever thirstier. They camped after about thirty miles at the base of a mountain where Thornton found a tiny spring; with a shovel he excavated a miniature reservoir that filled with agonizing slowness. The humans scooped enough for tea; each of the animals slurped half a pint.

Thornton hoped that Applegate's thirty-mile desert was now behind them. But the next day yielded more of the same. They marched the whole day, halting just before sunset to rest the animals. This time, though, they didn't stop for the night, as the oxen were wild-eyed with hunger and thirst. After an hour they resumed the march, and in the dwindling light Thornton could see a desert still more forbidding than that which they had already crossed.

"Nothing presented itself to the eye but a broad expanse of a uniform dead-level plain, which conveyed to the mind the idea that it had been the muddy and sandy bottom of a former lake, and that after the water had suddenly sunk through the fissures, leaving the bottom in a state of muddy fusion, streams of gas had broken out in ten thousand places and had thrown up sand and mud, so as to form cones, rising from a common plane and ranging some three to twenty feet in height. It seemed to be the River of Death dried up, and having its muddy bottom jetted into cones by the force of the fires of perdition."

Cattle staggered and fell, never to rise. The train moved on, desperate to discover water on the far side of this hellish region, if far side there was. Applegate had called this stretch the Black Rock Desert, and at the end of the second day the train reached the Black Rock. There they found water—but water so hot it scalded those who came close. Only with the greatest patience did the travelers let it cool enough for them to drink, and then they discovered that it turned the stomach, so laced was it with minerals. Yet it was better than nothing, and they choked it down.

After resting for two days they trudged on, through a landscape that grew more surreal with each mile. The trail passed beside a range of naked bluffs. "The tops of these bluffs or high hills appeared to be covered with volcanic scoria, or a substance resembling the slag formed in iron furnaces," Thornton wrote. "Their sides presented a great variety and blending of colors, including almost all those of the rainbow. These had evidently been produced by the action of intense heat, which had left different colors in different places, according to the degree of heat applied and the temperature of the atmosphere into which the masses had been suddenly projected while thus heated. Indeed, without attempting to account accurately for the phenomenon, the hills appeared to have been in some way scathed and blasted by subterranean fires."

The fires burned even yet. Sulfurous steam billowed from gashes in the earth; boiling water filled potholes beside the trail. Thornton inquisitively tested the depth of one pothole, a mere ten inches in diameter, lowering a weighted cord two hundred feet into the bubbling liquid without finding bottom. Another, much larger spring was aptly called the Great Boiling Spring. The spring itself was some thirty feet in diameter and filled the bottom of a basin or crater several hundred feet around. One of the emigrant women accidently stepped into the stream that drained the scalding water; leaping out, she pulled off her stocking and, with the stocking, a layer of skin.

Still they marched. They emerged from the desert and the volcanic zone into a broad valley. In the distance they spied a wide lake, named for the Klamath Indians. The animals revived on the fresh water and abundant grass of the valley; the spirits of the travelers were buoyed as well. Yet the humans, unable to survive on grass, measured their dwindling provisions and wondered how far they were from the Willamette Valley. David Goff tendered reassurance, but at this point no one in the train believed him.

They entered a forest of pine trees. "They were the first we had seen in many a weary league, through many a weary week, that could with propriety be said to be trees," Thornton recounted. "And now that we saw them it was like meeting old and much-loved friends." Yet the forest cloaked a mountain—called Siskiyou by Applegate—that grew formidable. The trail probed ravines over which the branches of the trees formed a gloomy canopy. The way steepened, taxing the long-suffering oxen to the limit. The emigrants were far past the point where they wished they had never heard of Jesse Applegate; now they cursed him with every second breath. "All that we knew of the mountain was vague and uncertain. Applegate had mentioned it by name, indeed, and had spoken of the ascent as being short and easy. But this—like almost every thing he had said of the road—we learned, by sad and painful experience, to be untrue. We only knew that many fierce savages prowled among its rugged recesses, and we only wished that they had prevented Applegate from passing through it."

The oxen could find no food in the forest, and more of them began to die. The larders of the emigrants were all but empty. They had budgeted provisions to last till the first of October, and it was now the final week of October. They felt the clutch of starvation. But there was nothing to do but press on. "We continued to hurry forward over this rough mountain-ridge, as though we were sensible that the Angel of Death was close behind us."

THEN CAME THE RAINS. THEY FELL DRENCHING AND COLD, making the trail more treacherous than ever and pushing animals and humans to the brink of soaking, shivering death by exposure. Thornton taxed himself bitterly for what he had brought upon his wife. "She did not complain in words, but she looked feeble, hungry, and haggard, and appeared to be suffering severely," he recalled. He cursed Jesse Applegate yet again.

And still their trials grew more severe. They agonizingly scaled one side of the Umpqua Mountains only to find that the trail descending the other side through a narrow canyon was all but impassable. "The canyon, which appears to have been rent asunder by some vast convulsion of nature, is about three miles long, having the whole of its width occupied by a very swift stream of cold snow-water varying from one foot and a half to four feet in depth and running over a bottom covered with boulders from four inches to five feet in diameter," Thornton wrote. "The rocky walls on each side are in many places perpendicular; in others they recede so as to form an angle of about forty-five degrees with the plane of the horizon."

They abandoned the wagons, packing what little remained of their property and possessions onto the draft animals. They stumbled and staggered down the canyon, often in the stream itself. One woman died of exhaustion and exposure. Thornton feared his wife might be next. "We each had a long stick in our hands to support ourselves, and to prevent the water from sweeping us into deep holes," he wrote. "Mrs. Thornton, upon suddenly descending into the cold snow-water above the waist, was much chilled, and I thought at first that she would perish." He rubbed her face and hands to revive her, and with a wan smile she indicated she could carry on.

They felt their way another mile, in the rushing stream nearly the whole way. Again Thornton thought his wife was slipping away from him. "Mrs. Thornton began to lose all sensibility upon one side. I supported her as well as I could, but at length she complained of indistinctness of vision, and soon became totally blind." She looked as though she were dead already. "Her lips were thin and compressed, and as white and bloodless as paper; her eyes were turned up in their sockets; her head fell back upon my arms, and every feature wore the aspect and fixedness of death."

Thornton began to reckon what he would do with her corpse. "I could not, for all the world, have carried her dead body out of that canyon." But there was no place to bury her, and in the time it would have taken, he would have been fatally chilled too. The dilemma increased his suffering.

He redoubled his efforts to revive her. "I rubbed her wrists violently, chafed her temples, shook her, and called aloud to her." After some minutes of this, she gradually stirred. Her vision partially returned, though her side remained numb. Yet she could walk, with his help.

They stumbled down the treacherous stream once more. They felt they were racing for their lives, though Thornton realized that they were moving no faster than yards per minute. Finally the walls of the canyon fell back, and they found a bank of the stream to crawl out on.

Ahead they saw a tent and a fire. Others in their party had preceded them and were drying and warming themselves. Thornton and his wife joined them and did the same. He rummaged in his shot-pouch for a morsel of food he still carried, and he and his wife shared it. Then they slumped to the ground before the fire and fell into the sleep of the utterly exhausted.

Yet they weren't finished with Canyon Creek. The trail now ran more often on the bank than in the stream, but they had to crisscross the torrent repeatedly. By Thornton's count they waded the creek thirty-nine times before they emerged onto the open bank of the Umpqua River.

Here Thornton learned that they might be saved. Jesse Applegate had gone far ahead to the Willamette Valley settlements, and though Thornton placed no faith in his willingness or ability to send back provisions, he hoped some of those who accompanied him would do so.

Thornton realized that survival would be by rescue alone. They were completely spent, and on the scant food they had left they couldn't regain strength. Thornton reflected on what they had lost, namely everything they owned but the wretched clothes they wore and a parcel of clothes he carried on his back, plus a little money in his pocket. His spirits began to fail. "I became greatly discouraged and depressed in mind, as well as reduced in my physical energies. I seemed to be approaching the eve of the breaking up of both." He couldn't shake his despondency, and he began to wonder if he could carry on. They had set out for Oregon with the highest hopes but now faced ruin, even assuming they survived. "A dark cloud rested upon the future and, intercepting every ray of hope, shut me up in the dark forebodings of a fearful issue."

Fortunately a rescue team appeared the next day. A party carrying flour on mules and driving a small herd of cattle arrived from the Willamette settlements. The cattle were slaughtered and the flour was distributed, and new life and hope were injected into the battered emigrants.

But it came at a price, and the price caused Thornton to conclude that everything that had befallen the emigrants since meeting Jesse Applegate had been part of a cynical profiteering plan. Applegate and others in the Willamette settlements had goods to sell, and they sought customers. Perhaps Applegate hadn't foreseen the extent of the suffering his plan would cause, but he certainly benefited from it. He had lured the emigrants to their ruin, depriving them of everything but what they could carry in their money belts, that he and his friends might relieve them of that.

"He first reduced us to the verge of starvation that he might thus be enabled to gather up the last dollar that remained to us," Thornton said.

Thornton and his wife eventually reached the settlements. They built new lives and attained what Thornton deemed a substantial portion of happiness. But he never forgave Jesse Applegate.

24

DESPERATE FURY

As HARD AS THE EMIGRATION WAS ON THE EMIGRANTS, IT was even harder on the native peoples of Oregon. The new-comers carried new diseases, which sorely afflicted the Indians. "In the fall of 1847 the emigration over the mountains brought the measles," Catherine Sager remembered. Catherine Sager was one of seven children who had lost their parents in the 1844 emigra-tion and landed, as orphans, on the doorstep of the Whitmans, who had taken them in. She was twelve years old in 1847 and, with many at the mission, contracted measles that autumn. "Whit-man's large family were all sick," she said, speaking of the extended household. She added, more significantly, "The disease was raging fearfully among the Indians, who were rapidly dying. I saw from five to six buried daily."

The measles epidemic appeared the coup de grace for the Cay-use. For decades the tribe had been declining, from other intro-duced diseases and from intertribal competition. The decline figured largely in their hostility toward the Whitmans, embodi-ments of the changes that were dooming them. By early 1847 the Cayuse numbered no more than a few hundred. The measles epi-demic threatened to wipe them from the face of the earth. "It was most distressing to go into a lodge of some ten or twenty fires," Henry Spalding wrote, "and count twenty or twenty-five, some in the midst of measles, others in the last stage of dysentery, in the midst of every kind of filth, of itself sufficient to cause sickness, with no suitable means to alleviate their inconceivable sufferings, with perhaps one well person to look after the wants of two sick ones. They were dying every day; one, two, and sometimes five in a day."

Some of the Indians blamed the new emigrants for bringing this final plague; others blamed Marcus Whitman. The Indians noted that though whites became ill like the Indians, the whites generally recovered while the Indians died. Whitman ministered to both groups; his medicine saved the whites but not the Indians. Observation of this fact, coming amid the flood of immigrants to Oregon, made plausible the arguments of some in the tribe that Whitman was killing the Indians to make room for the whites.

Another element added to the Indians' distrust. For some years Whitman had used arsenic to kill wolves that preyed on the mission's domestic animals. On at least one occasion Indians had eaten poisoned meat left out for the wolves, and become violently ill. They had recovered, thanks to Whitman's intervention, but the incident lodged in the memory of the Cayuse, who regarded Whitman as one whose medicine could kill as well as heal.

A small group of the Cayuse concluded that Whitman had to be killed before he wiped out their tribe. Their conclusion drew strength from stories circulated by a mixed-race man named Joe Lewis, recently arrived at Waiilatpu. Lewis had come with a group of emigrants but been stranded at Waiilatpu after alienating the others in his party. Marcus Whitman, recognizing Lewis's corrosive influence on those around him, tried to move him along. Lewis thereupon began spreading tales about Whitman that fit the Cayuse narrative of blame. The story that did the most damage to Whitman had Lewis improbably lying on a settee in Whitman's own house, apparently napping. Lewis asserted that he overheard Whitman speaking to Henry Spalding and Narcissa. Lewis said that Spalding asked Whitman why he didn't kill off the Indians faster. Whitman responded that they were dying fast enough. The old ones would perish this autumn; the young ones would die the next spring. Lewis told this story to a council of the Cayuse, warning them that if they didn't kill Whitman and Spalding, they all would die.

Joe Lewis attracted followers, and together they plotted the murder of the missionaries and the destruction of the mission. Their plan unfolded during the last days of November 1847. Whitman was called away to treat some ailing Cayuse at their camp on the Umatilla River. "The night was dark, and the rain beat furiously upon us," wrote Henry Spalding, who accompanied Whitman on the journey. Spalding said the two men reflected on the decade they had spent in Oregon and the troubles they were experiencing at present. Whitman said he was willing to leave if the Indians demanded his departure, but they hadn't done so yet. They arrived at the lodge of Stickus, a Cayuse chief who had been helpful and friendly in the past. Stickus warned Whitman that Joe Lewis and a Cayuse named Tamsucky had been talking angrily against him. Stickus urged Whitman to be careful.

Whitman did what little he could for the sick and turned back toward Waiilatpu. Spalding, who had injured his leg when his horse slipped and rolled on the rain-drenched trail, stayed behind. Whitman reached home several hours after sunset on Sunday evening, November 28. Narcissa, weary from tending the several sick children in the house, was asleep. The two oldest Sager children, John and Francis, were keeping watch. Whitman woke Narcissa to say he was home and sent the Sager boys to bed. Catherine Sager, herself sick, was lying on the settee in the main room, drifting in and out of sleep. "He examined the patients one after the other," Catherine recalled. "Coming to Helen"—Joe Meek's daughter—"he spoke and told his wife, who was lying on the bed, that Helen was dying. He sat and watched her for some time, when she rallied and seemed better. I had noticed that he seemed to be troubled when he first came home, but concluded that it was anxiety in reference to the sick children."

Whitman summoned Narcissa from the bedroom, saying he wanted to talk. "He related to her what Stickus had told him that day," Catherine remembered. He remarked that he had heard that the Cayuse were holding councils each night. This didn't seem good.

Catherine had tried to keep quiet while listening, but Whitman's message and demeanor caused her to start. "Observing that I was restless, he surmised that I had overheard the conversation. By kind and soothing words he allayed my fears and I went to sleep." Catherine added, "I can see it all now and remember just how he looked."

CATHERINE SLEPT THE NIGHT AND WOKE TO A COLD FOG OUTside. Whitman maintained watch, and though Catherine thought he seemed more serious than usual, nothing else drew her notice.

The family soon learned that more Indian children had died during the night. Their parents were bringing the bodies to the mission for burial. Whitman went to meet the grievers and conduct the funeral; he was surprised that none but the immediate relatives were in attendance. But there was a cow being butchered near the mill, and he supposed that the prospect of fresh beef might have drawn others to that location.

He returned about noon to the house, where he found Narcissa nervous. She had continued to try to keep Indians out of the house, but on this morning they had pushed their way in. "The kitchen was full of Indians, and their boisterous manner alarmed her," Catherine recounted. "She fled to the sitting room, bolting the door in the face of the savages who tried to pass in."

It wasn't Narcissa they wanted to see; it was Marcus. They pounded on the door and demanded to speak to the doctor.

Marcus and Narcissa exchanged glances. He tried to reassure her, saying he would calm the Indians down. But he didn't want to take chances on her safety. "Dr. Whitman told his wife to bolt the door after him," Catherine recalled. Whitman went through the door into the kitchen, and Narcissa bolted it.

She stood at the door, listening. Nothing more than voices, not especially loud, came from the other side of the door. She crossed the room, picked up Henrietta Sager, and cradled the little girl in her arms. She sat down to rock the child to sleep. Meanwhile the older children lined up to take a bath in a washtub. Margaret Osborn, the wife of a man who worked at the mission, had been sick and was staying with the Whitmans; she entered the living room from her adjoining bedroom. She found a seat near Narcissa.

"She had scarcely sat down when we were all startled by an explosion that seemed to shake the house," Catherine said. "The two women sprang to their feet and stood with white faces and distended eyes." Their alarm was contagious. "The children rushed out doors, some of them without clothes." Narcissa set Henrietta down and called the children back inside. She started toward the kitchen door, through which Marcus had gone, but changed her mind. "She fastened the door and told Mrs. Osborn to go to her room and lock the door, at the same time telling us to put on our clothes," Catherine remembered. "All this happened much quicker than I can write it."

The meaning of the explosion sank in. "Mrs. Whitman then began to walk the floor, wringing her hands, saying, 'Oh, the Indians! the Indians! they have killed my husband, and I am a widow!'" Catherine said.

Mary Ann Bridger, a mixed-race daughter of Jim Bridger, also living with the Whitmans, had seen what happened in the kitchen. Finding the kitchen door to the living room locked, she had run around the house and come in an outside door. "Her face was deathly white," Catherine remembered. "We gathered around her and inquired if father was dead. She replied, 'Yes.'"

One of the workers who had been butchering the cow came in the same door, his arm obviously broken. "Mrs. Whitman," he said through pain and shock, "the Indians are killing us all."

Narcissa pulled herself together. She brought a pitcher of water for the wounded man. She went around the house and locked all the doors to the outside. Then, steeling herself, she unlocked the kitchen door and opened it. "As she did so several emigrant women with their small children rushed in," Catherine recalled. Narcissa pushed past them.

She found Marcus lying in his own blood on the floor of the kitchen. She began dragging him toward the main room. "One of the women went to her aid, and they brought him in. He was fatally wounded, but conscious. The blood was streaming from a gunshot wound in the throat. Kneeling over him, she implored him to speak to her. To all her questions he whispered 'yes' or 'no,' as the case might be."

More loud reports outside the house caught the attention of all inside. "The roar of guns showed us that the bloodthirsty fiends were not yet satisfied," Catherine recounted. Narcissa stole a glance through the window. "Oh, that Joe Lewis is doing it all!" she said. Hardly had she spoken when Lewis reached the door and asked to be admitted. Narcissa demanded to know what he wanted. He said nothing and went away.

Andrew Rogers, another mission employee, ran toward the house, chased by Indians. "He sprang against the door, breaking out two panes of glass," Catherine said. "Mrs. Whitman opened the door, and let him in, and closed it in the face of his pursuers, who, with a yell, turned to seek other victims. Mr. Rogers was shot through the wrist and tomahawked on the head; seeing the doctor lying upon the floor, he asked if he was dead." Marcus Whitman retained sufficient consciousness to murmur that he wasn't, yet.

The schoolteacher at the mission, L. W. Saunders, had heard the guns and run to the house to see what was happening. He tried to get in, but Narcissa, not wanting to risk opening the door again, waved him off. He started to retreat. "He was seized by a savage who had a large butcher knife," Catherine wrote. "Mr. Saunders struggled and was about to get away when another burly savage came to the aid of the first. Standing by Mrs. Whitman's side, I watched the horrid strife until, sickened, I turned away."

As she did, she heard another rifle shot. "A bullet came through the window, piercing Mrs. Whitman's shoulder. Clasping her hands to the wound, she shrieked with pain, and then fell to the floor."

Catherine sought to do something. "I ran to her and tried to raise her up," she recounted. Narcissa shook her head. "Child, you cannot help me," she said. "Save yourself."

The other children watched in horror. "We all crowded around her and began to weep." Narcissa thought only of them. "She commenced praying for us, 'Lord, save these little ones.' She repeated this over many times."

The other adults in the room now took charge. "Mr. Rogers pushed us to the stairway." Catherine hesitated. "I was filled with agony at the idea of leaving the sick children and refused to go." Rogers quickly figured out how to get her to move. "Taking up one of the children, he handed her to me, and motioned for me to take her up. I passed her to some one else, turned and took another, and then the third and ran up myself." Rogers returned to Narcissa. He lifted her to her feet and half-carried her upstairs, where he laid her on a bed.

They hardly felt safe. "The crashing of doors informed us that the work of death was accomplished out of doors, and our time had come," Catherine said. The Indians entered the house and battered open the door that led to the stairway. Everyone upstairs braced for the worst. A wounded man named Nathan Kimball had come up with the others; he placed an old rifle he had found in the bedroom upon the banister, with its muzzle pointing down the stairs. This deterred the attackers, who retreated out of the house.

"All was quiet for awhile," Catherine related. "Then we heard footsteps in the room below, and a voice at the bottom of the stairway called Mr. Rogers. It was an Indian, who represented that he had just come; he would save them"—those in the upstairs room—"if they would come down." Rogers didn't believe him and refused. But he couldn't figure out how to escape, and the talking continued. "After a good deal of parleying he came up. I told mother that I had seen him killing the teacher, but she thought I was mistaken." The Indian had a grim message. "He said that they were going to burn the house, and that we must leave it."

Catherine hoped to save at least her youngest sibling. "I wrapped my little sister up and handed her to him with the request that he would carry her." The Indian initially refused. "He said that they would take Mrs. Whitman away and then come back for us."

Narcissa and the other women were guided down the stairs. "When they reached the room below mother was laid upon a set-tee and carried out into the yard by Mr. Rogers and Joe Lewis."

Then Lewis double-crossed Rogers and the rest. "Joe dropped his end of the settee, and a volley of bullets laid Mr. Rogers, mother and brother Francis, bleeding and dying, on the ground."

AMID THE ATTACK ON THE HOUSE, A GROUP OF INDIANS HAD gone to the school to seize the children there. The children had hidden in the attic of the schoolhouse but been discovered. They were brought to the main house and taken into the kitchen. "They were placed in a row to be shot," Catherine recalled. But the leader of the group changed his mind, and the children were left un-harmed, though still terrified.

For hours the Indians debated what to do with the children and the women they hadn't killed. They tentatively decided to keep them as hostages, guarantors against reprisal by the other whites in Oregon.

Catherine and the others gradually realized they wouldn't die that day, but they could do nothing for those who had been killed or were in their final agonies. "The November moon looked down, bright and cold, upon the scene, nor heeded the groans of the dy-ing who gave forth their plaints to the chill night air," Catherine recalled. In the darkness she heard Rogers pray for deliverance: "Come, Lord Jesus, come quickly!" Then she heard no more.

DURING THE NEXT FEW DAYS CATHERINE AND THE OTHER survivors pieced together the last moments of Marcus Whitman and the others killed at Waiilatpu. After Whitman went into the kitchen, he was confronted by two Indians, named Tiloukaikt and Tomahas. The lodge of the former had lost three children to measles the previous night; these were the ones Whitman had buried that morning. The two men demanded that Whitman give them medicine to stop the dying. The demand was a ruse to distract Whitman, for while Tiloukaikt engaged Whitman's attention, Tomahas pulled a tomahawk from beneath his blanket and struck Whitman in the head from behind. Whitman slumped to the floor, where Tomahas struck him again. A third Indian shot him in the neck, producing the blast Catherine and the others had heard from beyond the locked door.

John Sager, Catherine's oldest brother, was outside at the time of the attack. He, too, heard the shot, and he ran to the kitchen. Seeing Whitman on the floor, he fired a pistol at the Indians, evidently hitting two. The Indians fired back, wounding him fatally.

A mission worker named Hoffman was helping to butcher the cow when he heard the shooting. Some of the Indians assaulted him, but he used his butcher's ax to defend himself. He wounded some of his attackers yet was overpowered and killed. Catherine reported that he was disemboweled.

The schoolteacher, Saunders, also fought back. But he lacked a weapon and too was overpowered. He was slashed with knives and shot just before reaching what he hoped would be the safety of the house. His head was bludgeoned, either before or after he died.

One of the schoolchildren who witnessed the attacks out of doors later described the mutilation of the victims. "The bodies, or pieces of them, lay scattered all around, an arm here and a leg there," he said. "Some of the men had their breasts torn open and their hearts taken out. I saw two Indians each with a stick and a human heart stuck upon it."

A total of thirteen people were killed by the Indians. These were Marcus and Narcissa Whitman, the two Sager boys, Andrew Rogers, L. W. Saunders and seven others associated with the mission.

A fourteenth person, Peter Hall, managed to escape the initial attack but was never seen alive again.

More than fifty women and children were held by the Indians as prisoners. They didn't know if the killing had ended. "With hearts filled with fright, we awaited the coming of the murderers," Catherine Sager recalled.

25

AMBASSADOR FROM OREGON

IF EVER A MOMENT IN THE HISTORY OF THE OREGON country called for the strong, steady leadership John McLoughlin had exercised from Fort Vancouver for nearly a quarter century, it came in the critical hours and days after the massacre at the Whitman mission, when the lives of Catherine Sager and the other hostages hung in the balance. But McLoughlin no longer ruled the Hudson's Bay Company post. His generosity to the American emigrants, who often arrived hungry, ragged and woefully unprepared for their first winter, had caused his masters in the Bay Company to question his loyalty to their bottom line, and in 1846 they forced him to retire. McLoughlin crossed the Columbia River and took up residence at Oregon City, a town emerging at the falls of the Willamette River, twenty-five miles above its confluence with the Columbia. His new neighbors were hardly more grateful than his old employers; they thought he should have done *more* to save them from their own improvidence.

To Peter Skene Ogden, who in his days as a trapper and trader had given his name to the river later called the Humboldt, fell the task of filling McLoughlin's shoes. But an even larger task was managing the retreat of the Hudson's Bay Company, and of British authority in the Pacific Northwest, two hundred miles to the north. In the year Ogden took over from McLoughlin, the United States and Britain reached an agreement on the fate of Oregon. As expected, the two countries split the region, with Britain getting the northern part and America the southern. *Un*expectedly, the line of division was not the Columbia River, as McLoughlin and many others had assumed it would be, but rather the 49th parallel to salt water, and then the Strait of Juan de Fuca to the Pacific. Timing and context determined this outcome. James Polk had campaigned on an all-of-Oregon platform, but the prospect of war with Mexico over Texas put him in a compromising mood. Nor did the British push hard for the Columbia River. They were in the process of repealing their Corn Laws, as they called their ban on the importation of foreign grain. American wheat was cheaper than British wheat, and its import would encourage British industrialization by freeing—or forcing—British farmers to take jobs in the cities. Yet the repealers had to promise that wheat would not be used as a weapon against Britain. To make this promise plausible, they needed to keep the Americans happy. Hence the abandonment of Fort Vancouver and the withdrawal to modern British Columbia.

Ogden was still at Fort Vancouver when the shocking news of the Whitman massacre came down the Columbia. Humanitarianism aside, Ogden realized he had to free Catherine Sager and the other hostages lest their killing further inflame the spirit of vengeance the massacre was sure to kindle among the Americans on the Willamette. Until the retreat to the north was accomplished, the last thing Ogden wanted was a war between the Americans and the Cayuse, which might well become a war against all the Indians of Oregon, and of all the Indians against all the whites. So he packed a cargo of trade goods—the currency of ransom—into a Bay Company boat and headed upstream.

The negotiations proved easier than he feared. The elders among the Cayuse were as appalled at the massacre as any of the whites, for they understood what it might bring down upon them. They made clear to Ogden that the killings were the work of young hotheads and not of the tribe as a whole. They accepted his offer of the trade goods for the hostages. Ogden delivered blankets, cotton shirts, guns, ammunition, flints and tobacco; they delivered Catherine Sager and the other hostages.

THE BARGAIN DIDN'T END THE CRISIS, BUT MERELY KEPT IT from getting worse. Thirteen people were known to be dead and one presumed so; the Americans in the Willamette settlements demanded justice, if not vengeance. They demanded something else, as well, albeit of the United States government rather than of the Indians: territorial status for Oregon. Now that Oregon was definitively American, they insisted that Washington extend its protection to them.

In pursuit of justice and perhaps vengeance, the Oregonians launched the first organized war against Indians in the American West. Adapting an American tradition that ran back to the Mayflower Compact, the Willamette settlers created a provisional government, on no one's authority but their own. The provisional government raised a militia to capture the Cayuse killers and possibly punish the rest of the tribe. More than a few of the Oregon Rifles, as they called themselves, would have been happy to wipe out the entire Cayuse tribe. Some wished to teach all the Indians of Oregon a lesson.

They didn't get their way. The provisional government pursued a surprisingly sophisticated policy of negotiating amid hostilities. A peace commission met with the Cayuse chiefs and demanded the delivery of the murderers, even while the militia was moving against Cayuse warriors and potential allies. As a result, the Cayuse War didn't amount to much militarily. It was a conflict mostly of ambush and skirmish, punctuated by breaks for bad weather and furloughs for the militiamen to plant and harvest their crops. Eventually, almost three years after the slaughter at Waiilatpu, the exhausted and diminished Cayuse handed over five men for trial.

By then the settlers had accomplished their second goal: formal territorial government under American federal law. The provisional government drafted a petition citing the Whitman killings as evidence of the need for federal governance and protection. To carry the petition to Washington, in the dead of winter, the Oregonians chose Joe Meek. People who had known Meek only from the mountains would have been surprised by his adjustment to the life in the lowlands. His taste for farming never quite matched his way with words, but the latter enabled him to launch a modest political career. He took a part in creating the provisional government, and his good humor and solid sense caused his neighbors to look to him at moments when other men grew anxious and testy. At the time of the calling of the volunteers to fight the Cayuse, Meek thought his daughter Helen was one of the captives. He was tempted to ride to her rescue. But better than most of the settlers, he understood that direct action against the Cayuse might be the death of the captives, and he was willing to leave the negotiations to Peter Ogden. When the provisional legislature wrote its petition to Congress and sought a messenger to carry the crucial document across the winter mountains to Washington, Meek seemed just the man.

His journey east became the stuff of legend. Meek accompanied the Oregon Rifles as far as Waiilatpu. By this time he had learned that Helen was not one of the captives ransomed by Ogden; Meek assumed that Helen had died of the measles or been killed by the Cayuse. He learned that it was the former when, with the volunteers, he visited the scene of the massacre. A hasty burial given the bodies had been undone by wolves, which had devoured the flesh and scattered the bones of the corpses. Meek managed to identify Helen's body and ascertain that she had not been the victim of violence. He nonetheless blamed the Cayuse, concluding that she would have survived under Narcissa Whitman's care if Narcissa had not been murdered. He sorrowfully reburied his little girl in a deeper grave, beyond the reach of wild animals or any influence but passing time.

He took a last look at the remains of Narcissa. He recalled their first meeting at the Green River rendezvous, when she had laughed at his tales of the mountains. He remembered her fair face then—and shuddered at the battered, gnawed skull that now stared back at him. The only part of her that remained recognizable was her golden hair, which had beguiled mountain men and Indians alike. One of the volunteers snipped samples of the hair to give to her friends in the Willamette Valley.

Meek turned his face farther east. With a few other men he ascended the Blue Mountains, covered with snow in midwinter. He donned the red belt and distinctive Canadian cap of the Hudson's Bay Company in order to pass himself off as a friend of the Indians and one who benefited from the company's protection. The disguise served him well when his party encountered Bannock Indians, whose hostile first reaction softened when Meek explained that a large Bay Company trading party was following them at a day's distance. The Bannocks, eager for the trade goods, let Meek and the others go. Meek had no difficulty persuading his companions to march nonstop for forty-eight hours lest the Bannocks, angered upon learning of his deception, give chase and kill them.

They reached Fort Hall, where the wife of the absent director provided them a hot meal and offered warm beds. They declined the latter, choosing to resume their journey at once. In the high country above Fort Hall they ran into snowdrifts that defeated their horses. Dismounting, they made snowshoes of willow branches and, letting the horses find their way back to the fort, pressed on.

The surroundings reminded Meek of his mountain days, when he had often tramped about in the middle of winter. A relic of those days appeared in the form of Peg Leg Smith, a mountain man who now herded cattle for a rancher on the upper Bear River. They swapped stories and Smith killed a cow for a feast. Meek remarked that in the old days the meat would have been buffalo, but after the meager rations he and his partners had been on since Fort Hall, the beef was plenty satisfying.

At the headwaters of the Green River, Meek fell in with Jim Bridger. Meek had to convey the sad news that Bridger's daughter, like his own, had died in the aftermath of the Whitman massacre.

Bridger remarked that they shared a score to settle with the Cayuse. He gave Meek and the others four mules for their journey out of the mountains and down the Platte River.

They reached Fort Laramie, where the French trader in charge warned them against the Sioux farther east. Meek's group dodged the Sioux and reached St. Joseph, Missouri, just over two months after leaving the Willamette Valley. The Missouri River boatmen weren't easily impressed, but Meek's journey prompted one to christen his new vessel the *Joseph L. Meek*, with a sign affixed to the pilothouse that boasted "The Quickest Trip Yet."

ON THE MISSOURI, MEEK WAS A THROWBACK, A VESTIGE FROM the era of the fur trade; on the Mississippi and the Ohio he was a curiosity and then a celebrity. His mountain raiment grew more singular the farther from the mountains he traveled, and by the time his steamboat from St. Louis reached Wheeling, Virginia, he drew crowds in the dining parlor and on the foredeck. He played his role to the hilt, announcing that he was the ambassador from the "Republic of Oregon" to the president of the United States. To any who would treat him to refreshment he told tales of his fights with grizzly bears and savage Indians; the blanket that served as his coat and the wolf-skin cap that covered his head, together with his unshorn hair and fierce beard, lent credence and piquancy to his tales.

At Wheeling he boarded a stage for Cumberland, where he transferred to the train for Washington. He arrived in the capital to find Congress deadlocked over the Oregon question. Meek was surprised, as were many observers better versed in the ways of the nation's capital. Oregon had been, until very recently, an uncontroversial cause. American Protestants, who formed the great majority of the country's population, had cheered the missionary efforts of the Whitmans and their Protestant colleagues. John Frémont had become famous on the strength of his explorations of the Oregon country, as breathlessly recounted in narratives cowritten and publicized by his indefatigable wife, Jessie Benton

Frémont. It lent to Frémont's renown that he was dashingly hand-some and Jessie beautiful and politically connected. Their descriptions of the wonders of Oregon, not to mention of Frémont's feats of daring and courage in revealing them, added to Oregon's allure and romance at a time when it was the favored destination of westbound emigrants.

The example of the Whitmans, the exploits of Frémont, and the enthusiasm of the emigrants appeared to vindicate the prophets of Manifest Destiny. The high priest of the tribe, and the coiner of the phrase, was a journalist named John L. O'Sullivan, who in 1845 proclaimed that the United States had shared Oregon with Britain for too long. O'Sullivan demanded that the government advance America's claim to the whole of the Oregon country. "That claim is by the right of our manifest destiny to overspread and to possess the whole of the continent which Providence has given us for the development of the great experiment of liberty and federated self-government entrusted to us."

Americans, like most people, are easily flattered, and Manifest Destiny was flattery in its most seductive form. It cast American self-interest as a providential imperative. To oppose the acquisition of Oregon, to resist westward expansion, was to contradict God Himself.

Yet Manifest Destiny fell short. The United States split Oregon with Britain, and it never came close to overspreading all of North America. A principal reason for its failure was simultaneously the cause of Joe Meek's surprise at the end of his journey from Oregon: slavery. Slavery had nothing to do with Oregon per se; not in their wildest dreams did advocates of slavery imagine chattel workers plowing the fields of the Willamette Valley. But by the late 1840s slavery had everything to do with American politics, including the politics of the Oregon question. Southern lawmakers refused to create a government for Oregon that barred slavery or let the inhabitants of the territory do so. Oregon was the first American territory beyond the bounds of the Louisiana Purchase, where the slavery question had been resolved by the Missouri Compromise of 1820. Many Southern lawmakers now regretted having signed away slavery's rights to the northern part of the purchase, and they determined to make no such concession with Oregon. But the Oregonians didn't want slavery, Northern members of Congress didn't want it for them, and even the Southerners had difficulty describing a scenario under which slavery might actually take root in Oregon. Even so, as a matter of constitutional principle, the Southerners made slavery an issue, and in the spring of 1848 the Oregon question hung fire.

The arrival of Joe Meek transformed the situation. Meek's rustic appearance riveted the lawmakers, while the horrific news he brought of the Whitman massacre compelled them to put aside sectional rivalries and tend to the business of protecting American citizens in America's westernmost possession. Meek delivered the petition the provisional legislature in Oregon had composed, and he arranged a meeting with President Polk, who turned out to be a distant cousin.

Thomas Benton led the pro-Oregon forces in Congress. Benton had warned of the dangers of leaving Oregon without a government, and the recent events had, lamentably, proved his prescience. The Oregonians cried out for the protection of the government, he told the Senate. "In the depth of winter they send to us a special messenger who makes his way across the Rocky Mountains at a time when almost every living thing perished in the snow, when the snow was at such a depth that nothing could penetrate to the bottom of it." If Joe Meek could risk his life on behalf of his compatriots in Oregon, Congress could at least act on their petition. "They are in a suffering condition. Not a moment of time is to be lost."

Benton's argument carried the day, but not before Benton nearly came to blows on the Senate floor with Andrew Butler of South Carolina, who defended slavery and its asserted prerogatives to the last. Meanwhile Joe Meek caroused with Kit Carson, a mountain comrade—and a scout for John Frémont—who happened to be in Washington. And he regaled the women of the capital as he had regaled Narcissa Whitman at the Green River rendezvous. One of the ladies, taken by Meek's rugged good looks, inquired whether he was married.

"Yes, indeed," he answered. "I have a wife and several children."

"Oh, dear! I should think your wife would be *so* afraid of the Indians!"

"Afraid of the Indians?" rejoined Meek. "Why, madam, she is an Indian herself."

The woman nearly swooned.

JAMES POLK WAS SUFFICIENTLY IMPRESSED BY MEEK THAT when the Oregon bill passed, he appointed him to be the first United States marshal in the new Oregon Territory. In this capacity Meek returned to Oregon, reaching Oregon City, the capital of the territory, in time for the trial of the five Cayuse charged with the murder of the Whitmans and their associates. The trial proceeded swiftly, and the five were convicted and sentenced to hang. Yet they protested their innocence, and a vocal minority of the Oregonians believed them. The believers said the five were scapegoats given up by the tribe so that the Cayuse people as a whole would not be obliterated. A petition was raised to stay the execution. But the territorial governor was not in Oregon City, and his lieutenant declined to take responsibility for halting the execution.

At the appointed hour, the five were escorted to the scaffold. Joe Meek, doubtless thinking of Helen, swung a hatchet that cut the rope and sent the men to their deaths.

V

THE WORLD IN A
NUGGET OF GOLD

26

THE SECRET OF
THE SIERRA NEVADA

NEITHER JOE MEEK NOR ANY OF THE OTHER AMERICANS
who made their way up and down the Columbia River, and
not John McLoughlin or Peter Ogden or any of the British, could
have said how the rapids and falls of the Columbia River had come
to be. The state of geological knowledge left such things a mystery. The Indians who lived near the river had a story that made
as much sense as anything the outsiders could propose. Two great
chiefs—Wy'east, who lived south of the river, and Klickitat, on
the north—had fallen in love with the same beautiful maiden,
Loo-wit. Wy'east and Klickitat fought over the girl, who tended a
sacred fire on an ancient stone bridge that spanned the Columbia.
The chiefs enlisted their tribes, and war ensued. The Great Spirit
grew angry over what his people had done, and he turned the chiefs
and the woman into mountains. Wy'east became what the whites
called Mount Hood, Klickitat Mount Adams, and Loo-wit Mount
St. Helens. Yet the battle continued, with Wy'east and Klickitat
hurling boulders and spewing flames and ash at each other until
they shook down the stone bridge, which fell into the river.

The legend accounted for the Cascades of the Columbia, which
were nothing more than the remnants of the stone bridge. It explained the volcanic eruptions of the high peaks on either side of

219

the river, which had occurred within the historical memory of the Columbia tribes. And it made plausible the almost feminine grace and symmetry of Mount St. Helens compared with the craggier visages of Hood and Adams.

How the Indian legend would have dealt with the 1980 explosion of Mount St. Helen's, which spoiled the symmetry and left a ruined stump, is anyone's guess. By then the theories of the geologists had improved. In their new version, the crust of the earth is in constant motion, with large plates sliding across the surface of the globe. One plate holds most of North America, which moves steadily westward; as its leading edge slams into a plate beneath the Pacific Ocean, it is dragged downward. The downward bending of this front edge causes buckling in the plate behind; the buckling is what has raised the great mountain chains of the West: the Cascade-Sierra range and the Rockies. As the western edge of the continental plate descends into the abyss, it grows hotter and melts, and some of the molten rock finds its way to the surface in places weakened by the buckling. Thus the volcanoes of the Cascades. Where the molten rock, or magma, doesn't quite reach the surface, it heats groundwater to produce hot springs and geysers, as in the Yellowstone basin, which is the remnant of a giant crater left by a huge explosion when the molten rock *did* reach the surface.

The movement of the plates explains not simply the topography of the West but much about the region's climate. The prevailing westerly winds, caused by the earth's rotation, bring moisture from the Pacific, which falls on the western slope of the Cascades and Sierra Nevada, creating lush forests and valleys but leaving little for the eastern side. The rain shadow extends across the intermountain zone and is relieved only partially by the elevation of the Rockies, which cast their own rain shadow across the Great Plains.

The movement of the plates has had still other effects less noticeable at the earth's surface. The heat of the melting at the western edge of the continental plate distilled and separated various minerals found in the rock of the crust, in much the way the heat of a petroleum refinery distills and separates the constituents of crude oil. Transported under great pressure by superheated water, the minerals eventually precipitated out of solution when the water rose and cooled. The result was the gathering and deposit of certain minerals and metals in concentrations far higher than in the original rock. Gold, for example, is found in the crust of the earth at an average concentration of around five parts per billion; after the tectonic refining beneath the Sierra Nevada, it appears in veins of quartz at concentrations of one hundred million parts per billion.

The greatest part of those veins, and hence of the gold, remained far beneath the surface of the earth. But here and there the veins reached daylight when the overlying rock eroded away. The erosion carried small particles of the quartz and the gold down the slopes of the Sierra, often lodging them in streambeds, where they waited for someone to find them.

JAMES MARSHALL WAS NOT A GEOLOGIST, AT LEAST NOT before he reached California. Instead he was a sufferer of a malady that over the decades sent many to the West: unrequited love. Born in New Jersey, Marshall had sought his fortune in Missouri. He found not fortune but an enchanting young woman who, sadly for Marshall, didn't reciprocate his affections. He also contracted malaria. A doctor advised him he would never shake the fevers and chills if he remained in Missouri; Oregon was the place he must go. The fair object of Marshall's devotion seconded the opinion; she was in love with another man—a doctor, as it happened, quite possibly the same one who prescribed the Oregon cure.

Marshall joined an emigrant train and in 1845 reached the Willamette Valley. But he didn't stay for long. Still yearning for his lost love, unable to find solace and rest, he struck out for California. He ascended the Willamette River and crossed the Siskiyou Mountains—a rare western range that runs east to west rather than north to south—into the valley of the Sacramento River. He presented himself at a trading post operated by John Sutter, where the American River enters the Sacramento, and applied for work. Sutter asked what he could do. Marshall replied that he was handy in numerous ways. Sutter hired him.

Sutter had come to California for the same reason that Moses and Stephen Austin went to Texas: to escape debt. Sutter's home was Switzerland, and his Swiss creditors threatened him with prison for unpaid bills. Sutter fled to America, leaving behind a wife and children. He told them he would make his fortune, repay his debts and return. He never did return, or pay his debts. Instead he dropped out of sight, in the distant Mexican province of California. There he followed the Austin model, proposing to guard Mexico's northern frontier of California in exchange for land. He called his spread New Helvetia, in honor of his homeland, and became its grandee. He thought expansively, and was glad to hire James Marshall, whose skills would help him construct the commercial and landed principality he envisioned. He tasked Marshall with building a sawmill to supply lumber for construction and for sale.

But events elsewhere threw a crowbar into his plans. James Polk's campaign for president had included the acquisition of Oregon as one plank; the annexation of Texas was another. The arithmetic of the Senate and of the antislavery movement still prevented a treaty of annexation, but Polk's decisive victory prompted lame duck John Tyler, who lacked any other conspicuous accomplishment, to sponsor a joint resolution of annexation. This did the trick, as a joint resolution required simple majorities in the two houses of Congress rather than a two-thirds majority in the Senate. The lower, though broader, threshold proved achievable, and Texas entered the Union.

Yet not without embittering Mexico, which still hadn't acknowledged its loss of Texas. Beyond this, a dispute developed over the southern border of Texas. Texas, and now the United States, declared that border to be the Rio Grande. Mexico said it was the Rio Nueces, a hundred miles to the north.

The border dispute might have been settled if James Polk, by this time president, had wanted a settlement. Mexico could see it wasn't going to get Texas back. But Polk, the most aggressively expansionist of all American presidents, wanted not a settlement but California. When the Mexican government refused to entertain Polk's offers for California, he decided to force the issue by war. He sent American troops under Zachary Taylor to the disputed strip for the purpose of provoking a Mexican attack. For weeks the troops marched and taunted the Mexicans, yet the Mexicans refused to be provoked. Polk exasperatedly prepared a war request anyway, charging Mexico with bad faith, loose morals and sundry other sins.

But just before he was to deliver the request to Congress, he received word that the attack he had been praying for had happened. American blood had been shed on American soil, he told the lawmakers; they must declare war. Not all of them agreed, but a majority did, and the United States went to war against Mexico.

One American column drove south from the Rio Grande. A second landed at Vera Cruz and marched toward Mexico City. In due course the Americans occupied the capital. Peace negotiations began, but proceeded slowly due to the extreme weakness of the Mexican bargaining position. No Mexican leader wanted to take responsibility for the amputation of half the country. Ultimately, though, reality had its way, and the 1848 Treaty of Guadalupe Hidalgo was signed. Mexico renounced all rights to Texas, California and everything between; in exchange, the United States agreed to pay $15 million to Mexico. The payment allowed Polk and subsequent administrations to portray the transfer of land as by purchase rather than conquest.

The Mexican cession, augmented five years later by the Gadsden Purchase, which added a railroad-friendly strip of desert to the southern part of modern New Mexico and Arizona, completed the creation of the American West, as it was generally understood. Alaska would be purchased from Russia, but it was a world unto itself for many decades. Hawaii and other Pacific islands would hoist the Stars and Stripes far to the west of California, but they were yet another separate world.

The creation of the American West, as the *American* West, was arguably the greatest accomplishment in the history of the American federal government. The American East had been the handiwork of the original states, which antedated the Constitution and had claimed territory to the Mississippi. The West, by contrast, was called into American existence by the federal government. The overwhelming majority of land in the West was initially federal land; nearly all the Western states began life as parts of federal territories. In time many Westerners would become harsh critics of federal power—demonstrating the age-old habit of children being ungrateful to their parents.

The completion of the American West didn't exhaust the acquisitive spirit that had driven American expansion since the seventeenth century. But that spirit would assume new forms with the transformation of an agricultural economy into an industrial one. The need for new land would diminish. Anyway, as of the 1848 signing of the treaty with Mexico, the American West contained more than enough land for several generations of Americans. Almost half a century after the purchase of Louisiana, most of that territory remained unoccupied by any but the native peoples. The lands acquired from Mexico contained an even sparser population. Plains, mountains and deserts distanced California, the most attractive portion of the new region, from the settled portions of the United States. California might not come close to filling up before the beginning of the twentieth century.

JAMES MARSHALL HAZARDED NO SUCH PROJECTIONS. HE DIDN'T even know, when he set out for his morning inspection on January 24, 1848, that California was about to become American. Nor, more significantly, did the negotiators of the war-ending treaty, two thousand miles away, have any idea that Marshall was about to make California immeasurably more valuable than it had been the day before.

Marshall was supervising the digging of a millrace for Sutter's sawmill, on the middle fork of the American River, forty miles above Sutter's fort. During the workday the men would swing picks and shovels, moving rocks and sand; at night Marshall would open the headgate on the millrace and let running water amplify the men's labors. The morning of January 24 dawned crisp and bright; as the sun flashed over the peaks of the Sierra Nevada, its rays glinted on the quartz in many of the rocks, especially where the water had flowed overnight. Marshall walked the race, calculating where he would set the men to work this morning. The sparkles from the quartz caught his eye, but having seen it before, he gave it no mind.

But one glimmer seemed different, slightly duller and more yellow. Marshall bent down. "I picked up one or two pieces and examined them closely," he recalled later. "And having some general knowledge of minerals, I could not call to mind more than two which in any way resembled this—sulphuret of iron, very bright and brittle; and gold, bright yet malleable." He tested the malleability of one of the pieces by smashing it between two rocks. It didn't break but bent and flattened.

He showed the sample to one of the men, who asked what it was.

"Gold," replied Marshall.

The man was skeptical. Marshall called over another workman, who had a hammer in his hand. He directed him to pound the sample against a rock with the hammer. The result of repeated blows was a thin sheet of yellow metal—strong evidence of gold.

The camp cook was nearby, doing the laundry in a boiling cauldron of lye solution. The sample was dunked in the caustic bath. Instead of reacting, it came up clean, supporting the gold hypothesis.

Marshall mounted a horse and rode to Sutter's fort. In a hushed voice he told his boss what he had found. The two retreated to Sutter's office and consulted his copy of the *Encyclopedia Americana*, which had a detailed article on gold and its properties. The article prescribed aqua fortis—nitric acid—as a testing agent. Of the metallic substances that might be mistaken for gold, only gold

Sutter's Mill. Here James Marshall (in front) found the nugget that turned the world on its head.

itself would survive exposure. The acid was applied, and nothing happened.

Sutter and Marshall repeated the famous test of Archimedes to determine the density of the sample. Employing a two-armed scale, they balanced the sample against three silver coins. Then they immersed the whole apparatus in water, and the sample sank relative to the coins, proving its greater density.

They could draw but one conclusion. "I declared this to be gold," Sutter remembered of that fateful day.

YET IT WASN'T SUTTER'S DECLARATION THAT MADE THE DAY so fateful. Samuel Brannan was Sutter's competitor as commercial kingpin of California's Central Valley. Brannan was a son of Maine who had moved to Ohio and there encountered Mormonism, the heterodoxy that was struggling to become a religion. Something in the message of Joseph Smith touched Brannan's soul. Or perhaps it was the hostility the Latter-day Saints confronted. Brannan was still new to the faith when Smith was killed by an anti-Mormon mob, and Brannan threw himself into the effort to find a safer home for the faith and its adherents. While the main body of Mormons prepared to leave American soil and trek overland to Mexican California, Brannan was charged with reaching the same destination by ship, around Cape Horn.

Brannan got to California, but the main body of Mormons never did. Between the planning of the trek and its completion, the American war with Mexico began. California appeared certain to become American, and likely as hostile to Mormons as the states from which they were fleeing. Brigham Young, Joseph Smith's successor, decided that Utah would be a better home than California. Utah would become American, too, but once Young saw the valley of the Great Salt Lake, in all its daunting desolation, he judged that not many would follow his people there.

Brannan first guessed that the plans might be changing when his ship reached California after a voyage of nearly seven months. An American flag flew above what had been the Mexican customs house in the village of Yerba Buena on San Francisco Bay. "Damn that flag!" Brannan said. Yet he soon saw enough of California to conclude that, American or not, it might be a good place to settle. A message from Brigham Young explaining the decision to stop in Utah and summoning Brannan prompted a difficult journey across the Sierra Nevada and the desert beyond. Brannan spoke with Young and tried to convince him that California would be splendid for the Mormons. But Young had made up his mind.

So, too, had Brannan. He returned to California and gradually cut ties with Young and the Mormons. He opened a general store beside Sutter's fort in what would become Sacramento. He had been in business only weeks when James Marshall came down from the hills and told Sutter about the gold discovery.

The news leaked, and at once Brannan had an insight that would shape the California economy for decades. While Sutter and Marshall calculated how to make money from gold mining,

Brannan determined to make money from the gold *miners*. They would need picks and shovels, boots and trousers, flour and bacon. He would sell them what they needed. The business model of Sutter and Marshall prescribed keeping the existence of the gold secret, till they secured rights to as much of it as possible. The business model of Brannan dictated just the opposite: telling the whole world about the gold, so that miners would flock to the gold fields, stopping at his store on the way.

Acting on his vision, Brannan acquired enough gold dust from Marshall's workmen, now moonlighting as miners, to fill a jar. He traveled to Yerba Buena—which would become the city of San Francisco—and strutted about the village, holding up his jar of gold and shouting, "Gold! Gold! Gold from the American River!"

The news electrified the small community. One who heard it felt himself being swept away. "A frenzy seized my soul; unbidden my legs performed some entirely new movements of polka steps—I took several. Houses were too small for me to stay in; I was soon in the street in search of necessary outfits. Piles of gold rose up before me at every step; castles of marble, dazzling the eye with their rich appliances; thousands of slaves bowing to my beck and call; myriads of fair virgins contending with each other for my love—were among the fancies of my fevered imagination. The Rothschilds, Girards, and Astors appeared to me but poor people. In short, I had a very violent attack of the gold fever."

The fever depopulated Yerba Buena overnight. Nearly every able-bodied man headed for the hills. No one gave them permission to scour the streambeds and gravel bars for gold nuggets and gold dust, but neither did anyone stop them. Amid the frenzy arrived word that California was now American. The frenzy intensified, for while Mexican law on gold had tilted toward the government, American law favored the finder. The gold was there for the taking. Who got there first would get the most.

27

GOLD MOUNTAIN

S O BEGAN THE CALIFORNIA GOLD RUSH. THE NEWS SPREAD out from San Francisco Bay on the ships that visited there—those ships, that is, whose captains managed to keep their crews from deserting and joining the rush to the American River. The news reached Oregon, where farmers dropped their plows and headed for the gold fields. The news got to Mexico, which had a long history of mining. A thousand Mexicans marched north. The fact that California was no longer Mexican seemed not to matter; the gold didn't ask the nationality of those who took it. And neither, at this stage, did the other miners, who were too busy grabbing for themselves. The news arrived in Hawaii; soon ships of gold-seekers sailed the two thousand miles to San Francisco. The news hit Peru and Chile; ambitious young men pooled resources and bought passage north. The news crossed the Pacific to Australia, which had become Britain's outdoor prison after Georgia bolted the empire with the other American colonies. Transported felons booked passage for California. The news landed in China. Hundreds, eventually thousands, of Chinese set sail for Gum Shan—"Gold Mountain"—the name they gave to California.

Almost the last place to learn of the gold discovery was the American East. Few spots on earth were farther from New York than San Francisco in 1848, in terms of the time required to travel from one to the other. Fifteen thousand miles by sea, around Cape

Horn, or three thousand miles overland—several months either way. Not till the autumn of 1848 did word of the gold discovery arrive on the East Coast. Appearing amid the campaign to replace James Polk, who had declined to seek reelection, it initially drew less than the full attention of the nation's leading newspapers. "We have received some late and interesting intelligence from California," the *New York Herald* reported in a one-paragraph squib on the inside pages on September 15. "It relates to the important discovery of a very valuable gold mine. We have received a specimen of the gold." But the paper declined to say more. "Owing to the crowded state of our columns, we are obliged to omit our correspondence."

Yet this was enough to titillate readers. Or perhaps James Gordon Bennett, the *Herald's* editor, feared being scooped by his competitors. In any event, two days later he ran the letter. Bennett's correspondent warned that his report would be hard to credit. "Were I a New Yorker, instead of a Californian, I would throw aside your paper and exclaim, Bennett had better fill his paper with, at least, probable tales and stories, and not such outrageous fictions of rivers flowing with gold." Yet the reporter knew whereof he spoke. "This writer, among others, has visited the golden country, this *Placer*"—the Spanish name for the diggings—"in comparison to which the famous El Dorado is but a sand bank." The gold almost leaped into the miners' pockets. "There are cases of over a hundred dollars being obtained in a day from the work of one man." (In the East at this time, a manual worker was lucky to make five hundred dollars in a year.) "It requires no skill. The workman takes any spot of ground or bank he fancies, sticks in his pick or shovel at random, fills his basin, makes for the water, and soon sees the glittering results of his labor." There appeared to be no end to the gold-laden ore. "We are already aware of its being found over a space of one hundred miles in length, and but little of the Sacramento Valley has been explored."

Other papers picked up the story, each competing to outdo the others in eye-catching detail. The East soon thrummed with facts and surmises about America's new golden West. In December, James Polk put the government's seal of approval on the stories. "The accounts of the abundance of gold in that territory are of such an extraordinary character as would scarcely command belief were they not corroborated by the authentic reports of officers in the public service who have visited the mineral district and derived the facts which they detail from personal observation," the president declared.

POLK'S ANNOUNCEMENT ADDED ARMIES TO THE RANKS OF those already rushing to California. In every state young men dissatisfied with their present circumstances considered joining the race to California, where an ordinary fellow could earn as much in a summer as he might make in a decade in the East. Only a small portion of those who weighed the venture actually went, but they totaled perhaps eighty thousand in 1849, besides those who traveled from other countries to California. The great majority of the argonauts, as they styled themselves, were men; most intended to fill their pockets with California gold and return whence they had come, now able to buy the farm, the shop, the house of which they had dreamed.

Some traveled by sea, either by sailing ship around South America or, for the better-heeled, by the steamships that began plying the sea lanes from the East Coast to Panama and from Panama to San Francisco, with a land leg across the isthmus between. But the majority followed the lead of the emigrants to Oregon and traveled by horse, wagon and foot. The California Trail was simply the Oregon Trail to a fork west of Wyoming's South Pass; from there it angled southwest across the northern parts of what would become Utah and Nevada before ascending the eastern scarp of the Sierra Nevada north of Lake Tahoe and descending the western slope to Sacramento.

The forty-niners benefited from the travel experience of the earlier emigrants, but they brought problems of their own. The first was their haste. No one knew how much gold there was in

California, but no one wanted to arrive after the easy pickings were gone, or after the government changed the free-for-all rules under which it could be gathered. Even more than Oregon-bound emigrants like Quinn Thornton and his wife, who fell for Jesse Applegate's promise of a shortcut and nearly paid for it with their lives, the argonauts were susceptible to the temptation to try new routes that might save miles and time. Some did pay the ultimate price, dying of thirst or of disease brought on by exposure and fatigue. Death Valley earned its name when a party of forty-niners got lost. Only one of that group actually died there, but the rest had resigned themselves to the same fate before being rescued on the verge of expiration.

The second new challenge was the snow of the Sierra Nevada. The mountain passes of the Sierra were much higher than those of the Cascades on the route to Oregon, and the snow could trap laggard travelers, as the Donner party discovered in 1846. George Donner had quieted his wife's fears on separating from Quinn Thornton's Oregon train near South Pass by saying that the Hastings cutoff would get them to California in no time. And as the Thorntons stumbled through the mountains of southern Oregon and cursed Jesse Applegate for nearly killing them, they might have wished they had gone with the Donners. Only later did they discover the awful truth.

The Hastings route took the Donner party over the Wasatch Mountains and across the Great Salt Lake Desert. It was shorter in distance than the existing trail to California, but the ridges, boulders, arroyos and barrens it threw in the travelers' way made it longer in time. Not until late October did they reach the eastern rampart of the Sierra Nevada. Snow fell sooner that year than usual, and more heavily. The travelers couldn't usefully turn around, for their provisions were short and nothing behind them afforded a prospect of replenishment. They couldn't go forward, for the drifts grew deeper by the day. They made camp to wait out the winter.

As the snow continued to fall, and the provisions dwindled and vanished, the marooned travelers descended into the horrors of starvation. They ate their animals, including their dogs. They gnawed on shoes, belts and anything else of animal origin they could lay hands on. Some died, and the living ate the flesh of the dead. By the time relief arrived in the spring, the camp was strewn with human bones and dismembered corpses. Skulls had been smashed to get at the brains; torsos cut open for the livers and kidneys; femurs shattered to retrieve marrow. "A more revolting and appalling spectacle I never witnessed," declared a member of a U.S. army squadron sent to help.

The forty-niners all knew of the Donner party; they shuddered at the thought of a similar fate if they didn't crest the Sierra in time. And so, even as they labored hot and thirsty down the Humboldt River to its mysterious sink into the earth, they scanned the towering western horizon for sign of the first snowfall. They had to hurry; they couldn't rest. They had to get across before the snows came.

MOST DID. THEY HAD AN ADVANTAGE OVER THE OREGON emigrants, who traveled with families, herds of livestock, furniture and all the impedimenta of farmsteads, not to mention women and children. Traveling lighter, they could move faster. But they were ten times as many as had gone to Oregon each season, and the strain they and their mounts and draft animals put on the trail—grinding ruts deep into the earth, ruining fords, cropping the grass to the roots—compounded their difficulties. All the same, the great majority reached California safely, if bone-weary and thinner than when they had set out.

What they experienced in California was like nothing they or any other generation of Americans had ever been through. By the end of the summer of 1849, California had passed the threshold of the sixty thousand residents required for statehood, but it didn't possess even a territorial government. A military governor based in Monterey, on the coast, exercised a notional authority over the region, but he lacked the troops to enforce his orders. Like the infamous border region of East Texas in the late Mexican era, all of California was a no-man's-land, beyond any laws worth paying attention to. Like the Oregon settlers before the Whitman massacre, the Californians had to invent their own government.

They began in the gold fields. First on the American River but soon on other streams that drained the Sierra Nevada, gold hunters congregated wherever someone struck gold. The mining camps, as the communities were called, originated as tent villages but quickly added log cabins and other wood structures. Within a few months their populations could grow from nothing to ten thousand. To keep disputes over claims from turning too frequently violent, the camps crafted rules regarding the size of claims, how consistently claims had to be worked lest they lapse, to what degree operations on one claim could interfere with operations on neighboring claims, and so on. The camps chose committees that acted as de facto legislatures and courts.

These ad hoc governments guarded the rights of some miners more zealously than those of others. As the best claims were taken, Americans in the gold fields began to question the right of non-Americans to extract gold. Mexicans, the most numerous of the foreigners at first, came in for early scrutiny. Americans told each other that the recent war had been fought, and American blood been shed, to make California American. To them it seemed wrong that Mexicans should share in the bounty. Mexican miners were often harassed, sometimes attacked, occasionally killed, and generally made to feel unwelcome.

Chinese miners met similar treatment. Very few Americans had ever encountered Chinese people, and in an age when racism and ethnocentrism were considered venial sins, if sins at all, disdain for the Chinese was open and unapologetic. Chinese miners were often robbed or forced off their claims, and the perpetrators frequently went unpunished. Occasionally the Chinese banded together to defend themselves and their property. Sometimes they succeeded; sometimes their resistance made matters worse.

"THE GOLD IS IN FINE BRIGHT SCALES AND IS VERY PURE," William Sherman wrote after visiting the American River. Sherman was an officer in the U.S. army sent to California during the war with Mexico. He remained after the war as part of the military government, such as it was. The stories that came down to the army headquarters at Monterey from the gold diggings piqued his curiosity, and he traveled there to see what was going on.

Sherman observed miners gathering gold in the most rudimentary fashion. A broad washpan was loaded with a slurry of dirt, sand and water. The pan was rocked back and forth so that the water spilled over the sides, carrying away the dirt and sand and leaving the heavier particles of gold. The gold was plucked out, and the process was repeated, again and again. In reasonably good diggings, miners could do well by this primitive method, earning perhaps ten or fifteen dollars a day. The hundred-dollar days described by the correspondent of the *New York Herald* were rare, although they did occur.

Improvements were devised almost at once, as Sherman discovered. "The better plan is in a kind of inclined trough with cleats nailed across the bottom. A grate is placed over the highest part of this trough, upon which the gravel is thrown, afterwards the water. The gold passes into the trough, the gravel and stones are removed, and by a constant dashing of water and rocking the machine, the earthy matter is washed off, leaving the gold mixed with black sand in the bottom of the machine. These are separated by drying them in the sun and blowing off the sand, leaving the gold pure. You would be astonished at the ease with which the precious metal is obtained; any man by common industry can make $25 a day."

The sluice, which was what Sherman described, was complemented by other improvements. Vicente Pérez Rosales was a Chilean who had heard of California's gold from a ship calling

The sluice. This modest contraption was a first step up the ladder of mining technology.

at Valparaíso; he and some friends formed a company and sailed north. They staked claims on a tributary of the American River and began panning for gold. Early results were disappointing. But then they observed a device the local miners were calling the "California cradle." Pérez Rosales explained: "The cradle is a very simple and ingenious apparatus that has all the advantages of a scoop on a colossal scale, but is no larger than an actual cradle a yard and a half long by half a yard wide, placed so that the head rests on a base a fourth higher than the one at the foot. These bases are nothing more than wooden arcs that facilitate the rocking of the cradle. The upper end of the latter holds a rough sieve built of pieces of wood bored full of holes; the foot has no bottom. Along the floor of this singular device at intervals of four inches are nailed strips of wood a quarter of an inch square. These prevent the escape of the heavy particles mixed with the mud that runs down the inclined floor."

The cradle. This man's partners have left him to work alone
for the time being.

Significantly, the operation of the cradle required teamwork,
unlike panning, which was done alone. "One man feeds the
gold-bearing earth into the sieve, another pours buckets of water
over it, a third rocks the cradle, and finally still another takes out
by hand the stones that are too large to pass through the strainer,
examines them, and throws away such as do not contain gold,"
Pérez Rosales wrote. "The water rinses the earth through the sieve,
the mixture drops down and flows over the sloping bottom, and
the gold and other more or less heavy bodies lodge in the cleats
provided by the crosswise strips of wood. Every ten minutes the
work is interrupted and the gold dust and nuggets mixed with iron

that have been caught in these small angles are collected. This material is then placed in a hand trough for separation later, and the operation continues all day long."

Pérez Rosales and his Chilean partners became quite fond of the cradle. "In this device we lovingly rocked the infant gold and beheld it wax portentously," he gushed. "Our daily harvest varied between ten and twenty-two ounces of gold."

Sluices and cradles both had the purpose of increasing the amount of gold-laden material the miners could process. Placer mining—pronounced with a short "a"—was the general term for separating gold from dirt and sand, typically by the use of water, and was a matter of percentages. Where the percentage of gold in a sample of sand and gravel was high, simple panning could make miners rich. Where the percentage was lower, the miners required methods that multiplied their panning powers.

Over time the tendency was toward the more elaborate devices. As the miners examined the beds of rivers and creeks on the western slope of the Sierra, the rich deposits—the ones with a high percentage of gold—were claimed and worked first. Miners arriving later found slimmer pickings and required devices like sluice boxes and cradles to turn a profit.

Almost none of the miners were geologists on arrival in California, but most became amateur geologists before long. They inferred that the rushing streams had washed the gold down from the mountains, and that the greater density of gold than sand caused the former to cluster in the stream bottoms. As the miners scrambled over gravel bars and bluffs between streams, some noticed signs of old riverbeds, now dry. Perhaps those beds contained gold, they thought. Experiment demonstrated that the ancient beds did contain gold, and the miners pondered how to collect it. Some tried dry panning—panning without water—but the technique was inefficient. Some carried the materials of the ancient beds to existing streams, to use the water there for regular placer operations.

Others contrived to carry the water of existing streams to the ancient beds. They constructed dams and troughs to reroute the existing streams. In time—and again, significantly, with collective effort and resources—they built major waterworks. The acme of this approach was the use of water deployed under pressure to uncover buried streambeds. Mighty water cannons, rigged to pipes from dammed reservoirs far upstream, reduced whole mountainsides to slurry that was then run through oversized sluices.

A visitor to the gold fields described this hydraulic mining in action. "With a perpendicular column of water 120 feet high, in a strong hose, of which they work two, ten men who own the claim are enabled to run off hundreds of tons of dirt daily," the visitor wrote. "So great is the force employed that two men with the pipes, by directing streams of water against the base of the high bank, will cut it away to such an extent as to cause immense slides of earth, which often bring with them large trees and heavy boulders. . . . After these immense masses of earth are undermined and brought down by the streams forced from the pipes, those same streams are turned upon the tons of fallen earth, and it melts away before them, and is carried through the sluices with almost as much rapidity as if it were a bank of snow." The law of percentages applied; at this rate of processing, even low-grade ores yielded handsome returns.

NOR WAS HYDRAULIC MINING THE LAST WORD IN GOLD-gathering. The amateur geologists in the gold fields, with the help of a few professionals experienced elsewhere, figured out that the gold in the streambeds came from veins in the solid rock of the mountains. If they had been willing to wait another ten million years, that gold might have been washed down into existing and new streams. But they weren't willing to wait. Gold fever burned in their own veins. So they went into the bedrock of the Sierra Nevada, boring into the earth to pry the gold free.

An inquisitive newspaperman followed them. "We descended their shaft—but not before the workmen had offered and we had accepted the loan of an India-rubber suit of clothing—and on reaching the bottom of it we found a considerable stream of water running in the centre of the railway, constructed along the tunnel to the shaft," the correspondent wrote. "This water was removed by a pump in one corner of the shaft, working by steam power, both day and night. On we went, trying to keep a sure footing on the rail track, inasmuch as watertight boots even then became a very necessary accompaniment to the India-rubber clothing. Drip, drip, fell the water, not singly, but in clusters of drops and small streams."

The correspondent went deeper. "On, on; down, down we go, until we hear the sound of muffled voices issuing from somewhere deep down amid the darkness, and uttering something very indistinct and hard to be understood; when again we cross over to and enter a side drift; where in the distance we see lights glimmering, in shadow and smoke, and hear the voices become more and more distinct, until my guide asks the question, 'How does she look now, boys?' 'All right—better, sir.'"

The correspondent asked whether they had reached the bottom. Not even close, his guide said, and took him as far again into the earth, to nearly three hundred feet below the surface. The correspondent asked why they dug so deep. "The deeper we get, the richer the quartz becomes," his guide explained.

Quartz mining, as the process was called after the rock that held the gold, represented another, and for now a final, step in the chain of consolidation in gold country. In 1848 gold mining had been something an individual could do profitably with minimal investment, just enough to buy a pan and some beans and bacon. By 1849 the pans were being supplanted by sluice boxes and cradles, which required money to fashion and teamwork to operate. Hydraulic mining was more expensive still, demanding pipe, nozzles and fittings that had to be manufactured in the East and imported. Quartz mining multiplied the required investment even more. Heavy, specialized machinery—digging devices of various sorts, hoists for miners and ore, pumps to drain water from the mineshafts, giant stamps to crush the ore, chemical equipment to separate the gold from the quartz—necessitated capital amounting to many thousands of dollars. Joint-stock companies could sometimes raise the money; more frequently, outside investors—many of whom never set foot in the gold fields or even California—held the controlling interest.

The ironic result of all this was that in the 1850s America's farthest frontier was also its least frontier-like, in any traditional sense. It was an industrial frontier, with corporate boards and banks calling the tune. It was urban, rather than rural: the miners congregated in the towns they called camps, and most other Californians crowded into San Francisco, Sacramento and a few other cities that grew up to service the gold fields. Compared with the rest of the country, few Californians were farmers; increasingly they formed a working class of wage-laborers in the mines and service workers in the cities. Their days were governed not by the rising and setting of the sun, which for the quartz miners never penetrated their underground workplaces, but by steam whistles attached to powerful machines. America's Industrial Revolution unfolded over decades in most of the country; in the Far West it happened in just a few years.

28

CRIME AND PUNISHMENT

SAN FRANCISCO, THE QUEEN CITY OF THE GOLD RUSH, WAS unique among American cities. Eastern cities had grown slowly. Boston was two centuries old before its population reached fifty thousand. San Francisco passed that milestone in less than two years. Eastern cities connoted stability and permanence. In Philadelphia, the headquarters of the second Bank of the United States was a monument of marble modeled on Greek temples and intended to last as long as they had. San Francisco was a caravansary, a stopping point on the path to the gold fields. Its structures were tents, flimsy wooden buildings thrown up in haste, even abandoned ships in the harbor, left crew-less when the men went over the rail in search for gold. Too hurried to dismantle the ships and reuse the timbers, enterprising hoteliers and restaurateurs simply built rickety walkways over the water to their new places of business. In time, sand from dunes behind the city was hauled in and piled around the vessels; an expanding shoreline beached them forever. In the twenty-first century, construction crews would occasionally unearth hulks from the days of the gold rush, buried and forgotten as the city continued to grow.

Sarah Royce experienced San Francisco in its headlong phase. She was a rarity among the forty-niners: a woman. She had crossed the continent with her husband and their young daughter and begun to create a home in the gold country. She thought she had seen a lot on the journey west, but she never saw anything like the frenzy that characterized San Francisco. "In the immense crowds flocking hither from all parts of the world there were many of the worst classes, bent upon getting gold at all hazards, and if possible without work," she remarked. "These were constantly lying in wait, as tempters of the weak. A still greater number came with gold-getting for their ruling motive yet intending to get it honestly, by labor or legitimate business. They did not intend, at first, to sacrifice their habits of morality, or their religious convictions. But many of them bore those habits and held those convictions too lightly; and as they came to feel the force of unwonted excitement and the pressure of unexpected temptation, they too often yielded, little by little, till they found themselves standing upon a very low plane, side by side with those whose society they once would have avoided. It was very common to hear people who had started on this downward moral grade, deprecating the very acts they were committing, or the practices they were countenancing; and concluding their weak lament by saying, 'But here in California we *have* to do such things.'"

Journalist Frank Soulé was more worldly than Sarah Royce, but even he was shocked at what passed for normal in San Francisco. "No place in the world contains any thing like the number of mere drinking-houses"—as contrasted to restaurants—"in proportion to the population, as San Francisco," Soulé observed. "This, perhaps, is the worst feature of the city. The quantity of ardent spirits daily consumed is almost frightful. It is peddled out in every gambling-room, on the wharves, at almost every corner, and, in some streets, in almost every house. Many of the taverns are of the lowest possible description—filthy dens of vice and crime, disease and wretchedness. Drunken men and women, with bloated bodies and soiled garments, crowd them at night, making the hours hideous with their bacchanalian revels. Americans and Europeans, Mexicans and South-Americans, Chinese and even negroes, mingle and dissipate together, furnishing a large amount of business for the police department and the recorder's court."

Gambling was a favorite sport of the San Franciscans, which was unsurprising in that the entire gold rush was, for its participants, a grand gamble. Bayard Taylor was a writer in the service of Horace Greeley, the editor of the *New York Tribune*. Greeley would become famous for the admonition, "Go West!" given to a young man asking career advice. For now he realized that the California gold rush was the biggest story of the age, and he sent Taylor to California to gather and recount it for the *Tribune*'s readers. Taylor tested the gambling scene in San Francisco. "Denison's Exchange, the Parker House and Eldorado stand side by side; across the way are the Verandah and Aguila de Oro; higher up the plaza the St. Charles and Bella Union; while dozens of second-rate establishments are scattered through the less frequented streets," Taylor reported. "The greatest crowd is about the Eldorado; we find it difficult to effect an entrance. There are about eight tables in the room, all of which are thronged; copper-hued Kanakas, Mexicans rolled in their sarapes and Peruvians thrust through their ponchos, stand shoulder to shoulder with the brown and bearded American miners. The stakes are generally small, though when the bettor gets into 'a streak of luck,' as it is called, they are allowed to double until all is lost or the bank breaks. Along the end of the room is a spacious bar, supplied with all kinds of bad liquors, and in a sort of gallery, suspended under the ceiling, a female violinist tasks her talent and strength of muscle to minister to the excitement of play."

Taylor's observation that the gambling halls—or "hells," as they were often called—didn't discriminate among customers on racial or ethnic grounds reflected the fact that money trumped other considerations in the gaming trade. A Mexican's gold was as good as that of anyone else. Yet Taylor noted a difference in the gambling styles of the different groups. He reported from the Aguila de Oro, where the game was monte—favored in California because the odds were fairer to the players and the game was less prone to cheating. "The dealer throws out his cards with a cool, nonchalant air; indeed, the gradual increase of the hollow square of dollars at his left hand is not calculated to disturb his equanimity. The two Mexicans in front, muffled in their dirty serapes, put down their half-dollars and dollars and see them lost, without changing a muscle. Gambling is a born habit with them, and they would lose thousands with the same indifference." Americans reacted differently. "Their good or ill luck is betrayed at once by involuntary exclamations and changes of countenance, unless the stake should be very large and absorbing, when their anxiety, though silent, may be read with no less certainty. They have no power to resist the fascination of the game. Now counting their winnings by thousands, now dependent on the kindness of a friend for a few dollars to commence anew, they pass hour after hour in these hot, unwholesome dens. There is no appearance of arms, but let one of the players, impatient with his losses and maddened by the poisonous fluids he has drank, threaten one of the profession, and there will be no scarcity of knives and revolvers."

THE PREVALENCE OF KNIVES AND REVOLVERS WOULD BECOME a serious problem in San Francisco. But in the first years the more pressing concern was fire. A series of fires repeatedly destroyed large parts of the city. The first broke out on Christmas Eve in 1849. It began near Portsmouth Square, the center of the city, and spread in all directions, consuming a million dollars' worth of buildings and inventory before volunteer firefighters brought it under control by preemptively destroying buildings that lay in the fire's path. Deprived of standing fuel, the flames lost strength and flickered out.

A second fire occurred four months later. Most of the buildings consumed in the first fire had been replaced; many of the new buildings burned down. This time the firefighters were more reluctant; some demanded payment from the owners of threatened buildings before they would swing into action. And a curious phenomenon was observed after the flames had passed through a block. Even before the embers cooled, scavengers began sifting the ruins. San Francisco as yet lacked the institutions of a mature financial system, including banks and adequate paper currency. People walked around with gold in their pockets. Shops kept gold on hand. Hotels and restaurants collected gold from customers. And gold survives fire. The scavengers were looking for gold. One argonaut, newly arrived, hadn't yet reached the gold fields. He found his first sample of the precious metal in San Francisco in the wake of the fire. He sent his wife a picture of Portsmouth Square, marked to show the buildings destroyed. He included a souvenir. "I put into this a little piece of gold that I picked up on the square," he wrote. "The place I picked it up is marked by a cross thus X."

Again the city rebuilt; again it burned. The damage was greater than in the two previous fires combined. The city took an obvious lesson: that buildings made of wood were a fire hazard. When the property-owners rebuilt after the third fire, many employed brick and stone and iron, with iron for doors. The owners meanwhile pitched together to purchase firefighting equipment, reorganized fire companies, and trained with the engines and hoses to make ready for the next conflagration.

Which duly came, in September 1850. The better construction and the fuller preparation paid off. This fourth fire was fairly quickly contained; property damage was held below a million dollars.

San Franciscans began to think they had solved their fire problem. Then a fifth blaze erupted, and proved to be the worst of all. Heinrich Schliemann would become famous as the uncoverer of ancient Troy, but in 1850 he was an unknown German merchant looking for business in California's boom town. He arrived by sea and got a room at the Union Hotel on Portsmouth Square. Weary from travel, he turned in early. "I may have slept a quarter of an hour, when I was awakened by loud cries in the street: 'fire, fire,' and by the awful sounds of the alarm-bell," he remembered. "I sprang up in all haste and, looking out the window, I saw that a frame building only 20 or 30 paces from the Union Hotel was on fire. I dressed in all haste and ran out of the house, but scarcely had I reached the end of Clay Street when I saw already the hotel on fire from which I had just run out. Pushed on by a complete gale, the fire spread with an appalling rapidity, sweeping away in a few minutes whole streets of frame buildings. Neither the iron houses nor the brick houses (which were hitherto considered as quite fire-proof) could resist the fury of the element: the latter crumbled together with incredible rapidity, whilst the former got red-hot, then white-hot and fell together like cardhouses. Particularly in the iron houses people considered themselves perfectly safe, and they remained in them to the last extremity. As soon as the walls of the iron houses got red-hot, the goods inside began to smoke. The inhabitants wanted to get out, but usually it was already too late, for the locks and hinges of the doors having extended or partly melted by the heat, the doors were no more to be opened."

Astonishingly, even this wasn't the end. A month later a sixth fire broke out. It wasn't as large as the fifth, but it was the most heartbreaking to those who had somehow survived the previous blazes only to see their homes and businesses consumed in this one. Fire insurance was almost unknown in San Francisco at this point, and few of the victims had family nearby to fall back on. They were ruined; they had to start over.

RUIN AND STARTING OVER WOULD BECOME A MOTIF OF California, but in the meantime San Franciscans concluded that all these fires weren't happening by accident. Especially after residents saw scavengers raking through the smoldering embers, many concluded, almost certainly correctly, that the fires had been deliberately set.

Arson was but part of the city's crime problem, which was probably the worst of any city in America at the time. Some of the crime was simply the consequence of crowding too many young men into too small a space. The miners worked hard, then often drank hard, then fought hard. The knowledge that anyone intending a drink in a saloon, a meal in a restaurant, or a night in a hotel had gold in his pockets tempted the larcenous to waylay the unwary. Robbery became murder upon the victim's least resistance.

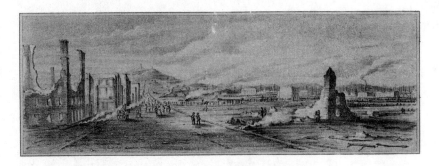

San Francisco in ashes. Such scenes were all too frequent in the early years.

San Francisco's cosmopolitanism contributed to the problem. By 1850 communities of Mexicans, Chileans, Chinese, Italians, French and African Americans existed among and beside the larger community of white Americans. Criminals could prey on these minority communities with little fear of incurring the wrath of the whites, who—like everyone else in the city—would rather be making money than tending to civic safety.

The most notorious criminals were organized into gangs. The Hounds consisted of veterans of the Mexican War who hadn't gone home. Their leaders had learned the arts of robbery, extortion, arson and murder in the Five Points and Bowery slums of New York. They gathered in a large tent they called Tammany Hall and posed as keepers of the public order under the name they gave themselves: Regulators.

Thomas Cary, an upstanding citizen, explained the dynamics of crime in San Francisco. "It will be asked why the more respectable part of the community did not exert themselves to put a stop to these proceedings," he said. "The answer is simple. The influential citizens, the merchants, lawyers and others, lived around what had been known as Yerba Buena Cove, while the Mexicans and Chileans lived at the back of the town among the sand-hills. They, therefore, knew little of what was going on out of sight and out of hearing. Everyone was too much interested in his own affairs to trouble himself about the misfortunes of others, and besides this, the Spanish-Americans were looked upon at that time very much as the Chinese are at the present moment"—Cary was writing in the 1880s—"as interlopers who should properly have been sent back to their own country, and these 'Hounds,' or 'Regulators' as they now called themselves, professed to be the guardians of the community against the encroachments of all foreigners."

In time the Hounds overreached, threatening the property and interests of the respectables, who resolved to respond. Sam Brannan's insight about mining the miners had made him the richest man in California, with property to protect. And he took offense at the lawless reputation that had become attached to San Francisco, to which he had moved his headquarters. Such a reputation was bad for business. He called a meeting of other property owners and declared that the Hounds must be reined in. A vigilance committee was formed, with two hundred deputies. The leaders of the Hounds were rounded up. A court convened by the vigilance committee tried the Hounds, including Sam Roberts, the head man. Roberts was convicted of conspiracy, robbery, riot and assault with intent to kill; eight others were convicted on lesser counts. Roberts and another man were sentenced to ten years at hard labor, the others to shorter terms.

At once arose a problem. There was no prison, and no one particularly wanted to pay to build and staff one. The vigilance committee didn't think the convicted men deserved death sentences, and lesser corporal punishment like whipping and branding had fallen out of favor outside the South, where it was confined to slaves.

So the committee contented itself with a stern warning to the convicted men and their fellow Hounds. They had better leave town. If they didn't, and persisted in their criminal ways, they would face execution.

THE WARNING WORKED; THE HOUNDS DISBANDED. BUT THE crime problem increased, as the demise of the Hounds gave room to an even more violent gang, the Sydney Ducks, sometimes called

Sydney Coves. They were from Australia, and found California appealing. "The voyage from Sydney to San Francisco was neither a very tedious nor an expensive one; and great numbers of ticket-of-leave men and old convicts who had served their time early contrived to sail for California," Frank Soulé explained. "There the field seemed so rich and safe for a resumption of their quondam pranks that they yielded to the temptation, and forthwith began to execute villainies that in magnitude and violent character far exceeded those for which they had been originally convicted. Callous in conscience, they feared nothing save the gallows. But that they had little reason to dread in merciful, gentle, careless California, where prosecutors and witnesses were few, or too busy to attend to the calls of justice; where jurors, not knowing the law, and eager to be at money-making again, were apt to take hasty charges from the bench as their sole rule of conduct; where judges, chosen by popular election, were either grossly ignorant of law, or too timid or careless, corrupt or incapable, to measure out the full punishment of crime; and where the laws themselves had not yet been methodically laid down, and the forms and procedure of legal tribunals digested into a plain, unerring system."

The Sydney Ducks ruled Sydney Town, a neighborhood of bars and brothels. They extorted protection money from the bar owners and madams; they robbed non-customers reckless enough to be passing through. They killed any who challenged their right to engage in nefarious activities. The police steered clear of Sydney Town, judging that those who ventured there were up to no good and deserved what befell them.

Reputable San Franciscans ignored the Ducks as long as they stayed in Sydney Town. But when the activity of the Ducks began to touch the rest of the city, and especially when evidence of arson in the later fires pointed toward the Ducks, civic leaders mobilized again.

This time their vigilance activity was better organized. A mass meeting was advertised; those who attended drafted a charter for a formal "Committee of Vigilance." The charter avowed its signees' devotion to the rule of law but complained that the law was being suborned by bribery of the police, intimidation of witnesses and other modes of malfeasance. The committee would fix that. "We are determined that no thief, burglar, incendiary or assassin shall escape punishment, either by the quibbles of the law, the insecurity of prisons, the carelessness or corruption of the police, or a laxity of those who pretend to administer justice," its charter said.

The committee soon had a chance to show its resolve. A store-owner reported a small safe missing. Shortly thereafter, a Duck named John Jenkins was seen exiting the waterfront neighborhood with something heavy and awkward under wraps—something that looked like a safe. Confronted, he stole a boat and made off into the bay. Several men pursued him in boats of their own. As they closed in, he dropped his burden into the bay. But the water was too shallow for concealment, and the object was retrieved. It was the missing safe.

That evening the bell of a fire company was rung to summon the Committee of Vigilance. Eighty members appeared. John Jenkins was brought in. Evidence against him was presented and evaluated. After a trial of two hours a verdict was handed down: guilty. The sentence: death.

By now it was past midnight. A large crowd had gathered outside the room where the trial had been convened. Sam Brannan, speaking for the committee, announced the verdict and sentence. The crowd shouted its approval.

The prisoner was brought out for execution. At this point the sheriff half-heartedly tried to intervene. He was let to know that if he valued his own life he should step aside. He did.

Jenkins's arms were tied behind his back. A noose was lowered over his head and adjusted to fit his neck. The other end of the rope was tossed over a sturdy timber standing out from the building. A few vigorous yanks by several strong men lifted Jenkins, swinging, off the ground. He struggled briefly and died.

The next day, the sheriff, emboldened by the dawn and the breakup of the crowd, ordered an inquest. Sam Brannan was questioned. He defended the work of the committee. "I believe the man had a fair and impartial trial," Brannan said of Jenkins. "He was tried before from sixty to eighty men. I believe the verdict of guilty was unanimous, and they came to the conclusion unanimously to hang him." The sheriff asked for names of those involved. Brannan declined to tell. "I have understood that threats have been made against their property and lives. I have heard the threats made, have heard it said that my own house would be burned. Threats have come to me from the prisoners in the county prison that I should not live ninety days."

The inquest board was satisfied. Its report described the events leading to Jenkins's execution, and it identified Brannan and other leaders of the Committee of Vigilance. But it declined to recommend action against them.

Yet even this meddling angered the committee and its supporters. Another mass meeting was held; the 184 men present condemned the inquest report and claimed equal responsibility with Brannan in the execution of Jenkins.

The committee dared the inquest board and the sheriff to come after them. It commenced another case, against a Sydney Duck named James Stuart, infamous for murder, extortion and other crimes. He was arrested, tried and sentenced to hang. "He did not struggle much," wrote Frank Soulé, who had mixed feelings about the vigilance phenomenon. "After hanging a few seconds, his hat fell off, and a slight breeze stirred and gently waved his hair. This was a sorry spectacle—a human being dying like a dog, while thousands of erring mortals, whose wickedness only had not yet been found out, looked on and applauded! But necessity, which dared not trust itself to feelings of compassion, commanded the deed and unprofitable sentiment sunk abashed. Reason loudly declared—*So perish every villain who would hurt his neighbor!* and all the people said *Amen!*"

29

THE SPIRIT OF '87

San Francisco's struggle to create order out of the chaos of the gold rush was paralleled by California's efforts to form a state government. By the late summer of 1849 California had more inhabitants than some states, and more people were arriving every day. The military government of the occupation couldn't keep order, let alone address the myriad civilian functions of state governments. Personal security depended on vigilante action, which was haphazard at best, alarming at worst.

Californians and friends of Californians pleaded with Congress to take action. At the least, they said, California should be given a territorial government. Because California lay beyond the bounds of the Louisiana Purchase, the Missouri Compromise didn't apply, leaving Congress without guidance on the slavery question. Most observers supposed California wasn't suited to slavery, but Southerners, having received nothing for giving Oregon a territorial government that didn't guarantee slavery, refused to do the same for California. The ensuing deadlock left California in limbo, neither territory nor state.

The military governor, General Bennet Riley, took matters into his own hands. Tired of bearing blame for not doing what he had no power to do, he called a constitutional convention. He lacked the authority to summon such a convention, but perhaps he remembered that the convention that wrote the federal Constitution in Philadelphia in 1787 had lacked authority to do what it did. Its work was made good in the denouement: the Constitution's ratification. Riley assumed, or at least hoped, that California's constitution would receive ex post facto approval too. "As Congress has failed to organize a new Territorial Government, it becomes our imperative duty to take some active measures to provide for the existing wants of the country," he said in the notice summoning the convention.

Corralling delegates wasn't easy. Most Californians were too busy seeking their fortunes to spare time for constitution-making. And most considered California their current place of work rather than their permanent home. What did they care how California developed over the next decade or the generations to come? They would be gone by then.

Nonetheless, forty-eight delegates gathered at Monterey in September 1849. Among them were seven native-born Californians, including one Indian, Manuel Dominguez of Los Angeles. Thirty-five had been born in the United States. Six had been born in Europe.

The Monterey convention adopted the Philadelphia convention as its model, augmented by experience. A first order of business was a bill of rights, which the Philadelphia convention had neglected. Significantly, the California bill of rights included a ban on slavery.

The significance of this provision lay in two facts: that it was the first pronouncement on slavery in the trans-Louisiana West, and that it was approved unanimously—by the delegates from America's slave states as well as those from the free states. More than a few Southern gold-seekers had brought slaves, whose status was ambiguous after they set foot on California soil. American law at the time allowed slaveholders to take slaves, typically as personal servants, to the free states of the North without jeopardizing the owners' legal title to them, so long as the stay in the North was temporary. America's courts had never ruled definitively on how long a temporary stay could last. And most of the Southerners in California didn't know how long they would be staying.

But the sentiment in California and at the Monterey convention was decidedly against slavery. Slavery stigmatized manual labor, and manual labor was the occupation of nearly all Californians. No free Californian wished to incur that stigma. Put otherwise, as one Californian did, "In a country where every white man makes a slave of himself, there is no use in keeping niggers."

Even while the convention voted to keep slaves out, several delegates wanted to keep *blacks* out, too. One delegate, formerly of Kentucky, considered free blacks a bane on a community. "They are idle in their habits, difficult to be governed by the laws, thriftless, and uneducated. It is a species of population that this country should be particularly guarded against," he said. Another delegate, lately from Louisiana, concurred, saying, "The free negro is one of the greatest evils that society can be afflicted with." Yet the proposed ban failed, stymied by a combination of egalitarian conscience and concerns about the constitutionality of such a ban, in a convention of dubious constitutionality itself.

The convention concluded with a grand celebration of its labors. The delegates and their guests feasted on beef, pig, turkey, tongue and pâté; toasted one another with wines of several varieties; and danced till dawn. Then they signed their names to the document, and cannons at the fort of Monterey fired thirty-one times, saluting California as the thirty-first state of the Union.

BUT BECOMING A STATE WASN'T AS EASY AS THAT. CONGRESS still had to approve. And any modestly knowledgeable observer of national politics could tell this was hardly guaranteed.

To carry their precious document, duly ratified by California voters, to Washington, the Californians chose John Frémont. "The Pathfinder of the West," as he was commonly called, had been lurking in Oregon and California ahead of the war with Mexico; when that conflict broke out, he raised the American flag over

California, inspiring Jessie Frémont to employ a new sobriquet for her husband, "Liberator of California." They aimed to settle in San Francisco, but a land swindle left them holding an apparently valueless tract on the Mariposa River, which turned out to sit atop the Mother Lode, the great ore body from which the Sierra gold had been eroding out all these eons. By dumb luck the Frémonts became fabulously wealthy. They were, metaphorically and almost literally, the golden couple of American national life in the early 1850s.

Congress was suitably impressed by Frémont on his arrival, California constitution in hand, in the late winter of 1850. Yet Southern members of the Senate were still loath to accept California's admission as a free state, which would tip the balance of states against their section. They dug in their heels.

The California question triggered a titanic political battle. On California's behalf arose Kentuckian Henry Clay, the author of the Missouri Compromise, who came out of retirement to fashion another compromise, lest the Union fall to pieces in the twilight of his career. John Calhoun of South Carolina, equally venerable and a legislator of no small gifts himself, would have stood toe-to-toe against Clay, if he could have stood at all. Calhoun was dying of consumption—tuberculosis—which had silenced his stentorian voice. Others had to read his speeches for him. But his fierce will was as strong as ever, and his eyes blazed with contempt for everything Clay was trying to accomplish.

California's fate hung in the balance. Calhoun rejected the right of the Californians to write a constitution for themselves. California didn't belong to them, he said. It belonged to the people of the United States, who had acquired it by war from Mexico. The people of the United States acting through Congress, not the people of California via illegitimate convention and bogus ratification, must determine California's fate.

Henry Clay riposted by wrapping California in a blanket of measures more acceptable to the South. Chief of these was a strengthened law governing the return of fugitive slaves. Northern abolitionists regularly subverted the clause of the federal Constitution requiring the return of fugitive slaves to their owners; Northern state legislators assisted by passing personal-liberty laws that forbade state officials from cooperating with slave-catchers. For years the South had been demanding a federal law with teeth to stop the practice. Clay proposed just such a law.

Calhoun wasn't satisfied. He demanded acceptance of the principle that slave-owners could take their slave property anywhere in the Union, just as owners of horses could take their horses anywhere. But Calhoun died amid the debate, and enough of his Southern colleagues yielded to Clay's appeals—and to the deft floor management of Stephen Douglas, a talented and ambitious young senator from Illinois—for what came to be called the Compromise of 1850 to win approval. The compromise might have failed at the last moment if not for another death. President Zachary Taylor, a Virginian and a slave-owner, looked askance at Clay's package and threatened a veto, but Taylor suddenly died in the final stages of the debate. His successor, Millard Fillmore of New York, favored the compromise and signed it.

In California the cannons boomed again, this time with authority.

30

TO BE DECENTLY POOR

Some in California groaned at the news of statehood. The treaty transferring California to the United States had specified that land titles acquired under Spanish and Mexican law be honored under American law. But California law, and especially California practice, diverged from American law, and in an age when no federal justice department even existed, local law and practice often trumped federal law. Many Mexicans in California lost their land through unfavorable statutes of the California government, adverse rulings in California courts, or outright theft.

Mariano Vallejo, a Californio, or native-born Californian of Spanish descent, was one of the largest landowners in California at the time of the gold discovery. He was also a practical man and a forward-thinking individual. He endorsed American annexation of California even before the war with Mexico, predicting that American rule would allow California to thrive as it had never done under Mexico. "When we join our fortunes to hers, we shall not become subjects but fellow citizens, possessing all the rights of the people of the United States," Vallejo told his fellow Californios. "We shall have a stable government and just laws. California will grow strong and flourish, and her people will be prosperous, happy, and free. Look not, therefore, with jealousy upon the hardy pioneers who scale our mountains and cultivate our unoccupied plains; but rather welcome them as brothers, who come to share with us a common destiny."

Alas, the Americans in California didn't reciprocate the good feeling. In 1846, just as the United States was going to war with Mexico, a group of Americans in California launched a revolt against the Mexican government there, proclaiming what they called the Bear Flag Republic. They arrested Vallejo as a symbol of the old order. He was held as a prisoner for six weeks, and contracted malaria in detention. When he was finally released, he discovered that his ranch in the Sonoma Valley had been robbed of large herds of horses and cattle. His standing crop of wheat had been stolen or simply destroyed. "All is lost," he lamented.

In fact there was much more for Vallejo to lose. Gold-hunters took up residence on his property, helping themselves to livestock, crops and anything else not firmly tied down. Lusters after his land hired lawyers to assail him in court. Comparing the attorneys to the Sydney Ducks of San Francisco, Vallejo said, "The bandits from Australia stole our cattle and horses, but these thieves in frock coats, wrapped about with the mantle of the law, took away our lands and buildings and, with no scruple whatsoever, enthroned themselves as powerful monarchs in our houses."

Yet Vallejo redoubled his commitment to the American way of doing things. He joined the Monterey convention as a delegate, and after Congress approved the constitution and statehood, he served as a state legislator. He donated land and money toward the construction of a state capital on a northern arm of San Francisco Bay. His gifts were accepted, but his fellow legislators chose Sacramento for their home away from home.

Vallejo's largesse and adoptive patriotism availed him little. The courts and Congress redefined the Treaty of Guadalupe Hidalgo in a way that shifted the burden of proof of ownership to the Californios. Because records and titles under Mexican law differed substantially from their American counterparts, the Californios often found it impossible to fend off challenges. Vallejo spent many thousands of dollars in legal fees, ultimately in vain. Once a rich man, he found himself deeply in debt. Formerly the lord of a vast domain, he now held but a few miserable parcels.

Yet Vallejo retained his dignity, or tried to. "I think I will know how to be decently poor when the time comes, just as I have known how to be rich," he said.

Not all those dispossessed by the Americans were as gracious as Mariano Vallejo. One who fought back violently was Joaquín Murrieta. So storied did Murrieta's exploits become that many in California believed he was a composite of several men. He apparently didn't mind having his powers exaggerated, the better to strike fear into the hearts of his enemies and tormentors.

Best evidence indicates that he was born in Sonora, Mexico, around 1830, and so was in his late teens when he followed the reports of gold to California in 1848 or 1849. He found enough gold to stay, even after harassment and violence against fellow Mexicans caused many to leave California and return home. Yet a series of traumatic events involving loved ones set him off on a campaign of revenge. The most common version of the Murrieta legend held that thuggish Americans raped his wife, killed his brother and horsewhipped Murrieta himself. Some of this might have been embellishment, as certainly was the part of the story that said he took his revenge only on those who had injured him, his wife or his brother.

More generally, Murrieta resented the labeling of Mexicans as "greasers" and "niggers" and their treatment as thieves for merely trying to gather gold. This attitude inspired the California legislature in 1850 to levy a tax on foreign miners. The tax was subsequently repealed, then reimposed, adding confusion to the insult Mexicans like Murrieta felt. They rejected the Americans' assertion that Mexicans were stealing American gold, rejoining that the Americans had stolen California.

In any event, Murrieta visited his resentment on the Americans in the gold fields. Violence had been common in the region since the start of the gold rush. Crowded clusters of unattached men who carried substantial wealth on their persons were a recipe for armed robbery and the mayhem that often accompanied it. As in San Francisco, much of the crime went unpunished when those not directly harmed judged they had better uses for their time. When the crime and violence afflicted Mexicans, Chinese or other scorned minorities, the American majority felt even less incentive to intervene.

But the first months of 1853 brought an escalation of violent crime. Then as later, crime sold newspapers, and the gold-country press recounted the sprees with gusto. "For some time back, a band of robbers have been committing depredations in the southern section of our county," a Calaveras County paper reported in January. "During the week a party of three Mexicans entered a Chinese tent at Yaqui Camp, near San Andres, and ransacked everything, despite the opposition of the inmates, carrying off two bags of gold dust, one containing $110 and the other $50." This was just the start. "Three armed Mexicans—supposed to be the same who committed the above outrage—entered another Chinese tent in the same vicinity, assaulted its inhabitants, holding loaded pistols to their heads to keep them quiet, and robbed them of two bags of gold dust, $90 and $60. One of the Chinamen, named Ah Kop, refused to give up his money and attempted to defend himself, when one of the ruffians drew his knife and ran the unfortunate celestial through the body, causing almost instant death." A second area paper, not to be outdone, recounted "the dreadful murders and outrages committed in the lonely gulches and solitary outposts" of the county, and identified the ringleader: "a robber named Joaquin, a very desperate man, who was concerned in the murder of four Americans some time ago at Turnersville."

The violence intensified and the coverage grew more lurid. "We publish today the details of fourteen horrible murders, all committed within seven days, in Calaveras county," a paper said in mid-February. "A condition of society exists in that important region far worse than that which prevailed in the early days of its settlement. No man dare travel a step unless armed to the teeth, or sleep without having fire-arms already in his grasp; life is not safe for a day and the utmost excitement prevails at every camp."

The story reached San Francisco, where it grew the more. "Joaquin was born in the Villa de Catoce, in the department of Jalisco," asserted *The Whig*. "He is aged about 35 years, and has ranked among the most crafty and daring guerrillas of Mexico. He is chief of a notorious band of robbers now infesting the vicinity of Mexico, and though living in California, has a regular chain of communication with his associates in his native country. He has been known to enter the capital cities disguised as a friar—has been arrested several times, but through the expertness and influence he wielded among the soldiery, he has been discharged. He is about six feet in height, and of immense muscular strength; is well versed in the use of arms, and in disposition cruel and sanguinary." Most of this was wrong, but no one except Joaquín could disprove it, and he had no incentive to do so.

Soon Joaquín Murrieta began popping up everywhere. He was sighted on the Salinas River, and then suddenly as far away as San Diego. Reasonable persons concluded that he couldn't have committed all the crimes laid to his account; unreasonable persons said he had almost superhuman powers, to travel that far that fast. He was impervious to gunfire. "When shot at, he receives the balls in the breast with a complacent smile," a gold-country paper reported. "It has been a matter of surprise to his pursuers that the balls fired at him have no effect." This writer was too practical to give Murrieta special powers. The bandit simply cheated. "We learn from a gentleman who shot from a short distance that he wears a coat of mail beneath his clothes. To what base use has the armor of the days of chivalry come!"

The news coverage forced local officials to order a manhunt, which made the story even better. "I have been engaged a week in hunting Mr. Joaquin and his party," the posse leader reported. "And we had a right lively time of it after the greasers. We followed them all over the country, and, while we were on their trail, they killed and wounded 15 Chinamen and stole seven or eight thousand dollars. We got one or two chances at them, but they were so well mounted that they beat us running all to hell."

The state legislature stepped in. The assembly appropriated funds to create a ranger squadron modeled on the Texas Rangers and headed by Harry Love, a former Ranger captain. Love mustered a company of frontier lawmen, guns-for-hire and Indian fighters. The governor of California placed a bounty of one thousand dollars on Murrieta's head.

Love and the California Rangers chased Murrieta across gold country. They captured one of his brothers-in-law. "He says he will take and show us to Joaquin if we will release him," Love reported. "I will try him a while to see what it will end in."

Love's Rangers, with the help of the prisoner—who likely inferred, not improbably, that he would meet a bad end if he did *not* betray his kinsman—tracked Murrieta's gang to a wooded camp. The Rangers charged, and one of the officers spied the leader. "This is Joaquin, boys," he shouted. "We have got him at last."

Not quite, as a correspondent who got the story from the Rangers recounted. "At the mention of the word Joaquín, seeing that he was recognized, the Mexicans threw off their cloaks and serapes and commenced firing and retreating. Joaquín, himself, was unarmed, having evidently just been awakened from a sound sleep, and in his hurry to get his horse forgot his weapons. However, he made a bold dash for the animal, jumped upon him unsaddled, hastily threw his lariat over the animal's nose and leaped down off the bluff, 14 or 15 feet in height, into the dry bed of the creek. One of the rangers followed him immediately down the bank and another down the side of the creek to cut him off. They had fired at him several times but without effect, and seeing that there was a danger of his escaping, they aimed at the animal and succeeded in bringing him down. Joaquin then commenced running, and had gone some thirty yards when he received two shots, and as he was falling cried *No tire mas, yo soy muerte*—Don't shoot any more, for I'm dead. He immediately expired."

Harry Love was a professional man-hunter. To reassure the citizens of California that he had got Murrieta, and to make certain he and his men received the bounty, he cut off Murrieta's head. Lacking a better preservative, he soaked it in a jar of whiskey.

The head persuaded the governor to pay up. And it convinced the papers that Joaquín Murrieta had met his end. Crime in the gold country didn't cease, but it was ascribed to lesser mortals. Murrieta began to appear in dime novels that cast him as the Robin Hood of El Dorado.

His pickled head became a curio in itself. To the soberly law-abiding, it was a symbol of justice vindicated. To Mexicans it represented a martyred hero. The last of Joaquín Murrieta finally rested in a San Francisco museum, where it gathered dust until the 1906 earthquake and fire, after which it was never seen again.

31

WHERE CAN WE GO?

O F THOSE THRUST TO THE MARGINS BY THE FLOOD OF Americans to California, none lost more than the Indians. The indigenous population of California had fallen by half during some eighty years of Spanish and Mexican rule, chiefly as a result of infectious disease. But the population appears to have stabilized, with the remaining 150,000 or so Indians finding an equilibrium with the much smaller number of European-descended friars, soldiers, civilian officials and settlers. Some of the Indian tribes lived in close proximity and contact with the Europeans; others remained aloof and largely untouched by white ways. Some tribes were comparatively peaceful; others more aggressive.

Things changed with the discovery of gold. The changes weren't all for the worse, at least not immediately. As elsewhere, native peoples adopted some elements of the new regime even as they resisted others. Gold wasn't unknown to the Indians of California, but they had never much valued it. Once they learned that white people *did* value it, and would trade useful items like guns, knives, steel pots and blankets for it, some of them joined the ranks of the miners. The first placer miners encountered by Vicente Pérez Rosales, the Chilean argonaut, were Indians, who often worked as families. "The system they employed for washing the earth was the same as that still used by our panners of gold, but more methodical," Pérez Rosales recalled. "With sticks hardened in the fire, or an occasional worn-out tool of civilization, the men dug until they came to the *circa*, one of the strata most largely composed of sand and of the heavy bodies deposited in the valleys by the water that drains into them. This sand the children loaded into tightly woven grass baskets and carried to the banks of the stream where a row of women with fine trays of the same material washed it, wrapping the gold in small packages to the value of about two Spanish gold pieces, for use in trading."

Indian participation in the mining process didn't last. Most of the immigrants had traveled thousands of miles to lay hands on California's gold, and many hardly thought twice about pushing the indigenous peoples aside. News of the gold discovery reached Oregon not long after the Whitman massacre; Oregon's males weighed their options: to stay in Oregon and avenge the killings, or go to California and claim their share of the nation's sudden fortune. Some decided to do both, traveling to California and then taking out their anger on the Indians they encountered there. The Oregonians acquired a reputation as Indian killers. A San Francisco newspaper, the *Daily Alta California*, explained how their "insatiated search for revenge" for the Whitmans had been visited upon even the most friendly tribes. "Their trail was marked with Indian blood," the paper said. It went on to assert that the Oregonians' attacks had started a cycle of violence. "The ire of the savages was stirred, and 'Indian outrages' alarmed the quiet diggers on the American River. . . . Here may be dated the commencement of disturbances between our people in the Placer and the Indian tribes of the North."

The San Francisco paper was too quick to blame the Oregonians for Indian troubles. The Oregonians simply happened to be the first Americans on the scene. Nearly every group of Americans treated the Indians with violence, which grew worse as the immigrant tide swelled. As with the Oregonians, attack begot reprisal, which triggered renewed attacks and additional reprisals. Before long the immigrants felt themselves as aggrieved as the Indians did.

In such a context it was no surprise that elected officials became some of the most ardent advocates of harsh Indian policies. Peter Burnett, after arriving in Oregon with the emigrant train of 1843, had ventured into politics and won election to the provisional government. Yet his career didn't advance swiftly enough to suit him, and on hearing of the gold discovery, he uprooted his family once more and trekked south. He dove into California politics and surfaced, in late 1849, as the first governor elected under the constitution Congress hadn't yet approved. Burnett kept his ear to the ground and a wetted finger in the air, and he retained his post when the constitution did take effect, in September 1850.

Burnett pronounced on the Indian question in terms that were chilling but not unlike those long heard on the frontier. He declared that the two races could never coexist; too great a gulf divided them. "The white man, to whom time is money, and who labors hard all day to create the comforts of life, cannot sit up all night to watch his property," Burnett said. "And after being robbed a few times, he becomes desperate, and resolves upon a war of extermination. That is the common feeling of our people who have lived upon the Indian frontier. The two races are kept asunder by so many causes, and having no ties of marriage or consanguinity to unite them, they must ever remain at enmity." Burnett thought the question transcended individual decision. "That a war of extermination will continue to be waged between the races, until the Indian race becomes extinct, must be expected. While we cannot anticipate this result but with painful regret, the inevitable destiny of the race is beyond the power or wisdom of man to avert."

Burnett's war of extermination took guerrilla form, primarily. In hundreds of incidents, thousands of Indians were killed, on the slightest provocation or no provocation at all. Hubert Howe Bancroft, an Ohio native who arrived in California the year after Burnett's declaration of war, and who would become California's leading historian, caustically summarized what followed the declaration and why: "The savages were in the way; the miners and settlers were arrogant and impatient; there were no missionaries or others present with even the poor pretense of soul-saving or civilizing. It was one of the last human hunts of civilization, and the basest and most brutal of them all."

YET NOT ALL THE WHITES WERE KILLERS, AND NOT ALL THE Indians merely victims. James Savage was a trader with the Indians of the central Sierra Nevada. "He is a man of about 28 years of age, rather small but very muscular and extremely active," wrote Robert Eccleston, who had taken up a claim on the Mariposa near the Frémonts' place. "His features are regular, and his hair light brown, which hangs in a negligé manner over his shoulders. He, however, generally wears it tied up. His skin is dark tanned by the exposure to the sun. He has, I believe, 33 wives among the mountain females of California, five or six only, however, of which are now living with him. They are from the ages of 10 to 22 and are generally sprightly young squaws. They are dressed neatly, their white chemise with low neck and short sleeves, to which is appended either a red or blue skirt. They are mostly low in stature and not unhandsome."

Savage's wives were evidence of more than his charm. As the gold rush commenced, he enlisted Indians to pan for gold, and he established a series of trading posts in the Mariposa region. He treated the Indians fairly, by the evidence of their willingness to work for him and the business they brought to his posts—business that was sometimes secured by wives, as deal-closers or guarantors of fulfillment.

His wives also served as early warners of dissatisfaction among the tribes. The Yosemite Indians—the name translated as "grizzly bear" and signaled their fierceness—were planning a war against the whites, one of his wives told him. Savage sought out the leaders of the nearby tribes and urged them not to join any war. The whites were too many, and they were vindictive; they would respond to any attack with overwhelming force and would crush the Indians.

One of the chiefs present at this parley scoffed. José Juarez, as he was called, declared that the whites wouldn't fight. They were too busy grubbing for gold. Yes, there were many whites at San Francisco. He had seen them there. And they had big ships with guns. But the ships couldn't come into the mountains.

José Juarez called for war at once. The numbers of whites were growing; they must be defeated and driven from the mountains now, before it was too late. All the tribes must band together.

José Rey, another chief, said his people would join. Not only would they save their country, they would seize the trade goods, gold and other property of the whites. The first to fight would win the most.

James Savage was dismayed, and he left the meeting fearing the worst. The next thing he heard was that the Indians of the region, conspicuously including the women and children, had disappeared into the mountains. This was ominous: the battlefield was being cleared of noncombatants.

Still Savage hoped to prevent the war. He gathered a small group of men and rode into the mountains to find the Indians. Their approach alerted the Indians, who warned him not to come close. He halted and shouted across a ravine that separated his men from the Indian camp. Adam Johnston, one of the men with Savage, later recounted the exchange. "Savage said to them it would be better for them to return to their village—that with very little labor daily, they could procure sufficient gold to purchase them clothing and food," Johnston said. "To this the chief replied it was a hard way to get a living, that they could more easily supply their wants by stealing from the whites. He also said to Savage he must not deceive the whites by telling them lies, he must not tell them that the Indians were friendly; they were not, but on the contrary were their deadly enemies, and that they intended killing and plundering them so long as a white face was seen in the country."

More discouraged than ever, Savage retreated from the mountains, and discovered that the war had begun, with an Indian attack on a mining camp on the Fresno River. "We reached the camp on the Fresno a short time after daylight," Adam Johnston recalled. "It presented a horrid scene of savage cruelty. The Indians had destroyed everything they could not use or carry with them. The store was stripped of blankets, clothing, flour, and everything of value; the safe was broken open and rifled of its contents; the cattle, horses, and mules had been run into the mountains; the murdered men had been stripped of their clothing, and lay before us filled with arrows; one of them had yet twenty perfect arrows sticking in him."

The Fresno River attack prompted Governor Burnett to authorize the raising of a militia battalion. It took a while. Even under attack, most of the miners didn't want to miss any days gathering gold. And the Indians had stolen most of the horses and mules, so replacements had to be found. But two hundred men eventually enlisted in the Mariposa Battalion, secured mounts, and set out.

James Savage served as the battalion's guide. "From his long acquaintance with the Indians, Mr. Savage has learned their ways so thoroughly that they cannot deceive him," battalion member T. G. Palmer remarked. "He has been one of their greatest chiefs, and speaks their language as well as they can themselves. No dog can follow a trail like he can. No horse can endure half so much. He sleeps but little, can go days without food, and can run a hundred miles in a day and night over the mountains and then sit and laugh for hours over a camp-fire as fresh and lively as if he had just been taking a little walk for exercise. With him for a guide we felt little fear of not being able to find them."

Savage knew the Indians would be on the lookout, and as he brought the battalion close to where the Indians had camped near one of their villages, he had them dismount. He chose sixty men to advance on foot. "About two o'clock"—in the morning—"we started in Indian file, as still as it was possible for sixty men to move in the dark," Palmer recalled. "For three long hours did we walk slowly and cautiously over the rocks and bushes, through the deepest ravines and up steep and ragged mountains, until within half a mile of the enemy. Here every one took off his boots, when we again pushed forward to about two hundred yards from the camp. Another halt was called to wait for daylight, while Savage went forward to reconnoiter."

There were more Indians than Savage had expected. He had hoped to strike the village by surprise, take some hostages, and use them as a bargaining chip toward a reestablishment of peace. But his band was badly outnumbered. He reconsidered his strategy.

The men shivered as day began to dawn. "We had been lying in our stocking-feet on the ground on the top of a mountain within a few paces of the snow for more than an hour, almost frozen by the intense cold, not daring to move or speak a word," Palmer remembered. "It was not yet light enough to see the sight of our rifles, when an Indian's head was seen rising on the hill before us. For a moment his eyes wandered, then rested on us, and with a yell like a coyote he turned for the rancheria"—the Indian village. "Never did I hear before such an infernal howling, whooping and yelling, as saluted us then from the throats of about six hundred savages, as they rushed down the hill into the gim-o-sell bushes below."

Savage didn't want to take on the whole camp of warriors, but he and his men had no choice. "Finding we were discovered, we charged on their town," Palmer said. "Fifty rifles cracked almost instantaneously; a dozen Indians lay groaning before their huts, and many supposed we had undisturbed possession. Our firing had ceased and we were looking around for plunder, when a rifle fired from the bushes below struck a young Texan, Charley Huston, standing by my side. He fell with a single groan, and we all supposed him dead."

This came as a particular shock to the battalion men, as they did not think the Indians had guns. "We were only expecting arrows," Palmer said. Palmer and the rest fled for their lives. "Before that shot was fired, I had always entertained the idea that I could run about as fast as common men (and I was one of the first in the charge), but by the time I had collected my wandering senses, I was nearly alone, the majority of the party some thirty paces ahead, and running as if they never intended to stop."

Eventually the Mariposa Battalion regrouped. And it adopted a new strategy—one that exploited the principal advantage the whites possessed over the Indians in the gold country. The Indians had women and children to protect; the whites didn't. The whites didn't have to catch and kill the Indian warriors; they could starve out the women and children.

Which was precisely what the Mariposa Battalion did. After the Indian warriors had moved farther into the mountains, the battalion entered their village. "We burned a hundred wigwams, several tons of dried horse and mule meat," Palmer explained.

And so the Mariposa war proceeded. The whites seldom killed or even encountered the Indian fighters, nor did they find the women and children, who remained in the mountains. But the Indians couldn't stay in the mountains forever. Their food stores—the acorns, pine nuts, wild grains and dried meat that would sustain them through the winter—were back at the villages, unguarded. These and the Indian houses were put to the torch. "Burnt over 5000 bushels of acorns, and any quantity of old baskets," one of the battalion men wrote at the end of a busily destructive day. After a similar outing: "We burnt over 1000 bushels of acorns and also a good many old Rancherias, some of which were not long deserted."

The scorched-earth policy worked. With starvation staring them in the face, the tribes came out of the mountains, one by one, and sued for peace.

ONLY A SINGLE BAND OF YOSEMITES REMAINED. THE MARIPOSA militia captured an old Yosemite chief named Teneiya. He asked to see the body of his son, who had been killed by the whites. The son had surrendered, then was allowed to break his fetters so he could be shot trying to escape. Seeing his son dead, with bullet wounds in his back, the old chief turned to the officer in charge. "*Kill me*, sir captain!" he cried. "Yes, *kill me*, as you killed my son;

as you would kill my people if they would come to you! You would kill all my race if you had the power."

The chief proceeded to cast a curse on his tribe's tormentors. "When I am dead I will call to my people to come to you," he said. "They shall hear me in their sleep, and come to avenge the death of their chief and his son. Yes, sir American, my spirit will make trouble for you and your people, as you have caused trouble to me and my people. With the wizards, I will follow the white men and make them fear me. You may kill me, sir captain, but you shall not live in peace. I will follow in your footsteps; I will not leave my home but be with the spirits among the rocks, the water-falls, in the rivers and in the winds. Wheresoever you go I will be with you. You will not see me, but you will fear the spirit of the old chief, and grow cold."

Indians in that part of the mountains believed in the spirits the Yosemite chief summoned. The home ground of the Yosemites was a deep valley guarded by unscalable cliffs and thought to be enchanted. "We are afraid to go to this valley, for there are many witches there," the chief of another tribe told the Mariposa men.

But the Mariposa men didn't fear the spirits. Some of them forced Teneiya to show them the way to the valley. Initially he balked, but then he concluded that only surrender would spare the Yosemite women and children from starvation.

The Mariposa contingent was the first group of whites to enter Yosemite Valley. They marveled at its waterfalls, its soaring granite ramparts, and the dark forests along the Merced River at its bottom. Some began to think it might be enchanted after all. And they appreciated why the Yosemites were so reluctant to surrender—to trade this wonderland for the comparative wastes of the low country.

But the Indians had no choice. "Where can we now go that the Americans will not follow us?" one of their chiefs said. "Where can we make our homes, that you will not find us?"

VI

STEEL RAILS
AND SHARPS RIFLES

32

STEPHEN DOUGLAS'S
BRAINSTORM

JAMES MARSHALL'S 1848 GOLD DISCOVERY, BESIDES
triggering a mass rush of peoples to California, making that
place the most cosmopolitan spot in America, transforming San
Francisco from a quiet village into a raucous city, causing the Industrial Revolution to hurtle half a continent from America's East
to its Far West, and sealing the demise of California's Indians—
besides all this, the gold discovery set America on a course that ran
rapidly downhill to the Civil War.

The Compromise of 1850 let California into the Union as a
free state, but it said nothing about slavery in the other territories
taken from Mexico. Its very silence provoked an uproar, especially
among that Northern majority in the House of Representatives
that had repeatedly endorsed the Wilmot Proviso, a measure that
would bar slavery from the new territories. The South stymied the
proviso in the Senate, so it never became law. But it signaled that
a majority in Congress thought the West—save Texas—should
remain free of slavery.

Stephen Douglas thought otherwise. The Illinois senator
wanted to build a railroad to California. One reason was to keep
California from spinning out of the Union. It occurred to more
than a few Californians that their new home might be better off as

an independent country. Americans had seceded from the British empire in 1776 in part because of the great distance that separated the colonies from the seat of government. Thomas Jefferson had suspected, after the Lewis and Clark expedition, that America's Western slope had a political destiny separate from that of the East. Distance and difficulties of travel aside, California had something that made going it alone seem entirely plausible and attractive—namely, all that gold. Douglas judged that a railroad would neutralize California separatism. Once forty-niners who had walked or ridden horseback or wagon for five or six months to make the journey west discovered that they could make the return trip east in four *days*, they would remember what they loved about the land of their birth.

The second reason for the railroad was that it would be good for the business of Douglas's home state. Chicago was becoming the gateway to the West, linking the Eastern seaboard, via the Erie Canal, to the prairies and plains of the upper Mississippi and Missouri valleys. Douglas determined to expand Chicago's reach to the Far West: California. The fact that he had business interests that would prosper from Chicago's boom simply strengthened his desire to build a railroad to the Pacific.

Yet no one had ever built such a long railroad, through such largely unpopulated regions. Potential investors demanded governments that could secure land titles and guard against Indian attack. Douglas proposed to give them just that. He sponsored a bill that would create territorial governments for Kansas and Nebraska, through which the railroad would run.

Southern members of Congress asked what was in the bill for them. The railroad would benefit the West and the North, not the South. Why should they approve?

Douglas had an answer. His bill would repeal the Missouri Compromise's ban on slavery in the northern part of the Louisiana Purchase, including Kansas and Nebraska. Some Southerners actually considered emigrating with their slaves to Kansas, whose eastern portion looked much like next-door Missouri, a slave state; more important to most Southerners was the principle of nondiscrimination against slave property. The Douglas bill promised just that, and Southerners were pleased to support it.

Northern antislavery groups recoiled in horror. They had thought they had slavery quarantined in the South. The Douglas bill would let it spread to the West and, if the underlying principle caught on, even reinfect the North.

Douglas cleverly cast his bill as an exercise in democracy. "Popular sovereignty," he called the concept. Americans would travel from other parts of the country and settle in Kansas and Nebraska. Some would take slaves; some would not. When the population of the territories reached the threshold for statehood, residents would vote. If they wanted slavery, they would have it. If they didn't want it, they would not. What could be more democratic?

And so the Douglas bill became the Kansas-Nebraska Act of 1854. America's attention, lately riveted on the Far West of California, abruptly refocused on its Near West, in Kansas.

ON A DARK NIGHT IN MAY 1856 JOHN BROWN SET OUT FROM A camp near Pottawatomie Creek in Kansas, a two-days' ride southwest of the bend in the Missouri River from which the early emigrant trains to Oregon embarked. Several men accompanied him, including four of his sons. Brown alone knew the purpose of their mission, but the others, attached to Brown by filial devotion and his strange charisma, would obey his orders, whatever they might be.

Brown had opposed slavery all his life. At first his opposition had been moral and private; he spoke against slavery among friends. But in 1837, when he was thirty-seven years old and living in Ohio, an abolitionist editor was murdered in Illinois by a mob of slavery sympathizers, and Brown took the killing personally. He stood up in church and said, "Here, before God, in the presence of these witnesses, from this time, I consecrate my life to the destruction of slavery."

Brown joined the Underground Railroad, the network of roads, buildings and people that transported fugitive slaves from the South to freedom in Canada. He settled in upstate New York among free black homesteaders. He trained his children—there were twenty altogether, by two wives—to despise slavery and work for its abolition.

Yet progress came too slowly for John Brown. He passed the half-century mark of his life, and slavery seemed to be gaining strength, not losing it. The Kansas-Nebraska Act opened the West to slavery. Brown realized he might die with nothing to show for his life's mission.

But the Kansas law also pointed a way forward for Brown. The two sides—proslavery and antislavery—recruited men and some women to travel to Kansas and settle there, so that when the residents voted to make Kansas a slave state or a free state, their side would win.

The proslavery side had the advantage of proximity. Kansas abutted Missouri, and the first settlements in Kansas were an easy ride from Missouri towns. Missourians could pitch tents in Kansas or even throw up hasty houses, establish residence of a sort, and return to their real homes in Missouri by nightfall.

The antislavery side had the advantage of zeal and organization. Antislavery groups established emigrant aid societies that helped get free-state settlers to Kansas. They provided the settlers with "Beecher's Bibles"—rifles named for the abolitionist minister Henry Ward Beecher, who said that in the struggle against slavery, one rifle was worth a hundred Bibles.

John Brown joined the fight. He traveled to Kansas and with his boys looked for a chance to strike a blow for freedom. They arrived in time to learn of a raid on Lawrence, a free town, by a crowd of slavery men. The only person killed in the raid was one of the raiders, who was hit by falling bricks, but newspaper offices were looted, printing presses smashed, and a large hotel burned. The point of the raid was terrorism: to scare the antislavery settlers and drive them away.

John Brown, whose theology favored the Old Testament over the New, vowed to take an eye for an eye, and then some. He gathered his sons and the other men and proceeded, under cover of night, to a small community of proslavery settlers on the north bank of Pottawatomie Creek. At Brown's direction the raiders forced their way into three cabins and seized several men. Five were selected for execution. Under Brown's implacable gaze, the victims were slashed to death with broadswords. Leaving the mangled corpses for their loved ones to find, Brown and his men disappeared into the night.

THE POTTAWATOMIE MASSACRE OUTRAGED THE SOUTH AND sparked an escalation in the Kansas struggle. Proslavery militias poured into Kansas and hunted for Brown and his band. In a fight at Osawatomie, they killed several of Brown's followers, including one of his sons. Brown became a hero to the abolitionists, who called him "Osawatomie Brown"—in preference to "Pottawatomie Brown," since even the archest abolitionists had trouble owning the slaughter of that dark night.

The violence in Kansas transfixed the country. "Bleeding Kansas," headlined the *New York Tribune.* The paper's editor, Horace Greeley, an abolitionist, extended the leader: "Startling News from Kansas. The War Actually Begun." The *New York Times* chimed: "The War in Kansas. Murders Thickening." Southern papers reported much the same thing. The image of Kansas drenched in blood etched itself in American minds.

The image was misleading. Both sides in the slavery debate had an incentive to exaggerate the violence in order to motivate and mobilize their supporters. And the newspaper owners and editors, like their counterparts in California amid the Joaquín Murrieta scare, knew that lurid headlines sold papers.

But even if the violence was exaggerated, the struggle in Kansas said something significant about the West and its relation to the rest of the country. When Americans in the 1850s thought in sectional terms, they usually thought of North versus South. But that struggle had suddenly and dramatically spilled over into the West. The West had always seemed the future of America, and until recently that Western future had excluded slavery. It no longer did so, and the bloody trail left by John Brown was the evidence.

33

NORTH, SOUTH, WEST

A T THE AGE OF NINETEEN, ABRAHAM LINCOLN MADE THE grand tour of the West, as it existed then and as his means allowed. He traveled as a flatboat deckhand down the Mississippi River to New Orleans. Feeling the power of the great river, and observing the armada of boats and barges bringing produce, lumber, minerals and other goods from the far reaches of the Mississippi Valley, he understood how central the West was to America's present and future.

A quarter-century later, as a Springfield lawyer of some reputation and a politician of unfulfilled ambition, Lincoln read of the struggle in Kansas and thought, once more, that as the West went, so the country would go. Lincoln's single term in Congress, as a Whig, hadn't led to anything more in the political field by the time the Whigs disintegrated in the early 1850s. Lincoln joined the new Republican party, along with many former Whigs and Free Soilers. He scored points for the party and for himself by criticizing Stephen Douglas on the Kansas-Nebraska Act. Being a man of peace and a moderate among the opponents of slavery, he shuddered at the news of the Pottawatomie massacre and watched with concern as the violence in Kansas escalated.

Lincoln grew alarmed when the Supreme Court in 1857 handed down a decision that threw nearly the whole West open to slavery. In the Dred Scott case, the court decreed that Congress had no power to prevent slaveholders from taking their slaves into the Western territories. The Missouri Compromise had been unconstitutional all along. By this decision, the court cut the ground from under Republican moderates who, while granting that the Constitution protected slavery in the states where it existed, held that Congress could, and must, keep slavery out of the Western territories. The Dred Scott verdict killed this option.

But it revitalized Lincoln's career. In 1858 he challenged Stephen Douglas for the Senate seat Douglas held. In a series of debates that summer, the two tramped up and down Illinois, with Lincoln on the attack against the Dred Scott decision, as well as the Kansas-Nebraska Act and other parts of the Douglas record. Lincoln didn't win the election; Douglas was returned to office. But the effort gained Lincoln a name among Republicans. He was thoughtful and articulate. He was determined to keep slavery out of the West. And at a time of rising voices all across the country, he understood how to make his points without making a fuss. He was moderate not merely in views but in temperament and manner. The experienced political hands among the Republicans took note especially of this. Their reading of the electoral college convinced them that the Republican nominee in 1860, if he didn't scare away moderates in the North, had an excellent chance of becoming the next president. Lincoln might be their man.

The value of moderation increased in 1859, when the slavery debate took another violent turn, once more the work of John Brown. Though wanted for murder in Kansas, Brown traveled freely around the North, albeit under assumed names. Abolitionists shielded him and gave him money, and he plotted a blow against slavery more telling than the murder of a handful of slavery men. He projected an insurrection of slaves in Virginia that would spread across the South and lead to the overthrow of the slave system.

His first step was the seizure of the federal arsenal at Harpers Ferry, Virginia. Brown and his followers entered the town at night in October 1859. Meeting little resistance, they occupied the arsenal and made prisoners of its guards. Meanwhile other Brown men moved quietly about the neighborhood spreading word to slaves that freedom was at hand. The slaves should come to Harpers Ferry, where they would receive weapons and instructions for their war of liberation.

The slaves rejected Brown's plan. They wanted nothing to do with him or his war. Some were less unhappy with their lot than Brown had supposed; others simply reckoned that his plan was crazy and would only get them killed.

Awaiting reinforcements that never appeared, Brown and his men became trapped in the arsenal by local authorities who quickly summoned militia. Regular marines arrived from Washington by train, commanded by U.S. army colonel Robert E. Lee. After Brown refused to surrender, Lee ordered the storming of the engine house where Brown and the others were holed up. Several of Brown's men were killed; Brown himself was wounded but taken alive.

Virginia prosecutors charged him with treason against the commonwealth. Brown was tried, convicted and sentenced to hang. But before his execution he was allowed to speak, and his eloquence in indicting the slave system seared the consciences of Northern abolitionists who asked themselves why they hadn't had the courage to put their lives on the line for their beliefs, as Brown had done. Brown's death was observed by the tolling of church bells in the North and his canonization by many Northerners as a martyr to liberty.

The South was appalled by every part of this. A race war had been the nightmare of the white South for decades; Brown's raid on Harpers Ferry rendered the nightmare chillingly plausible. And then, when the North made a saint of this terrorist, Southerners despaired that they could ever be safe within the Union.

ABRAHAM LINCOLN DISTANCED HIMSELF FROM JOHN BROWN. He sincerely disagreed with Brown's violent approach. But Lincoln also recognized that the path to the presidency for a moderate

Republican required keeping clear of a militant like Brown. John Brown was no Republican, Lincoln told all who would listen, including a crowd at the Cooper Institute in New York, to which Lincoln had been invited by fellow Republican moderates. The crowd sized up Lincoln as a possible nominee for president, and most liked what they saw and heard. Lincoln passed subsequent tests on his way to the Republican national convention, where he got the nod of the party.

The election was divisive but the outcome foreordained. Lincoln didn't have to win a single electoral vote in the South in order to carry the election. He didn't, and he did.

Even before his inauguration, Southern states began to secede: first South Carolina, then six more. The last two of the seven— Louisiana and Texas—were crucial. Had secession been limited to states east of the Mississippi, many Northerners, conceivably including Lincoln, might have been tempted to let them go. They would never be more than a rump country on the wrong side of history, weighed down by slavery while the rest of the civilized world, under the double inspiration of democracy and industrialization, was abandoning the feudal institution.

But when secession leaped the Mississippi, it put Lincoln in the position Benjamin Franklin and Thomas Jefferson had been in when they rejected the idea that any part of the great river could be in foreign hands. Most goods and cargoes continued to travel by water; the Mississippi still held the key to the American West. Franklin hadn't been willing for Britain or Spain to threaten access to the West; Jefferson wouldn't suffer France to do the same thing. Now Lincoln refused to let the Confederacy endanger the West and jeopardize America's future.

34

FREE SOIL

THE WAR CAME. AND THOUGH IT BROUGHT TREMENDOUS
trials to the North and the South, it conferred great good
fortune on the West. Westerners fought in the war: most Texans
on the Confederate side, and nearly all other Westerners with the
Union. But very little fighting took place in the West. And the
politics of the Civil War served Western interests quite well.

More precisely, the politics of the war served *particular* Western
interests. Secession and the war enabled a revolution in American
policy toward the ownership of Western land. What emerged as
the Homestead Act had its roots in the audacious land grab by settlers in the Willamette Valley in the 1840s, the one they hoped to
legitimize by the Linn bill that had inspired Peter Burnett to strike
out for Oregon. The Linn bill caught the coattails of the Free Soil
movement, which started as a wing of abolitionism but evolved
into a program championing the rights of ordinary people to the
possession of land. "Free soil" meant soil free of slavery, but also
soil given for free to free farmers, in family-sized homesteads. The
idea was that family farms would preempt large plantations and
form a bulwark against slavery. They would also allow the creation
of new free states that would eventually crack the Southern veto
of restrictive legislation on slavery. The concept drew adherents
among antislavery groups in the East, but it was most passionately

supported in the West, where the great majority of federal land was located.

The Free Soil party didn't last, but its philosophy was adopted by the Republican party. Meanwhile the homestead idea gave the Linn proposal the boost it needed to win congressional assent. In September 1850 the federal legislature approved the Donation Land Claim Act, granting 320 acres to each unmarried male and 640 acres to each married couple resident in Oregon before December 1, 1850. Smaller plots of land were allowed to those who arrived later, up to the time the law expired in 1855. The Oregon squatters had won.

They might not have if the South had cared more about Oregon. Slavery advocates disliked the homestead concept for the same reason slavery opponents liked it. Southerners let the Oregon bill pass because Oregon was far away and unsuited to slavery, and because the Oregon bill was largely retrospective and time-limited. Southerners refused to countenance anything like a general homestead bill, which reached the national platform of the Republicans but advanced no farther by the end of the 1850s.

The breakthrough came amid the Civil War. Southern secession made the Republicans the dominant force in national affairs, and in 1862 the Republican-controlled Congress passed the Homestead Act. Modeled after the Oregon land law but temporally open-ended, the Homestead Act authorized every head of family or single adult to receive 160 acres of federal land for free, providing that he or she—women were included—lived on the land for five years and improved it. Transferrable title could be acquired sooner, after one year, by the payment of $1.25 per acre. The law applied to American citizens and to immigrants who had declared an intention to become citizens.

The effective date of the Homestead Act was January 1, 1863, which not coincidentally was the day the Emancipation Proclamation was issued. The twin measures affirmed the ideology of freedom the Republicans had inherited from the Free Soilers. And just as the Emancipation Proclamation promised to revolutionize

life in the South, the Homestead Act appeared certain to revolutionize life in the West. "We cannot but feel that the passage of
the Homestead Bill will form a new era in Western emigration,"
declared the Kansas *Junction Union*, in a sentiment echoed in a
hundred Western papers. "The field is now fully open to the honest and energetic farmer, who wishes to secure himself a home on
easy terms."

From colonial days the cost of land had acted as a filter on the
westward movement. Land was cheaper on the frontier, to be sure,
but it wasn't free. It had to be purchased, often from speculators
who had negotiated deals with Indian tribes or the government.
People of modest means could move west, but those of lesser resources frequently could not. This was why Texas, where the Mexican government had offered its own homestead policy, had been
such a magnet for American settlers. The Homestead Act held out
the promise that anyone, of whatever means, could take part in the
American dream of land ownership.

THE REPUBLICANS HAD MORE TO GIVE THE WEST. THOUGH
a Pacific railroad had been the congressional brainchild of Democrat Stephen Douglas, it got nowhere so long as the South wielded
a veto in the Senate. The eastern end of the projected railroad
would lie in the North, funneling the gold of California into the
Northern economy, to the comparative detriment of the South.
The departure of the South suddenly made the railroad possible,
and the Republicans moved at once. In the same session that adopted the Homestead Act, Congress approved the Pacific Railway
Act, which decreed federal support for the construction of a line
from the Missouri River to California. Participating rail companies would receive land grants from the federal domain and loans
from the federal treasury. The loans would cover the cost of construction; they would be repaid with revenues from the sale of the
granted lands and from the operating revenues of the railroads.

The Pacific railroad would accomplish the unifying purpose of
Stephen Douglas, who was unable to appreciate even the irony of

its signing by his archrival, Abraham Lincoln, since Douglas had died in 1861. Indeed, unification was a more pressing issue than ever upon the outbreak of the Civil War. Southern sympathies were strong in California, and that state's gold would have been a godsend to the Confederacy. Lincoln was prepared to move heaven and earth to keep California in the Union, and while he couldn't relocate California, he could bring it effectively closer by means of a railroad. As soon as the railroad bill was passed, the secessionist rumblings in California ceased, as they did in neighboring Nevada, where the silver mines of the Comstock Lode had lately made that territory a rival to California in production of precious metals. No one doubted that the Pacific railroad would be expensive, but Lincoln would have paid thrice the price if necessary to secure the Far West and its glittering wealth.

35

HELL ON WHEELS

THE CONSTRUCTION OF THE PACIFIC RAILWAY WAS THE grandest project of its kind in American history until then. It was certainly the greatest thing the West had ever seen. Two companies took charge of the building. The Union Pacific Railroad Company started in Omaha, Nebraska, and worked west; the Central Pacific started in Sacramento and worked east. Though separated at first by fifteen hundred miles, they were in competition with each other, for the federal funding was keyed to the miles of track laid. Differentials were devised to account for the greater difficulty of building in the Sierra Nevada as compared with the Great Plains, but from the moment the initial grading began, the race was on to see which company could cover more ground and thereby win more of the public subsidy.

In the 1860s railroads were the largest enterprises in America by far. At a time when a big mine might employ several hundred workers, and a big factory about the same, the Pennsylvania Railroad employed many thousands. The Union Pacific and the Central Pacific didn't operate on that scale at first, but they were engines of economic development nonetheless. They pulled in workers by the trainload, including immigrants willing to do hard and dangerous labor for modest pay.

The Union Pacific favored Irish immigrants, who had been fleeing their birth land for America since the potato famine of the

1840s. The Irish were greeted with curses and brickbats by many Easterners, who despised them for being Catholic and for depressing the wage scale. When the Union Pacific advertised for laborers on its great Western project, thousands of Irish took up the offer.

The Central Pacific expected to rely on Irish workers as well. James Strobridge, construction chief for the Central Pacific, had dealt with the Irish before and intended to do so again. But there weren't enough Irish in California to keep them complaisant. "Four or five of the Irishmen on pay day got to talking together," recalled Charles Crocker, one of the four principals in the Central Pacific. "And I said to Mr. Strobridge there is some little trouble ahead." The trouble took the form of a demand for higher wages. "I told Mr. Strobridge then to go over to Auburn"—a town in the gold country—"and get some Chinamen and put them to work," Crocker continued. Strobridge was skeptical. He didn't doubt that Chinese would work cheap. But what did they know about construction? Crocker retorted, "Did they not build the Chinese Wall?"

The Chinese soon displaced the Irish on the Central Pacific, and they became the unsung heroes of the construction assault on the Sierra Nevada. Collis Huntington, another of the Central Pacific partners, had argued for avoiding fanfare at the groundbreaking ceremony; looking east from Sacramento, Huntington explained, "Those mountains over there look too ugly, and I see too much work ahead of us. We may fail, and if we do, I want to have as few people know it as we can."

The mountains looked even uglier up close. Their passes were higher than those on any railroad in America; the approaches to the passes were forbiddingly steep. The surveyors and engineers did their best to wind the route along rivers and make looping curves that eased the grade. But some stretches required brute force, and no little courage. One section rounded a cliff face called Cape Horn for its resemblance to that daunting South American landmark. Try as they might, the engineers could not find an alternative to cutting a roadbed out of the thousand-foot-tall, solid granite face. No one in America had ever accomplished such a feat. James Strobridge stared at the cliff and wondered if it could be done. The head man of one of the Chinese crews approached him and said it could. He said his people had done similar work in the gorges of the Yangtze River at home. They could crack this nut. Strobridge told him to have at it.

The Chinese said they'd need reeds from the Sacramento delta. From these they wove baskets big enough to hold a man. Ropes anchored at the top of the cliff dangled the baskets and the men inside them to the level of the proposed rail grade. The basket men swung hammers that drove steel drills into the granite, making holes into which they tamped black powder. Upon lighting the fuses, they signaled up the ropes to be hauled out of the way before the powder went off. The powder roared and the loosened rock thundered down into the valley below, and the aerial sappers inched their way around Cape Horn.

Crocker, Huntington and the other two Central Pacific partners—Leland Stanford and Mark Hopkins—came to appreciate the value of the Chinese crews. "Without them it would be impossible to go on with the work," Hopkins declared.

Even so, the Central Pacific foursome demurred when the Chinese demanded a wage hike. They wanted a raise to $40 per month, more than the Irish had been making, and a reduction in the workday from eleven hours to ten. They put down their tools and said they wouldn't pick them up until their terms were met.

The partners refused, judging that this demand would be followed by others. They said that if the Chinese wouldn't work, neither would they eat. Deep in the mountains, the construction crews depended on the company for provisions. The partners halted food shipments. The workers felt the pinch. "They really began to suffer," said Edwin Crocker, brother of Charles, and a lawyer and member of the Central Pacific board of directors. "None of us went near them for a week—did not want to exhibit anxiety. Then Charles went up, and they gathered around him, and he told them that he would not be dictated to, that he made the rules for them and not they for him." Some of the strikers said they wanted to go back to work but feared retribution from their fellows. "Charley told them that he would protect them, and his men would shoot down any man that attempted to do the laborers any injury. He had the sheriff and posse come up to see that there was no fighting."

The strikers' hunger and the threat of violence drove them back to the job. The construction resumed.

The Union Pacific, plowing across the plains of Nebraska and Wyoming, had labor issues of its own. During the first phase of construction, while the Civil War continued, the Union Pacific had to compete with the Union army for manpower. Irish immigrants sometimes deemed labor on the railroad preferable to service in the military, but not always. The end of the war freed up soldiers to become track layers, yet by making the alternative to railroad work less onerous, it made that work comparatively less attractive. The construction never stopped for lack of workers, but it sometimes slowed.

The Union Pacific crews, on the Great Plains, covered ground much faster than the Central Pacific crews in the Sierra Nevada. As the westbound line extended from Nebraska into Wyoming and on toward the mountains, it dragged in its wake a rolling construction camp that looked much like the mining camps of the California gold country, only mobile. "Hell on wheels" was what the wide-eyed press called the gaggle of saloons, brothels and gambling halls that did their best to relieve the workers of their hard-earned money, typically with the workers' enthusiastic cooperation. The first permanent towns along the Union Pacific route included pieces of the caravan that dropped off as the construction passed on.

The Union Pacific confronted one challenge the Central Pacific was largely spared. By the 1860s the Indians of California had been so devastated and demoralized that they posed little threat to the construction crews. But the tribes of the Great Plains were as formidable as they had ever been. Epidemics had scourged them, if not as badly as some of the tribes that lived in closer quarters, yet those who survived developed a degree of resistance to the diseases. The Plains tribes, including the Sioux, Cheyennes and Arapahos, understood that the railroad signaled a mortal threat. The Indians had harassed the wagon trains heading to Oregon and California, stampeding horses and cattle or exacting tribute for not doing so, but because the emigrants typically traveled in large groups, and because they clearly were just passing through the Indian lands, the tribes saw little reason to contest their passage.

The railroad was a different matter. Where the emigrant trains left tracks that blew away in the next prairie wind, the railroad tracks were fixed to the earth for all time, apparently. The railroad tracks disrupted the movement of the buffalo, on which the Plains peoples depended. The towns and depots the Union Pacific planted along the line sat squarely in territory the Indians called their own. Until now the Plains tribes had been spared the experience of the Eastern tribes, the Oregon tribes and the California tribes: of being physically displaced by large numbers of settlers. The railroad suggested that the Plains exception was coming to an end.

The tribes fought back. War parties of Sioux and Cheyennes attacked the surveyors and construction crews. At first the attacks were demonstrative, involving the theft of horses, destruction of equipment and removal of survey markers, but little loss of life. In time they grew more serious. Indian raiders in 1867 killed several workers, mutilated the dead and left the remains as warning to the others.

The most spectacular, though not the most lethal, attack involved a trainload of government officials, investors and journalists brought from Washington to inspect and publicize the construction. A band of a hundred Indians surrounded the train and its military escort. The visitors weren't injured physically, but their composure was wounded, and they returned east with tales of the ferocious savages that still roamed the West.

Their stories prompted demands that the government take action against the Plains tribes. "We've got to clean the damn Indians out or give up building the Union Pacific Railroad," said Grenville Dodge, superintendent of construction for Union Pacific. "The government may take its choice!" Thomas Durant, overall head of the Union Pacific project, appealed to Ulysses Grant, the ranking general at the War Department. "Unless some relief can be afforded by your department immediately," Durant said, "I beg leave to assure you that the entire work will be suspended."

TRAVELERS THROUGH THE SIERRA NEVADA HAD THE GOOD sense to avoid winter crossings. The Donner party had demonstrated what became of those caught by the snows that buried the passes in drifts twenty, forty, sixty feet deep.

The crews of the Central Pacific set aside such sense, yielding to the demands of the partners to build as many miles of track as possible before meeting the Union Pacific. The crews battled the snow till it drifted so deep in the passes they couldn't shovel it aside. Winters in the Sierra aren't uniformly cold; mild winds off the Pacific often lift daytime temperatures above freezing. The snow would start to melt. But overnight it would freeze again, now into solid masses of ice that defied any number of shovels. The crews turned to picks, then to explosives.

Eventually the construction engineers concluded that the best way to keep the route clear was to catch the snow before it hit the ground. The crews built long shed roofs over the roadbed. These allowed the track-laying work to proceed regardless of the weather and, once the rails were in place, protected the line from the elements.

For most of the way across the mountains, the crews carved the roadbed from the mountain faces. But in several spots they had no choice but to bore through the mountains themselves. They took cues from the miners, who had been boring and blasting mine shafts into the Sierra for more than a decade. The process was dangerous. The black blasting powder could prematurely ignite; loose rock could cave down on the crews. And it was slow, with progress measured in inches per day.

Snow shed. This structure and others like it kept the route and track clear of the deep Sierra drifts.

The Central Pacific partners grew impatient. Though the federal payout per mile in the mountains was three times the price for the plains, Leland Stanford and company knew that the Union Pacific was covering far more than three times as much ground as the Central Pacific crews. The tunnels were costing the partners money.

The Central Pacific engineers explained to Stanford and the others that there was an alternative to black powder: nitroglycerin. It was new, and it had a reputation for being touchy. An early experiment by the Central Pacific with nitro had resulted in several deaths when a worker inadvertently hit some nitro with his hammer.

The slow pace of progress in the mountains grew more frustrating by the day. The crew of hundreds of men could go no faster

Chinese workers on the Central Pacific. Here they are tackling the crest of the Sierra Nevada, digging and blasting the Summit Tunnel.

than the few who could crowd into the tunnel and do the blasting and mucking. Eventually James Strobridge determined to try nitro again. He enlisted a Scottish chemist named James Howden, an expert on nitroglycerin and its properties. Howden trained the blasters in its use, and before long it became another tool among many. It was still dangerous, of course. "Many an honest John went to China feet first," recalled a Central Pacific engineer.

But the nitro was several times as powerful as the black powder, with the additional benefit that it was smokeless, so the muckers could move right in and start hauling out the rubble. The faster progress seemed worth the danger. Mark Hopkins heard from Charles Crocker after an inspection. "Charles has just come from the tunnel and he thinks some of them are making three feet per day," Hopkins noted. "Hurrah for nitroglycerine!"

WHILE THE CENTRAL PACIFIC WAS DOMESTICATING NITRO-glycerin, the U.S. army was taming the Plains Indians, at least sufficiently for the work of the Union Pacific crews to proceed. More soldiers arrived, and they kept the Indians away from the workers. The Central Pacific was still grappling with the Sierra granite when the Union Pacific crested the Rockies in southwestern Wyoming. The Union's Thomas Durant shared the news with the Central's Leland Stanford. "We send you greeting from the highest summit our line crosses between the Atlantic and the Pacific Oceans, 8200 feet above tidewater," Durant wrote. "Have commenced laying iron on the down grade westward."

Stanford knew that Durant's teams had built many more miles of road than his own had. And he understood that Durant was rubbing this accomplishment in his face. But Stanford also knew that the Union's greatest challenge, the Wasatch Mountains, lay ahead, while the Central's, the Sierra Nevada, would soon be behind. He refused to be provoked. "Though you may approach the union of the two roads faster than ourselves, you cannot exceed us in earnestness of desire for that event," Stanford said. "We cheerfully yield you the palm of superior elevation; 7042 feet has been quite sufficient to satisfy our highest ambition."

Though Stanford yielded to Durant in elevation, he wasn't going to yield in anything else. Once the Central crews came out of the mountains, they tore across the desert of Nevada as swiftly as the Union crews had flown across the plains. Yet still their chiefs pressed them to go faster, even at the sacrifice of construction quality and road safety. "Make it cheap," the Central's Collis Huntington demanded of the crews. "Run up and down on the maximum grade instead of making deep cut and fills, and when you can make any time in the construction by using wood instead of stone for culverts &c., use wood, and if we should have now and then a piece of road washed out for the want of a culvert, we could put one in hereafter."

Huntington's partners agreed. Mark Hopkins, noting that the Railroad Act required construction to meet the approval of federal inspectors before the company was paid, remarked that approval wouldn't be a serious problem. The Central Pacific—and the Union Pacific—had friends in the right places. "We *know* the commissioners will readily accept as poor a road as we can wish to offer for acceptance," Hopkins said.

As the crews of the two companies drew closer to each other, negotiations began over where the actual meeting would take place. Neither side wished to concede any mileage to the other it could possibly claim for itself. A committee of Congress finally decreed that the joining of rails should take place at Promontory Summit, on the north side of the Great Salt Lake.

Nothing at so remote a spot in America had ever received such broad national attention. Reporters rode special trains, one from Omaha, the other from Sacramento. Dr. James Stillman traveled in the train that carried Leland Stanford. Spring had already arrived in the lowlands of California, but snow still clogged the passes of the Sierra Nevada. Yet the sheds allowed easy passage. "We are cribbed in by timbers, snow-sheds they call them; but how strong!" marveled Stillman. "Every timber is a tree trunk, braced and bolted to withstand the snow-slide that starts in mid-winter from the great heights above, and gathering volume as it descends, sweeps desolation in its path; the air is cold around us; snow is on every hand; it looks down upon us from the cliffs, up to us from the ravines, drips from over head and is frozen into stalactites from the rocky wall along which our road is blasted, midway of the granite mountain."

From the sheds they passed into the tunnels drilled through the rock. "We are in pitchy darkness in the heart of the mountain," Stillman wrote. They emerged into the brilliant light of a sunny day at high altitude. Below and to the right lay Donner Lake. Stillman and the others couldn't help thinking that no one crossing these mountains would ever again suffer the fate that had befallen the poor party trapped there two decades before.

Yet dangers persisted. Work crews cutting trees above the track, uninformed of the schedule of the special train, had felled a large trunk that lay athwart the track. The train, rounding a bend, had to apply full brakes. A reporter riding the pilot, or cowcatcher, in front of the engine dove to the side to save his life. The engine was damaged; the cars had to be hitched to a substitute.

Stanford's train included forty-niners who recalled the trials of the Nevada desert. "Several of our party were among the overland emigrants," Stillman wrote, "and they pointed out where, one by one, their animals perished, where they abandoned their wagons, and where their guns—the last article they could afford to part with—were planted, muzzle downward, into the hillocks in the desperate struggle for water and life." Even as the veterans of the trail recollected the old days, they savored the new. "It was a country that one could not travel over too fast."

The joining ceremony was delayed when the train carrying Thomas Durant and the Omaha contingent was held up by Union Pacific crews who hadn't been paid on time. The crews demanded $200,000 before they would let the officials and reporters go. They eventually settled for $50,000, amid suggestions that the kidnapping was a sham, a trick devised by Durant to speed payment of money owed him and his partners. In time much greater shenanigans would be uncovered in the financing of the Union Pacific; for now the ploy, if such it was, seemed in keeping with Durant's close-to-the-vest approach to management. "Durant is so strange a man that I am prepared to believe any sort of rascality that may be charged against him," one of his associates declared.

The epic moment came in May 1869. Not since Lee's surrender to Grant at Appomattox had the nation so eagerly awaited news of national importance. Telegraph wires were linked to the rails and to a symbolic golden spike that would tie the two ends of the line together; upon the moment of joining, an electric signal flashed to both coasts. News correspondents appended their breathless accounts. "THE LAST RAIL IS LAID!" shouted the Associated Press. "THE LAST SPIKE IS DRIVEN! THE PACIFIC RAILROAD IS COMPLETED! THE POINT OF JUNCTION IS 1086 MILES WEST OF THE MISSOURI RIVER AND 690 MILES EAST OF SACRAMENTO CITY."

The meeting of the rails. At length the epic project was completed, at Promontory Summit, north of the Great Salt Lake.

The Liberty Bell was rung in Philadelphia; cannons were fired in Washington; church bells clanged in New York and Boston and other cities. San Francisco had celebrated earlier, when the original ceremony was supposed to be held; it celebrated again, with cannons, rifles, side-arms, bells and whistles.

36

SAINTS AND SINNERS

M OST WESTERN SETTLERS APPLAUDED THE APPROACH OF the railroad, delighted that it would bring the outside world closer. If they noticed that it embodied the largest federal subsidy given to any part of the country in American history until then, they didn't obviously fret. Only later would the legend of Western individualism develop; at the time, the Westerners were happy for all the help they could get. Those many thousands of Westerners who took advantage of the Homestead Act, another huge federal subsidy, felt doubly blessed.

One particular group of Westerners, however, had decidedly mixed feelings upon the approach and completion of the Pacific railroad. The Mormons had encountered unremitting hostility in the East, and been driven from one state to another; their prophet, Joseph Smith, had been killed by an anti-Mormon mob in Illinois. Smith's successor, Brigham Young, decreed that the earthly safety of the Latter-day Saints required leaving the United States. At that time—the mid-1840s—Mexico still lay to America's west as much as to its south. Young determined to cross the Rocky Mountains and find a home for the Saints in Mexican territory, beyond the reach of American law and the baleful influence of American gentiles.

Then the American war with Mexico began, threatening to frustrate the Mormon exodus by Americanizing the Saints' projected home. But Young could be flexible when necessary. He shifted from expatriatism to patriotism, coordinating with the U.S. army in raising several hundred young men to serve against Mexico. And he apprised the government of the Mormons' plans in moving west. "The cause of our exile we need not repeat; it is already with you," he wrote to James Polk. "Suffice it to say that a combination of fortuitous, illegal and unconstitutional circumstances have placed us in our present situation, on a journey which we design shall end in a location west of the Rocky Mountains, and within the basin of the Great Salt Lake, or Bear River valley, as soon as circumstances shall permit, believing that to be a point where a good living will require hard labor, and consequently will be coveted by no other people."

Other Saints were less diplomatic. "We owe the United States nothing," declared one Mormon editorialist. "We go out by force, as exiles from freedom. The government and people owe us millions for the destruction of life and property in Missouri and Illinois. The blood of our best men stains the land, and the ashes of our property will preserve it till God comes out of his hiding place, and gives this nation a hotter portion than he did Sodom and Gomorrah."

The Mormon trek became a defining chapter in the history of the Latter-day Saints, combining adventurous elements of the westward movement generally with religious sentiments that might have been pulled from the Book of Exodus. Like Moses and the Israelites, Young and the Mormons left for the West when they could, not when they would. Too late to cross the Rockies before the first snows, they established winter quarters on the west bank of the Missouri River in Nebraska Territory. The Mormons' previous flights had sharpened their evacuation skills; now the group functioned like a well-trained army. Within weeks they built a regular village of sod houses, log cabins and even a few brick buildings. Their town had streets and blocks, and zoning: this part for residences, that for stores and workshops, and that over there for stockyards and slaughterhouses. Young and the other church elders combined religious and secular authority; their dual mandate made their community more orderly than any other on the frontier, or perhaps anywhere in America. Yet authority and obedience couldn't keep all the Saints alive; infectious disease swept through the town, as it recurrently swept through all the river towns. Several hundred died.

In the spring of 1847 Brigham Young led a vanguard out of their winter quarters up the Oregon Trail, which they followed to South Pass. Beyond the pass they met Jim Bridger, the mountain man, who, in response to Young's queries, expressed doubt about the Salt Lake basin as a spot for a large settlement. It was very dry, he observed, shaking his head.

Sam Brannan showed up a short while later. Brannan made his pitch for California, but the very things that attracted Brannan to California—its fine weather, fertile soil and good harbors (gold hadn't been discovered yet)—repelled Young. For Young, the *less* attractive a place was, the more he liked it. The Mormons wouldn't be escaping the jurisdiction of the United States, but they could still hope to elude its close supervision.

Young's party headed southwest. Young fell ill; he was riding in a wagon when the train emerged from the Wasatch Mountains east of present Salt Lake City. Raising his eyes to take in the desolate wastes of the Salt Lake desert, he declared that this was the place. This was where the new Zion would be planted in the wilderness.

THE MORMON MIGRATION TO UTAH OVERLAPPED THE AMERican emigrations to Oregon and California. It was like those emigrations in some ways but distinct in others. Tens of thousands of Saints made the same dusty journey across the plains and mountains the emigrants to Oregon and California made. Most were American citizens, but a striking number, many more than in the migrations to the Far West, were immigrants fresh off the boat. Mormon missionaries were active in Europe; thousands of new converts crossed the Atlantic before crossing North America.

The most important distinction of the Mormon migration was its religious motive. Except for a few missionaries, Oregon was settled by people looking for land, health and other earthly goals. California's lure was its gold. The Mormons went west seeking eternal salvation. Their zeal for Zion gave them energy to accomplish great feats of endurance on the trail. But it occasionally led to disaster and tragedy.

By the 1850s the Oregon Trail—now the Oregon and California Trail—was a well-trod route, with trading posts at convenient intervals and guides conversant with the best practices for cross-continent travel. Yet Brigham Young thought he could improve on the standard model. Theology and politics prompted his desire to innovate. For Young and other Mormons, the physical gathering of Zion was a crucial part of their belief system; all Mormons should come to Utah as soon as possible. Politically, filling Utah with Mormons would serve the purpose of securing the new Zion against gentiles who might want to settle there. After the Kansas-Nebraska Act of 1854 enshrined the principle of popular sovereignty—that the settlers in a territory had the right to determine their own government—Young sought to ensure that when the residents of Utah drafted a state constitution, Mormons controlled the process.

But getting to Utah cost money, especially for those European converts who had to sail the Atlantic first. Many of the Europeans were poor. No small part of the appeal of Mormonism was its promise, by something called the Perpetual Emigrating Fund, of financial assistance to immigrants who chose to make a new life in America. Yet the Mormon church wasn't wealthy. Simply building Salt Lake City, and dealing with the problems that beset the Mormon farmers—including drought and plagues of grasshoppers—stretched the church's finances. Brigham Young was eager to discover any device or method that trimmed the travel cost to Utah.

The biggest single outlay for most overland emigrants was a covered wagon and its team. If emigrants could do without wagons, they could travel at much less expense. One of the early Mormon trains had overtaken a thrifty Scotsman who carried his goods in a wheelbarrow. Questioned about this novelty, the fellow praised his choice of transport. He didn't have to worry about feeding and tending horses, he said, or about Indians stealing them.

When Brigham Young heard the story, he was fascinated. He concluded that substituting wheelbarrows—or handcarts—for covered wagons could cut the cost of emigration dramatically. As a young man he had worked as a carpenter, and he now devised specifications for the ideal vehicle. "Take good hickory for the axle trees," he wrote to one of his subordinates, "and make them, say, two inches in diameter at the shoulder and 1¼ at the point, say four and a half feet from point to point; make the hubs out of hardhack or iron wood, or if they cannot be had, get young hickory, small and tough and turn them out about six inches long and five or six inches in the diameter." The wheels should be four-and-a-half or five feet in diameter. "The axle should be up high enough for a man to draw on the level. The rims should be split out of hickory like the rim to a spinning wheel, only thicker, fastened and lined with green hides when they can be obtained." Forgoing iron rims, by itself, would reduce the cost dramatically. Young recognized that a handcart could not carry all the provisions a family would need, but the Mormons in Utah would take care of that. "If it is once known that such a company is on the plains, there will be no difficulty in having the brethren from this place meeting them with provisions nearly if not quite half way."

Not all the Mormons thought the handcart scheme wise. It was difficult enough simply to walk across the plains and the Rockies. To have to push loaded carts would tax the strength of even healthy young men, let alone the women who might be called into service. Moreover, wheels rimmed with iron sometimes failed on the trail; wholly wooden wheels would fare much worse.

Yet Young's word was law among the Saints. The church leadership endorsed the project. The challenges it entailed should be considered a test of faith, they declared. "Families might start from Missouri river, with cows, hand-carts, wheel-barrows, with little flour, and no unnecessaries, and come to this place quicker, and with less fatigue than by following the heavy trains with their cumbrous herds, which they are obliged to drive miles to feed," an epistle from the leadership declared. "Do you not like this method of travelling? Do you think salvation costs too much? If so, it is not worth having."

The rank and file responded. "The Lord has promised, through His servant Brigham, that the hand-cart companies shall be blessed with health and strength, and be met part way with teams and provisions from the Valley," declared Jean Jaques, a British convert. "And I am not afraid to prophesy that those who go by hand-carts, and continue faithful and obedient, will be blessed more than they ever dreamed."

Five companies set out in the summer of 1856. The first three left Iowa City, in eastern Iowa, in June. They comprised nearly eight hundred emigrants, mostly from England, Wales and Scandinavia, with some Italians thrown in. Problems arose at once. The design and construction of the carts fell short of what the journey required. "We had them to eternally patch—mornings, noons and nights," one of the trekkers recalled. The wheels and axles lacked sufficient grease, making them harder to push than necessary. And the racket they created took a toll on the travelers' nerves. "They mowed and growled, screeched and squealed, so that a person could hear them for miles."

The biggest problem was hunger. Even with provisions presumably awaiting them at the halfway mark, the handcarts couldn't carry enough to keep the trekkers decently fed. "There was very little food to cook, and we were too tired to cook it," one of the migrants remembered. Another said, "I never was so hungry in my life." A woman who had been twelve years old on the journey remarked, "At night we often went to bed without supper." She had been enchanted, amid her hunger and weariness, by a stream-side spot. She turned to her father and said, "Let's build a little log house and stay in this place always." He looked at her and asked what they would do about food. She replied, "Do as we're doing now—go without."

In their race against time—that is, against the dwindling of their rations—the leaders of the handcart companies resorted to separating the children from the adults and compelling them to make a head start on the day. "There were 30 children in the company and early every morning they were sent on ahead of the grownups all in one bunch," recounted one of the travelers, an immigrant from Iceland. "Some of them had very little clothing but they all wore hats. They were driven along with willows and had to keep walking as long as they could. No use to cry or complain." The practice wrung the hearts of the parents of the children. "It was hard for parents to see their little 5 and 6 year olds driven along like sheep." But the leaders of the train had decreed it, and so it was done.

For all their suffering, the three trains made it to Utah, with total casualties not much worse than wagon trains typically suffered. They were greeted at Salt Lake City by a brass band and by Brigham Young himself. "And thus has been successfully accomplished a plan devised by the wisdom and forethought of our President"—Young—"for gathering the poor," proclaimed the *Deseret News*, the paper of the church.

THERE WAS ANOTHER CHAPTER TO THE HANDCART STORY that year. Two other trains were slow hitting the trail. One set out in mid-August, the other in early September. Everyone who knew about the challenges of the plains and mountains realized that starting so late in the season was risky, yet the emigrants put their faith in God. "They expect to get cold fingers and toes," wrote one of the Mormon officials directing the emigration. "But they have this faith and confidence towards God that he will overrule the storms that may come in the season thereof and turn them away, that their path may be free from suffering more than they can bear."

The handcart companies went ahead, and the suffering started
soon enough. September snows are not unusual on the high plains;
October snows are normal. The handcart emigrants were unprepared for serious cold; constrained by what the carts could carry,
they lacked anything like winter gear. Making matters worse was
the fact that handcarts, unlike covered wagons, offered no shelter
from storms. In rain, sleet and snow, the emigrants overnighted in
the open or in tents chosen for lightness rather than warmth. Their
bodies shivered, desperately burning calories to fend off hypothermia; the shivering aggravated the shortness of their rations.

Long before they reached South Pass, the emigrants battled
deep snow. "A severe day," wrote Levi Savage, a captain of a group
of a hundred handcarts, on October 23. "The wind blew awful cold
and hard." The trail climbed Rocky Ridge, the sharpest pitch of
the route, and the snows kept the emigrants struggling until long
after dark. The night camp afforded little respite. "Few tents were
pitched," Savage said, "and men, women and children sit shivering with cold around their small fires." The last stragglers arrived
just before dawn, in one of the few wagons that accompanied the
handcart train. "Some badly frozen, some dying, some dead. It was
certainly heartrending to hear children crying for mothers, and
mothers crying for children."

Hope appeared at Devil's Gate, where the Sweetwater River
cuts a gash in a line of granite. Six wagons sent to provision the
handcart trains met the emigrants there. But the food and clothing
they brought fell far below the need.

The suffering worsened. Part of one train took refuge from the
freezing wind in a ravine just off the trail. The weather pinned
them down. "We stayed in the ravine five or six days on reduced
rations," a member of the group recalled. "One night a windstorm
blew down almost every tent. Many perished of cold and hunger at
this place." A member of the rescue party wrote Brigham Young
from Devil's Gate, characterizing the emigrants as he found them:
"between five and six hundred men, women and children, worn

down by drawing hand carts through snow and mud; fainting by the way side; falling, chilled by the cold; children crying; their limbs stiffened by cold; their feet bleeding and some of them bare to snow and frost."

The rescue parties saved the two trains from utter annihilation. Eventually enough wagons came to feed the surviving emigrants and carry them to Salt Lake City. Brigham Young's loyalists lauded the rescue effort, which would be etched in Mormon history as an example of how the Saints looked out for one another, and God looked out for them all. "Notwithstanding some deaths and the suffering and frost bite since leaving the North Fork of the Platte River, we can plainly recognize the kind hand of an overruling Providence in opening a way of escape for so many, in dictating wise and timely counsels to the living Oracles," the *Deseret News* asserted.

The deaths, in fact, ran into the hundreds—perhaps the highest toll suffered by any body of emigrants in the history of the West. A survivor remembered the journey as "one long funeral march." Jean Jaques, the British Mormon, was not usually a critic of Brigham Young, but he thought the handcart debacle a needless tragedy. "It was cruel to a degree far beyond the power of language to express," Jaques said, "and the more so for the reason that the worst parts of the experience were entirely unnecessary, because avoidable by timely measures and more sagacious management."

THE QUESTIONING OF YOUNG'S LEADERSHIP MIGHT HAVE BEEN more intense had Mormons not felt the need, at just this moment, to band together against the outside world. At one time or other, in every federal territory—which was to say, in every part of the West except Texas and California, which became states without having been federal territories—friction developed between federally appointed officials and the locals. The latter typically looked on the former the way American colonists had looked on British officials just before the Revolutionary War: as outsiders who had legal authority but no moral right to tell them how to behave. The locals knew that, under the Constitution, they one day would inherit political power. They chafed at restrictions in the meantime.

Nowhere did the friction between federals and locals rise to more acrimonious levels than in Utah Territory during the 1850s. Many Mormons looked askance at secular government of any sort; the point of their fleeing to the desert Zion was to be governed by Saints, not sinners. Most of the American Mormons had memories of mistreatment at the hands of American gentiles and so were sensitive about anything that smacked of more of the same.

Federal officials, in turn, distrusted the Mormons. They knew that Brigham Young and the Mormons had intended to escape American jurisdiction by their flight west; Washington could only assume that the separatist hopes still burned in Mormon hearts. And at a time when Southerners were threatening to bolt the Union over slavery, the nation's government was in no mood to abide Mormon challenges to federal authority.

Nor did the American public at large have any love for Mormons. Most American Christians considered Mormonism a species of heresy. The bounds of tolerance of the Protestant majority were already being tested by the Catholic immigration from Ireland. But at least the Catholics ascribed the same primacy to the Bible that the Protestants did, and they hewed to essentially the same understanding of God's history with humans. The Mormons, with their own holy book and their own sacred history, were beyond the pale. And when, in 1852, Brigham Young made public the Mormon embrace of polygamy, the sect seemed more threatening still.

President Millard Fillmore sought to smooth things by appointing Brigham Young as Utah's territorial governor. The appointment had the desired effect with the Mormons, but not with other federal officials in Utah. Judges and Indian agents repeatedly found themselves blocked by Young; they complained that he was determined to govern Utah with the same unchecked authority he wielded over the Latter-day Saints. Their complaints fed the anti-Mormon feeling in American politics. In 1856 the Republican party ran John Frémont for president on a platform demanding that the federal territories be rescued from "those twin relics of barbarism—polygamy and slavery." Democrat James Buchanan, the election's winner, decried the "despotism of Brigham Young" and vowed to bring the Mormons to heel.

Buchanan appointed a new governor and ordered a large force of U.S. army regulars to Utah. The Mormons responded with alarm, contending that Washington was declaring war on them and their religion. Brigham Young called out the Mormon militia and prepared to defend the new Zion, perhaps to the death.

AMID THE MOUNTING TENSION IN THE LATE SUMMER OF 1857, a wagon train from Arkansas, bound for California, entered southern Utah. Most non-Mormon emigrants tried to avoid the Mormons if they could. The main route to California and Oregon ran well north of the Great Salt Lake, and the California Trail crossed into Utah Territory, which then included modern Nevada, only far west of Salt Lake City. But sometimes the emigrants needed provisions or, if too late on the trail, a place to winter. In the latter case, a tense sojourn often followed. After the 1853 killing of U.S. army captain John Gunnison and eleven of his men in southern Utah by Ute Indians, rumors circulated among gentiles that Brigham Young had goaded the Indians into the slayings. Gentiles crossing Mormon lands grew even more nervous.

The 1857 Arkansas train included some Missourians as well. Mormons held much against Missouri, where their persecution in earlier days had been especially severe; this train was watched with gravest suspicion. Brigham Young had ordered the faithful to husband resources against a possible clash with the U.S. army; consequently the Arkansans and Missourians, who had expected to purchase grain and other provisions, found themselves shut out. The emigrant train included a large herd of cattle, which the Mormons judged they could use in the event of war. The cattle also tempted resident Paiute Indians, with whom the Mormons had developed good relations. In fact, so good were Mormon relations with the Indians that Brigham Young could credibly threaten to unleash the tribes against westbound emigrant trains. "If the government dare to force the issue, I shall not hold the Indians by the wrist any longer," he told a U.S. army officer. "If the issue comes, you may tell the government to stop all emigration across the continent, for the Indians will kill all who attempt it."

The alarm among the Mormons that they might once again have to flee a home they had made, their resentment at decades of mistreatment at the hands of gentiles and the American government, their feeling of strength in their fortress community amid the mountains, a desire to signal to America at large that the Saints were not to be trifled with, the annoyance of dealing with yet another party of emigrants crossing their territory, this one with property worth stealing—all these thoughts and emotions gave rise to a murderous scheme among Mormons in southern Utah.

The decision to massacre the emigrants might have developed in stages. Mormon leaders in Cedar City signaled to the Paiutes that these emigrants were fair game for attack. When the Paiutes, accustomed to mere rustling of a few cattle from passing trains, registered reluctance at a frontal assault, Mormon militiamen promised to join them. The attack was made at a place called Mountain Meadows. Several of the emigrants were killed; the rest gathered their wagons into a defensive circle. A siege ensued.

The leaders of the Mormon plot concluded that they had got themselves in too deep to turn back. The besieged emigrants knew that white men, and not just Indians, had been involved in the murders of the deceased. Should word get out to this effect, with U.S. troops on the way, it would strengthen the case of those who wanted to crush the Mormons. The plotters decided to kill all the witnesses. They would blame the Paiutes.

They devised a new plan. One of their number would approach the emigrants and offer assistance in escaping the Paiutes. This man, John Lee, would explain that the Indians had consented to safe passage for the emigrants, under strict conditions. The emigrants must put down their arms. They must agree to leave their cattle behind. The women and children must come out first. The men could follow.

The emigrants were suspicious of these conditions. And they queried Lee about the white men who had joined the Paiute attack. But Lee deflected the questions and convinced the emigrants that, whatever their suspicions, they had little alternative. They were short of water. Those wounded in the attack were especially suffering. The tight circle of wagons had become a prison. The emigrants' only hope was to trust Lee. They accepted his terms.

Out came the women and children, some in wagons, some walking along the dusty road. They proceeded past members of the Mormon militia, who presented themselves as the emigrants' protectors against the Indians.

After the women and children were clear of the camp, the men followed. All were tired from the siege; the wounded were in obvious pain.

When everyone was out in the open, unarmed and undefended, the leader of the militia shouted, "Halt!" This was less an order to the emigrants than a signal to the militiamen and their Paiute accomplices. The militia opened fire on the emigrant men. Most fell in the initial volley. Those who weren't killed outright were dispatched by close-range fire or by knife. The ones who tried to flee were run down and killed.

The Paiutes fell upon the women and children. With guns, arrows, knives, clubs and stones, they killed them brutally and swiftly. The only survivors were children deemed too young to bear witness to the carnage.

Within minutes the deed was done. To cover the crime, the militiamen and the Paiutes looted the bodies and carried away the emigrants' property. When the world learned that more than 120 emigrants had been killed, the Mormons blamed the Paiutes. For years they stuck to their story, obstructing investigation and denying responsibility. They largely succeeded; only one man, John Lee, was eventually convicted. Their success owed something to the very enormity of the crime. Even in the West, where killings of Indians by whites hardly raised an eyebrow, and killings of whites by Indians were not unexpected, the cold-blooded mass slaughter of whites by whites was hard to believe. For many in Utah and beyond, it was easier not to.

37

ONCE WE WERE HAPPY

"I AM A LAKOTA OF THE OGLALA BAND," BLACK ELK TOLD an interviewer. "My father's name was Black Elk, and his father before him bore the name, and the father of his father, so that I am the fourth to bear it." Black Elk recalled his earliest days. "I was born in the Moon of the Popping Trees on the Little Powder River in the Winter When the Four Crows were killed"—December 1863—"and I was three years old when my father's right leg was broken in the Battle of the Hundred Slain."

The Battle of the Hundred Slain was a turning point in the history of the Lakotas, or western Sioux, and it stuck in Black Elk's memory. "I had never seen a Wasichu then, and did not know what one looked like," he said. *Wasichu* was what the Lakotas called white people, though it didn't refer to their skin color; African American soldiers in Lakota country were called black Wasichus. "But every one was saying that the Wasichus were coming and that they were going to take our country and rub us all out and that we should all have to die fighting. It was the Wasichus who got rubbed out in that battle, and all the people were talking about it for a long while." With hindsight, Black Elk added, "But a hundred Wasichus were not much if there were others and others without number where those came from."

Only later did Black Elk learn what the battle was all about. "Up on the Madison Fork the Wasichus had found much of the yellow metal that they worship and that makes them crazy, and they wanted to have a road up through our country to the place where the yellow metal was; but my people did not want the road. It would scare the bison and make them go away, and also it would let the other Wasichus come in like a river. They told us that they wanted only to use a little land, as much as a wagon would take between the wheels; but our people knew better. And when you look about you now, you can see what it was they wanted."

Black Elk's memory flitted backward to a time before the white men came, and forward to a much later date: "Once we were happy in our own country and we were seldom hungry, for then the two-leggeds and the four-leggeds lived together like relatives, and there was plenty for them and for us. But the Wasichus came, and they have made little islands for the four-leggeds, and always these islands are becoming smaller, for around them surges the gnawing flood of the Wasichu; and it is dirty with lies and greed."

Black Elk resumed his story: "And so when the soldiers came and built themselves a town of logs there on the Piney Fork of the Powder, my people knew they meant to have their road and take our country and maybe kill us all when they were strong enough. Crazy Horse was only about nineteen years old then, and Red Cloud was still our great chief. In the Moon of the Changing Season"—October—"he called together all the scattered bands of the Lakota for a big council on the Powder River, and when we went on the warpath against the soldiers, a horseback could ride through our villages from sunrise until the day was above his head, so far did our camp stretch along the valley of the river; for many of our friends, the Shyela and the Blue Clouds, had come to help us fight." The Shyela were the Cheyennes and the Blue Clouds the Arapahos. "And it was about when the bitten moon"—the last quarter moon—"was delayed in the Time of the Popping Trees"— December—"when the hundred were rubbed out."

BLACK ELK'S BOYHOOD OCCURRED AMID A REVOLUTION IN THE ecology of the Great Plains. Or perhaps it was simply evolution accelerated. When humans first arrived in North America via the Bering land bridge, the continent they invaded teemed with animals large and small. Some were prey to the arriving hunters; these were what drew the invaders on. The biggest game included mammoths and mastodons, elephant kin that taxed the cleverness and courage of the hunters but provided a fat payoff when a hunt succeeded. So clever and bold were the hunters that they sorely strained the populations of the beasts, leading—perhaps in conjunction with the same climate changes that trapped hunters and prey alike on the eastern side of the Pacific—to the animals' extinction. A broad principle was demonstrated: that the introduction of new organisms, in this case humans, into a habitat could wreak havoc on the existing ecology.

Members of the genus *Equus* were among the species that greeted the human invaders but didn't long survive their coming. Whether hunting or changing climate was the larger cause of their demise is as uncertain as with the mammoths, but by the time the Spanish reached mainland North America in the early sixteenth century, the ancient horses weren't even a memory among the indigenous peoples. The horses the Spanish brought gave their soldiers a tremendous advantage in their campaigns against the Indians, demonstrating that the disruption attendant upon the introduction of a new species could be cultural as well as ecological. The Spanish took pains to preserve their advantage by keeping the horses away from the Indians. But horses occasionally escaped. Possibly some got loose from Coronado's expeditionary force in the 1540s, or from that of fellow Spaniard Hernando de Soto, who explored the Mississippi Valley at about the same time.

Yet no evidence shows horses in the possession of native peoples until a century later. More was involved in adopting the horse than simply capturing horses. The Indians had to learn how horses and humans interact. The Spanish settlements in New Mexico placed horses and Indians in close proximity for decades; the Indians watched and learned what horses could do, how they could be trained for riding, and how herds of them might be managed.

The first horses acquired by Indians might have been gifts from Spanish missionaries to Indians who converted to Catholicism and adopted Spanish ways. Some horses might have been stolen by Indians. A revolt by the Pueblo people in the late seventeenth century put hundreds of horses in Indian hands, at a time when Indians had learned what to do with them.

Over the following decades the Indians and the horses adapted to each other. Settled peoples like the Pueblos found horses to be a convenience but not a life-changer. But for the migratory tribes of the Great Plains, who acquired horses by sale and theft from the Pueblos, horses upended thousands of years of habit. The Plains peoples, from the Apaches in the south to the Sioux in the north, suddenly became vastly more mobile than before. They had hunted buffalo on foot; now they could hunt on horseback. Dogs had dragged their tepees and other equipment; a horse could do the work of ten dogs. Dogs, being carnivores, had to be fed, in effect competing with the Indians for buffalo meat and other killed flesh. Horses, as herbivores, could eat the prairie grasses humans and dogs couldn't.

Horses changed the nature of warfare on the plains. Raiders now could roam over thousands of square miles, striking far from their camps and disappearing quickly. Spanish soldiers on horses had seemed almost godlike to the first Indians they encountered; Indian soldiers on horseback possessed a comparable advantage over tribes that still moved and fought afoot. Some tribes, most notably the Comanches, took military horsemanship beyond what the Spanish had accomplished, and seemed to their enemies a terrifying hybrid of man and beast.

Horses weren't an unmitigated blessing. The lore of the Cheyennes told of tribal elders making a choice for their people: to adopt the horse culture, as their neighbors the Comanches had done, or to stick to the traditional ways. The elders prayed to their principal god, who answered them through the senior priest. "If you have horses, everything will be changed for you forever," the god said. "You will have to move around a lot to find pasture for your horses. You will have to give up gardening and live by hunting and gathering, like the Comanches. And you will have to come out of your earth houses and live in tents. I will tell your women how to make them and how to decorate them. And there will be other changes. You will have to have fights with other tribes, who will want your pasture land or the places where you hunt. You will have to have real soldiers, who can protect the people. Think, before you decide."

The elders chose horses. The prophecy came true.

LIKE THE COMANCHES ON THE SOUTHERN PLAINS, THE SIOUX on the northern plains were a people on the move. The western Sioux—the Lakotas—had broken away from the eastern branch of their tribe, a forest people of Minnesota, in the seventeenth century, as the Ojibwa and other tribes from farther east, feeling pressure from tribes still farther east and from whites, pushed into their territory. The Lakotas lacked horses when they emerged onto the northern plains, and they developed pedestrian techniques for exploiting the primary resource of the plains, the buffalo. They would set fire to the grass when the wind was blowing toward a place where the level surface was broken by a ravine; the buffalo would flee the flames and be pinned at the edge of the ravine. Yet the weight of the herd behind would push many over the side; they would fall and break their legs. The Sioux hunters would kill them with spears and arrows.

The Lakotas discovered horses on the plains yet didn't immediately adopt them. Their existing life suited them well, and they might have anticipated the bargain described by the Cheyenne priest. Even when the Sioux began riding horses, they didn't at once become full nomads. During their time on the plains they had contrived to dominate the regional trading network. Lewis and Clark had encountered the Sioux dominance, in the form of the tribe's blockade of the upper Missouri River. The Sioux valued their stranglehold on the Missouri trade, and they were loath to jeopardize it by adopting the full horse culture and its nomadic requirements.

In fact, the Sioux expanded their commercial activities by joining the fur trade. They had no use for beaver pelts, but on learning that white people would pay for them, they began collecting the pelts and trading them for items they did value. They became adept in their new line. "The Sioux tribes are those who hunt most for the beaver and other good peltries of the Upper Missouri," a French trader observed. "They scour all the rivers and streams."

They scoured so well that the beaver disappeared. Like Joe Meek, the Sioux were compelled to find other work. At this point they turned fully toward the horse, and with it, the buffalo, which the horse allowed them to hunt more efficiently. The buffalo provided them sustenance; it also gave them a new item of commerce. The Sioux traded robes, dried meat and tongues to other Indians and to white traders.

They exhibited their characteristic energy, and ruthlessness. They eliminated or conquered all who stood in their way, wiping out entire villages of rivals and compelling others to pay tribute. They became the lords of the northern plains—respected, feared, obeyed.

They were an anomaly among Indian peoples in that their population increased at a time when the populations of other tribes were declining, often drastically. Their secret was employment of a vaccine against smallpox, acquired from some of their American trading partners. Between the beginning of the nineteenth century and the 1850s, the Sioux population quintupled, if only to around twenty-five thousand.

Observers predicted that the strength of the Sioux would continue to increase. "The day is not far off when the Sioux will possess the whole buffalo region, unless they are checked," a federal agent wrote.

To provide such a check, the U.S. government in 1851 called a peace conference, to be held at Fort Laramie. Ten thousand Indians came, from dozens of tribes. But the only tribe that really mattered—the one for which the conference had been called—was the Sioux. And on account of the Sioux the conference failed. The American officials tried to persuade the Sioux to stay north of the Platte River, the main emigrant route to Oregon and California. Black Hawk, the leader of the Oglala Sioux, refused. His people had conquered the lands the Americans sought to deny them, he said. "These lands once belonged to the Kiowas and the Crows, but we whipped those nations out of them, and in this we did what the white men do when they want the lands of the Indians." And this they would continue to do.

A clash was inevitable. The discovery of gold in Colorado in 1858 triggered a rush to that territory, smaller in scale than the rush to California, but sufficient to alarm the tribes of the plains. The miners—and the shopkeepers, saloon owners, hoteliers and all the others who followed the miners—meanwhile demanded protection, and such was the reputation of the Sioux that Congress swiftly complied. A territorial government was created for Colorado in 1861, and a governor—John Evans—appointed. As a first order of business, Evans oversaw the raising of a territorial militia, commanded by Colonel John Chivington.

Neither Evans nor Chivington displayed any desire for peace with the Indians. Upon receiving a peace offer from a delegation of Arapahos and Cheyennes, Evans responded, "What shall I do with the Third Colorado Regiment if I make peace? They have been raised to kill Indians, and they must kill Indians." The Civil War had begun, and Evans knew that if he didn't put the militia to use, they might be called into service against the Confederacy.

Chivington was even more bloody minded. He had been a Methodist minister, but he found a new calling as an Indian fighter. "Kill all the Indians you come across," he ordered his troops. That included women and children. "Nits make lice," he explained.

His soldiers got their chance in November 1864. Chivington led them against a camp of Cheyennes and Arapahos on Sand

Creek in eastern Colorado. Most of the men of the bands were away hunting; the camp consisted primarily of women, children and the old. There was no confusion about this. "I saw five squaws under a bank for shelter," an eyewitness recalled. "When the troops came up to them they ran out and showed their persons to let the soldiers know they were squaws and begged for mercy."

They received not mercy but the most brutal violence. "The soldiers shot them all," the witness continued. "There were some thirty or forty squaws collected in a hole for protection. They sent out a little girl about six years old with a white flag on a stick. She had not proceeded but a few steps when she was shot and killed. All the squaws in that hole were afterwards killed." After death came mutilation. "Every one I saw dead was scalped. I saw one squaw cut open with an unborn child, as I thought, lying by her side. . . . I saw one squaw whose privates had been cut out."

The soldiers reveled in the atrocities. "I did not see a body of man, woman, or child but was scalped," a soldier said. "And in many instances their bodies were mutilated in the most horrible manner—men, women, and children's privates cut out, &c.; I heard one man say that he had cut out a woman's private parts and had them for exhibition on a stick. . . . I also heard of numerous instances in which men had cut out the private parts of females and stretched them over the saddle-bows and wore them over their hats while riding in the ranks."

THE SAND CREEK MASSACRE SPARKED A WAR ON THE PLAINS that would last a decade. The Cheyennes and the Arapahos allied with the Sioux for a reprisal campaign against white settlements in eastern Colorado. In early 1865 the allies attacked the town of Julesburg, killing all the settlers they could find, scalping the dead and burning the buildings. They cut telegraph wires and closed the road to Denver, isolating the territorial capital and threatening it, in the middle of winter, with starvation.

The leader of the Indian alliance was Red Cloud, war chief of the Sioux. Red Cloud made clear that his fight was to the bitter end. "The white men have crowded the Indians back year by year until we are forced to live in a small country north of the Platte," he told a council of American officials and fellow Indians held during a pause in the fighting. "And now our last hunting ground, the home of the People"—the Sioux—"is to be taken from us. Our women and children will starve, but for my part I prefer to die fighting."

The council had been called by federal officials who hoped to negotiate a road to Bozeman in Montana Territory, where gold had been discovered. This was the road Black Elk spoke of. Despite Red Cloud's opposition, the whites built the road, and fortified it with military posts at various points along the way.

Red Cloud's Sioux and the allied Arapahos and Cheyennes attacked construction crews and ambushed travelers on the road. The attacks had little lasting effect, as the army stepped up patrols to protect the crews and travelers.

Red Cloud's young lieutenant, Crazy Horse, had a better idea. He and a small party of Indians jumped a wagon train on the Bozeman road and inflicted modest damage. The train took refuge at Fort Phil Kearny, where the officer second in command, Captain William Fetterman, expressed outrage that a handful of savages would have the nerve to stage such an attack. Fetterman had fought in the Civil War, and he was certain the Indians were far inferior as fighters to the Confederates he had defeated. "A single company of regulars could whip a thousand Indians," he declared. "With eighty men I could ride through the Sioux nation."

In fact he had eighty-one men when he sallied forth in pursuit of Crazy Horse's raiders. His commanding officer ordered him to go no farther than Lodge Trail Ridge, several miles from the fort, in case he ran into trouble and required reinforcement. But Fetterman knew better: he must catch the raiders before they got away.

Fetterman's company galloped up Lodge Trail Ridge and kept going. Just beyond the ridge, Crazy Horse sprang his trap. Two thousand Sioux, Arapahos and Cheyennes fell upon Fetterman's column and cut it to pieces. All eighty-one bluecoats were killed. Many of the corpses were mutilated.

THIS WAS THE BATTLE OF THE HUNDRED SLAIN OF BLACK Elk's boyhood, the one in which his father's leg was broken. The Sioux recalled it as a great victory, the one that marked Crazy Horse as the one who might save them and their land from the Wasichus.

As Black Elk got older, he took part in more of the activities of the tribe. He remembered his first buffalo hunt. "One morning the crier came around the circle of the village calling out that we were going to break camp. The advisers were in the council tepee, and he cried to them: 'The advisers, come forth to the center and bring your fires along.' It was their duty to save fire for the people, for we had no matches then. 'Now take it down, down!' the crier shouted." The people dismantled their tepees and loaded them on the pony drags.

The crier said, "Many bison, I have heard; many bison, I have heard! Your children, you must take care of them!" The crier meant that the children had to be kept close and quiet, lest they scare the buffalo. "Then we broke camp and started in formation, the four advisers first, a crier behind them, the chiefs next, and then the people with the loaded pony drags in a long line, and the herd of ponies following," Black Elk recalled. He rode in the rear with the young boys. "Something exciting was going to happen, and even the ponies seemed to know," he said.

At noon they camped. "While the women were cooking all around the circle I heard people saying that the scouts were re- turning, and over the top of a hill I saw three horsebacks coming. They rode to the council tepee in the middle of the village and all the people were going there to hear. I went there too and got up close so that I could look between the legs of the men. The crier came out of the council tepee and said, speaking to the people for the scouts: 'I have protected you; in return you shall give me many gifts.'" They gave him a pipe filled with the bark of red willow. He lit, smoked, and passed it to the scouts. He said, "The nation has depended on you. Whatever you have seen, maybe it is for the good of the people you have seen." He asked for their report.

One of the scouts said, "You know where we started from. We went and reached the top of a hill and there we saw a small herd of bison."

The adviser asked for more information.

The scout said, "On the other side of that, we saw a second and larger herd of bison."

Tell me more, the adviser directed.

The scout said, "On the other side of that, there was nothing but bison all over the country."

The adviser responded, "*Hetchetu aloh*!"—It is so, indeed.

Then the crier sang out to all within earshot, "Your knives shall be sharpened; your arrows shall be sharpened. Make ready, make haste; your horses make ready! We shall go forth with arrows. Plenty of meat shall we make!"

Everyone did as instructed. Knives and arrows were sharpened; the best horses were brought forward.

"Then we started for where the bison were," Black Elk recalled. "The soldier band went first, riding twenty abreast, and anybody who dared go ahead of them would get knocked off his horse. They kept order, and everybody had to obey. After them came the hunters, riding five abreast. The people came up in the rear."

The head man of the advisers selected the best hunters on the fastest horses. To them he gave encouragement: "Good young warriors, my relatives, your work I know is good. What you do is good always; so today you shall feed the helpless. Perhaps there are some old and feeble people without sons, or some who have little children and no man. You shall help these, and whatever you kill shall be theirs." The young men listened and nodded; this was a great honor.

"Then when we had come near to where the bison were, the hunters circled around them, and the cry went up, as in battle, '*Hoka hey!*' which meant to charge," Black Elk said. "Then there was a great dust and everybody shouted and all the hunters went in to kill—every man for himself. They were all nearly naked, with their quivers full of arrows hanging on their left sides, and they would ride right up to a bison and shoot him behind the left shoulder. Some of the arrows would go in up to the feathers, and sometimes those that struck no bones went right straight through. Everybody was very happy."

Black Elk was too young to join the killing, but he rode his pony in the rear and cheered the hunters on. As the carcasses littered the plain where the hunt took place, the butchering began. The hunters cut long strips of meat and draped them over their horses' backs. The livers were a special delicacy. "On the way back to the hunting village all the hunting horses were loaded, and we little boys who could not wait for the feast helped ourselves to all the raw liver we wanted," Black Elk said. "Nobody got cross when we did this."

The women made ready at the camp to dry the meat the hunters brought in. The hunters threw the meat in great piles atop leaves that had been spread on the ground. The advisers praised the hunters for their good work. All gathered around.

Black Elk remembered the moment, and the hours that followed. "The women were all busy cutting the meat into strips and hanging it on the racks to dry. You could see red meat hanging everywhere. The people feasted all night long and danced and sang. Those were happy times."

38

THERE WOULD BE
NO SOLDIERS LEFT

WILLIAM SHERMAN'S FATHER HAD ADMIRED INDIANS enough to give his son the middle name Tecumseh, for the Shawnee chief who gathered tribes of the Ohio and Mississippi valleys into an alliance intended to drive whites out of North America's heartland and back across the mountains to the Atlantic shore. As a boy he had been called Tecumseh, or Cump. As an adult, after the Civil War, in which he had become the second most famous soldier in the Union, behind Ulysses Grant, it fell to him to suppress an effort like that his namesake had organized.

Sherman received command of a military district that comprised the entire West north of Texas. He watched from his St. Louis headquarters as the fighting that followed the Sand Creek massacre escalated. At first he blamed the white settlers for most of the trouble. The settlers would provoke the Indians, he said, be attacked in response, and then cry for the army to come and kill all the Indians. He wanted nothing to do with it. Characterizing the Indians as "pure beggars and poor devils more to be pitied than dreaded," he pledged, "I will not permit them to be warred against as long as they are not banded together in parties large enough to carry on war."

Yet the Indians didn't get Sherman's message, and if they had, they would have ignored it. The Sand Creek killings demonstrated what white men would do to Indians if the Indians didn't defend themselves. The Sioux and their allies refused to count on Sherman's goodwill; they gathered in parties of the kind Sherman forbade, and carried on war.

Sherman responded with the implacability that had made his reputation during the Civil War. "We must act with vindictive earnestness against the Sioux, even to their extermination: men, women, and children," he wrote to Grant, his Washington superior, after the slaughter of the Fetterman column. The Plains tribes must be broken. "Both the Sioux and the Cheyennes must die, or submit to our dictation."

Sherman elaborated on this brutal dichotomy at an 1867 council on the Platte River. Speaking for the federal government, he offered the Sioux a reservation, amounting to the western half of the modern state of South Dakota. The concept of reserved areas for Indians ran back to colonial times; it subsequently motivated the establishment of what was called the Indian Territory—essentially modern Oklahoma—in the 1820s. Sherman offered the Sioux a northern equivalent. They would also be allowed to hunt on the Powder River, and the government would give up the Bozeman road. The government would provision the Indians on the reservation and pay them an annual stipend.

Sherman told the Indians that this was the best offer they would get. "If you don't choose your homes now, it will be too late next year," he said. The Indians might win a battle or two against the whites, but they could never win the war. The whites were coming, and they would continue to come, in ever larger numbers. "You can see for yourselves that travel across the country has increased so much that the slow ox wagons will not answer the white man. We will build iron roads, and you cannot stop the locomotive any more than you can stop the sun or moon." Sherman repeated that they would receive no better offer. "Live like white men, and we will help you all you want," he said. The alternative was the

Indians' destruction. "Our people in the East hardly think of what you call war out here, but if they make up their minds to fight you, they will come out as thick as a herd of buffalo, and if you continue fighting you will all be killed."

The Sioux chiefs took Sherman's ultimatum as an insult. They stalked out of the council and galloped away. Sherman wasn't surprised, and he wasn't unprepared. He ordered Phil Sheridan, his theater commander, to do everything necessary to enforce the government's policy. "Go ahead in your own way and I will back you with my whole authority," Sherman said. "If it results in the utter annihilation of these Indians, it is but the result of what they have been warned of again and again." Sherman continued, "I will say nothing and do nothing to restrain our troops from doing what they deem proper on the spot, and will allow no mere vague general charges of cruelty and inhumanity to tie their hands, but will use all the powers confided to me to the end that these Indians, the enemies of our race and of our civilization, shall not again be able to begin and carry out their barbarous warfare on any kind of pretext they may choose to allege."

Sheridan was happy to comply. He had been as ruthless in the Shenandoah Valley during the Civil War as Sherman had been in Georgia, and he judged Indians to be beneath the consideration of whites. During a campaign in Texas, a Comanche chief surrendered to Sheridan, calling himself a good Indian. Sheridan sneered, "The only good Indians I ever saw were dead."

Sherman's threats changed the minds of some of the Sioux, including Red Cloud. The aging chief, recognizing the essential truth behind Sherman's warning of annihilation, led a delegation to another council at Fort Laramie, in 1868, and accepted the reservation Sherman offered.

IN THE SUMMER OF HIS TENTH YEAR, BLACK ELK HAD A VISION. He had fallen ill with a fever, and for many days lingered at death's door. His vision appeared to him while he was unconscious. He felt himself rising out of his body and being lifted high into the clouds. The clouds became hills covered with snow. "I looked and saw a bay horse standing there, and he began to speak," he recounted. The horse directed him to look west. "I looked, and there were twelve black horses yonder all abreast with necklaces of bison hoofs, and they were beautiful, but I was frightened because their manes were lightning and there was thunder in their nostrils."

The horses carried him to a council of the elders of the four corners of the earth. "Younger brother," said the Grandfather of the South, "with the powers of the four quarters you shall walk, a relative. Behold, the living center of a nation I shall give you, and with it many you shall save." The Grandfather of the South stretched out his arm, and in his hand was a bright red stick that came alive. "As I looked it sprouted at the top and sent forth branches, and on the branches many leaves came out and murmured, and in the leaves the birds began to sing. And then for just a little while I thought I saw beneath it in the shade the circled villages of people and every living thing with roots or legs or wings, and all were happy." The living stick had a message for Black Elk, the Grandfather of the South said. "It shall stand in the center of the nation's circle, a cane to walk with and a people's heart, and by your powers you shall make it blossom."

The twelve horses now spoke to Black Elk, interpreting what the Grandfathers had done. "They have given you the sacred stick and your nation's hoop," the horses said. "In the center of the hoop you shall set the stick and make it grow into a shielding tree, and bloom."

The horses carried Black Elk to a village filled with the laments of mourning. "When I looked around I saw that in nearly every tepee the women and the children and the men lay dying," Black Elk recalled. But a voice told him to plant the stick and the hoop. "I took the bright red stick and at the center of the nation's hoop I thrust it in the earth. As it touched the earth it leaped mightily in my hand and was a *waga chun*, the rustling tree, very tall and full of leafy branches and of all birds singing. And beneath it all the animals were mingling with the people like relatives and making happy cries. The women raised their tremolo of joy, and the men shouted all together: 'Here we shall raise our children and be as little chickens under the mother *sheo*'s"—sage hen's—"wing."

BLACK ELK'S VISION BECAME THE GUIDING FORCE OF HIS LIFE. The Sioux respected the power of visions, and they provisionally respected Black Elk's. His father was a medicine man, and so were several uncles. The boy might grow up to be a medicine man himself. The test would be whether Black Elk's vision provided sound guidance in decades to come.

His friends and neighbors were more immediately impressed with the vision of Crazy Horse, who happened to be Black Elk's second cousin. Crazy Horse's vision told him that the world people saw in everyday life was but a shadow of the true world that existed beyond the shadows. His vision gave him access to the true world, and when he stepped into it, nothing in the shadow world could harm him. It also gave him great confidence. "When he went into a fight," Black Elk remembered, "he had only to think of that world to be in it again, so that he could go through anything and not be hurt."

Crazy Horse had a magnetic effect on those around him. "His eyes looked through things and he always seemed to be thinking hard about something," Black Elk said. "All the Lakotas like to dance and sing, but he never joined a dance, and they say nobody ever heard him sing." Yet he clearly put the interests of his people before his own. "He never wanted to have many things for himself, and did not have many ponies like a chief. They say that when game was scarce and the people were hungry, he would not eat at all." Without trying, Crazy Horse became a natural leader of the Lakotas. "They would do anything he wanted or go anywhere he said."

GOLD PROSPECTORS IN THE WEST BUCKED THE NATURAL TIDE of migration. While the emigrant trains were moving west, they moved east. This was an accident of history. James Marshall had stumbled over gold in California, with the result that the initial center of mining was in the region farthest west. After the returns there diminished, the prospectors had nowhere to go but east. They struck gold and especially silver in Nevada in the late 1850s, and gold in Colorado about the same time. They found gold and silver in Idaho in the early 1860s, and copper in Montana and Arizona. By the 1870s they had almost run out of promising geology. But one spot conspicuously remained: the Black Hills of Dakota. So long as other regions remained unexplored, prospectors had given the Black Hills a wide berth, for the district was sacred to the Sioux, who defended it fiercely.

The Sioux knew the Black Hills held gold. And they knew the whites coveted gold. So they did their best to embargo the knowledge of the gold the Black Hills held. But as easy gold grew scarcer elsewhere in the West, the Black Hills grew more alluring to the prospectors. Some wondered if Sioux stories of ghosts and wizards in the Black Hills might be part of a deception campaign. Intrepid souls would occasionally slip into the Black Hills, and rumors of gold discoveries would leak out. But they remained rumors as of 1873, when a financial panic seized the nation's railroads and compelled the Northern Pacific, which had been building across Dakota, to suspend construction. Local business owners desperate for replacement revenues agitated to open the Black Hills to prospectors and miners. A Dakota editor denounced the Fort Laramie treaty, reserving the Black Hills to the Sioux, as an "abominable compact." "They will not dig the gold or let others do it," the editor said of the Sioux. "They are too lazy and too much like mere animals to cultivate the fertile soil, mine the coal, develop the salt mines, bore the petroleum wells, or wash the gold. Having all these things in their hands, they prefer to live as paupers, thieves and beggars; fighting, torturing, hunting, gorging, yelling and dancing all night to the beating of old tin kettles."

The Dakotans and their friends in Washington demanded that the federal government ascertain whether the rumors of Black

Hills gold were true or not. Ulysses Grant, now president, was reluctant. The antithesis of the remorseless Sherman and Sheridan, Grant hoped that whites and Indians could live in peace. He sincerely tried to honor the treaties the government had negotiated with the Indians. He replaced venal Indian agents with Quakers and others of firmer conscience, and did his best to keep whites off the Indian reservations.

But he was merely president, and amid the economic depression that followed the financial panic, he faced overwhelming pressure to allow almost anything that would stimulate the American economy. Nothing would provide a kick like a new gold discovery. Grant grudgingly approved a federal expedition to determine the truth or falsity of the rumors of gold in the Black Hills.

COMMAND OF THE EXPEDITION WENT TO GEORGE ARMSTRONG Custer, of the army's 7th Cavalry. Grant had doubts about Custer, a Civil War hero but also a prima donna. Yet the long-haired colonel had supporters, including many in Congress, and Grant yielded to their wishes to see Custer head the Black Hills exploration.

Custer played to his following. Besides soldiers to defend the expedition against Sioux attack, and scientists to extract and assay the ore they found, Custer brought newspapermen on the journey. He made every effort to give them material for stories—about him, whenever possible. The one thing they didn't get, which would have suited him perfectly, was a fight against the Indians, who kept their distance.

Grant wished the expedition would *dis*prove the existence of gold in paying quantities in the Black Hills. But geology was against him, and so was Custer. The scientists found gold, which Custer showed to the reporters that they might inform the world. "STRUCK IT AT LAST!" one local paper hurrahed, in full Sam Brannon mode. "MINES OF GOLD AND SILVER REPORTED FOUND BY CUSTER. PREPARE FOR LIVELY TIMES!" Another paper, slightly calmer but no less boosterish, declared, "This immense section bids fair to become the El Dorado of America."

The headlines had the desired effect, and a rush to the Black Hills began. Grant vainly tried to stop it. He ordered violators of the treaty arrested, their outfits seized and their wagons burned. But the rushers drastically outnumbered the soldiers, and Grant recognized that it was politically impossible to order soldiers to shoot gold rushers, especially when most of the country thought the rushers were right and the president wrong.

As a fallback, Grant tried to negotiate the purchase of the Black Hills from the Sioux. Red Cloud was prepared to strike a bargain, having concluded that what the Sioux didn't sell, the whites would simply take. But the negotiations bogged down over the price. Anyway, as even Red Cloud had to acknowledge, he didn't speak for all the Sioux. Crazy Horse and Sitting Bull, a powerful medicine man, publicly rejected his authority and made clear they were going to fight to defend the Sioux lands.

They forced Grant's hand. By this time the gold rush to Dakota was in full roar. Ten thousand miners crowded the Black Hills seeking their fortunes. Their presence was illegal, but Grant, now facing complaints about corruption in his administration, in addition to the anger over the economy, was in no position to drive them out. He ordered the army to compel Crazy Horse, Sitting Bull and the other treaty opponents to recognize the authority of the government and move to the reservation.

Once more George Custer rode at the head of the 7th Cavalry. Reports placed Crazy Horse on the Yellowstone River; Custer pursued him there. Americans knew enough about Crazy Horse, and more than enough about Custer, to devour every news story of the coming clash between the wily war chief and the gallant cavalryman. Crow and Arikara scouts marched with Custer against the Sioux; Custer was heard to boast to them that there would soon be a new Great Father in Washington—Custer himself. It wasn't an outlandish thought. America's fondness for victorious soldiers was well known. Grant would leave office after his second term. William Sherman, the obvious one next in line, had repeatedly asserted his distaste for politics. The way seemed open for a new hero to ride into the White House.

ON THE MORNING OF JUNE 25, 1876, BLACK ELK'S FATHER warned him to be careful. The boy, thirteen years old, and several others his age were tending horses along the river they called the Greasy Grass—a stream the whites called the Little Bighorn. "If anything happens, you must bring the horses back as fast as you can," Black Elk's father said. "Keep your eyes on the camp."

The camp, and the adjacent camps of other bands, were tense. Crazy Horse had gathered warriors for the showdown with Long Hair, as the Indians called Custer. Most were Sioux, either outright treaty rejectionists like himself and Sitting Bull, or tribe members who wintered on the reservation and decided to spend the summer reliving the old ways, perhaps for the last time. Some Cheyennes and Arapahos joined them in their stand against the white invaders.

As Custer approached, Crazy Horse made his preparations. A part of his army engaged Custer's lieutenant, George Crook, then broke off and disappeared. Custer pursued them, uncertain how many warriors Crazy Horse had, but unworried by his ignorance. He was sure his men could rout several times their number of savages. His only concern was how to make Crazy Horse fight. He didn't want to spend all summer chasing him.

Crazy Horse let the soldiers approach. Custer's column made contact again, through his Crow scouts, who caught sight of the Sioux camps. The Crows were surprised at the size of the gathering; they warned Custer that there were more of the enemy than he had counted on. He waved aside their fretting. He was close; he would move in for the kill.

He aimed to attack the Sioux camps from two directions. Major Marcus Reno would ride directly toward the camps from the south. Custer would circle to the north with a second column and close off any escape. The hammer would meet the anvil, and the renegade Indians would be crushed.

The approach of the bluecoats was what prompted the warning of Black Elk's father. The son heeded the words. All morning he and the boys watched for any sign that the Wasichus were at hand. Hours passed, and they saw nothing. The day's heat and their youth caused their attention to flag. One suggested they swim in the river to cool off. Black Elk hesitated. "I did not feel well," he said afterward. "I felt queer. It seemed that something terrible was going to happen." But the laughter of the other boys caused him to dismiss the thought. He joined them in the cold water, which seemed to wash away his forebodings.

Suddenly they heard a cry from the nearest camp, of the Hunkpapas. "The chargers are coming!" the criers said. "They are charging! The chargers are coming!" The warning rapidly spread. "The crier of the Oglalas shouted the same words," Black Elk recalled, "and we could hear the cry going from camp to camp northward clear to the Santees and Yanktonais."

All the warriors ran for their horses. Black Elk and the other boys leaped on their own mounts. "My older brother had a sorrel, and he rode away fast toward the Hunkpapas," Black Elk remembered. "I had a buckskin." Black Elk's brother was a warrior, but he had left behind a few guns. Black Elk's father brought up the guns and told Black Elk to chase down the brother and give him the guns. "I took the guns, jumped on my pony and caught my brother."

He discovered what all the shouting was about. "I could see a big dust rising just beyond the Hunkpapa camp and all the Hunkpapas were running around and yelling, and many were running wet from the river. Then out of the dust came the soldiers on their big horses. They looked big and strong and tall and they were all shooting."

Reno's column struck the Hunkpapa camp and inflicted sharp casualties. But a warrior named Gall, sometimes referred to as Pizi, rallied his comrades. "A cry went up," Black Elk remembered: "'Take courage! Don't be a woman!'"

The counterattack knocked some of the white soldiers off their horses. The bluecoats took shelter in trees beside the river. The fighting grew more intense. "The valley went darker with dust and smoke," Black Elk related. "There were only shadows and a big noise of many cries and hoofs and guns. On the left of where I was I could hear the shod hoofs of the soldiers' horses going back into the brush, and there was shooting everywhere. Then the hoofs came out of the brush, and I came out and was in among men and horses weaving in and out and going upstream, and everybody was yelling, 'Hurry! Hurry!' The soldiers were running upstream and we were all mixed there in the twilight and the great noise. I did not see much, but once I saw a Lakota charge at a soldier who stayed behind and fought and was a very brave man. The Lakota took the soldier's horse by the bridle, but the soldier killed him with a six-shooter. I was small and could not crowd in to where the soldiers were, so I did not kill anybody. There were so many ahead of me, and it was all dark and mixed up."

On one corner of the battlefield some of the Sioux were stripping dead and downed bluecoats of their weapons and uniforms. Black Elk watched in fascination. "There was a soldier on the ground and he was still kicking," he recalled. "A Lakota rode up and said to me, 'Boy, get off and scalp him.' I got off and started to do it. He had short hair and my knife was not very sharp. He ground his teeth. Then I shot him in the forehead and got his scalp."

By now Custer realized that his plan had miscarried. The Indians were more numerous than he had imagined, and they fought better than he had thought they would. Reno's troops, far from driving the Sioux into Custer's fatal grasp, were pinned down and fighting for their own lives. What Custer met was not an Indian band in confusion but a disciplined force led by Crazy Horse himself. "Hoka hey!" the war chief cried, at the head of the charge. "It is a good day to fight! It is a good day to die!"

The Indians struck the bluecoats from the front, the sides and eventually the rear. Custer ordered his men to the highest ground in the area, where they dismounted and fired at the mass of Indians swirling around them. He hoped to hold off the Indians until reinforcements arrived or night fell. Then they might escape.

But Crazy Horse had no intention of letting them go. His only chance of victory, not just in this battle but in the longer struggle, was to inflict such a defeat on the invaders that they would back off and leave the Sioux in peace.

His warriors swirled closer and closer, raining gunfire and arrows on the surrounded soldiers. The latter fought with the courage of desperation. None wanted to be taken alive, knowing that torture awaited.

"We could not see much of the battle for the big dust," Black Elk said. "But we knew there would be no soldiers left."

Within half an hour, he was right. "We rode across the Greasy Grass to the mouth of a gulch that led up through the bluff to where the fighting was," Black Elk remembered. "Before we got there, the Wasichus were all down, and most of them were dead, but some of them were still alive and kicking. Many other little boys had come up by this time, and we rode around shooting arrows into the Wasichus. There was one who was squirming around with arrows sticking in him, and I started to take his coat, but a man pushed me away and took the coat for himself. Then I saw something bright hanging on this soldier's belt, and I pulled it out. It was round and bright and yellow and very beautiful, and I put it on me for a necklace. At first it ticked inside, and then it did not any more. I wore it around my neck a long time before I found out what it was and how to make it tick again." Black Elk continued across the killing ground. "There was a soldier who was raising his arms and groaning. I shot an arrow into his forehead."

39

ADOBE WALLS

IT WAS A BRILLIANT VICTORY FOR CRAZY HORSE AND THE Sioux, yet ultimately futile. The news of "Custer's Last Stand," as it was called in the popular press, reached the American East amid the festivities surrounding the centennial of American independence. The continuing economic depression took some of the shine off the celebration, making the country hungry for a demonstration that the American way remained the path to the future. Ulysses Grant thought Custer no hero. "I regard Custer's massacre as a sacrifice of troops, brought on by Custer himself, that was wholly unnecessary, wholly unnecessary," he told a reporter. But the lame-duck president couldn't resist the pressure to avenge the 260 men lost on the Little Bighorn. The 7th Cavalry, now under George Crook, was reinforced and given orders to capture Crazy Horse and his followers. The chase filled the summer and autumn of 1876. Occasional skirmishes were indecisive. What finally defeated Crazy Horse was what defeated most other Indian resisters: the destruction of Indian villages and food stores. Crazy Horse and his band somehow survived the winter, but spring found them starving. Crazy Horse yielded to the inevitable and agreed to come onto the reservation. The war for the northern plains was over.

WHAT THE SIOUX WERE TO THE NORTHERN PLAINS, THE Comanches were to the southern. They had always been warlike.

Their own name for themselves, like that of many Indian tribes, was simply "the People," but to the Utes, whom the Comanches encountered upon emerging from the southern Rockies in the early eighteenth century, they were "anyone who wants to fight me all the time." When the Ute word for this phrase was rendered by the Spanish, it became "Comanche."

About the time they descended from the mountains, the Comanches acquired horses, which had an even more profound effect on their culture than horses had on the life of the Sioux. The Comanches became the utter equestrian people, roaming thousands of miles after buffalo and after more horses. Their skills at mounted warfare were legendary. "He makes but an awkward figure enough on foot," an eyewitness said of the Comanche fighter, "though he is no sooner mounted than he is transformed, and with no other aid than that of the rein and heavy whip he makes his horse perform the most incredible feats." Another observer drew a classical parallel, calling the Comanche warrior "the model of the fabled Thessalian centaur, half horse, half man, so closely joined and so dexterously managed that it appears but one animal, fleet and furious."

The Comanches were divided into several bands, each with its own leaders and making its own decisions. The principal leader of the most formidable band was Quanah Parker, son of a Comanche chief and a white woman named Cynthia Ann Parker. Stolen from her family at the age of ten or eleven in an 1836 attack on Fort Parker, Texas, for the same reason Indians stole other children from the whites and from one another—in order to rebuild their disease-ravaged populations—Cynthia Ann grew up among the Comanches and assimilated into the tribe. She married and had children, whom she raised as Comanches. By the time Texas Rangers recaptured her in 1860, she considered herself a Comanche; she was repatriated to the white settlements only by force.

Her husband died trying to defend her, and so Quanah, then about fifteen, was effectively orphaned. As the boy became a man he exhibited traits of leadership and courage that won him a following among the Quahadis, the most independent of the Comanche bands. The Quahadis defied efforts by the federal government to confine them to a reservation, and they roamed at will across the Llano Estacado, living by hunting buffalo and raiding white settlements. The U.S. army sent expeditions in pursuit of Quanah and the Quahadis, but the troopers rarely even spotted the Indians. On one occasion the cavalrymen didn't discover the Comanches' proximity until Quanah and his warriors were riding off with the federals' horses.

WHAT THE SOLDIERS COULDN'T ACCOMPLISH, THE BUFFALO hunters did. Seth Hathaway was a buffalo hunter who joined a hunting party from Colorado in the spring of 1874 for an expedition across the Llano Estacado. Hathaway made the fourth of a four-man group. Jerry Gardner, a veteran plains hunter, owned and directed the operation; the two other men were buffalo skinners. Hathaway and the two skinners would receive a monthly stipend and a percentage of the hides; as the junior member of the outfit, Hathaway was expected to tend the camp while the others were at work and to run errands as necessary. "When I told them I was no tenderfoot they only laughed," he remembered. "So all I could do was to keep still and show them what I could do when the time came."

The hunters were well-equipped. "For our ammunition we carried six or seven hundred pounds of lead, and two or three thousand shells with primers," Hathaway said. "The arms of the party consisted of two 50-caliber three-band needle guns"—breech-loading rifles in which a steel needle penetrated the paper cartridge to ignite the powder—"for the wagon, and two 50-caliber 120-grain Sharp's rifles, weighing sixteen and eighteen pounds, for hunting. A number of knives for skinning, one grindstone and our blankets completed the equipment."

The hunters made their way to Willow Creek, where they encountered several other parties. They continued south toward Palo Duro Canyon, with its broken bluffs and red rimrock. They killed a few buffalo but ran short of salt. The four men expected to live on buffalo meat for months at a time, but they couldn't stand it unsalted. Gardner told the others to keep hunting; he'd find someone to trade him salt. As he left, one of the skinners, Tom Cox, told Hathaway, "Kid, you have been talking about your killing buffaloes. Here is your chance. Show us what you can do."

Hathaway hefted one of the needle guns and ran to a small gully from which a portion of the buffalo herd was emerging. "The herd came along at an easy lope, and when they were close enough I turned loose, killing five before they got out of range," he said. Gardner heard the shooting from a distance and feared that Indians had jumped his crew; he hurried back to the camp. "When he rode up and found out what I had done," Hathaway recalled, "he said, 'You are a regular Seth Green on shooting.' And from that day on I have been called Seth. I never found out who Seth Green was, but reckon he was a good shot, as Gardner named me after him."

Gardner got his salt, and the party moved on. Eventually they found a spot Gardner liked. Hathaway considered himself a good buffalo hunter, but Gardner carried the craft to a higher level. Hathaway observed and learned. "This is very particular work," he later explained, "and requires a great deal of experience to do it successfully, as every herd has a number of its members, more or less according to the size of the bunch, straggling out from the main herd from forty to sixty yards. These buffaloes act as sentinels. At the first sign of any danger they start and run. This action sets the whole herd in motion, and in a minute all you will see is rising and falling humps in a cloud of dust."

The hunter had to use the wind to his advantage. "The buffalo has a very acute sense of smell, and the first scent of man they catch they are off," Hathaway said. "So in crawling up, the hunter works towards them against the wind if he possibly can. This is hard on a still day. To determine the direction of the wind a handful of grass is thrown in the air. After he has got the direction he starts crawling, at the same time watching the straggling buffaloes. If the nearest animal raises his head, the hunter lays flat on the ground and keeps quiet, out of sight if possible. If the country is rolling, he takes advantage of the ground. In a flat country he is always in sight, and it is very hard to approach a herd and not be discovered." The buffalo weren't keen of vision, but they were wary. "If the buffalo discovers a hunter, he will watch him for as long as five minutes some times. If he is satisfied that there is no danger, he will start to feeding again. If, on the other hand, he is not satisfied—and a buffalo is a mighty suspicious animal—he will twist his tail over his back and go. Then it is up to the hunter to find a new herd and start all over again. Patience is a virtue in hunters, as I have seen it take one hour and a half to work up close enough to shoot."

Getting in position was just the start, Hathaway said. "After the hunter has worked up to what he considers a good range, say from 150 to 225 yards, he will pick out the bull he thinks is the leader of the bunch, take good aim at the center of the body, just back of the fore shoulder, and blaze away. At the crack of the gun they will all start on the run, though if the shot is a good one, if the animal stops and blood flows from his mouth and nostrils, in a moment he will stagger and fall. Scenting the blood, the rest of the herd will stop. The hunter will then work up a little closer, place the rest sticks for his gun, and kill all the buffaloes he can before they recover themselves." Rest sticks were props used to hold up the muzzles of the heavy guns. "Sometimes the hunter would get five, ten, or perhaps fifteen buffaloes before the herd moved too far away. I have seen Gardner kill at one stand forty-six. In one of my hunts with Gardner I killed thirty-three."

When the shooting stopped, the skinners moved in. This far from civilization, the only part of the animal that could be transported to market economically was the hide, which the skinners swiftly separated from the thousand pounds or so of meat and bone. The hides were stretched taut and pegged to the ground, to dry in the sun and wind of the plains. While the hides were drying, the men molded new bullets from the lead they carried, refilled the spent cartridges with powder, and visited with any other hunters who happened to be in the area. After several days, depending on the weather, the hides were stacked in the wagon and the hunting party moved on.

IF THE HUNTERS EXPECTED TO RETURN TO A PARTICULAR SITE on the way back to the railroad, where they would sell the hides, they might cache supplies in a hole in the ground. Gardner's group did this, only to discover, on the return, that wolves had smelled the cache and raided it. Gardner hadn't wanted to purchase any more supplies, as this far out, merchants charged extortionate prices. But he had no choice, and so sent Hathaway to a trading post at a place called Adobe Walls, near the Canadian River.

The adobe walls in question were the ruins of a fort built in the late 1840s by private traders hoping to do business with the Co- manches and their neighbors. Some Comanches did patronize the fort, but others drove the traders away. In 1864 the walls served as refuge for Kit Carson and a regiment of New Mexican volunteers besieged by thousands of Comanches and Kiowas in one of the largest battles ever fought on the plains. Carson's heavier arma- ments, including howitzers, eventually drove the Indians off, but not before the engagement reminded the whites that they were mere intruders in a land still controlled by the Comanches and their allies. Though traders returned to the site several years later, their position at the time of Seth Hathaway's visit was precarious.

"Nothing of interest occurred on the trip until I got within a few miles of the place," Hathaway recalled. "Riding up on a hill, I came in sight of the Adobe Walls, situated in a beautiful val- ley from a half mile to a mile wide, and sloping each way from the creek out to the hills." At his distance Hathaway thought he saw dozens of small houses scattered about the valley, but closer inspection proved these to be piles of buffalo hides awaiting trans- port to the railroad in Kansas, hundreds of miles away. Several other hunting parties had found themselves in predicaments sim- ilar to Gardner's and had sent men to reprovision. Hathaway met some of them in the store of the post, where the proprietor, a fellow named Myers, traded flour, corn meal, bacon, horse feed, and lead for buffalo hides and cash. Hathaway paid cash for the few supplies he needed, and then, the day being too far gone for him to start the return journey, joined the other hunters for recreation. This included shooting-matches, card-playing and "swapping lies with one another," as Hathaway put it.

Normally the men would have slept under the stars, but a storm drove most of them into the cramped quarters of the compound. A few others slept in their wagons. Between the weather and the crowding, no one got much sleep. Before dawn a hunter named Billy Dixon, deciding he might as well end the long night, volunteered to go to the creek and round up the horses. The others began preparing breakfast.

Moments later they heard rifle shots. Dixon arrived back at a run. "Indians, boys, Indians!" he shouted. "Lots of them!" He said he hadn't seen the Indians but had heard them singing. "I might state here," Seth Hathaway explained, "that Indians always sing before they go into action, just as white warriors have bands playing to inspire them." The gunshots were Dixon's, fired to warn the men in the compound.

The men began piling flour sacks as makeshift barriers to Indian bullets and peered through the half-light of dawn. "We could see that the savages were riding abreast in a line two deep, which stretched across the valley," Hathaway recalled. "It was the grandest and most aweing sight I have ever seen. Their many colored blankets and the eagle feathers in their war bonnets waved in the wind as they came riding on at an easy canter, chanting a war song." Seen together, they appeared to number between three and four hundred, or fifteen to twenty times as many as the hunters who now watched from behind the adobe walls. "When about five hundred yards from the house, they broke into a war cry. It was a sound I shall never forget, that yell of defiance and hate coming from those savage throats."

LEADING THE CHARGE WAS QUANAH PARKER. DURING THE previous few years Quanah had come to realize that the buffalo hunters were a greater threat to the independence of the Quahadis than the soldiers. The soldiers could be eluded, but the hunters were killing the buffalo, without which the Comanches would be forced to accept the terms of the federals.

The buffalo had been under pressure for decades, from before the arrival of the white hunters. Their sheer numbers made them susceptible to population crashes in periods of drought, which occurred at irregular intervals on the plains. The intrusion of horses onto the buffalo range added a competitor species that hadn't existed before. Introduced diseases, including anthrax, which seems to have jumped from cattle to buffalo, had devastating effects on parts of the herd not unlike the effects new diseases had on many of the Indian tribes. The shift of pedestrian hunters like the Sioux to horseback made the buffalo more vulnerable to human predation, which increased with the Indians' acquisition of firearms, and increased again when the beaver trade declined and the Sioux and other tribes switched to buffalo robes as a staple of commerce. The arrival of the white hunters supplied the coup de grace, making a bad situation imminently terminal.

Quanah Parker didn't know every detail of the chain of causation in the decline of the buffalo, but he understood where it all was leading. And in the early summer of 1874 he laid plans for an attack against the white hunters at the trading post at Adobe Walls. On June 27, the day after Seth Hathaway arrived, the operation commenced.

The assault force comprised perhaps seven hundred warriors: Comanches, Cheyennes and Kiowas. Beside Quanah rode Isatai, a Comanche medicine man who claimed to be able to stop the bullets of the white hunters with his magic. "Those white men can't shoot you," he declared. "With my medicine I will stop up their guns. When you charge, you will wipe them all out." Fortified by this promise, Quanah raised the war cry and led the assault. "We charged pretty fast on our horses, throwing up dust high," he later remembered. The thunder of thousands of hooves shook the walls of the trading post as the Indians surged forward.

Behind the adobe walls, the hunters waited till the Indians closed to within a hundred yards, then aimed low to hit the horses. Dozens of the animals went down, pitching their riders to the dirt. But the others continued to come, surging forward until they were inside the compound itself. "I got up into the adobe houses with another Comanche," Quanah Parker said. "We poked holes through the roof to shoot."

A semblance of coordination marked the hunters' initial volleys, but soon they were firing at random, as quickly as they could reload. "It was each man for himself," Hathaway said. "The house soon filled up with smoke, and as of course every chink was closed up but the loopholes, it became stifling in the place, and every man perspired freely."

The Indians fell back after the first charge, then regrouped and charged again. Hathaway got a clear view of an Indian warrior even younger than himself. "In the second charge, one young Indian, a mere boy, had been shot through the chest. Instead of retreating with the rest, he rode his horse full tilt around the ranch house before he fell dead."

The hunters beat back the second charge, and the Indians took cover behind the hide piles outside the walls. From there they sniped at the trading post and kept the hunters pinned down. The latter gained heart, after an hour of the rifle duel, from a welcome sound. "The clear notes of a cavalry bugle sounded in the distance, which raised a cheer from the powder-begrimed, besieged men in the close, bad-smelling ranch house," Hathaway remembered. "Crouching behind sacks and boxes, every eye was glued to the loopholes to catch the first sight of the rescuers, every nerve and muscle drawn to the fullest tension. The suspense was fearful, as every moment we expected to see a party of cavalrymen dash on to the scene."

The Indians, however, seemed unperturbed by the apparent approach of a relief column, and presently the hunters learned why.

"One of the men discovered that the bugle blower was a big negro, supposed to be a deserter from one of the colored regiments then stationed at Fort Will, Indian Territory, that had joined the Indians," Hathaway recalled. The disappointment of the hunters gave way to anger as the turncoat continued to play. "One of the boys said, 'I am going to shoot that damned nigger the first chance I get.'" The black man mistakenly thought he was out of the range of the hunters' rifles. "Three shots sounded through the ranch house, and before the reports died away, the bugle notes were cut off as though the instrument had been snatched from the lips of the blower. A man they called Dutch Henry shouted, 'I got the damned nigger, boys. That will end the music!' And to him the honor was given. It was a long shot but a good one."

By now, though, the hunters had other problems. "The men suffered greatly from thirst," Hathaway said. "The place was choked with powder smoke, and the men's tongues began to swell, so that they could only speak in whispers." The Indians, with access to the water of the creek, appeared willing to wait the men out.

One of the hunters, refusing to die of thirst, began to dig in a corner of the dirt floor of the house. Most of the others thought he was crazy. But a few took turns digging. At five feet they struck water. "Although there was plenty of alkali in it, the men drank eagerly," Hathaway said. "The change that came over the men was wonderful. One would not suppose it was the same party. Some tried to sing, others to whistle as well as their parched lips would allow." They helped themselves to the inventory of the place. "Canned fruit, crackers and other eatables were brought out, and we made quite a meal."

Perhaps the changed mood of the besieged men was somehow transmitted to the besiegers. Perhaps the remarkable range of the buffalo guns dispirited the Indians. "One Indian about eight hundred yards off climbed on top of a hide pile and started to dance, but a bullet from one of the buffalo guns ended his career as a dancer," Hathaway remarked. Evidently the attack had not gone the way the Indians had believed it would. Hathaway and the others learned later of Isatai's promise that the white men's bullets wouldn't harm the attackers. "It was on account of this faith in the strong medicine that they made so fierce a charge," Hathaway said. When the promise proved false, Quanah and the others reconsidered. "As is well known among those familiar with the Indian mode of warfare, they will not attack at a disadvantage unless they are convinced that the disadvantage of numbers is overbalanced by the potency of their medicine."

The Indians now weighed the benefits of starving the hunters out against the costs of doing so, and determined to settle for looting the wagons and stealing the horses caught in the open. "The buffalo hunters were too much for us," one of the Comanches conceded afterward. "They stood behind adobe walls. They had telescopes on their guns. Sometimes we would be standing way off, resting and hardly thinking of the fight, and they would kill our horses. One of our men was knocked off his horse by a spent bullet fired at a range of about a mile." The shooter was Billy Dixon, and the wondrous shot would become etched in the lore of the southern plains.

The attackers concluded that against such firepower they had no chance. By twos and threes they slipped away, firing to keep the hunters' heads down. By the end of the day they had disappeared.

"All the boys went out into the fresh air and looked around," Hathaway said. "In front of the Adobe Walls lay seven dead Indians, and from ten feet out to a thousand yards in all directions lay any amount of dead and crippled horses." The Indians normally carried away their dead, but these were too close to the house to retrieve. The hunters lost three men dead, including one who had been caught out in his wagon and whose corpse had been mutilated, and several wounded.

THE INDECISIVE OUTCOME OF THE BATTLE SIGNALED THE beginning of the end of Comanche control of the southern plains, and indeed of Comanche independence. Quanah Parker could see the buffalo dwindling and the white presence on the plains swelling, and in failing to annihilate the hunters at Adobe Walls, he lost his last chance to keep these twin dangers at bay. During the following months Phil Sheridan and the U.S. army mounted a new campaign to force the Comanches onto a reservation. As always, the bluecoats hit the Indians at their most vulnerable point: burning their villages and destroying their food supplies. They also shot Comanche horses. The approaching winter held nothing but hunger, exposure and disease, especially for the women and children of the tribe. Some accepted Sheridan's terms and took refuge on a reservation near Fort Sill, in the southwestern corner of Indian Territory.

Quanah Parker and a band of diehards hung on for several months more. But in the summer of 1875, they too acknowledged the inevitable and rode onto the reservation.

40

LOST RIVER

QUANAH PARKER AND CRAZY HORSE, WHILE ULTIMATELY losing their battles against the soldiers, won the respect of many in the United States for their courage and resourcefulness. The leader of another resistance movement, by contrast, became a watchword for treachery.

Captain Jack was the name whites used for a chief of the Modoc people of southern Oregon and northern California. The Modocs had been relatively unaffected by the migration to the Willamette Valley that ravaged the Cayuse and resulted in the Whitman massacre. And they survived the transit of Oregonians to California upon the discovery of gold on the American River. But after gold was discovered in southern Oregon, they became part of the cycle of killing, reprisal, escalation and atrocity that left whites and Indians feeling reciprocally aggrieved. The Indians of southern Oregon determined to defend their homelands; whites who had lost friends and kin would have been happy to exterminate the whole lot of the natives. Numbers, always growing, favored the whites; knowledge of the terrain helped the Indians.

In time the same factors that wore down Indians elsewhere took hold in southern Oregon, and by the 1870s nearly all the tribes had been compelled to sign away most of their lands and settle on reservations. The last holdouts were Captain Jack's band of Modocs. Jack resented the whole reservation system, but especially the failure of the government to honor its treaty promise to furnish supplies and protect the Modocs from the larger tribes on the reservation they all were supposed to share. In protest, Jack led his several dozen warriors and their wives and children to their ancestral lands along the Lost River on the border of Oregon and California. Those lands were occupied by white settlers, who complained to the government. The army launched a campaign to force Captain Jack and his followers back to the reservation.

The campaign proceeded by skirmish and negotiation. The Modocs didn't seem numerous enough to justify an all-out war. But the negotiations broke down at critical moments, from bad faith and misunderstanding on one side and then the other. The settlers, for their part, wanted no compromise. Neither did diehards among the Modocs, who preferred death in battle to confinement on the reservation.

In protest of the failure of the talks, Captain Jack led his band into some lava beds beside Tule Lake in northernmost California. The lava beds—a local expression of the tectonic forces that shaped the rest of the West—made an impenetrable stronghold, their frozen waves of stone forming nooks, crannies, caves and clefts. The soldiers chased the Modocs into the beds, only to be picked off by rifle fire from shooters they never saw.

The army regrouped, and the government reconfigured its peace commission. Alfred Meacham, a Methodist minister and superintendent of Indian affairs for Oregon, headed the commission; he was advised by General Edward Canby, the army commandant for the Pacific Northwest, and Eleazar Thomas, another minister. Frank Riddle and his wife, Tobey, a Modoc woman, served as interpreters.

Captain Jack recognized that his band couldn't hold out against the army forever, even in the lava beds. He was prepared to negotiate. "General, we can make peace quick if you will meet me even half way," he told Canby, through the interpreters. "If you will only agree to half of what I and my people want, why, we can get along fine."

Lava beds. In this geological maze, Captain Jack and the Modocs held out against the U.S. army.

Canby would brook no compromise. "Captain Jack, I want you to understand that you are not to dictate to me," he replied. "I am to make peace with you, nothing else."

"General, I hardly think *you* ought to dictate to *me*," Jack said. "I think you ought to be aware of the fact that I am not your prisoner or slave, not today, anyway. All I ask of you is to give me a reservation near Hot Creek or Fairchild's ranch." Hot Creek and Fairchild's ranch were close to the lava beds.

"Jack, you know I cannot do that."

"Then give me these lava beds for my home. No white man will ever want to make homes here."

Alfred Meacham spoke up. "Jack, the general or any of us can't promise you any place until we make peace."

Canby told Jack what he must do. "Get all your people together and come out under a flag of truce. A white flag means peace. No one will hurt you under the white flag."

"Look here, Canby, when I was a boy a man named Ben Wright called forty-five of my people under the flag of truce," Jack said. "How many do you think got away with their lives?" He held up his hand, showing five fingers. Then he curled his thumb and two of the fingers, and with the two remaining fingers pointed in the direction of the lava beds. "Two of them are there, alive today. You ask me to come out under a flag of truce. I will not do it. I cannot do it."

"That was wrong," Canby said.

"Your white people at Yreka didn't say it was wrong. They gave him a big dinner and dance at night, called him the hero."

Meacham answered, "Jack, we are different men. We are not like Wright. We want to help you people so you can live in peace."

"If you want to help us, give me and my people a home here in our own country. We will harm no one."

Eleazar Thomas appealed to a higher authority. "God sent me here to make peace with you, brother," he told Captain Jack. "We are going to do it. I know it. God says so."

"Brother Thomas, I may trust God," Jack said. "But what good will that do me? I am sorry to say I cannot trust these men that wear blue cloth and brass buttons."

Canby reacted as though insulted. "What have these blue cloths and brass buttons done to you?" he queried sharply.

"They shot our women and little babies," Jack said, his voice rising.

"Did not your men kill settlers, and them innocent?"

"The men killed were not innocent. They were the first to fire on my people on the north banks of Lost River."

At this point Tobey, the interpreter, spoke in her own voice. "Mr. Canby, do not get mad," she told the general. "You cannot make peace this way." She turned to Captain Jack. "You, too, Jack, be a man. Hold your temper."

Tobey's words calmed things a bit but didn't produce an agreement. Jack went back to the lava beds; Canby and the others returned to their camp.

WHEN JACK TOLD CANBY HE COULDN'T MAKE PEACE ON THE white men's terms, he wasn't speaking figuratively. Leadership among the Modocs was even more tentative than among the Comanches or the Sioux. A chief wielded authority only as long as the others in the tribe chose to follow him. The irreconcilables among the Modocs were angry at Captain Jack for merely talking to the whites, and they expressed their displeasure plainly at the next council meeting. One asserted that the peace talks were a ruse to allow time for more soldiers to arrive. Another, Black Jim, agreed, and said, "I for one am not going to be decoyed and shot like a dog by the soldiers. I am going to kill my man before he gets me. I make a motion that we kill the peace-makers the next time we meet them in council. We may just as well die a few days from now, as die a few weeks from now." Black Jim called for a show of support. More than a dozen warriors stepped forward.

Jack acknowledged the difficulty of the negotiations. "I just do not know how to commence," he said. "I have a hard fight ahead of me in the coming councils, to save my men that killed the settlers, or to win my point to secure a piece of land in this country for our future home." Yet he was confident, sort of. "I shall win— at least I think I will."

"You will never save your people," Black Jim shouted. "Are you blind, my chief? Can't you see soldiers arriving every two or three days? Don't you know the last soldiers that came brought big guns with them that shoot bullets as big as your head?" He glared at Jack. "The commissioners intend to make peace with you by blowing your head off with one of those big guns. You mind what I tell you, Jack. The only way we can get an even start with the peace-makers is to kill them next council. Then all we can do is to fight until we die."

The other diehards gave their approval. Black Jim, encouraged, almost spat in Jack's face: "Promise us you will kill Canby next time you meet him."

"I cannot do it, and I will not do it," Jack said.

Another irreconcilable pushed forward. "You will kill Canby or be killed yourself," he told Jack. "You are not safe any place. You will kill or be killed by your own men."

The diehards crowded around Jack. One pushed a woman's hat down on his head. Another draped a woman's shawl over his shoulders. Several shoved him to the ground. "You coward! You squaw!" they mocked. "You are not a Modoc. We disown you. Lay there, you woman, you fish-hearted woman!"

Jack struggled to his feet. He threw off the hat and the shawl. He looked from one to the other of the diehards. "I will do it," he said. "I will kill Canby, although I know it will cost me my life and all the lives of my people." He paused a moment, then continued, "I know it's a coward's work. But I will do it."

THE CLASH IN THE COUNCIL, AND CAPTAIN JACK'S SUBMISSION to the irreconcilables, became known to all the Modocs, including Tobey. She felt an obligation to Alfred Meacham, who had done her family a good turn, and so she told her husband, Frank Riddle, who just before the next meeting warned the commissioners that their lives were in danger. "Do not go," Riddle said. "You will all be killed if you do."

Edward Canby dismissed the warning. His scouts had been watching the council tent. Only four Modocs had arrived. Should any more approach, Canby said, his men had orders to attack. He would not be frightened by the words of a woman.

Eleazar Thomas likewise deemed the warning unreliable. In any case, the minister said, he was willing to put his fate in the hands of God.

Meacham knew the Modocs better than Canby and Thomas did. And he knew Tobey Riddle. He didn't think she frightened easily, and he trusted her honesty. He shared his view with Canby and Thomas. Neither changed his mind.

Meacham thereupon wrote a letter to his wife. "You may be a widow tonight," he said. "You shall not be a coward's wife. I go to save my honor." He added, "The chances are all against us. I have done my best to prevent this meeting. I am in no wise to blame."

The commissioners proceeded to the tent. Canby opened the meeting by appealing once more to Captain Jack to come in from the lava beds and take up life on the reservation. Resistance was hopeless, he said. "If you kill all these soldiers, the Great Father will send more soldiers. You cannot kill all of them." The Modocs had no choice. "The white man's law is straight and strong."

Jack, clearly agitated, stood up and walked around. He seized a sagebrush stick that was lying in the dirt and held it out toward Canby. "Your law is as crooked as this," he said. He bent down and made a scrawl in the dirt with his finger. "The agreements you make are as crooked as this."

"What have I done?" Canby asked calmly. "Tell me."

Jack said that Canby had promised not to make war so long as the peace talks continued. But he had been reinforcing his troops and bringing up new weapons, including artillery. "Does that look like peace?" Jack demanded. "We cannot make peace as long as these soldiers are crowding me." He was getting worked up. "Take away your soldiers. Take away your big guns. And then we can talk peace. Either do that or give me a home at Hot Creek."

The other Modocs present, including Hooker Jim, an irreconcilable, began talking angrily over Jack. Alfred Meacham tried to calm them down. Canby seemed unperturbed.

"Canby, do you agree to what I ask of you or not?" demanded Jack, trying to regain control of the meeting. "Tell me. I am tired of waiting."

Meacham nervously implored Canby to answer Jack. "General, for heaven's sake, promise him," he said.

Another of the Modocs tried to get Meacham to make the promise. "Meacham, give us Hot Creek," he said. "Give us Hot Creek."

Meacham said all he could honestly say: "I will ask the Great Father at Washington."

While Tobey was translating Meacham's reply, Jack took a step toward Canby. In Modoc he declared to the other Indians, "Let's do it." He drew a pistol from under his shirt and took aim at Canby, a few feet away. He squeezed the trigger, and the hammer fell. But the charge didn't ignite. He pulled the hammer back again, and squeezed the trigger once more. This time the bullet fired, and it hit Canby in the face, just under his right eye. Yet the bullet missed Canby's brain, and the general tried to run. A Modoc named Bogus Charley tripped him, then fell upon him and fatally slit his throat.

Another Indian shot Eleazar Thomas in the chest. The minister fell to the ground, asked God to have mercy on his soul, and died.

Alfred Meacham, believing Tobey's warning, had brought a small pistol to the meeting. He now aimed the pistol at one of the Modocs, named Schonchin. He squeezed the trigger, but the gun failed to fire. Schonchin fired at Meacham, hitting him in the left shoulder. Meacham retreated and Schonchin kept firing, but to little further effect. When Schonchin ran out of bullets, he produced another pistol. By the time he took aim, Tobey had stepped between him and Meacham. "Don't kill him!" she said. "Don't kill Meacham. He is the friend of the Indians."

Schonchin ignored her. He fired and hit Meacham in the forehead. Miraculously Meacham wasn't killed outright. Another bullet slammed into Meacham's right arm. Yet another nicked his right ear. And still another grazed the right side of his head. He fell to the ground, all but dead.

One of the Indians began to scalp him. Tobey rushed at the Indian and tried to pull him off the prostrate, dying Meacham. The Modoc threw her aside.

Thinking quickly, she shouted, "The soldiers are coming! The soldiers are coming!"

The Modocs froze, then started running to the lava beds. In seconds they were gone.

The soldiers were *not* coming, but Tobey's words saved Meacham, who kept his scalp and somehow survived his wounds.

THE KILLING OF EDWARD CANBY AND ELEAZAR THOMAS MADE a prophet out of Captain Jack. Canby was the highest-ranking officer—the only general—to be killed by Indians in all the wars of the West. And Thomas was a man of the cloth. The murder of the two, under a peace flag, abruptly erased the sentimental support that had existed in parts of white America for Captain Jack and the outnumbered Modocs. "All the Modocs are involved," William Sherman declared. "Do not pretend that the murder of General Canby was the individual act of Captain Jack. Therefore the order for attack is against the whole, and if all be swept from the face of the earth, they themselves have invited it." Not everyone in America would have put the matter as harshly as Sherman did, but almost no one contradicted the sentiment.

The Modocs were not—quite—swept from the face of the earth. The soldiers' ranks were reinforced until they outnumbered the Modoc warriors twenty to one. With their artillery they pounded Captain Jack's lava-bed stronghold. The Modocs slipped the cordon one moonless night, but they didn't elude their pursuers for long. After a few more skirmishes, short but sometimes bloody, they surrendered.

Most of the survivors of Jack's band were sent into exile in Oklahoma. Jack and three others, convicted of the murder of Canby and Thomas, were sentenced to death. They were hanged at Fort Klamath, near the reservation they had refused.

41

THE PRIDE OF YOUNG JOSEPH

THE AMERICAN POLITICAL SYSTEM HAD LONG BEEN OF two minds about the Indians. Americans who lived closest to the Indians, who stood to benefit from the seizure of Indian lands and felt at risk of Indian attack, tended to support repressive, dispossessive policies. Americans who lived at a greater distance, with less to gain or lose, often displayed greater sympathy toward Indians and supported more accommodating policies. Put simply, the East liked Indians a lot more than the West did.

The East liked no Indian more than Joseph, chief of the Nez Perce. "The Nez Percé comes into history as the white man's friend," the *New York Times* editorialized in 1877. The paper quoted Lewis and Clark: "The Pierced-Nose nation are among the most amiable men we have seen—stout, well-formed, well-looking, active, their character placid and gentle, rarely moved into passion, yet not often enlivened by gayety." The editorialist noted that until the very recent past, there was no record of a full-blooded Nez Perce having killed a white man. "With the Nez Percés we have always been at peace; and when we have had wars with other neighboring tribes, the Nez Percés have invariably been the allies of our army."

All of which, the *Times* declared, made the U.S. army's war against the Nez Perce, beginning in the summer of 1877, so incomprehensible. The paper blamed the U.S. government. "These harmless and peaceful neighbors, these faithful allies in every war, were the nation that we drove to desperation and deeds of blood." Acknowledging that the immediate responsibility was obscure, given the convoluted chain of events triggering the war, the paper nonetheless condemned the conflict as "a gigantic blunder and a crime."

The Nez Perce war, like many other Indian wars, had roots in the distributed nature of governance in the tribe. Starting in the 1850s various bands of the tribe had agreed to relinquish land claims to the U.S. government in exchange for annuity payments of food and blankets. But other bands refused to sign. Among these were the followers of Joseph, the son of a chief who had been given the Christian name Joseph by Henry Spalding, Marcus Whitman's missionary partner. The younger Joseph took pride in his father's peaceful reputation. "There was no stain on his hands of the blood of a white man," he said. "He left a good name on the earth."

He also left young Joseph some advice. The elder Joseph and other Nez Perce of his generation had watched as whites came to their land. "At first our people made no complaint," the younger Joseph said. "They thought there was room enough for all to live in peace, and they were learning many things from the white men that seemed to be good. But we soon found that the white men were growing rich very fast, and were greedy to possess everything the Indian had. My father was the first to see through the schemes of the white men, and he warned his tribe to be careful about trading with them. He had a suspicion of men who seemed so anxious to make money. I was a boy then, but I remember well my father's caution. He had sharper eyes than the rest of our people."

Some Nez Perce yielded to white pressure to sell the tribe's lands. Old Joseph did not. "I have no other home than this," he said. "I will not give it up to any man. My people would have no home." He never changed his view. As he grew older, his son became chief of the band. Another council was called by the whites, and the younger Joseph made ready to represent the band. "When

Joseph. The Nez Perce chief became eastern
America's model of the noble warrior.

you go into council with the white man, always remember your
country," the father told the son. "Do not give it away. The white
man will cheat you out of your home."

Young Joseph heeded his father's advice. At the council he told
the government officials, "I did not want to come to this council,
but I came hoping that we could save blood. The white man has no
right to come here and take our country. We have never accepted
any presents from the government." Other chiefs had agreed to sell
the lands of Joseph's band, but they had no right to do so. "It has
always belonged to my people. It came unclouded to them from
our fathers, and we will defend this land as long as a drop of Indian blood warms the hearts of our men."

The Indian agent at the council said Joseph and his people *must*
move. They had been assigned land on a reservation. They must
go there.

"I will not," Joseph answered. "We have plenty, and we are contented and happy if the white man will leave us alone. The reservation is too small for so many people with all their stock." The agent offered presents; Joseph rejected them. "You can keep your presents. We can go to your towns and pay for all we need. We have plenty of horses and cattle to sell, and we won't have any help from you. We are free now; we can go where we please. Our fathers were born here. Here they lived; here they died; here are their graves. We will never leave them."

Shortly thereafter, Joseph's father lay dying. He called for his son. "Always remember that your father never sold his country," he said. "You must stop your ears whenever you are asked to sign a treaty selling your home. A few years more, and white men will be all around you. They have their eyes on this land. My son, never forget my dying words. This country holds your father's body. Never sell the bones of your father and your mother."

Joseph nodded. "I pressed my father's hand and told him I would protect his grave with my life. My father smiled and passed away to the spirit-land."

JOSEPH REMAINED TRUE TO HIS FATHER'S ADMONITION, THOUGH the task became increasingly difficult. "White men had found gold in the mountains around the land of winding water"—the Wallowa Valley, the home of Joseph's band. "They stole a great many horses from us, and we could not get them back because we were Indians. The white men told lies for each other. They drove off a great many of our cattle. Some white men branded our young cattle so they could claim them. We had no friend who would plead our cause before the law councils. It seemed to me that some of the white men in Wallowa were doing these things on purpose to get up a war. They knew that we were not strong enough to fight them."

Government agents repeatedly told Joseph that he and his people had to move to the reservation. Joseph replied, equally often, that they would not. Finally came General Oliver Howard, who summoned Joseph to the reservation for a talk. He said he had many soldiers at his back, and would soon have more. "The country belongs to the government," Howard told Joseph. "And I intend to make you go upon the reservation."

Joseph responded, "We are all sprung from a woman, although we are unlike in many things. We can not be made over again. You are as you were made, and as you were made you can remain. We are just as we were made by the Great Spirit, and you can not change us. Then why should children of one mother and one father quarrel? Why should one try to cheat the other? I do not believe that the Great Spirit Chief gave one kind of men the right to tell another kind of men what they must do."

"You deny my authority, do you?" demanded Howard. "You want to dictate to me, do you?" Howard grew angry. "The law says you shall go upon the reservation to live, and I want you to do so. But you persist in disobeying the law. If you do not move, I will take the matter into my own hand, and make you suffer for your disobedience."

A Nez Perce who had accompanied Joseph answered Howard. "Are you the Great Spirit? Did you make the world? Did you make the sun? Did you make the rivers for us to drink? Did you make the grass to grow? Did you make all these things, that you talk to us as though we were boys? If you did, then you have the right to talk to us as you do."

"You are an impudent fellow," Howard said. "I will put you in the guard house." He ordered him arrested.

The others in Joseph's party looked to him to stop the arrest. "I counseled them to submit," Joseph recalled. "I knew if we resisted that all the white men present, including General Howard, would be killed in a moment, and we would be blamed."

The council broke up that day, with no violence. Howard returned twenty-four hours later with an ultimatum. Joseph had thirty days to move his people and their belongings to the reservation. "If you are not here in that time, I shall consider that you want to fight, and will send my soldiers to drive you on."

Joseph concluded from this that Howard had already decided on war. It would be physically impossible to round up all the band's cattle and horses, cross the melt-swollen Snake River, and reach the reservation in thirty days. "I am sure that he began to prepare for war at once," Joseph said.

JOSEPH RETURNED TO HIS PEOPLE. HE CALLED A COUNCIL. HE said he didn't want war. Some of the young men *did* want war, in revenge for Nez Perce slain by whites in the past. While the council was meeting, a party of the young men, led by one whose father had been killed by whites, rode into a white settlement and killed four people. The leader of the party came back to the council and denounced those who still sought peace. "Why do you sit here like women?" he said. "The war has begun already."

Joseph realized that his hand had been forced. "I knew that their acts would involve all my people," he recounted. "I saw that war could not then be prevented."

But it was a war unlike any other in the history of the American West. Joseph recognized that he couldn't stand against Howard and the army; his people would be destroyed. Instead, he and the chiefs of some allied bands determined to conduct a fighting retreat into the mountains, and through the mountains to the buffalo country of the Great Plains.

The Nez Perce withdrew from Wallowa; the soldiers followed. The Nez Perce doubled back and ambushed the soldiers, killing a few, slowing their progress, and then resuming the retreat. The Nez Perce crossed the Salmon River, intending for Howard to follow. When he did, the Indians got behind him and cut his supply lines. The Nez Perce knew the terrain better than Howard and the soldiers did; in the few pitched battles, the soldiers almost always came off worse. Scanty ammunition imposed discipline on the Nez Perce warriors. "When an Indian fights, he only shoots to kill," Joseph said. "But soldiers shoot at random." The Nez Perce held themselves to a higher standard than the soldiers and other tribes. "None of the soldiers were scalped," Joseph explained. "We do not believe in scalping, nor in killing wounded men. Soldiers do not kill many Indians unless they are wounded and left upon the battlefield. Then they kill Indians."

Howard's force got help from a separate column coming from the east, under John Gibbon. Gibbon caught the Nez Perce off guard and inflicted the heaviest losses of the campaign: thirty warriors killed and fifty women and children. The Nez Perce changed direction, angling north into the Yellowstone basin.

En route they came upon isolated white settlements. "We captured one white man and two white women," Joseph recalled. "We released them at the end of three days. They were treated kindly. The women were not insulted. Can the white soldiers tell me of one time when Indian women were taken prisoners, and held three days and then released without being insulted?" They captured two white men several days later. "One of them stole a horse and escaped. We gave the other a poor horse and told him he was free."

A third column intercepted them, under Samuel Sturgis. The warriors fought the new soldiers to a standstill while the women and children were moved out of reach.

Finally a fourth column—which, like each of the others, alone outnumbered the Nez Perce fighters—engaged them. This one was led by Nelson Miles, the captor of Crazy Horse. Another pitched battle followed, ending in a truce offer by Miles to Joseph.

Joseph weighed the offer. His people were hungry and weary. They had traveled over a thousand miles. The original plan, to find refuge on the plains, had been thwarted by the appearance of Sturgis and Miles. Joseph considered crossing into Canada and linking up with Sitting Bull and other Lakotas who had refused to join Crazy Horse on the Sioux reservation.

But winter was coming, and the Nez Perce were not a people of the plains. One reason, besides its surpassing beauty, that Joseph and his people were so attached to the Wallowa Valley was that the mountains that encircled it protected them from winter winds like those that raked the plains.

Joseph could have left the women, children and wounded behind and dashed across the border, now only forty miles away. "I knew that we were near Sitting Bull's camp in King George's land," he said. But he wouldn't leave the defenseless to the mercy of the soldiers. "We had never heard of a wounded Indian recovering while in the hands of white men."

Nelson Miles had made a pledge to Joseph. "If you will come out and give up your arms, I will spare your lives and send you to your reservation."

Joseph thought Miles an honorable man. "General Miles had promised that we might return to our own country with what stock we had left. I thought we could start again. I believed General Miles, or I never would have surrendered."

Joseph returned to the truce tent. He handed his rifle to Miles. "It is cold and we have no blankets," he said. "The little children are freezing to death. My people, some of them, have run away to the hills and have no blankets, no food; no one knows where they are—perhaps freezing to death. I want to have time to look for my children and see how many I can find. Maybe I shall find them among the dead. Hear me, my chiefs. I am tired; my heart is sick and sad. From where the sun now stands I will fight no more forever."

VII

THE MIDDLE BORDER

42

ABILENE

NO IMAGE IN AMERICAN HISTORY HAS BEEN SO POWERFUL—so evocative not simply of romance and adventure but of what it means to be American—as that of the cowboy. Astride his horse, etched against a lonely horizon, the cowboy epitomizes individualism, integrity, strength. The cowboy guards his herd; he guards his nation's identity.

Strikingly, given its power and persistence, the image of the cowboy was rooted in a specific time and place, and in a peculiar set of circumstances. Cattle came to America with the Spanish, in the same ships as the horses, and they escaped into the wild at about the same time the horses did. Yet while horses revolutionized the lives of some of the native peoples, cattle had almost no effect on them. Horses gave the natives something they didn't have: increased mobility. Cattle merely duplicated something they *did* have: meat. Cattle were no improvement over buffalo. Cattle meat didn't taste better than buffalo meat, to the Indians. If anything, cattle were a poor substitute for buffalo, lacking the buffalo's hardiness and exquisite adaptation to the rigorous environment of the Great Plains.

But cattle caught on in Mexico, south of the buffalo's range. And they gradually spread north. They reached the plains of south Texas by the early nineteenth century. Those that had gone wild acquired some of the buffalo's hardiness. The longhorns of Texas weren't much to look at, from a butcher's perspective, being mostly bone and muscle—and of course those horns. Their meat was tough. But so was their constitution. They could thrive on withered grass and scrub that would starve the domestic breeds of cattle common in the East. They could roam many miles from water and find their way back. No predator daunted them. And they multiplied. And multiplied. By the beginning of the Civil War, millions made Texas their home.

As the cattle spread, so did a cattle culture. The Spanish had taught the Mexicans to tend cattle; the Mexicans taught the Texans. The cowboy was initially the *vaquero*. His hat was the sombrero; his rope *la reata*, or lariat; his leggings *chaparejos*, or chaps. Many of the first cowboys in American Texas were in fact Mexicans, often from families that had been in Texas since Spanish times.

Until the Civil War, Texas cattle were largely unknown in the rest of the United States. Indeed, beef cattle of any sort weren't common. Americans were pork eaters. Pigs, being omnivores, were more versatile than cows. They could be raised on the smallest farms and fed nearly anything. Americans knew cattle as dairy animals, valued for their milk. Beef was a by-product rather than the purpose of raising the cows.

The Civil War changed things. Armies have to be fed, and soldiers don't get to be picky. Texas cattle became a mainstay of the Confederate army. An industry developed gathering Texas cattle and sending them off to the front.

But two years into the war, the Union capture of Vicksburg cut off the cattle from their market. The cattle in Texas continued to multiply, until by the end of the war there were so many cattle in Texas that they could be had almost for the taking.

Something else multiplied during the war: the Northern appetite. The war stimulated the Northern economy, creating jobs in emerging industries in booming cities. The jobs drew armies of workers from American farms and from foreign countries, and like soldiers in the field, they couldn't feed themselves. And they couldn't be picky. Most came preferring pork, but if someone could put beef on their tables at modest cost, they would add steak to their culinary repertoire.

JOSEPH MCCOY AIMED TO BE THAT SOMEONE. ILLINOISAN BY birth, McCoy made his living in the stock market—the original stock market, in which cattle and other animal stock were sold. He began monitoring prices in Chicago stockyards as a young adult, and he watched the prices rise during the Civil War. He meanwhile observed the blockade on Texas cattle during the war's last two years, and at war's end he noted an enormous price disparity between cattle on the range in Texas and those at a stockyard's gate in Chicago. A cow in Texas cost two or three dollars; that same cow in Chicago could fetch thirty or forty. The profit potential made McCoy's mouth water.

All he had to do was get that Texas cow to Chicago. By this time trains regularly transported livestock, but no trains reached the cattle regions of Texas. Small herds of cattle—and pigs and other animals—had been driven from place to place in America for centuries, afoot over ordinary roads. But McCoy aimed to move cattle in great herds, of thousands. These were far too many for roads. And far too many for the neighbors living along those roads. Cattle had to eat, and if driven through regions inhabited by farmers, they would eat the farmers' crops. The farmers wouldn't stand for it.

The only way to move Texas cattle en masse to the East was to drive them north, up the Great Plains. There were few farms on the plains, and plenty of grass. The plains were a natural highway for cattle, just as they had been for buffalo. The buffalo were diminishing, under the multiple pressures upon them. The highway was sufficiently clear and getting clearer.

Joseph McCoy monitored not only cattle prices but the progress of railroad construction. The Kansas Pacific was working its way west from Kansas City; in 1867 its trains ran as far as Salina, well out on the plains. McCoy's plan was to make some Kansas town the link between the cattle range and the slaughterhouse. "In short, it was to establish a market whereat the Southern drover and Northern buyer would meet upon an equal footing," he explained afterward.

He traveled to Kansas City in the spring of 1867 and bought a ticket on the Kansas Pacific. He rode the line to Junction City and spoke to one of the town's leading businessmen. He had learned that a Texas herd was coming north, its destination yet undetermined. McCoy proposed to make Junction City that destination. He would purchase a plot of ground large enough to gather the Texas herd and prepare it for loading on the train. Junction City would become the hub of the Western plains.

The Junction City man was unimpressed. He responded in a way that stung and puzzled McCoy. "An exorbitant price was asked," McCoy recalled. "In fact a flat refusal to sell at any price was the final answer of the wide-awake Junctionite." McCoy still shook his head years later. "So by that one act of donkey stupidity and avarice, Junction City drove from her a trade which soon developed to many millions."

He returned to Kansas City. He pitched his project to the president of the Kansas Pacific, hoping that the backing of the railroad would change the minds of men like the one who had turned him down in Junction City. McCoy explained that the cattle trade could become a handsome addition to the business of the railroad. The president was no more impressed than the Junction City man had been. He dismissed McCoy's scheme as chimerical.

McCoy traipsed to the office of the Missouri Pacific, which traversed Missouri. What would that railroad charge to ship cattle if McCoy could get them to the Missouri border? The immaculately attired Missouri Pacific president took one look at McCoy's dress—"rough, stodgy, unblacked boots, a slouch hat, seedy coat, soiled shirt, and unmentionables that had seen better days twelve months previous," McCoy admitted—and concluded that he wasn't worth his time. "Get out of this office," the president said, "and let me not be troubled with any more of your style."

McCoy's confidence was shaken. Were his critics right? Was his plan *that* implausible? He made one last attempt. And, finally, he found his partner, in the modest Hannibal & St. Joseph Railroad. The company would furnish the cattle cars McCoy needed; he would ship the cattle on the cars, via the Kansas Pacific.

McCoy bought another ticket on the Kansas Pacific. He headed back out on the prairie, looking again for the place where the range cattle and the iron horse could meet. Abilene lay west of Junction City, farther from civilization. It wasn't much to look at. "A very small, dead place, consisting of about one dozen log huts, low, small, rude affairs, four-fifths of which were covered with dirt for roofing," was how McCoy described it. "The business of the burg was conducted in two small rooms, mere log huts. And of course the inevitable saloon, also in a log hut."

The residents were more picturesque than the buildings. "The proprietor of the saloon was a corpulent, jolly, good-souled, congenial old man of the backwoods pattern, who in his younger days loved to fish and hunt and enjoyed the life of the frontiersman. For his amusement a colony of pet prairie dogs were located on his lots, and often the old gentleman might be seen feeding his pets." He sold prairie dogs to tourists riding the train.

But Abilene had what McCoy was looking for. The grasslands surrounding the town on all sides formed one great pasture. Reliable creeks supplied water. It was more than a hundred miles from the farm settlements. And it was on the railroad.

McCoy sent word to the drovers on the trail that Abilene would welcome them, and he threw himself into making his promise true. "From Hannibal, Missouri, came the pine lumber, and from Lenape, Kansas, came the hard wood, and work began in earnest and with energy," he recalled. "In sixty days from July 1st a shipping yard that would accommodate three thousand cattle, a large pair of Fairbank's scales"—to weigh the animals—"a barn and an office were completed, and a good three story hotel was well on the way toward completion."

Meanwhile McCoy sent word to Northern buyers that Abilene would be the great market of the West. Thousands of cattle would be available for purchase.

His gamble paid off. The first herd arrived and was sold for a good price. Word flashed back down the trail, and a second herd followed the first. Then a third, and a fourth. By the end of the season some thirty-five thousand cattle had boarded railcars at Abilene for the stockyards and slaughterhouses of Chicago and cities farther east.

THE CATTLE INDUSTRY WASN'T MUCH DIFFERENT, CONCEPTU-ally, from the trades in beaver pelts and buffalo hides. In each case profit required connecting a Western resource to consumers in distant cities. Joseph McCoy, probably without drawing the parallel, intended to become the John Jacob Astor of cattle.

And Charles Goodnight would be John McLoughlin. Goodnight was a gatherer of cattle, an organizer of trail drives from Texas to Kansas. With practice he got his part of the business down to a science. "The ordinary trail-herd in the years following the Civil War numbered about 3,000 head of cattle," Goodnight recalled. "The outfit consisted of sixteen or eighteen men, each of whom had two good horses; a mess-wagon, drawn by four mules, which were driven by the cook; and a horse-wrangler, who had charge of the horse-herd." Goodnight had made a name as a Texas Ranger; his reputation helped him recruit the best trail hands. "We aimed to have as many experienced men as possible with our outfit," he said. "After a few years, there had been developed on the trail a class of men that could be depended upon anywhere."

The best trail hands earned wages of five dollars a day, which meant that at the end of a drive they could pocket several hundred dollars in cash. They worked long hours. "We broke camp at daylight and were in the saddle until dark," Goodnight said. "It was a rough, hard, adventurous life, but was not without its sunny side, and when everything moved smoothly the trip was an agreeable diversion from the monotony of the range."

Of course, things did not always move smoothly. There were rivers to cross, which involved either wading or swimming the herd. In the former case, the cattle could hit quicksand—a bottom so soft as not to bear their weight. Physics worked in the cattle's favor; if they kept calm, they could float and be pulled out by ropes. But the cattle often panicked, and could become exhausted and drown. Swimming a stream entailed risks of its own, again involving panic, exhaustion and drowning. The cowboys waded and swam in the thick of the herds; danger to the cattle became danger to them. Ironically, drowning was a common cause of death on the prairies, hundreds of miles from the ocean and any large bodies of water. It didn't help that many cowboys couldn't swim.

Snakes posed another danger, more to the cowboys than to the cattle. A prairie-dog hole could catch the hoof of a galloping horse, breaking the leg of the horse, which then had to be shot, and throwing the rider head over mane, at risk to the rider's neck, spine and limbs. Summer storms brought lightning, besides torrential rain; on the open plains a man on horseback was the tallest thing around, and the likeliest to attract the thunderbolts.

But the greatest danger was stampedes. "Nothing the cattlemen so feared as the stampede," Charlie Goodnight recalled. The Texas longhorns, being skittish by temperament—their wariness was an evolutionary advantage—were particularly prone to bolting. Stampedes were most likely early in a drive, before the rhythm of the trail set in and the hierarchy of the herd developed. "Everybody was on the alert," Goodnight said of the early days of the drive. "The men slept on the ground with the lariat wrapped around the wrist and with the horse so close that he could be mounted at a bound. Sometimes the demands were so urgent that a man's boots would not be taken off his feet for an entire week. The nerves of the men usually became wrought up to such a tension that it was a standing rule that no man was to be touched by another when he was asleep until after he had been spoken to. The man who suddenly aroused a sleeper was liable to be shot, as all were thoroughly armed and understood the instant use of the revolver or the rifle."

Despite the precautions, stampedes occurred. Often a night-time storm was the trigger. "The herd of 2,500 or 3,000 cattle might be lying on the bed-ground in the most perfect peace and security, with everything as quiet as a graveyard, when, in a second and without the slightest warning to the eye or ear of man, every animal would be on its feet, and the earth would tremble as the herd swept off through the darkness. The experience was one of the most thrilling a man ever could know. Every person in camp would be up and away. No one, not even the most experienced trailman, could, at the beginning of the stampede, guess the direction of the flight. The course appeared to be at random, for the cattle would plunge headlong against any obstacle and down any precipice that stood in their way."

The drovers did what they could. "The task of the men was to gain control of the herd and gradually turn the cattle until they were moving in a circle. Then, although they might break each other's horns off and crush one another badly, the great danger was past. A well-trained night-horse needed but little guidance, and knew that if the herd came his way, all that he had to do was to lead. The speed of the herd was terrific, but the position at the head of the stampede was just what the trailman desired, for there he was in a position to start the herd to turning. Advantage was taken of level ground, and when the leaders were started toward moving in a circle, the victory practically had been won."

A stampede was a force of nature. "The heat developed by a large drove of cattle during a stampede was surprising," Goodnight explained. "The faces of men riding on the leeward side of the herd would be almost blistered, as if they had been struck by a blast from a furnace; and the odor given off by the clashing horns and hoofs was nearly overpowering."

Yet against this force the men and their mounts worked miracles. "In the excitement of a stampede a man was not himself, and his horse was not the horse of yesterday. Man and horse were one, and the combination accomplished feats that would be utterly

Cowboy guarding his herd. All is calm on this Texas day.

impossible under ordinary circumstances." Together the hands and horses choreographed a bovine ballet that shook the earth, singed the grass and threatened everything near with horrible, instant death, but usually ended without more than minor damage. "The stampede then gradually came to an end; the strain was removed; the cowboys were the happiest men on earth; and their shouts and laughter could be heard for miles over the prairie."

THE COWBOY DEVELOPED OTHER SKILLS. HE COULD THROW A lariat around a running cow as easily as a city dweller tossed his wallet in a drawer. On his favorite pony he could cut a single cow from a herd in seconds. Cowboys sang to each other over the campfire; they also sang to the cattle, to calm them in the night and to keep them from stampeding.

The men learned to live on the simplest fare. "Corn bread, mast-fed bacon and coffee constitute nine-tenths of their diet," Joseph McCoy wrote. "Occasionally they have fresh beef and less often they have vegetables of any description. They do their own cooking in the rudest and fewest possible vessels, often not having a single plate or knife and fork other than their pocket knife, but gather round the camp kettle in true Indian style, and with a piece of bread in one hand proceed to fish up a piece of sow belly and dine sumptuously, not forgetting to stow away one or more quarts of the strongest coffee imaginable."

They took things as they came, the bad with the good. "The life of the cowboy is one of considerable daily danger and excitement," McCoy observed. "It is hard and full of exposure, but is wild and free, and the young man who has long been a cowboy has but little taste for any other occupation." The cowboy's path was uncluttered. "He lives hard, works hard, has but few comforts and fewer necessities. He has but little, if any, taste for reading. He enjoys a coarse practical joke or a smutty story; loves danger but abhors labor of the common kind; never tires riding, never wants to walk, no matter how short the distance he desires to go. He would rather fight with pistols than pray; loves tobacco, liquor and women better than any other trinity. His life borders nearly upon that of an Indian."

Occasionally cowboys advanced to become ranch owners. McCoy cited William Perryman, who began his career tending his father's stock, with the agreement that he could keep for himself every third calf born. "In a few years he was able to buy out his father's stock and then set out exclusively for himself," McCoy noted. "He has now been ranching for seventeen years and has acquired a fortune of princely magnitude. His ranches aggregate fully twenty-five thousand acres of land, all under fence, of which he cultivates but few acres, only sufficient for the necessities of his own house and one or two fancy saddle horses kept for his own private use. The balance of his lands are devoted to grazing. His stock of cattle numbers twenty-five thousand head, and annual increase varies from four to five thousand."

But most cowboys had no such ambition. They took their pay at the end of the drive and did more or less what Joe Meek and the fur trappers did at the annual rendezvous in the Rocky Mountains. "When the herd is sold and delivered to the purchaser, a day of rejoicing to the cowboy has come, for then he can go free and have a jolly time," Joseph McCoy said. "And it is a jolly time they have. Straightway after settling with their employers the barber shop is visited, and three to six months' growth of hair is shorn off, their long-grown, sunburnt beard set in due shape and properly blacked. Next a clothing store of the Israelitish style"—peddlers were often Jews or presumed to be—"is gone through, and the cowboy emerges a new man, in outward appearance, everything being new, not excepting the hat and boots." The well-dressed cowboy went out on the town. "The bar-room, the theatre, the gambling-room, the bawdy house, the dance house, each and all come in for their full share of attention."

Fun included fighting. "In any of these places an affront or a slight, real or imaginary, is cause sufficient for him to unlimber one or more 'mountain howitzers'"—heavy revolvers—"invariably found strapped to his person, and proceed to deal out death in unbroken doses to such as may be in range of his pistols. Whether real friends or enemies, no matter; his anger and bad whisky urge him on to deeds of blood and death."

The gunfights of Abilene and other cattle towns became legendary. As often happened with the West, especially in matters relating to cowboys, the legend outran the reality. Street life in the West was less lethal than in such notorious Eastern neighborhoods as New York's Five Points. And rarely did Western gunfights assume the stylized form depicted by novelists and, later, filmmakers, in which two antagonists faced each other on a dusty street, and victory went to the one with the quicker draw. The most famous of all the gunfights, at the O.K. Corral in Tombstone, Arizona

Territory, didn't take place at the O.K. Corral but in an unnamed empty lot, and there was nothing stylized or orderly about it. Dozens of shots were fired in a spasm of close-range violence. Three men died in the brawl; the other six walked away. The story almost died, too; not till decades later did it travel much beyond the West, reaching the national consciousness only when a breathless biographer included it in his life of Wyatt Earp, one of the survivors.

JOSEPH McCoy was proud of Abilene and its prosperity. Yet he was hardly uncritical of some of the people the town attracted. "At frontier towns where are centered many cattle and, as a result, considerable business is transacted, and many strangers congregate, there are always to be found a number of bad characters, both male and female, of the very worst class in the universe, such as have fallen below the level of the lowest type of the brute creation," McCoy said. "Men who live a soulless, aimless life, dependent upon the turn of a card for the means of living. They wear out a purposeless life, ever looking blear-eyed and dissipated, to whom life, from various causes, has long since become worse than a total blank; beings in the form of man whose outward appearance would betoken gentlemen but whose heart-strings are but a wisp of base sounding chords, upon which the touch of the higher and purer life have long since ceased to be felt." These were the bad men: the gamblers, gunfighters and renegades.

The bad women were even more dangerous. "When the darkness of the night is come to shroud their orgies from public gaze, these miserable beings gather into the halls of the dance house and 'trip the fantastic toe' to wretched music, ground out of dilapidated instruments by beings fully as degraded as the most vile." Yet the ladies of the night were catnip to the cowboys. "In this vortex of dissipation the average cowboy plunges with great delight. Few more wild, reckless scenes of abandoned debauchery can be seen on the civilized earth than a dance hall in full blast in one of the many frontier towns."

The cowboys had dreamed of this on many lonely nights on the trail, and they were not to be denied. "The cowboy enters the dance with a peculiar zest, not stopping to divest himself of his sombrero, spurs, or pistols, but just as he dismounts off of his cow pony, so he goes into the dance." The dancing cowboy made quite a figure. "With the front of his sombrero lifted at an angle of full forty-five degrees; his huge spurs jingling at every step or motion; his revolvers flapping up and down like a retreating sheep's tail; his eyes lit up with excitement, liquor and lust; he plunges in and 'hoes it down' at a terrible rate, in the most approved yet awkward country style, often swinging his partner clear off the floor for an entire circle, then 'balance all' with an occasional demoniacal yell, near akin to the war whoop of the savage Indian."

Periodically the "waltz to the bar" was called. The cowboy was expected to treat his partner to whiskey, and of course drink some himself. By this means the bars made their money and the dancing women earned their keep. No self-respecting cowboy, pockets full of cash, declined. The more he danced, the more he drank, and the more he drank, the less careful of his money he became. McCoy could have mentioned the other ways certain working women of Abilene separated the cowboys from their money, but he left that topic to his readers' imaginations.

"Such is the manner in which the cowboy spends his hard-earned dollars," McCoy concluded. "After a few days of frolic and debauchery, the cowboy is ready, in company with his comrades, to start back to Texas, often having not one dollar left of his summer wages." Yet he took back memories of high living that would last the year.

Some took back softer memories as well. Mrs. Lou Gore owned and managed the Drovers' Cottage, a hotel for cowboys. She looked after them when their drinking made them ill or their fighting plugged them with bullets. "She was the Florence Nightingale to relieve them," McCoy said. "Many a sick and wearied drover has she nursed and tenderly cared for until health was

Drovers' Cottage, Abilene. A pillow and a bed were most welcome after months on the trail.

restored; or in the event of death soothed their dying moments with all the kind offices that a true sister only so well understands how to perform. Many western drovers, rough, uncouth men, such as nature and the wild frontier produces, will ever hear the name of Mrs. Lou Gore mentioned only with emotions of kindest respect and tenderest memory."

43

HARD LESSON

THE ERA OF THE CATTLE DRIVES FROM TEXAS TO KANSAS was remarkably brief. It lasted less than a decade, ending when railroads reached the plains of Texas. Cowboys still rounded up cattle and drove them to the railheads, but these were now mere days from the cattle's home range rather than months.

The exception was a particular kind of drive, of cattle meant not for market but for stocking new ranges. The Texas longhorns were surprisingly resilient; though creatures of the scorching plains of south Texas, they could survive the bone-chilling winters of the northern plains, as the cattlemen discovered when cows driven north to the railroad didn't find buyers. The animals weren't worth driving back to Texas, and so were simply left to fend for themselves through the winter. Not only did they survive, they reproduced. In doing so they suggested to cattlemen that there was a whole new realm to be added to the cattle kingdom. Conveniently for the cattlemen, the longhorns showed their cold-resistance just as the buffalo hunters were completing the near-extermination of the previously dominant species. No sooner had the ecological niche opened than it began to be refilled.

One of those who helped in the filling was Theodore Roosevelt, who bought his Dakota ranch and became a cattleman at just this time. There were many others. In the early 1880s a boom mentality seized the range-cattle industry, a mentality not unlike that of the California gold rush. The range was finite, and those who arrived first could choose the best spots—near the railroad, with good water and streamside timber for building.

The cattle rush had its Sam Brannans: the boosters who shouted of the fortunes to be made on the range. James Brisbin had spent the dozen years after the Civil War on duty in the West as an officer in the army; he guessed that he could improve his pay by writing and selling a book called *The Beef Bonanza*. Brisbin concocted a letter, as from one brother to another, with the former urging the latter to come west and make a fortune in beef, just as he had. "Dear Brother," he wrote, "I have bought a cattle ranch, and as you have long wished to engage in business out West, I do not know of a better thing you can do than raise cattle. As you have no knowledge or experience in breeding, I will tell you what I think, with proper care, we can make out of it. The ranch is twenty-two miles from a railroad, and contains 720 acres of land, 600 acres of which is hay or grassland, and 120 acres good timber. The meadow will cut annually 2½ tons of hay to the acre, and there is a living stream on the land. The timber is heavy and will furnish logs for stables, corrals, and fuel for many years to come. The hills in the vicinity afford the best grazing, and we can have a range ten miles in extent."

Brisbin's alter ego made a specific proposal. "You can put in $2,500, and I will duplicate it and add $1,000 for bulls. For $5,000 we can get 400 head of Texas cows to start with, and I will add a sufficient number of Durham bulls to breed them." The Durhams added meat to the bony frames of the Texas longhorns. "At the end of one year the cows would have 400 calves, each worth $7.00. I count full yield, for in cross-breeding there is not one cow in a hundred barren." Already the money would be rolling in. "Our first year's profit is 400 calves, $7.00 each, $2,800." Addition became multiplication: the second year would yield $4,800; the third year $6,800; the fourth $10,200; the fifth $14,600. The writer would sell his share over time to the younger brother. "What business on earth is there that can equal this?" he asked. "You have often said you wished me to put you into a good business and show you how to make some money, and now, sir, I think I have pointed you out the way to a fortune, and the good wife too. In eleven years you can, by care, be at the head of a blooded-stock farm worth $100,000, and very soon afterwards its sole owner."

Brisbin's promise was echoed by writers of similar tracts. Some, like Brisbin, hoped to profit primarily from the sale of the books and pamphlets. Others—railroad companies, most notably—had land they wanted to sell. Still others were boosters of particular towns, counties and states.

The sales pitch worked. Investors lavished money on the cattle business, filling the northern plains with livestock and causing cities to emerge where mere rail stops had existed before. Cheyenne, the capital of Wyoming Territory, became the San Francisco of the cattle rush. "Sixteenth Street is a young Wall Street," a Wyoming editor remarked. "Millions are talked of as lightly as nickels, and all kinds of people are dabbling in steers." Speculation became abstracted from the cattle themselves, and developed a dynamic all its own. "Large transactions are made every day in which the buyer does not see a hoof of his purchase, and very likely does not use more than one half of the purchase money in the trade before he has sold and made an enormous margin in the deal." People quite ignorant of cattle and their habits jumped into the speculation with both feet. Lawyers were oddly susceptible, and apparently successful, the editor said. "A Cheyenne man who don't pretend to know a maverick from a mandamus has made a neat little margin of $15,000 this summer in small transactions and hasn't seen a cow yet that he has bought and sold."

THE BOOM LASTED UNTIL THE MID-1880s. AND THEN THE boosters, the investors, the ranchers and the cowboys discovered something crucial about the northern plains. The weather there could vary dramatically from year to year. The Indians might have told them this, had the Indians been asked. Some summers were drier than others; some winters colder. In the lifetime of an elderly

Sioux, drought had stricken the plains several times, searing the grass and causing buffalo numbers to plunge. The Indians recalled these as hungry times. When a cold winter followed a dry summer, they suffered even more.

The cattlemen learned the lesson in the punishing winter of 1886–1887. The massive die-off that terrible season cured tyros like Theodore Roosevelt of the notion that they might become cattle barons almost overnight. With much of his inheritance having floated down the Little Missouri on the ghoulish tide of frozen flesh, Roosevelt lacked the wherewithal to replenish his ranches. He refocused his energy on his first ambition, politics.

Those who stayed in the cattle business retrenched and built a new industry on sturdier foundations. It wasn't just the weather that produced the winter's slaughter; it was the overstocking of the range. Most of the ranchers on the northern plains owned little of the land their cattle grazed on. The land was in the public domain, with the grass free for the taking by whoever got there first. Existing ranchers used strong-arm tactics to keep newcomers from encroaching on what they considered their territory. After Roosevelt had bought his ranch, he received a visit from a squad of gunslingers in the employ of one of his neighbors, a French aristocrat named the Marquis de Morès, who was projecting a cattle empire of his own. Roosevelt was away at the time, hunting bears in the Rockies, but the leader of the gunmen, a rough character named Paddock, left a message. Roosevelt could *purchase* grazing rights in the area from the marquis, or he could get out.

Roosevelt, with confidence boosted by having bagged his grizzly, returned Paddock's call. Armed with pistol and rifle, he demanded to know what Paddock meant by his message. Paddock—and the marquis—evidently had thought that the greenhorn from the East could be easily intimidated. When Roosevelt demonstrated that he wouldn't go without a fight, Paddock explained that there had been a misunderstanding. Nothing more was said about Roosevelt's paying de Morès for the right to graze on public land.

Roosevelt's refusal to back down was a personal triumph, but it contributed to the public problem: too many cattle for the range to support. The cattle were already overgrazing the range before the bad winter hit. Roosevelt himself had helped organize an association of ranchers on the Little Missouri as a first step toward dealing with the issue. Similar groups gathered elsewhere; the Wyoming Stock Growers' Association was ceded control of the range by the Wyoming territorial legislature. But the cattle population on the range continued to grow. A first symptom of distress was falling prices for cattle. A second, much sharper, was the die-off of 1886–1887, which would have been less severe had the range and the cattle been in better shape before the blizzards came.

The winter accomplished what the cattlemen couldn't accomplish on their own. It convinced them they couldn't rely so heavily on public lands in running their operations. Of their own volition they limited the size of their herds; they purchased land on which to grow hay for winter fodder; they fenced their land to keep others' cattle out; they rotated their herds among fenced fields to let the range recover. They drilled wells to ensure a water supply. They imported Durhams and other breeds that, although less hardy than the longhorns, produced better beef.

In sum, in a shift that mirrored the transformation of the mining industry, they moved from the model in which a person with few resources could enter the cattle business and thrive to one that required major investments. The corporatization of the cattle business, like the corporatization of mining, squeezed out most individual entrepreneurs.

And it left the cowboy in the dust. Cowboys had always been hired hands. But they had had a great deal of freedom, and during much of the year they had plenty of leisure. Now they became industrial laborers, distinguishable from factory minions chiefly by working outdoors. "Cowboys don't have as soft a time as they did eight or ten years ago," one who experienced the transition remarked. "I remember when we sat around the fire the winter through and didn't do a lick of work for five or six months of the year, except to chop a little wood to build a fire to keep warm by. Now we go on the general roundup, then the calf roundup, then comes haying—something that the old-time cowboy never dreamed of—then the beef roundup and the fall calf roundup, and gathering bulls and weak cows, and after all this, a winter of feeding hay. I tell you times have changed."

44

INTO THE GREAT UNKNOWN

Times were changing all across the West. Territories settled earlier were filling up and becoming states. California (1850) had been followed by Oregon (1859), Kansas (1861), Nevada (1864), Nebraska (1867) and Colorado (1876). Utah, where the armed conflict that had loomed in 1857 fizzled without a shot being fired, would have been granted statehood if not for the Mormons' polygamy. Regions skirted by the early settlers as too remote or inhospitable yielded to exploration, typically sponsored by the federal government. The Lewis and Clark expedition of the nineteenth century's first decade had its post–Civil War counterparts in journeys of discovery led by John Wesley Powell and Ferdinand Hayden.

Powell tackled the great mystery of Western geography, a mystery that had its origins in the very first organized exploration of the West, by Coronado in the 1540s. Since Coronado's lieutenant García López de Cárdenas had stumbled upon the Grand Canyon of the Colorado River, almost nothing in detail and little enough in outline had been confirmed about the canyon, the river or the broad plateau the river bisected. By the middle of the nineteenth century, explorers and cartographers had surmised that the Grand River of Colorado and the Green River of Wyoming were upper branches of the river that ran through the canyon, and from the canyon to the Gulf of California, but this surmise came by process of elimination rather than by observation. The two northern rivers had to empty somewhere, and the southern river had to rise somewhere, and the likeliest conclusion was that the answer to each half of the puzzle was the other half. But no one had ever proven this. No one had started down the Green River or the Grand and emerged on the Colorado.

No one, that is, had made the voyage and lived to tell of it. Lewis Manly and a party of forty-niners had sought a shortcut to California via the Green River and more than once nearly drowned. They finally abandoned the river at the urging of an Indian they met, who in sign language told them they could never survive its lower course. The canyon had swallowed all who had gone before. The alternative Manly's party chose was only a little better; their group was the one that gave Death Valley its name.

John Wesley Powell considered the ignorance about the Colorado an affront to modern science and a challenge to himself. Powell was a professor of geology and a Union veteran of the Civil War who had lost his right arm at the battle of Shiloh. He could have taken a medical discharge, but he was a stubborn fellow who insisted on finishing what he had started. By war's end he commanded Union artillery in the Department of the Tennessee. He commanded, too, the respect of his superiors for his determination and grit.

Powell's reputation served him well after the war. He had previously floated down the Ohio and the Mississippi and concluded that there was no better way to learn about a country than by following its rivers. He conceived of applying the same principle to the Green and the Colorado. He would start in the Green and, braving its canyons, prove its connection to the Colorado and *its* canyons.

Powell persuaded the army to sponsor him. He made his case in terms of science: the expedition would expand human knowledge about the geography and geology of the Colorado Plateau and of the large forces that shape the earth. He added an economic element: the river or its tributaries might be dammed, providing

John Wesley Powell. The scientist, soldier and
explorer completed the map of the West.

water for irrigated agriculture. It wasn't inconceivable that the
Colorado could be made navigable by dams and locks, giving the
Rocky Mountain region a southern outlet to the Pacific.

To all this Powell added an emotional, even romantic argument. He related a tale the Indians told of the creation of the
Grand Canyon. "Long ago, there was a great and wise chief, who
mourned the death of his wife, and would not be comforted until
Ta-vwoats, one of the Indian gods, came to him, and told him she
was in a happier land, and offered to take him there, that he might
see for himself, if, upon his return, he would cease to mourn,"
Powell wrote. "The great chief promised. Then Ta-vwoats made
a trail through the mountains that intervene between that beautiful land, the balmy region in the great west, and this, the desert

home of the poor Nú-ma. This trail was the canyon gorge of the Colorado. Through it he led him; and when they had returned, the deity exacted from the chief a promise that he would tell no one of the joys of that land, lest, through discontent with the circumstances of this world, they should desire to go to heaven. Then he rolled a river into the gorge, a mad, raging stream, that should engulf any that might attempt to enter thereby."

Powell added, in his own voice, "More than once I have been warned by the Indians not to enter this canyon. They considered it disobedience to the gods and contempt for their authority, and believed that it would surely bring upon me their wrath."

But he was determined to dare the gods and make the journey. With army support he organized an expedition. In May 1869, Powell and nine comrades set out. "The good people of Green River City turn out to see us start," he wrote in the log of the journey. "We raise our little flag, push the boats from shore, and the swift current carries us down." Powell had designed the boats and had them constructed in Chicago, whence they had been transported by train to Green River City, where the recently completed Union Pacific crossed the Green River.

Powell described the four vessels on which the success of the expedition, and the lives of the men, depended. "Three are built of oak; stanch and firm; double-ribbed, with double stem and stern posts, and further strengthened by bulkheads, dividing each into three compartments. Two of these, the fore and aft, are decked, forming watertight cabins. It is expected that these will buoy the boats should the waves roll over them in rough water." The three boats were twenty-one feet long and, emptied of cargo, could be carried by four men each. "The fourth boat is made of pine, very light, but sixteen feet in length, with a sharp cut-water, and every way built for fast rowing, and divided into compartments as the others." This was Powell's flagship.

They carried rations for a journey of ten months. They expected to winter on the river, and so packed warm clothing. They brought

Into the unknown. Powell's crew sets off down the Green River.

rifles and ammunition for hunting and self-defense, and traps to catch game. They brought tools for repairing boats and building cabins. Powell's scientific instruments included chronometers, sextants, thermometers, barometers and compasses. The provisions, tools and instruments were divided among the boats, so that if any one boat were lost, the expedition wouldn't wholly lack something essential.

The gear burdened the boats. "Only with the utmost care is it possible to float in the rough river without shipping water," Powell recorded. They hadn't traveled two miles before one of the flotilla ran into a sandbar. "The men jump into the stream and thus lighten the vessels, so that they drift over, and on we go." A short while later, one of the boats broke an oar trying to avoid a rock. "Thus crippled, she strikes. The current is swift, and she is sent reeling and rocking into the eddy." Two other oars were lost overboard and the men thoroughly disconcerted before the boat was freed from the eddy and the good oars retrieved.

The men gradually got the feel of the boats, and three days passed with no greater mishaps. Then the Green River met the Uintah Mountains, and the canyon country began. "On the right, the rocks are broken and ragged, and the water fills the channel from cliff to cliff," Powell wrote. The walls of the canyon were bright red sandstone; Powell called it Flaming Gorge. "Now the river turns abruptly around a point to the right, and the waters plunge swiftly down among great rocks; and here we have our first experience with canyon rapids."

Powell took the lead, standing on the deck of his boat to see as much of the way ahead as possible, and to be seen amid the waves by the boats behind. "Untried as we are with such waters, the moments are filled with intense anxiety," Powell recorded. "Soon our boats reach the swift current; a stroke or two, now on this side, now on that, and we thread the passage with exhilarating velocity, mounting the high waves, whose foaming crests dash over us, and plunging into the troughs."

The four boats passed this first serious test; in less than a mile they shot out into calmer water. The men decided they liked their adventure. "Today we have an exciting ride," Powell wrote on June 1. "The river rolls down the canyon at a wonderful rate, and, with no rocks in the way, we make almost railroad speed. Here and there the water rushes into a narrow gorge; the rocks on the side roll it into the center in great waves, and the boats go leaping and bounding over these like things of life."

They reached calm water, only to hear an ominous roar in the distance. Powell advanced carefully and discovered a waterfall. He directed the boats to shore. The men unloaded the vessels while he looked for a path around the falls. Several of the men lowered the lightest boat by rope to the brink of the falls. When they could no longer hold it against the force of the current, they let it go over the edge. Empty, and putting its watertight compartments to good use, it survived the plunge, bobbing on top of the waves below the falls. Others of the party, having been positioned below the falls, reeled it in via a rope tied to the bow.

They repeated the process with the other boats, repacked the cargo, and continued on their way.

A short distance farther Powell spied an inscription on the canyon wall, above the high water mark. "Ashley 1835," it read, or "Ashley 1855"; the third digit was obscure and the men couldn't agree. Powell recalled having heard from an old mountain man that someone named Ashley had descended the river. Apparently he had made it this far. Powell also recalled that several members of Ashley's party had not come out of the canyon alive. "We resolve on great caution," he recorded. "Ashley Falls is the name we give to the cataract."

In fact, William Ashley, the principal of the company that first hired Joe Meek, had been on the river in 1825, which accounted for the fading of the inscription. And indeed, most of his party had drowned in rapids below this spot.

The canyon displayed the immense forces at work in the creation of the rapids and falls. "The river is very narrow; the right wall vertical for two or three hundred feet, the left towering to a great height, with a vast pile of broken rocks lying between the foot of the cliff and the water," Powell wrote. "Some of the rocks broken down from the ledge above have tumbled into the channel and caused this fall. One great cubical block, thirty or forty feet high, stands in the middle of the stream, and the waters, parting to either side, plunge down about twelve feet, and are broken again by the smaller blocks into a rapid below."

The men got better at handling the boats in rough water. But not quite good enough. Powell landed his boat above another falls, and signaled for the others to do the same, so that he could reconnoiter on foot. Two of the three boats did, but not the third. "I hear a shout, and looking around, see one of the boats shooting down," he recounted. "I feel that its going over is inevitable." The drop was steeper than he had thought. "The first fall is not great, only ten or twelve feet, and we often run such; but below, the river tumbles down again for forty or fifty feet, in a channel filled with dangerous rocks that break the waves into whirlpools and beat them into foam." He ran along the bank, fearing the worst. "I pass around a great crag just in time to see the boat strike a rock, and, rebounding from the shock, careen and fill the open compartment"—where the men sat—"with water. Two of the men lose their oars; she swings around, and is carried down at a rapid rate, broadside on, for a few yards, and strikes amidships on another rock with great force, is broken quite in two, and the men are thrown into the river."

Powell scrambled over the rocks on the bank even while trying to keep the men, clinging to the wreckage of the boat, in view. "Down the river they drift, past the rocks for a few hundred yards to a second rapid, filled with huge boulders, where the boat strikes again, and is dashed to pieces, and the men and fragments are soon carried beyond my sight."

Powell ran on. "I turn a bend, and see a man's head above the water, washed about in a whirlpool below a great rock." The man was Frank Goodman, and he tried to get a grip on the rock, but his hands kept slipping. Another of the men approached Goodman from an island onto which the other man had been washed. "He comes near enough to reach Frank with a pole"—a stick on the island, apparently—"which he extends toward him. The latter lets go the rock, grasps the pole, and is pulled ashore." A third man also managed to make the island.

Yet they were hardly safe. On either side of the island, the river raged past. And below the island lay another waterfall.

A rescue was set in motion. A man named Sumner took the light boat and, starting far above the island, succeeded in reaching its head. Then the three stranded men and Sumner, wading in the river neck-deep, pulled the boat as far upstream as possible from the head of the island. They knew the current would suck them toward the falls as soon as they tried to cross to the bank, and they wanted to give themselves a fighting chance to make the crossing before they went over. When they had gotten as far up as they could, they hauled themselves into the boat and rowed for their lives toward the bank. To the great relief of Powell and the others, they made it. "We are as glad to shake hands with them as though they had been on a voyage around the world, and wrecked on a distant coast," Powell concluded.

The good feeling was tempered by the knowledge that the four boats were now three. And the rations and equipment had shrunk proportionally. How many miles remained of the voyage, no one knew. How many more falls they would encounter, and how much worse they might be than the ones passed so far, were equally unknown. Their losses were all too obvious.

CURIOSITY, AS MUCH AS ANYTHING ELSE, HAD ENTICED Powell into the canyon. Curiosity nearly prevented his getting out. He made a habit, while the men were pitching camp or resting after supper, of climbing the walls of the canyon for a better view. George Bradley sometimes accompanied him, as Bradley did on June 18. "We start up a gulch; then pass to the left, on a bench, along the wall; then up again, over broken rocks; then we reach more benches, along which we walk, until we find more broken rocks and crevices, by which we climb, still up, until we have ascended six or eight hundred feet," Powell wrote. "Then we are met by a sheer precipice." There seemed no way forward. But Powell wasn't discouraged easily. "Looking about, we find a place where it seems possible to climb. I go ahead, Bradley hands the barometer to me, and follows." The barometer was for measuring altitude. "So we proceed, stage by stage, until we are nearly to the summit. Here, by making a spring, I gain a foothold in a little crevice, and grasp an angle of the rock overhead."

On the entire journey till now, the men had marveled at Powell's ability to do everything they could do, but with one arm. His lack became apparent at this point. "I find I can get up no farther, and cannot step back, for I dare not let go with my hand, and cannot reach foot-hold below without." Powell did something he almost never did. "I call to Bradley for help."

Bradley tried to give it. "He finds a way by which he can get to the top of the rock over my head, but cannot reach me. Then he looks around for some stick or limb of a tree, but finds none."

Powell was weakening. "My muscles begin to tremble. It is sixty or eighty feet to the foot of the precipice. If I lose my hold I shall fall to the bottom, and then perhaps roll over the bench, and tumble still farther down the cliff." Serious injury, likely death, would be the inevitable result.

His companion had an idea. "It occurs to Bradley to take off his drawers, which he does, and swings them down to me. I hug close to the rock, let go with my hand, seize the dangling legs, and, with his assistance, I am enabled to gain the top."

THE JOURNEY CONTINUED, AND REVEALED A LANDSCAPE unlike any Powell had imagined. "We pass through a region of the wildest desolation," he recorded. "The canyon is very tortuous, the river very rapid, and many lateral canyons enter on either side. They usually have their branches, so that the region is cut into a wilderness of gray and brown cliffs. In several places, these lateral canyons are only separated from each other by narrow walls, often hundreds of feet high, forming passages from one canyon into another. These we often call natural bridges; but they were never intended to span streams. They had better, perhaps, be called side doors between canyon chambers."

In mid-July, after seven weeks on the river, the party reached the confluence of the Grand River with the Green, the two forming the Colorado River. Powell, again joined by Bradley, climbed to another vantage point. "What a world of grandeur is spread before us!" he wrote. "Below is the canyon through which the Colorado runs. We can trace its course for miles, and at points catch glimpses of the river. From the northwest comes the Green, in a narrow, winding gorge. From the northeast comes the Grand, through a canyon that seems bottomless from where we stand. Away to the west are lines of cliff and ledges of rock—not such as you may have seen where the quarryman splits his blocks, but ledges from which the gods might quarry mountains that, rolled out on the plain below, would stand a lofty range; and not such cliffs as you may have seen where the swallow builds its nest, but cliffs where the soaring eagle is lost to view ere he reaches the summit."

In early August they reached the head of the Grand Canyon itself. "We are now ready to start on our way down the Great Unknown," Powell wrote. "Our boats, tied to a common stake, are chafing each other, as they are tossed by the fretful river. They ride high and buoyant, for their loads are lighter than we could desire. We have but a month's rations remaining. The flour has been resifted through the mosquito net sieve; the spoiled bacon has been dried, and the worst of it boiled; the few pounds of dried apples have been spread in the sun, and reshrunken to their normal bulk; the sugar has all melted, and gone on its way down the river; but we have a large sack of coffee. The lighting of the boats has this advantage: they will ride the waves better, and we shall have but little to carry when we make a portage."

The Grand Canyon dwarfed anything they had seen so far. "We are three-quarters of a mile in the depths of the earth, and the great river shrinks into insignificance as it dashes its angry waves against the walls and cliffs that rise to the world above; they are but puny ripples, and we but pigmies, running up and down the sands or lost among the boulders."

They continued to lack crucial information. "We have an unknown distance yet to run; an unknown river yet to explore. What falls there are, we know not; what rocks beset the channel, we know not; what walls rise over the river, we know not." But the members of the expedition were in good spirits. "The men talk as cheerfully as ever; jests are bandied about freely this morning." On Powell, though, the weight of responsibility hung heavily. "To me the cheer is somber and the jests are ghastly."

No canyon that Powell ever heard of was like the one the party was penetrating. "The walls, now, are more than a mile in height—a vertical distance difficult to appreciate." Powell knew his journal would be read by Easterners; he tried to give a sense of proportion. "Stand on the south steps of the Treasury building, in Washington, and look down Pennsylvania Avenue to the Capitol

Park, and measure this distance overhead, and imagine cliffs to extend to that altitude, and you will understand what I mean; or, stand at Canal Street, in New York, and look up Broadway to Grace Church, and you have about that distance; or, stand at Lake Street Bridge, in Chicago, and look to the Central Depot, and you have it again."

The river boiled along at a frightful pace. The men ran some rapids, portaged around others. They had hair-breadth escapes. "The boats are entirely unmanageable," Powell wrote of one stretch. "No order in their running can be preserved; now one, now another, is ahead, each crew laboring for its own preservation." The rapids seized the boats, swamping one. "A great wave fills the open compartment; she is waterlogged and drifts unmanageable. Breaker after breaker rolls over her, and one capsizes her. The men are thrown out; but they cling to the boat, and she drifts down some distance, alongside of us, and we are able to catch her. She is soon bailed out, and the men are aboard once more; but the oars are lost."

One afternoon, while the men pitched camp, Powell explored a side canyon. He came across the ruins of some rock houses, obviously very old. A milling stone, for the grinding of corn by hand, lay in one of the rooms. Broken pottery was strewn outside. Footpaths worn into the rock indicated someone's long residence. But who? And why there? "It is ever a source of wonder to us why these ancient people sought such inaccessible places for their homes," he remarked. "They were, doubtless, an agricultural race, but there are no lands here, of any considerable extent, that they could have cultivated." Perhaps they had built terraces on the steep faces. "But why should they seek such spots? Surely the country was not so crowded with population as to demand the utilization of so barren a region." Powell guessed that these canyon dwellers might have been fugitives from Spanish rule. "Those old Spanish conquerors had a monstrous greed for gold, and a wondrous lust for saving souls. Treasures they must have; if not on earth, why, then, in heaven; and when they failed to find heathen temples,

bedecked with silver, they propitiated Heaven by seizing the heathen themselves."

By mid-August the provisions were running dangerously low.
"We have now only musty flour sufficient for ten days, a few dried
apples, but plenty of coffee," Powell wrote. "We must make all
haste possible."

The summer sun blazed overhead, and the canyon walls focused
its beams on the voyagers. Most of the party lacked hats; none had
an entire suit of clothes. And despite the day's heat, the nights
were chilly. "So we gather drift wood, and build a fire; but after
supper the rain, coming down in torrents, extinguishes it, and we
sit up all night, on the rocks, shivering, and are more exhausted by
the night's discomfort than by the day's toil."

At every turn Powell and the others stared agape at the geological record that unfolded before them. Slates, shales, sandstones,
limestones, granites, marble and lava lay stacked like pages in the
history of the earth. "The book is open, and I can read as I run,"
Powell wrote.

To their surprise they discovered an active vegetable garden,
planted by Indians, currently absent, in a side canyon apparently
accessible from the canyon rim. The corn was not yet ripe. "But
there are some nice, green squashes. We carry ten or a dozen of
these on board our boats, and hurriedly leave, not willing to be
caught in our robbery, yet excusing ourselves by pleading our great
want." They cooked the loot and gobbled it down. "Never was fruit
so sweet as these stolen squashes."

They entered a granite canyon where the river plunged faster
and louder than at any place on the journey so far. They landed,
and Powell reconnoitered. He got himself in a fix again. "In my
eagerness to reach a point where I can see the roaring fall below,
I go too far on the wall, and can neither advance nor retreat. I
stand with one foot on a little projecting rock, and cling with my
hand fixed in a little crevice. Finding I am caught here, suspended
400 feet above the river, into which I should fall if my footing fails,
I call for help. The men come, and pass me a line, but I cannot

let go of the rock long enough to take hold of it. Then they bring two or three of the largest oars. All this takes time which seems very precious to me; but at last they arrive. The blade of one of the oars is pushed into a little crevice in the rock beyond me, in such a manner that they can hold me pressed against the wall. Then another is fixed in such a way that I can step on it, and thus I am extricated."

This solved Powell's immediate problem, but it left the question of whether this stretch of river could be run. They hadn't seen anything so frightful. "The lateral streams have washed boulders into the river, so as to form a dam, over which the water makes a broken fall of eighteen or twenty feet; then there is a rapid, beset with rocks, for two or three hundred yards, while, on the other side, points of the wall project into the river. Then there is a second fall below; how great, we cannot tell. Then there is a rapid, filled with huge rocks, for one or two hundred yards. At the bottom of it, from the right wall, a great rock projects quite half way across the river."

Against appearances, Powell declared the pitch passable. "I announce to the men that we are going to run it in the morning." He wasn't sure their food would last if they took the time for what would be a difficult portage.

His decision provoked a mutiny. The men had repeatedly tempted fate on Powell's orders, but three of them, including two brothers, now concluded that this wasn't so much a tempting as a date with certain death. The elder of the two took Powell aside and urged him to reconsider. They all could abandon the river, the man said, climb out of the canyon, and find their way to Mormon settlements on the rim above.

For the first time Powell wondered if he was doing the right thing. "All night long, I pace up and down a little path, on a few yards of sand beach, along by the river. Is it wise to go on? I go to the boats again, to look at our rations. I feel satisfied that we can get over the danger immediately before us; what there may be below I know not." Powell wasn't even sure they could climb out of the canyon at their present location. Nor, given their dearth of provisions, was it likely they could reach the Mormon settlements, which were at least seventy or eighty miles away, across desert and mountains. Farther down the river, the walls appeared to be still more forbidding. They might well become trapped, if they weren't already. And the settlements, should they get out of the canyon, would be that much farther away.

He made a decision for himself. "For years I have been contemplating this trip. To leave the exploration unfinished, to say that there is a part of the canyon which I cannot explore, having already almost accomplished it, is more than I am willing to acknowledge, and I determine to go on."

Come morning he polled the men. The voyage had been underwritten by the army, but it was not a military expedition, and the men were free to go if they pleased. The three objectors said they remained opposed; they were leaving. The other six said they would go forward with Powell.

Powell gave the three leavers weapons: two rifles and a shotgun. They accepted these. He ordered that the scant provisions remaining be divided with the leavers. They rejected this offer, saying they could shoot something once they got out of the canyon. But the cook prepared a pan of biscuits, and left them for the three to take.

The expedition had been incommunicado with the outside world since the day they launched the boats on the Green River. Powell had kept a double set of records, lest one be lost in an overturning or a wreck. He now gave one set to the leavers, with orders that they be forwarded to the government. He wrote a letter to his wife and likewise handed it over. One of the remainers gave the leavers his watch, that it be sent to his sister in case he was never heard from again.

The three leavers once more asked Powell and the others to reconsider. "They entreat us not to go on," Powell wrote, "and tell us that it is madness to set out in this place, that we can never get safely through it; and, further, that the river turns again to the south into the granite, and a few miles of such rapids and falls will exhaust our entire stock of rations, and then it will be too late to climb out. Some tears are shed; it is rather a solemn parting; each party thinks the other is taking the dangerous course."

THE DEPARTING TRIO CLIMBED UP A SIDE CANYON; POWELL and the rest headed down the river again. They lowered the boats by rope over the first fall, then put out into the stream. "We glide rapidly along the foot of the wall, just grazing one great rock, then pull out a little into the chute of the second fall, and plunge over it. The open compartment is filled when we strike the first wave below, but we cut through it, and then the men pull with all their power toward the left wall, and swing clear of the dangerous rock below all right."

They started feeling better about their prospects. As bad as the stretch had appeared from above, it proved no worse than others they had run before.

Then things *did* get worse. "A little stream comes in from the left, and below there is a fall, and still below another fall," Powell recorded. "The river tumbles down, over and among the rocks, in whirlpools and great waves, and the waters are lashed into mad, white foam." They tried one side of the channel, then realized that it was becoming impassable. Pulling hard on the oars, they backed up the stream and crossed over. The canyon walls were too close to the water and too steep for a portage. Powell scaled a high basalt escarpment that overlooked the first fall and decided to lower the boats by a rope secured at that height. One man would remain in each boat to keep it off the rocks.

But the rope wasn't long enough. Bradley was the one standing in the first boat, and the rope was secured to the stem-post. The men played out all the rope they had, yet this left Bradley and the boat in the swiftest part of the stream, being bounced from left to right by the current, and crashing into the rocks on either side. A second rope was brought up, and the men prepared to attach it to the first. Bradley couldn't see this from the boat, and in any event all his attention was devoted to keeping the boat from wrecking on the rocks.

Powell leaped up on a rock in what he hoped would be Bradley's line of sight. He waved his hat and shouted over the roar of the cataract. But Bradley didn't notice.

"Just at this moment, I see him take his knife from its sheath, and step forward to cut the line," Powell wrote. "He has evidently decided that it is better to go over with the boat as it is, than to wait for her to be broken to pieces." But even this decision came too late. "As he leans over, the boat shears again into the stream, the stem-post breaks away, and she is loose. With perfect composure Bradley seizes the great scull oar, places it in the stern rowlock, and pulls with all his power (and he is an athlete) to turn the bow of the boat down stream, for he wishes to go bow down, rather than drift broadside on. One, two strokes he makes, and a third just as he goes over, and the boat is fairly turned, and she goes down almost beyond our sight, though we are more than a hundred feet above the river. Then she comes up again, on a great wave, and down and up, then around behind some great rocks, and is lost in the mad, white foam below."

Powell and the others strained their eyes from their elevated vantage, looking for Bradley and the boat to reappear beyond the rocks. But they saw nothing except the furious water. "Bradley is gone, so it seems." They glanced at one another, saying not a word.

Finally, far down the stream, something bobbed on the frothy surface. "It is evidently a boat. A moment more, and we see Bradley standing on deck, swinging his hat to show he is all right. But he is in a whirlpool." The other men had the boat's stem-post at the end of their rope. They couldn't tell how badly the craft was disabled.

Powell at once decided to go to Bradley's rescue. While two of the men tried to make their way along the bank, Powell and the others challenged the falls and rapids directly. "Away we go over the falls. A wave rolls over us, and our boat is unmanageable.

Another great wave strikes us, the boat rolls over, and tumbles and tosses, I know not how." Powell apparently hit his head on a rock and lost consciousness, for the next thing he knew, Bradley was hauling him out of the water.

Somehow they all survived. But they were down to a boat and a half, and they still had no idea how much canyon they had left to cover.

Yet the gods of the canyon were smiling on them. The next day, August 29, 1869, Powell wrote in the log: "We start very early this morning. The river still continues swift, but we have no serious difficulty, and at twelve o'clock emerge from the Grand Canyon of the Colorado."

45

THE ARID REGION

JOHN WESLEY POWELL'S VOYAGE DOWN THE COLORADO made him a celebrity and a national hero. It filled in a large blank space on the map of the American West, and his journal of the expedition, after he published it, allowed armchair explorers to share the dangers and thrills of a trip none but a handful would ever take.

Yet Powell remained a scientist, and he employed his fame as a platform from which to speak on the fundamental problem of the West, as he conceived it. In a document titled *Report on the Lands of the Arid Region*, written for the federal secretary of the interior, Powell declared that the distinguishing characteristic of the West—what made it different from the East—was that the West was dry. East of the Great Plains—specifically, east of the 100th meridian—farmers could reasonably expect to grow crops with the water nature provided as rain and snow. West of the 100th meridian, natural precipitation had to be supplemented by irrigation. There were exceptions: the Pacific Northwest and parts of coastal California. But otherwise, aridity was the rule, and the problem to be overcome.

This meant that policies, laws and customs that had evolved in the East had to be modified, or wholly transformed, if the West was to thrive. Individualism had built the East, but it would fail in the West unless complemented by large doses of collective action.

The yeoman farmer of the East could succeed on his own efforts and those of his family; farmers in the West needed help. "The redemption of all these lands will require extensive and comprehensive plans, for the execution of which aggregated capital or cooperative labor will be necessary," Powell wrote. "Here, individual farmers, being poor men, cannot undertake the task."

Irrigation was the central task, and irrigation, above all, demanded collective effort. Where rain was scarce, successful farming required that what fell on a broad area be collected and delivered to a small area. This in turn necessitated dams, canals and pipelines. No individual farmer had the ability to build such infrastructure. But farmers acting together *could* marshal the requisite authority and funding. Powell cited the Mormons, who, working in unison, had built irrigation systems and created flourishing farms in the valley of the Great Salt Lake. What the Mormons had done in the name of their religion, other Americans could do in the name of democracy.

Powell prescribed specific changes in laws. The Homestead Act had been written from the experience of the humid East; it should be amended for application to the arid West. The quarter-section, which suited a family in the East, was too small or too large for the West. It was too small if the Western farmer grew wheat without irrigation, or if he ran a cattle ranch. It was too large if the land was irrigated, for no single farmer could cultivate that much irrigated land, and other worthy claimants would get squeezed out. The homestead law should be adjusted accordingly. Laws regarding water rights should be revised as well. The first Western water laws had been written in California, to suit mining operations. The state laws there permitted water rights to be sold separately from land rights. This pleased the mining industry, but applied to farming, it fostered monopolies of water supplies, to the detriment of whole farming communities. State water laws should be rewritten or preempted by federal law.

The process had begun, Powell said. "Customs are forming and regulations are being made by common consent among the people in some districts already." Cattlemen's associations like Theodore Roosevelt's in Dakota came to mind. These instances should be extrapolated. Most of the lands in the West were federal lands; the federal government was the appropriate agency to accomplish the extrapolation. The Mormons had made their part of the desert bloom; under Washington's wise guidance, much of the remainder of the West might see a similar efflorescence.

POWELL'S CALL FOR PUBLIC MANAGEMENT OF WESTERN WATER dovetailed with a movement envisioning similar custody for special places in the West. At the moment when Powell was designing the boats that would carry his party down the Colorado, a Scottish immigrant to America embarked on a journey of his own, to the Yosemite Valley of California. "The landscapes of the Santa Clara Valley were fairly drenched with sunshine, all the air was quivering with the songs of the meadow-larks, and the hills were so covered with flowers that they seemed to be painted," John Muir wrote of his departure from the southern end of San Francisco Bay. Muir took his time, wandering across the Central Valley and into the Sierra foothills. He followed the Merced River upward, toward its origins deep in the mountains, till he reached the goal of his one-man expedition.

"No temple made with hands can compare with Yosemite," Muir wrote. "Every rock in its walls seems to glow with life. Some lean back in majestic repose; others, absolutely sheer or nearly so for thousands of feet, advance beyond their companions in thoughtful attitudes, giving welcome to storms and calms alike, seemingly aware, yet heedless, of everything going on about them. Awful in stern, immovable majesty, how softly these rocks are adorned, and how fine and reassuring the company they keep: their feet among beautiful groves and meadows, their brows in the sky, a thousand flowers leaning confidingly against their feet, bathed in floods of water, floods of light, while the snow and waterfalls, the winds and avalanches and clouds shine and sing and wreathe about them as the years go by, and myriads of small winged creatures—birds, bees, butterflies—give glad animation and help to make all the air into music. Down through the middle of the Valley flows the crystal Merced, River of Mercy, peacefully quiet, reflecting lilies and trees and the onlooking rocks; things frail and fleeting and types of endurance meeting here and blending in countless forms, as if into this one mountain mansion Nature had gathered her choicest treasures, to draw her lovers into close and confiding communion with her."

Muir was the most ardent of Yosemite's lovers; the valley and its environs became the object of his enduring affection and the subject of his literary raptures. He returned to Yosemite the next year and subsequently made it his home. From his cabin on Yosemite Creek he explored every creek and rill, every cliff and waterfall, every ridge and dome of the valley and the land around it. He climbed to the top of Yosemite Falls, edging dangerously close to the point at which it leaps into space, a thousand feet above the valley floor. "The last incline down which the stream journeys so gracefully is so steep and smooth one must slip cautiously forward on hands and feet alongside the rushing water, which so near one's head is very exciting," he wrote. "But to gain a perfect view one must go yet farther, over a curving brow to a slight shelf on the extreme brink. This shelf, formed by the flaking off of a fold of granite, is about three inches wide, just wide enough for a safe rest for one's heels. To me it seemed nerve-trying to slip to this narrow foothold and poise on the edge of such precipice so close to the confusing whirl of the waters; and after casting longing glances over the shining brow of the fall and listening to its sublime psalm, I concluded not to attempt to go nearer; but, nevertheless, against reasonable judgment, I did. Noticing some tufts of artemisia in a cleft of rock, I filled my mouth with the leaves, hoping their bitter taste might help to keep caution keen and prevent giddiness. In spite of myself I reached the little ledge, got my heels well set, and worked sidewise twenty or thirty feet to a point close to the out-plunging current. Here the view is perfectly free down into the heart of the bright irised throng of comet-like streamers into which the whole ponderous volume of the fall separates, two or three hundred feet below the brow."

Winter gave Yosemite a different look. Blizzards filled the valley and cloaked the mountains with slabs of snow that grew unstable as the snows deepened. Avalanches thundered down the slopes—to Muir's delight. "One fine Yosemite morning after a heavy snowfall, being eager to see as many avalanches as possible and wide views of the forest and summit peaks in their new white robes before the sunshine had time to change them, I set out early to climb by a side canyon to the top of a commanding ridge a little over three thousand feet above the Valley," he recalled. The looseness of the snow made the climbing tedious. "Most of the way I sank waist deep, almost out of sight in some places." He struggled for hours and hours. Yet he still hoped to make the summit, if only to see the sunset. "But I was not to get summit views of any sort that day, for deep trampling near the canyon head, where the snow was strained, started an avalanche, and I was swished down to the foot of the canyon as if by enchantment. The wallowing ascent had taken nearly all day, the descent only about a minute. When the avalanche started I threw myself on my back and spread my arms to try to keep from sinking. Fortunately, though the grade of the canyon is very steep, it is not interrupted by precipices large enough to cause outbounding or free plunging. On no part of the rush was I buried. I was only moderately imbedded on the surface or at times a little below it, and covered with a veil of back-streaming dust particles; and as the whole mass beneath and about me joined in the flight there was no friction, though I was tossed here and there and lurched from side to side. When the avalanche swedged and came to rest I found myself on top of the crumpled pile without bruise or scar. This was a fine experience."

Even finer was an earthquake. Muir's examination of the rocks of Yosemite had convinced him that glaciers had carved the valley. This view contradicted conventional wisdom among geologists, which held that earthquakes had caused the floor of the valley to sink thousands of feet relative to the highlands around it.

The earthquake theory wasn't implausible, given the frequency of quakes in the region. Muir felt one himself in 1872. "At half-past two o'clock of a moonlit morning in March, I was awakened by a tremendous earthquake, and though I had never before enjoyed a storm of this sort, the strange thrilling motion could not be mistaken, and I ran out of my cabin, both glad and frightened, shouting, 'A noble earthquake! A noble earthquake!' feeling sure I was going to learn something. The shocks were so violent and varied, and succeeded one another so closely, that I had to balance myself carefully in walking as if on the deck of a ship among waves, and it seemed impossible that the high cliffs of the Valley could escape being shattered." One cliff worried him particularly. "I feared that the sheer-fronted Sentinel Rock, towering above my cabin, would be shaken down, and I took shelter back of a large yellow pine, hoping that it might protect me from at least the smaller outbounding boulders. For a minute or two the shocks became more and more violent—flashing horizontal thrusts mixed with a few twists and battering, explosive, upheaving jolts—as if Nature were wrecking her Yosemite temple, and getting ready to build a still better one."

But the temple was not wrecked. Nor was it apparently enlarged or deepened. The earthquake theory was weakened, if only slightly. In time, Muir's glacialism supplanted it.

The flora of Yosemite and the surrounding Sierra sent Muir into raptures of another sort. The dominant species of the valley was the Ponderosa pine. Individual trees could be eight feet in diameter and more than two hundred feet tall. Muir felt obliged to experience the species for himself. "Climbing these grand trees, especially when they are waving and singing in worship in windstorms, is a glorious experience," he said. "Ascending from the lowest branch to the topmost is like stepping up stairs through a blaze of white light, every needle thrilling and shining as if with religious ecstasy."

Yet the monarch of the forest was the giant sequoia. "The immensely strong, stately shafts are free of limbs for one hundred and fifty feet or so. The large limbs reach out with equal boldness in every direction, showing no weather side, and no other tree has foliage so densely massed, so finely molded in outline and so perfectly subordinate to an ideal type. A particularly knotty, angular, ungovernable-looking branch, from five to seven or eight feet in diameter and perhaps a thousand years old, may occasionally be seen pushing out from the trunk as if determined to break across the bounds of the regular curve, but like all the others it dissolves in bosses of branchlets and sprays as soon as the general outline is approached. Except in picturesque old age, after being struck by lightning or broken by thousands of snow-storms, the regularity of forms is one of their most distinguishing characteristics. Another is the simple beauty of the trunk and its great thickness as compared with its height and the width of the branches, which makes them look more like finely modeled and sculptured architectural columns than the stems of trees, while the great limbs look like rafters, supporting the magnificent dome-head."

JOHN MUIR WASN'T THE FIRST PERSON TO HAVE A RELIGIOUS experience in Yosemite. The Indians for whom the valley was named thought it enchanted, as did the neighboring tribes who kept clear of it. During the decade after the first penetration of the valley by whites, a political consensus emerged that this was a special place, worth preserving as nature had made it. In 1864 Abraham Lincoln took a moment from monitoring Ulysses Grant's campaign against Robert E. Lee to sign an act transferring control of Yosemite from the federal government to the state of California, subject to the condition that the valley should be preserved for "public use, resort, and recreation . . . for all time."

Before long, disputes would develop over what constituted public use. And so when people who felt about Wyoming's Yellowstone region—the Colter's Hell traversed by Joe Meek—the way John Muir felt about Yosemite, they employed a different model of preservation. Because no one quite trusted the testimony of Meek and the other mountain men, Congress sponsored a scientific expedition to Yellowstone, led by Ferdinand Hayden, an army doctor during the Civil War and a geologist since. The Hayden survey confirmed everything that Meek and the others had said about the geysers and hot springs, and added convincing testimony on the great falls and canyon of the Yellowstone River and the shimmering expanse of Yellowstone Lake.

The Hayden report lent decisive support to a campaign to set aside the Yellowstone region as America's first national park—that is, a natural preserve retained and operated by the federal government. While his official report was being printed, Hayden provided a layman's summary in *Scribner's Monthly*, in which he concluded, "The intelligent American will one day point on the map to this remarkable district with the conscious pride that it has not its parallel on the face of the globe. Why will not Congress at once pass a law setting it apart as a great public park for all time to come?"

The main reason why not was that privatization remained the default mode of American policy on Western land and other natural resources. The public domain existed to be transferred to private hands as quickly as possible. Privatization was what had made the California gold rush happen. Privatization had justified the grant of federal land to railroads to spur construction. Privatization was the heart of the Homestead Act. The idea of setting aside federal land for a park cut directly against the privatization grain. It would deprive individuals of resources they could have put to commercial use, and it would deprive the government of revenues that could have been realized from the sale of such resources.

For this reason, the advocates of a Yellowstone park emphasized the utter worthlessness of the region for anything *but* a park. "The entire area comprised within the limits of the reservation contemplated in this bill is not susceptible of cultivation with any degree of certainty, and the winters would be too severe for stock-raising," one of the bill's proponents explained. Nor would rich ores be discovered in the mountains that surrounded the Yellowstone basin. "These mountains are all of volcanic origin, and it is not probable that any mines or minerals of value will ever be found there." No buyer would come forward if the land were offered for sale. "The withdrawal of this tract, therefore, from sale or settlement takes nothing from the value of the public domain, and is no pecuniary loss to the Government."

A crucial ally of the park advocates was tycoon Jay Cooke, who had rescued the Union from insolvency during the Civil War by canny management of the government's bond sales. Cooke had pocketed a fortune for himself in the process, and after the war he employed it, and his continuing political connections, to launch construction of another cross-country railroad, the Northern Pacific. Cooke's first concern was that the Yellowstone park might infringe on the land grants his railroad was due from the government. But once he learned that it wouldn't—that *he* couldn't claim the Yellowstone wonders—he moved to make sure no one else could. He decided to promote tourism on his line, and he didn't want to have to pay private parties for the privilege. "It is important to do something speedily, or squatters and claimants will go in there," he wrote to an associate. "We can probably deal much better with the government in any improvements we may desire to make for the benefit of our pleasure travel than with individuals."

The Yellowstone bill passed Congress in early 1872 and was signed into law by President Grant. Immediately the local interests Jay Cooke had worried about began complaining. The *Rocky Mountain Gazette*, of Helena, Montana, condemned the Washington-knows-best attitude of Congress and the park advocates. "The effect of this measure will be to keep the country a wilderness, and shut out, for many years, the travel that would seek that curious region if good roads were opened through it and hotels built therein," the paper said.

But Easterners applauded. The *New York Herald* praised the new park, and the park movement generally. "Why should we go to Switzerland to see mountains, or to Iceland for geysers?" the *Herald* inquired. "Thirty years ago the attraction of America to the foreign mind was Niagara Falls. Now we have attractions which diminish Niagara into an ordinary exhibition. The Yosemite, which the nation has made a park, the Rocky mountains and their singular parks, the canyons of the Colorado, the Dalles of the Columbia, the giant trees, the lake country of Minnesota, the country of the Yellowstone, with their beauty, their splendor, their extraordinary and sometimes terrible manifestations of nature, form a series of attractions possessed by no other nation in the world."

46

MORE LIKE US

Y ET NATIONAL PARKS WERE THE RARE EXCEPTION; privatization remained the rule. The West was filling in, but it was hardly filling *up*. Six new states were formed in 1889 and 1890: South Dakota, North Dakota, Montana, Washington, Idaho and Wyoming. That left Oklahoma, New Mexico and Arizona in federal hands, as well as Utah, where Mormon hands were at least as powerful. People were still scarce in the West, and the public domain seemed almost endless.

In American history it has been common to think of the frontier as moving steadily westward. This was accurate enough from the seventeenth century to the middle of the nineteenth century. Settlement crept inland from the Atlantic, then crested the Appalachian chain and spilled over into the Ohio Valley. In some places the edge of settlement moved more rapidly than in others, but on the whole the advance took place along a broad front.

Things changed when Americans hit the Great Plains. The frontier stalled, blocked by the barrier of aridity John Wesley Powell described. Some maps denoted the plains as the Great American Desert. Indians roamed the plains longer than elsewhere, partly because the Sioux and the Comanches were formidable warriors, but mostly because white Americans saw little of value there. Instead they looked beyond the plains and mountains to Oregon, and then to California. The emigrants to the Willamette Valley and then the argonauts to California caused the frontier to leap-frog to the Pacific coast.

During the following decades the frontier backfilled as min-ers developed the Comstock Lode in Nevada, the deposits around Denver, and finally the Black Hills of Dakota.

Sections of the Middle Border, as the Great Plains were some-times called, were among the last to be settled. Farmers crept out onto the eastern part of the plains in Kansas and Nebraska, where the climate was only marginally drier than farther east. They turned the prairie sod with improved steel plows and planted win-ter wheat, which squeezed moisture out of winter's snows to go with spring's rains. On the western plains, cattlemen like Theodore Roosevelt and his more persistent colleagues carved a niche where the buffalo had been.

One big chunk of the plains remained off limits to most white settlement. In the 1880s Oklahoma was what remained of the In-dian Territory, Arkansas having been peeled off to form a state decades earlier. Oklahoma was where the government sent the hardest cases of Indian resistance, including Geronimo, the last of the holdouts. Geronimo had lived on an Arizona reservation for a time, but he had become unwilling to stand the confinement. In 1881 he led a band of his Chiricahua Apaches off the reserva-tion and into the wilderness along the border between the United States and Mexico. After a few years of raiding settlements in both countries, Geronimo was talked back onto the reservation, but he broke away again. He was chased; he agreed to return; he changed his mind; the chase resumed.

Among his pursuers were members of the 10th Cavalry Reg-iment, a special unit established at the end of the Civil War. During that conflict some two hundred thousand African Ameri-cans, many of them escaped and emancipated slaves, served in the Union military; upon the war's end, the government decided to employ some of them and other blacks who chose to enlist in new regiments on the Western frontier. The deployment was in the nature of an experiment, for though the black soldiers had shown they could fight, they were hardly loved by all in the army. And they were loved least by white Southerners, who had formed a large part of the U.S. army before the Civil War and were expected to do so after. The rank-and-file of the regiments were black, the officers mostly white. This model reflected prejudice in the military but also the fact that many of the enlisted men were illiterate, having been barred as slaves from being taught to read and write.

The experiment commenced with the creation of the 9th and 10th Cavalry Regiments, which were complemented by four infantry regiments. In the first years the black soldiers guarded the construction crews of the Union Pacific; before long they were engaged in the war of attrition against the various Plains tribes. "We destroyed everything in their village," a black sergeant reported after a raid against one band in northwestern Texas. "They had many guns, mostly citizens' rifles, and a good supply of ammunition besides bows, arrows, quivers, lances, etc. These we destroyed. We found a vast amount of buffalo robes, of which each man made choice of the best—the rest were destroyed. Their tents were made of poles over which hides were stretched, and these were all burned."

The more responsibility they were given, the better the black troops typically performed. Frances Roe was the wife of an officer of the 10th; she followed her husband from fort to fort on the plains and wrote letters to friends in the East. "The officers say that the negroes make good soldiers and fight like fiends," she said. She added, "The Indians call them 'buffalo soldiers,' because their woolly heads are so much like the matted cushion that is between the horns of the buffalo."

Mrs. Roe's 1872 letter seems to be the first recorded use of the term "buffalo soldier." It was seconded in an article that appeared in *The Nation* the following year. The magazine's correspondent was writing from Fort Sill, Indian Territory. "This is the best arranged and most complete military post I have yet seen," he said.

"The barracks, officers' quarters, and quartermaster's buildings are built of limestone around a square parade-ground of near ten acres area. Hard by are a fine hospital and guard-house. All are kept in fine order by a garrison of (just now) five companies of colored cavalry of the Tenth Regiment, and two companies (colored) and one (white) of infantry. The colored troops (called by the Comanches the 'buffalo soldiers,' because, like the buffalo, they are woolly) are in excellent drill and condition. The Indians at first treated them with utter contempt, and when they chanced to kill one would not take his scalp. After a while, when they had had a taste of their fighting qualities, they began to respect them, and to show their respect by scalping a few that they have managed to kill." The correspondent, who had observed many soldiers, was impressed by the quality of the black troops. "These 'buffalo soldiers' are active, intelligent, and resolute men; are perfectly willing to fight the Indians whenever they may be called upon to do so, and appear to me to be rather superior to the average of white men recruited in time of peace. Their officers explain this by saying that the best colored young men can be recruited in time of peace, while, under the same condition, only indifferent or inferior whites can in general be induced to enlist."

The black troops, though better behaved than the many of the white troops, weren't uniformly virtuous. Racial friction sometimes caused trouble, as did the overall strain of service on the frontier. Deserters included the black man killed by the buffalo hunters in the battle of Adobe Walls. This soldier evidently concluded he'd fare better with the Indians than with his white commanders and black comrades-in-arms.

On the whole the army was pleased with its experiment. Most of the trouble was minor, and much of the performance was truly meritorious. Sergeant Emanuel Stance was leading a small command on a "scout," or reconnaissance, when he spied a band of Indians stealing government horses. Though badly outnumbered, he leapt into action. "I immediately attacked them by charging them," he reported afterward. "They tried hard to make a stand to get their herd of horses off, but I set the Spencers"—his men's rifles—"to talking and whistling about their ears so lively they broke in confusion and fled to the hills, leaving us their herd." They eventually regrouped and decided to retrieve their booty. "They skirmished along my left flank to the eight mile water hole, evidently being determined to take the stock. I turned my little command loose on them at this place, and after a few volleys they left me to continue my march in peace."

Sergeant Stance was too modest in his account of the action. After the details were relayed to Washington, he was awarded the Medal of Honor.

GERONIMO EVENTUALLY SURRENDERED TO NELSON MILES, the captor of Crazy Horse and Joseph, in 1886. He was sent first to Florida and then to Oklahoma. What made Oklahoma different from the other federal territories was that while they contained Indian reservations, Oklahoma *was* an Indian reservation. And the essence of reservation status was that Indians on reservations had their own governments. They were, as John Marshall had put it in the defining Supreme Court case *Cherokee Nation v. Georgia*, "domestic dependent nations." But there was another option for the Indians, held out by the executive branch and articulated by Andrew Jackson. In calling on Congress to pass the Indian Removal Act of 1830, which mandated the removal of the Cherokees, Chickasaws and other southeastern tribes across the Mississippi to the Indian Territory, Jackson said the Indians could stay where they were, only not as autonomous tribes. "If they remain within the limits of the states they must be subject to their laws."

The question of autonomy or assimilation persisted. Many Indians assimilated informally, by the expedient of leaving their reservations and living in the larger non-Indian community. This was seldom easy, but it was least problematic for Indians who married whites or were the children of such unions. Assimilation was the goal of the missionaries to the Indians. Marcus and Narcissa Whitman sought to teach the Indians not merely the religion of the whites but the way of living of the whites. Americans of the nineteenth century almost unanimously considered farming superior, as a way of life, to hunting and gathering. If the Indians would settle down and become farmers, the missionaries and other reformers said, they might enjoy the blessings all Americans enjoyed.

Such was the philosophy behind the Dawes Severalty Act of 1887. Supporters of the law concluded that the reservation system wasn't working. Reservation Indians, under tribal government and typically on the dole of the U.S. government, had little incentive or opportunity to better their lot. Land was owned in common, preventing hardworking individual Indians from enjoying the full benefits of their labors. The key to improvement, the law's supporters said, was individual ownership of land. The Dawes Act, named for Henry Dawes of Massachusetts, would provide individual ownership by apportioning reservation lands among the individuals of the various tribes. Each head of family received 160 acres, with an additional 40 acres for each child. Each single person eighteen years of age or older got 80 acres, as did each orphan under eighteen. When the apportioning of lands was completed, the reservations would be dissolved and the tribes disbanded, and the Indians would become citizens with the same rights and responsibilities as other citizens.

The Dawes Act mirrored the Homestead Act in transferring land to individuals. It was hailed by its supporters as an emancipation proclamation for Indians, freeing them from bondage to tribal collectivism. Philanthropists hoped it would stir the Indians into the melting pot of America and allow them to achieve what other groups, immigrants primarily, had achieved.

Yet philanthropists weren't the only ones behind the Dawes Act. The total acreage of the allotted lands, determined by the arithmetic of the law, came to only a third of the reservation holdings. The rest would be opened to white ownership. Land speculators and prospective settlers, recognizing the Dawes Act as the latest device for expropriating Indian lands, kept their voices low during the discussion of the bill. But they made ready for the day when the excess lands would be theirs for the taking.

THAT DAY CAME, IN OKLAHOMA, IN APRIL 1889. THE FEDeral government sponsored a one-day version of the gold rush, except in land. The land rush was advertised to begin at noon on April 22. William Howard, a reporter, took part, and he explained how it unfolded. "The preparations for the settlement of Oklahoma had been complete, even to the slightest detail, for weeks before the opening day," he wrote. "The Santa Fe Railway, which runs through Oklahoma north and south, was prepared to take any number of people from its handsome station at Arkansas City, Kansas, and to deposit them in almost any part of Oklahoma as soon as the law allowed." Other settlers chose different modes of transport. "Thousands of covered wagons were gathered in camps on all sides of the new Territory waiting for the embargo to be lifted."

The race for land was unprecedented in American history, and Howard thought it was unprecedented anywhere. "The rush across the border at noon on the opening day must go down in history as one of the most noteworthy events of Western civilization," he said. Many lives hung on the outcome of the day's events. "At the time fixed, thousands of hungry home-seekers, who had gathered from all parts of the country, and particularly from Kansas and Missouri, were arranged in line along the border, ready to lash their horses into furious speed in the race for fertile spots in the beautiful land before them."

The spring weather on the day of the rush couldn't have been finer, with bright sun, blue skies and balmy temperatures. As the starting hour approached, the contestants for the Indian lands grew nervously expectant. And then: "The clear, sweet notes of a cavalry bugle rose and hung a moment upon the startled air. It was noon. The last barrier of savagery in the United States was broken down. Moved by the same impulse, each driver lashed his horses furiously; each rider dug his spurs into his willing steed; and each man on foot caught his breath and darted forward. A cloud of dust rose where the home-seekers had stood in line, and when it had drifted away before the gentle breeze, the horses and wagons and men were tearing across the open country like fiends."

It wasn't long, though, before something appeared amiss. "The fleetest of the horsemen found upon reaching their chosen localities that men in wagons and men on foot were there before them." The only inference that could be drawn was that these men had cheated, sneaking across the line ahead of the official start. William Howard didn't report any shootings of the cheaters, but he predicted litigation. "It is not to be expected that the man who ran his horse at its utmost speed for ten miles only to find a settler with an ox team in quiet possession of his chosen farm will tamely submit to this plain infringement of the law."

Yet, as Howard observed, the race wasn't always to the swift or the dishonest. A rusher on foot, with a keen sense of where he was going, could do just as well. "One man left the line with the others, carrying on his back a tent, a blanket, some camp dishes, an axe, and provisions for two days," Howard said. "He ran down the railway track for six miles, and reached his claim in just sixty minutes. Upon arriving on his land he fell down under a tree, unable to speak or see. I am glad to be able to say that his claim is one of the best in Oklahoma."

The rushers who raced by train dealt with challenges of their own. "The train left Arkansas City at 8:45 o'clock in the forenoon," Howard said. "It consisted of an empty baggage car, which was set apart for the use of the newspaper correspondents, eight passenger coaches, and the caboose of a freight train. The coaches were so densely packed with men that not another human being could get on board. So uncomfortably crowded were they that some of the younger boomers climbed to the roofs of the cars and clung perilously to the ventilators. An adventurous person secured at great risk a seat on the forward truck of the baggage car."

The train was bound for the town of Guthrie, which was being planted this day. Or so the passengers thought. "It was an eager and an exuberantly joyful crowd that rode slowly into Guthrie at twenty minutes past one o'clock on that perfect April afternoon," Howard wrote. The mood changed abruptly. "Men who had expected to lay out the town site were grievously disappointed at the first glimpse of their proposed scene of operations. The slope east of the railway at Guthrie station was dotted white with tents and sprinkled thick with men running about in all directions."

"We're done for," declared one of the train-borne town builders. "Some one has gone in ahead of us and laid out the town."

"Never mind that," answered another. "Make a rush and get what you can."

This attitude seized them all. "Hardly had the train slackened its speed when the impatient boomers began to leap from the cars and run up the slope," Howard recorded. "Men jumped from the roofs of the moving cars at the risk of their lives. Some were so stunned by the fall that they could not get up for some minutes. The coaches were so crowded that many men were compelled to squeeze through the windows in order to get a fair start at the head of the crowd. Almost before the train had come to a standstill the cars were emptied. In their haste and eagerness, men fell over each other in heaps; others stumbled and fell headlong, while many ran forward so blindly and impetuously that it was not until they had passed the best of the town lots that they came to a realization of their actions."

Howard wasn't seeking a town lot for himself, but rather a story for *Harper's Weekly*. He ran alongside the others until he found a good spot from which to view the surge, and to catch his breath. As he straightened up, he realized he was standing beside a tent. A man was chopping holes in the prairie sod with a shiny new axe.

"Where did you come from, that you have already pitched your tent?" asked Howard.

"Oh, I was here," said the man.

"How was that?"

"Why, I was a deputy United States marshal."

"Did you resign?"

"No, I'm a deputy still."

"But it is not legal for a deputy United States marshal, or any one in the employ of the government to take up a town lot in this manner."

"That may all be, stranger. But I've got two lots here, just the same, and about fifty other deputies have got lots in the same way. In fact, the deputy-marshals laid out the town."

William Howard considered this perversion of the system outrageous. So, presumably, did the others on his train. But they were too busy grabbing what they could do dispute the matter. The deputies had laid out the main street of the town until they all had their lots. The train-men took things from there. "They seized the line of the embryo street and ran it eastward as far as their numbers would permit," Howard said. Another train arrived. "The second train load of people took it where the first left off, and ran it entirely out of sight behind a swell of ground at least two miles from the station." More trains came. "The following car loads of home-seekers went north and south, so that by the time that all were in for the day a city large enough to hold 100,000 inhabitants had been staked off."

As the town site became crowded, tensions increased. "Disputes over the ownership of lots grew incessant, for the reason that when a man went to the river for a drink of water, or tried to get his baggage at the railway station, another man would take possession of his lot, notwithstanding the obvious presence of the first man's stakes and sometimes part of his wearing apparel. Owing to the uncertainty concerning the lines of the streets, two and sometimes more lots were staked out on the same ground, each claimant hoping that the official survey would give him the preference."

Yet the disputes did not lead to gunplay. Howard polled the participants to discover why. Their answers pointed in a single direction: the absence of alcohol. "The peaceful way in which Okla-

Oklahoma land rush. After the rushers staked their claims, they had to register them at land offices like this one.

homa was settled was due entirely to its prohibition," Howard wrote. He added, as a word to the wise, "When Congress gives Oklahoma some sort of government, the prohibition of the sale of intoxicating liquor should be the first and foremost of her laws."

Howard traveled around the new territory in the following days. He visited Oklahoma City, where the mad rush for lots mirrored that in Guthrie, including the illegal preemption by the deputy marshals. "The actual home-seekers were compelled to take what was left," he noted. This was the case throughout the territory. Insiders got the good land, those without connections the remainder. Many of the rushers, often the ones most in need, wound up with little to show for their high hopes. "The poverty and wretched condition of some of the older boomers who have been waiting for years for the opening of Oklahoma were painfully apparent," Howard observed. "Men with large families settled upon land with less than a dollar in money to keep them from starvation. How they expected to live until they could get a crop from their lands was a mystery which even they could not pretend to explain. Like unreasoning children, they thought that could they but once reach the beautiful green slopes of the promised land, their poverty and trouble would be at an end. They are now awakening to the bitter realization that their real hardships have just begun."

47

IT GREW VERY COLD

MORE BITTER WAS THE REALIZATION OF OKLAHOMA'S Indian tribes that once again they were the victims of the whites' insatiable hunger for land. For surviving Indians all across the West, the end of days—or at least of anything like the life they had known—seemed fast approaching.

For this reason many were attracted to a rising millenarian cult. Black Elk was curious when he first heard of it, for he was having questions about his own vision. He had been twelve at the time of the Lakota victory at the Greasy Grass; he was thirteen when Crazy Horse was killed by a military guard who claimed he was resisting arrest. "I was frightened," Black Elk recalled of the moment, "because everything felt the way it did that day when we were going up to kill on the Greasy Grass, and it seemed we might all begin fighting right away." But there was nothing for the Lakotas to fight with; their weapons had been taken away.

He grew to manhood on the Sioux reservation. He adjusted to life under the new order on the plains. He met William Cody, a former scout and buffalo hunter who likewise was trying to adjust to the new life. Cody, sensing nostalgia in the East for the life that was being lost in the West, created a traveling show called "Buffalo Bill's Wild West." He offered Black Elk a job, and Black Elk toured the East with the show. Cody took the troupe to Britain, and while there, Black Elk separately visited mainland Europe.

The journey was enlightening but enervating. "All the time I was away from home across the big water, my power was gone, and I was like a dead man moving around most of the time," Black Elk recalled. "I could hardly remember my vision, and when I did remember it, it seemed like a dim dream."

He returned to discover his people debilitated. The Sioux reservation had been cut in half since the 1870s. Hunger and measles befell the Lakotas, now dependent on government aid, which was always inadequate and often late. Black Elk's healing powers revived somewhat, but for many he could do nothing. "There were more people sick that winter when the whooping cough came and killed little children who did not have enough to eat," he said. "Our people were pitiful and in despair."

Amid their distress the Lakotas grasped at straws. "That summer when I came back from across the water, strange news had come from the West, and the people had been talking and talking about it," Black Elk recounted. "This news said that out yonder in the West, at a place near where the great mountains stand before you come to the big water"—the Sierra Nevada—"there was a sacred man among the Paiutes who had talked to the Great Spirit in a vision, and the Great Spirit had told him how to save the Indian peoples and make the Wasichus disappear and bring back all the bison and the people who were dead, and how there would be a new earth." The Lakota elders had discussed the strange news, and they decided to send three envoys to meet the holy man and hear more about his vision. The envoys undertook the journey and came back convinced that the Paiute messiah spoke the truth.

Black Elk demurred. "I thought maybe it was only the despair that made people believe, just as a man who is starving may dream of plenty of everything good to eat," he recalled.

Yet the envoys remained convinced. The Paiute messiah had insisted that a new world was coming, they said. "It would come in a whirlwind out of the West and would crush out everything in this world, which was old and dying. In that other world there was plenty of meat, just like old times; and in that world all the dead

Indians were alive, and all the bison that had ever been killed were roaming around again."

The messiah had given the Lakota envoys two eagle feathers and some red paint. He told them what to do. The people must daub the paint on their faces and do a dance—a ghost dance, for the dead Indians—that the messiah taught the envoys. "If they did this, they could get on this other world when it came, and the Wasichus would not be able to get on, and so they would disappear." The eagle feathers were for a sign. "Receive these eagle feathers and behold them, for my father will cause these to bring your people back to him."

During the winter of 1889–1890 the Lakotas could talk of little else. They sent more envoys west; these returned with the same message as the others. Tribes all across the West were dancing the Ghost Dance. The Lakotas must join, lest they not be able to enter the new world when it came.

The Lakota dancing began. Black Elk heard that some of his people were dancing at the head of Cheyenne Creek, and that the dancers there had seen their dead relatives and spoken to them. He heard of dancing on Wounded Knee Creek, with similar results. He was still skeptical. But his father had recently died, and he started to wonder if the dance would bring him back. He mounted his horse and rode to Wounded Knee Creek.

"I was surprised, and could hardly believe what I saw, because so much of my vision seemed to be in it," he recounted. "The dancers, both women and men, were holding hands in a big circle, and in the center of the circle they had a tree painted red with most of its branches cut off and some dead leaves on it." The holy tree in his vision was dying, and the circle of dancers was like the sacred hoop that would bring the tree back to life.

At first Black Elk was sad. "It all seemed to be from my great vision somehow, and I had done nothing yet to make the tree to bloom." But reflection yielded insight, and gratification. "All at once a great happiness overcame me, and it all took hold of me right there." He would help make the vision—his vision and the messiah's vision—come to pass. "The dance was over for that day, but they would dance again the next day, and I would dance with them."

THE DANCING WENT ON THROUGH THE SUMMER AND INTO the fall. The white soldiers in Dakota took alarm. Those whites with a knowledge of history knew that messianic movements among the native peoples often preceded violent attempts to hasten the coming of the new world. Those without such knowledge simply didn't like to see the Indians join a cult that preached the annihilation of whites. The dancing alone was scary; the dancers kept at it for hours or days, falling into a trance state where the ordinary rules of fear and self-preservation didn't apply.

The soldiers warned the Sioux to stop dancing. The federal agent on Clay Creek gave a cease-and-desist order. The dancers rejected it. "They would not stop, and they said they would fight for their religion if they had to do it," Black Elk recalled. "The agent went away, and they kept on dancing. They called him Young-Man-Afraid-of-Lakotas."

The effort to stop the dancing merely made it spread. "I heard that the Brulés were dancing over east of us," Black Elk said. "And then I heard that Big Foot's people were dancing on the Good River reservation; also that Kicking Bear had gone to Sitting Bull's camp on Grand River, and that the people were dancing there too. Word came to us that the Indians were beginning to dance everywhere."

Black Elk and the other Sioux learned that the soldiers were moving in, apparently to stop the dancing. "We heard that there were soldiers at Pine Ridge and that others were coming all the time. Then one morning we heard that the soldiers were marching toward us, so we broke camp and moved west to Grass Creek. From there we went to White Clay and camped awhile and danced."

Black Elk by now had developed a reputation as a leader of the dancers. An Indian policeman, a Lakota who worked with the

Lakota camp. This image is from the era of the Ghost Dance. Note the wagons, which the Sioux adopted from whites, after adopting the horses generations earlier.

federal agents, tipped him off that he and another dancer, Good Thunder, were going to be arrested.

Black Elk and Good Thunder decided not to wait around. They rode to the camp of the Brulés on Wounded Knee Creek.

They learned that Sitting Bull had been killed by Indian policemen at his cabin on the Grand River. The federal authorities had suspected Sitting Bull of being behind the Ghost Dance, and they ordered his arrest. When some of the other Lakotas tried to prevent the arrest, a struggle ensued, in which Sitting Bull was shot dead.

"It was now near the end of the Moon of Popping Trees"— December—"and I was twenty-seven years old," Black Elk said. News came that Big Foot was coming to Wounded Knee with four hundred men, women and children, including some from Sitting Bull's band. They were in desperate condition. "They were all starving and freezing, and Big Foot was so sick that they had to bring him along in a pony drag."

On the evening of December 28, Black Elk rode to Pine Ridge. While he was there he saw soldiers preparing to march out, toward Big Foot's camp. "I felt something terrible was going to happen," he recalled. "That night I could hardly sleep at all. I walked around all night."

The next morning, when he went to gather his horses, he heard shooting in the east, in the direction of Big Foot's camp. "I knew from the sound that it must be the wagon-guns"—cannons— "going off. The sounds went right through my body."

He donned his sacred shirt, painted his face and put an eagle feather in his hair. He mounted his horse and rode toward the shooting. Several other young men joined him as he rode, till they totaled about twenty. They reached the crest of a ridge, from which they could see a crooked, dry gulch.

What Black Elk then witnessed became etched in his brain. "Wagon guns were still going off over there on the little hill," he recounted, decades later. "And they were going off again where they hit along the gulch. There was much shooting down yonder, and there were many cries, and we could see cavalrymen scattered over the hills ahead of us. Cavalrymen were riding along the gulch and shooting into it, where the women and children were running away and trying to hide."

Black Elk and his small party charged toward the shooting. Black Elk had no gun, only a sacred bow, which he held out in front of him as the soldiers turned their fire on them. "The bullets did not hit us at all," he said.

Yet without a gun he could do nothing. Anyway, he and the others had arrived too late. "We followed down along the dry gulch, and what we saw was terrible. Dead and wounded women and children and little babies were scattered all along there where they had been trying to run away. The soldiers had followed along the gulch, and they ran, and murdered them in there. Sometimes they were in heaps because they had huddled together, and some were scattered all along. Sometimes bunches of them had been killed and torn to pieces where the wagon guns hit them. I saw a little baby trying to suck its mother, but she was bloody and dead."

Black Elk learned from one of the few survivors how the massacre had begun. The soldiers had entered Big Foot's camp and demanded that the warriors relinquish their weapons. Most did, seeing that they were outnumbered and badly outgunned, with the cannons trained on them. But one man refused to give up his rifle. A soldier tried to take it from him, and in the scuffle the rifle went off and killed the soldier. At this another soldier, standing over the bedridden Big Foot, shot and killed the chief. The rest of the soldiers opened fire on the camp, sparing none their weapons could reach.

Black Elk remembered that the day had dawned clear. "But after the soldiers marched away from their dirty work, a heavy snow began to fall. The wind came up in the night. There was a big blizzard, and it grew very cold. The snow drifted down in the crooked gulch, and it was one long grave of butchered women and children and babies, who had never done any harm and were only trying to run away."

48

LESS CORN AND MORE HELL

THE MASSACRE AT WOUNDED KNEE—AT LEAST 150
Lakotas, and perhaps twice that many, were killed—marked
the end of the violent struggle for control of the lands of the American West. The indigenous peoples had lost; the invaders had won.

A different marker of the passing age caught the eye of Frederick Jackson Turner, a young historian from Wisconsin who addressed a convention of his colleagues in Chicago during the summer of 1893. Turner asked his audience to conjure a parade of American history from two points in time. The first was in the late eighteenth century. "Stand at Cumberland Gap and watch the procession of civilization, marching single file—the buffalo following the trail to the salt springs, the Indian, the fur-trader and hunter, the cattle-raiser, the pioneer farmer," Turner said. He paused. "And the frontier has passed by." He then asked his listeners to jump forward to a more recent time. "Stand at South Pass in the Rockies a century later, and see the same procession with wider intervals between." And the frontier had passed by there, too.

Turner proposed a theory of America's westward expansion that embraced successive kinds of frontiers. "The unequal rate of advance compels us to distinguish the frontier into the trader's frontier, the rancher's frontier, or the miner's frontier, and the farmer's frontier. When the mines and the cow pens were still near the fall line, the traders' pack trains were tinkling across the

Alleghenies, and the French on the Great Lakes were fortifying their posts, alarmed by the British trader's birch canoe. When the trappers scaled the Rockies, the farmer was still near the mouth of the Missouri."

The multiphase frontier accounted for the distinctive features of American civilization, Turner said. It afforded individual opportunity; it leveled social differences; it nurtured democracy. If not for the frontier, America would have been much like Europe.

Turner noted that the director of the U.S. census, referring to the 1890 tally, had observed that a clear line separating the settled regions of the country from the unsettled regions no longer existed. The frontier had disappeared. Turner inferred from this that America had reached a turning point in its history. "Since the days when the fleet of Columbus sailed into the waters of the New World, America has been another name for opportunity, and the people of the United States have taken their tone from the incessant expansion which has not only been open but has even been forced upon them." Those days of westward expansion were over. "Never again will such gifts of free land offer themselves."

With the passing of those days ended the distinctive frontier experience—the distinctive *American* experience. "What the Mediterranean Sea was to the Greeks, breaking the bond of custom, offering new experiences, calling out new institutions and activities, that, and more, the ever retreating frontier has been to the United States directly, and to the nations of Europe more remotely. And now, four centuries from the discovery of America, at the end of a hundred years of life under the Constitution, the frontier has gone, and with its going has closed the first period of American history."

HISTORIANS WOULD SPEND DECADES DEBATING THE VALIDITY of Turner's frontier thesis. Few bought the whole argument, but the fact that skeptics devoted so much time to refuting it suggested he was onto something.

A Turnerian gloom was in the American air in the last decade of the nineteenth century. Financial troubles in London shook markets across the Atlantic; American banks large and small collapsed by the dozens per week. The effects of the panic spread to the larger economy, forcing railroads to seek bankruptcy protection, factories to close, mines to cancel shifts, and furloughed workers to scrounge for other sources of income.

For Western farmers, the depression that followed the panic of 1893—the worst depression in the nation's history until then—merely added to the stresses they had been feeling for decades. Since the 1870s farm prices had been falling relentlessly, pushing prosperous farmers into the ranks of the marginal, and marginal farmers into ruin. Ironically, a principal cause of the price decline was the farmers' very success: they produced more corn, wheat, cotton, pork and so on than the markets for those commodities could absorb. Some of the overproduction was the result of the increase in farm acreage, notably under the Homestead Act. Some was the consequence of the mechanization of the farm process.

But farmers didn't like hearing this explanation. It demeaned their labor and accomplishment. They were suffering because they had succeeded *too well*? It made no sense. And it implied that some of them—maybe very many of them—would have to go out of business.

So the farmers blamed something else: the money system. A Nebraska farmer wrote to the editor of a local farm journal in 1891 lamenting the hard year he and his neighbors were having. "The hot winds burned up the entire crop, leaving thousands of families wholly destitute, many of whom might have been able to run through the crisis had it not been for the galling yoke put upon them by the money loaners and sharks—not by charging 7 per cent per annum, which is the lawful rate of interest, or even 10 per cent, but the unlawful and inhuman country-destroying rate of 3 per cent a month, some going still farther and charging 50 per cent per annum," he said. "We are cursed, many of us financially beyond redemption, not by the hot winds so much as by the swindling games of the bankers and money loaners, who have taken the money and now are after the property, leaving the farmer moneyless and homeless."

The farmer explained how the system worked against those like him who had to borrow to run their businesses. "I have borrowed, for example, $1,000. I pay $25 to the commission man. I give my note and second mortgage of 3 per cent of the $1,000, which is $30 more. Then I pay 7 per cent on the $1,000 to the actual loaner. Then besides all this I pay for appraising the land, abstract, recording, etc., so when I have secured my loan I am out the first year $150." Things get worse. "This is on the farm, but now comes the chattel loan. I must have $50 to save myself. I get the money; my note is made payable in thirty or sixty days for $35, secured by chattel of two horses, harness and wagon, about five times the value of the note." The note comes due; the farmer asks for a few days. "No, I can't wait," says the lender. "I must have the money." Says the farmer, to himself and the editor: "If I can't get the money I have the extreme pleasure of seeing my property taken."

The editor remarked that he received such letters every day. They revealed how conditions on the Middle Border were beating the average farmer down. "Take a man, for instance, who labors hard from fourteen to sixteen hours a day to obtain the bare necessaries of life. He eats his bacon and potatoes in a place which might rather be called a den than a home; and then, worn out, lies down and sleeps. He is brutalized both morally and physically." His work had kept him from attaining the higher things in life, or even realizing that they existed. "He has no ideas, only propensities. He has no beliefs, only instincts. He does not, often cannot, read. His contact with other people is only the relation of servant to master, of a machine to its director." This man was a product of a system of finance that threw one farmer against all the others in a cutthroat competition for survival of the fittest. "Deny it if you can; competition is only another name for war. It means slavery to millions; it means the sale of virtue for bread; it means for thousands upon thousands starvation, misery, and death. After four thousand years of life, is this the best that we can achieve?"

MARY ELIZABETH LEASE THOUGHT NOT. THE DAUGHTER OF Irish immigrants, Mary Clyens moved to Kansas and married a druggist named Lease. She lost two children in infancy, and as her other children grew older she filled her free time by studying law and gaining admission to the bar. But she found political advocacy more fulfilling than the legal kind. She spoke for women's suffrage, prohibition and, increasingly, the rights of farmers against the banks, railroads and other corporations that beset them. "Wall Street owns the country," she declared. "It is no longer a government of the people, by the people, and for the people, but a government of Wall Street, by Wall Street, and for Wall Street. The great common people of this country are slaves, and monopoly is the master. The West and South are prostrate before the manufacturing East. Money rules." The inequality of wealth and opportunity in America was shocking. "There are thirty men in the United States whose aggregate wealth is over one and one-half billion dollars; there are half a million looking for work."

Mary Lease joined the Populist party, which put farmers' issues front and center. Speaking for the Populists, and especially for the farmers of Kansas, she spelled out their demands: "We want money, land and transportation. We want the abolition of national banks, and we want the power to make loans direct from the government. We want the accursed foreclosure system wiped out. Land equal to a tract thirty miles wide and ninety miles long has been foreclosed and bought in by loan companies of Kansas in a year. We will stand by our homes and stay by our firesides by force if necessary, and we will not pay our debts to the loan-shark companies until the government pays its debts to us. The people are at bay; let the bloodhounds of money who have dogged us thus far beware."

Mary Lease's most famous line was one she might not have uttered but which she didn't disavow: "What you farmers need to do is to raise less corn and more hell."

THE POPULIST REVOLT AGAINST THE EASTERN ESTABLISHMENT was something new in the history of the West, a product of the post-frontier age. The fight over land had been settled, in the favor of whites. The fight over politics—to determine which of the whites would rule in the West, and what policies they would adopt—was just beginning.

William Allen White weighed in against the Populists. White was more Kansan than Mary Lease, having been born in Emporia, grown up in El Dorado, studied at the University of Kansas, and become owner and publisher of the *Emporia Gazette*. He refused to let Mary Lease, or any of the Populists, speak for Kansas. "What's the matter with Kansas?" he asked in a blistering 1896 editorial against the Populists. The answer: the Populists themselves. A recent survey revealed that the economy of the country had resumed its growth, but Kansas continued to languish. "In five years ten million people have been added to the national population, yet instead of gaining a share of this—say, half a million—Kansas has apparently been a plague spot and, in the very garden of the world, has lost population by ten-thousands every year." The Populists, with their rants against money and wealth, were driving good people away. "Every moneyed man in the state who could get out without loss has gone. Every month in every community sees someone who has a little money pack up and leave the state. This has been going on for eight years. Money has been drained out all the time. In towns where ten years ago there were three or four or half a dozen money-lending concerns, stimulating industry by furnishing capital, there is now none, or one or two that are looking after the interests and principal already outstanding."

White acknowledged that life on the Middle Border could be challenging. But other states were doing all right. Nebraska, the birth twin of Kansas, was gaining wealth and population. He demanded again: "What's the matter with Kansas?"

And he answered again: the Populists, who couldn't abide that anyone should succeed when they did not. "We have an old moss-back Jacksonian who snorts and howls because there is a bathtub in the State House; we are running that old jay for Governor. We have another shabby, wild-eyed, rattle-brained fanatic who has said openly in a dozen speeches that 'the rights of the user are paramount to the rights of the owner'; we are running him for Chief Justice." In a direct swipe at Mary Lease, White added, "Then, for fear some hint that the state had become respectable might percolate through the civilized portions of the nation, we have decided to send three or four harpies out lecturing, telling the people that Kansas is raising hell and letting the corn go to weed."

"Oh, yes, Kansas is a great state," said White, dripping sarcasm. "Here are people fleeing from it by the score every day, capital going out of the state by the hundreds of dollars; and every industry but farming paralyzed, and that crippled, because its products have to go across the ocean before they can find a laboring man at work who can afford to buy them. Let's don't stop this year. Let's drive all the decent, self-respecting men out of the state. Let's keep the old clodhoppers who know it all."

"What's the matter with Kansas?" he asked once more. "Nothing under the shining sun. She is losing wealth, population and standing. She has got her statesmen, and the money power is afraid of her. Kansas is all right. She has started in to raise hell, as Mrs. Lease advised, and she seems to have an over-production. But that doesn't matter. Kansas never did believe in diversified crops."

WHITE WAS A REPUBLICAN, AND THE NATIONAL PARTY SOON elevated him to the status of sage of the West for showing that the Populists didn't speak for all the West, or even all Kansas. The Democrats looked to another Westerner, William Jennings Bryan of Nebraska, in seeking to hold the White House that season. Bryan had been a congressman and an editorialist, but he was, above all, an evangelist—a preacher of the gospel of democracy and respect for the ordinary men and women of America. Bryan attended the Democratic national convention as a relative unknown; he emerged as the party's nominee after delivering a powerful speech that praised America's farmers for their devotion to traditional values, condemned the money changers for their insistence on the debtor-strangling gold standard, and concluded with a call to arms: "Having behind us the producing masses of this nation and the world, supported by the commercial interests, the laboring interests, and the toilers everywhere, we will answer their demand for a gold standard by saying to them: You shall not press down upon the brow of labor this crown of thorns! You shall not crucify mankind upon a cross of gold!"

Bryan's speech carried the Democratic convention, and it won him the Populist nomination as well. His opponent was William McKinley, who represented all the interests Bryan attacked. Bryan stormed around the country campaigning, while McKinley stayed home in Canton, Ohio. Bryan shouted himself hoarse, speaking morning, noon and night; McKinley rocked in his chair on his front porch, smiling and waving at those who came to pay their respects. Bryan lit a prairie fire that spread west from Nebraska; he wound up carrying every state in the West but North Dakota, Oregon and California. He also won the traditionally Democratic South. Yet the industrial states of the Northeast and the Great Lakes went for McKinley, and their large populations and numerous electoral college votes put him over the top.

49

BONANZA

WILLIAM ALLEN WHITE'S ANTI-POPULIST BROADSIDE earned him not merely a reputation in the East but space in the columns of Eastern papers and magazines. In 1897 *Scribner's* enlisted him to report on a striking new form of Western agriculture: the bonanza farm. Bonanza farms were giant operations devoted to the cultivation of wheat; ranging in size from several thousand acres to seventy thousand, they applied modern factory methods to a process with roots in the Neolithic era.

Bonanza farms sprang up in the Central Valley of California and the Palouse district of eastern Washington, but the most impressive were found in the Red River Valley of North Dakota. White traveled there to see the phenomenon for himself. The first thing he noticed was that the giant farms were a function of American law as much as of North American geography. The Red River—of the North, to distinguish it from the Red River of Oklahoma, Texas and Louisiana—is that rarity in the United States: an important stream that flows from south to north. (The Willamette River of Oregon is another.) The Red River drains North Dakota before passing into Canadian Manitoba on its way to Lake Winnipeg. A striking disparity was obvious to the most casual observer who visited both sides of the boundary line. "When the river crosses the Canadian border," White wrote, "the bonanza farms are not found in its valleys, and even smaller farms have not been established universally upon the rich soil, as they have been a few score of miles south in Yankeedom."

White didn't track down the reasons for the disparity, which related to the larger rewards to entrepreneurialism in the United States, and America's greater tolerance for corporate gigantism. He suggested that Canada might one day catch up. But for now the American phenomenon was enough to astonish any student of agriculture. White wasn't even sure whether this counted as agriculture. It looked more like industry. "In the valley upon the American side there is not a barren acre," he said. "Wheat stretches away from the car-window to the horizon, over a land flat as a floor. The monotonous exactness of the level makes one long for the undulating prairies of the Middle West." White appreciated that the monotony made for greater efficiency. "The very evenness of the plain has a commercial value, and makes the location here of the great wheat-farms possible. For in a rolling country there is waste land: here an 'eighty'"—acres—"on a hill-top, there a 'forty' in a swamp. But in bonanza farming every foot of land must be productive with the expenditure of the least possible amount of human labor upon it."

All aspects of the bonanza farms were huge, from their physical extent to the tools employed in their cultivation. "In the lexicon of the Dakota farmer there is no such word as 'hoe,'" said White. "The smallest implement upon a big wheat farm is a plough. And from the plough to the elevator—from the first operation in wheat-farming to the last—one is forced to realize how the spirit of the age has made itself felt here." That spirit began with a celebration of size. John Rockefeller built an empire of oil, Andrew Carnegie of steel. No one person dominated farming as Rockefeller and Carnegie did oil and steel, but the county-sized farms of Dakota were to the quarter-sections of Ohio as Carnegie Steel was to the shop of the village blacksmith.

The spirit of the industrial age also glorified the power of machines. Human muscle power had been replaced by machine

power on the big farms, White said. "The man who ploughs uses
his muscle only incidentally in guiding the machine. The man who
operates the harrow has half a dozen levers to lighten his labor. The
'sower who goeth forth to sow' walks leisurely behind a drill and
works brakes. The reaper needs a quick brain and a quick hand, but
not necessarily a strong arm nor a powerful back." Steam engines
drove harvesters and threshers, replacing not only men but horses.
The trend appeared certain to continue.

White remarked a profound convergence between industry
and agriculture, between East and West. "The farm laborer in the
West today, where machinery is employed, finds himself advanced
to the ranks of skilled labor and enjoys a position not widely different from that of the mill-hand in the East. Each is a tender of a
machine." Like the Eastern industrialist, the Dakota wheat grower
had to match output to market demand. "His profits are large or
small according to the caprices of the market," White said. Yet
here the wheat man was at a disadvantage to the iron-monger or
textile-weaver. He was at the mercy of forces of nature beyond his
control. "The rain, the hail, or the drought may cut his crop short
fifty per cent, within a fortnight of the harvest." When it did, the
unit cost of the farmer's output doubled.

The bonanza farms had not grown organically the way other
farms did. They had not originated in the homestead laws, or
evolved by the amalgamation of many small properties. They were
born big, offspring at one remove from the federal government.
The government had granted millions of acres of public land to the
Union Pacific, the Central Pacific, and other railroads built on the
same model; the railroads then sold the land, in very large parcels,
to the current owners of the bonanza farms. "The railroad people
interested capitalists, and the establishment of the farms came naturally," White observed.

The result was something strange to the American mind. "It
is difficult to present the idea of the bigness of these farms to the
person whose preconceived notion of a farm is a checker-board
lying upon a hillside or in a valley," White said. A farm of many

thousands of acres operated more like a principality than a farm. "Crews of workmen living at one end of the farm and operating it may not see the crews in other corners from season's end to season's end." The fields were so vast that it didn't pay for the crews to eat lunch at a mess hall, which might be a half-hour's walk away. Instead the mess halls were put on wheels and rolled out to the workers in the fields.

The giant farms generated mind-boggling statistics. "Averaging twenty bushels to the acre, as many farms will this year, the total number of bushels in a crop on a bonanza farm would be 140,000." White supposed a farm of seven thousand acres—not especially large for the Red River Valley. "Putting five hundred bushels of that crop in a freight car, and allowing forty feet to the car, the train which would haul the crop from the farm would be two miles long." If the crop were bundled the old-fashioned way and transported on mule-back, the train of mules would stretch more than halfway from Brooklyn to Buffalo.

The economy of the West had always been tuned to the markets of the East and Europe; the fur trade died when tastes in London and New York changed. The same linkage was evident in bonanza farming, only it was instantaneous and farther reaching. "The business office of every big wheat farm in the Red River Valley is connected by wire with the markets at Duluth, and Minneapolis, and at Buffalo," White wrote. "The superintendent keeps in the closest touch with his agents in the world's great wheat-pits. When the telegraph ticker indicates the arrival of a good price, the farm's agent—a commission merchant at some city board of trade—is instructed to sell." The telegraph brought the world to Dakota's door; no arable region was too remote to escape the attention of the managers of the bonanza farms. "A rainfall in India or a hot wind in South America is felt upon the Dakota farm in a few hours. The nerves of trade thrill around the globe."

What another century would call globalization reached Dakota in the 1890s. "The wages of the harvester in the Red River Valley are fixed by conditions in the fields in Russia, or in Argentina, or in India. The distance between the fields has been lost. The world's great wheat-crop might as well lie in one field, for the scattered acres are wired together in the markets, and those markets are brought to the farmer's door."

SOMEWHERE THE GHOST OF THOMAS JEFFERSON SHUDDERED. Dakota was part of Jefferson's Louisiana Purchase, the vast tract he had considered a guarantee of the independence of generations of yeoman farmers, who in turn would guarantee the independence of the American republic. Independence was nowhere in sight on the bonanza farms. The men who did the work on the farms were beholden to their bosses, and the bosses were entangled in a web of global commerce that controlled them far more than they controlled it. The republic might survive, but not by any path Jefferson had envisioned.

VIII

THE COWBOY IN
THE WHITE HOUSE

50

ROUGH RIDING

THEODORE ROOSEVELT HAD BEEN A NEW YORK STATE assemblyman before turning cowboy; when the disaster of 1886–1887 drove him back to politics, he ran for mayor of New York City. He didn't win, but he gained enough positive exposure that when a post came open on the city's police board, he got the job. He tilted against criminals and corrupt policemen in a way that made headlines but little headway, and meanwhile moonlighted as a cheerleader for the Republican party. He stumped on behalf of William McKinley in 1896 and called William Jennings Bryan every kind of dangerous radical. When McKinley won, Roosevelt lined up for a job in the new administration.

The one he landed was assistant secretary of the navy. It was the closest he could get to war during peacetime, and war was his heart's desire. Roosevelt's struggle to shake his early weakness would culminate, he dreamed, in the ultimate test of manhood: war. If he could show his courage under fire, he would finally have become a man.

As it happened, there was a war looming. A nationalist revolt in Cuba, one of the last Spanish colonies in the Americas, had triggered repression against the rebels and sympathy among Americans for the rebel cause. Roosevelt wasted little sympathy on the rebels, but he did want a chance to fight Spain. He urged war upon McKinley at all opportunities, which weren't many, given that he was a mere assistant navy secretary. McKinley rebuffed Roosevelt's advances.

But Roosevelt had a friend, Leonard Wood, an army surgeon with experience in the West, and also the president's doctor. Wood agreed with Roosevelt on the need for American action against Spain, and he saw McKinley almost daily. In time the machinations of Roosevelt and Wood became a joke with McKinley. "Have you and Theodore declared war yet?" McKinley typically asked Wood, while the latter was taking his pulse. "No, Mr. President, but we think that *you* should," Wood replied.

The pressure mounted on McKinley, from many besides Roosevelt and Wood. New York newspapers, locked in a circulation battle and reckoning that war would boost sales, shamelessly agitated for American belligerence. Eventually McKinley sent a battleship, the *Maine*, to Havana to register American concern. The ship mysteriously blew up, allowing Roosevelt and the war hawks to blame the Spanish. The pressure on McKinley increased, and finally he succumbed. The president asked Congress for a declaration of war, and Congress obliged.

The legislature thereupon authorized the creation of volunteer regiments, including three of cavalry. Leonard Wood was given command of the 1st Cavalry Regiment, with Roosevelt as his lieutenant colonel. At the suggestion of Roosevelt and Wood, the regiment would be drawn primarily from the Western territories. Word went out, and the one thousand positions were quickly oversubscribed.

Roosevelt was thrilled. He was tickled to be lieutenant to Wood, whose career under arms had included much more than doctoring. "He had served in General Miles's inconceivably harassing campaigns against the Apaches," Roosevelt observed, "where he had displayed such courage that he won that most coveted of distinctions—the Medal of Honor; such extraordinary physical strength and endurance that he grew to be recognized as one of the two or three white men who could stand fatigue and hardship as well as an Apache; and such judgment toward the close of the campaigns he was given, though a surgeon, the actual command of more than one expedition against the bands of renegade Indians."

The enlisted men of the regiment were hardly less impressive to Roosevelt. "They came from the four territories which yet remained within the boundaries of the United States"—New Mexico, Arizona, Oklahoma and Indian Territory—"that is, from the lands that have been most recently won over to white civilization, and in which the conditions of life are nearest those that obtained on the frontier when there still was a frontier." The recruits possessed traits Roosevelt had long envied. "They were a splendid set of men, these Southwesterners—tall and sinewy, with resolute, weather-beaten faces, and eyes that looked a man straight in the face without flinching," he said. "In all the world there could be no better material for soldiers than that afforded by these grim hunters of the mountains, these wild rough riders of the plains. They were accustomed to handling wild and savage horses; they were accustomed to following the chase with the rifle, both for sport and as a means of livelihood."

A few hailed from frontier towns. "But most were from the wilderness, having left their lonely hunters' cabins and shifting cow-camps to seek new and stirring adventures beyond the sea." Some of the noncommissioned officers of the regiment were military veterans of the Indian wars. Other had worn badges. "They were sheriffs, marshals, deputy-sheriffs, and deputy-marshals—men who had fought Indians, and still more often had waged relentless war upon the bands of white desperadoes." Bucky O'Neill was "a famous sheriff throughout the West for his feats of victorious warfare against the Apache, no less than against the white road-agents and man-killers." A regimental captain from New Mexico had been in numerous scrapes. "He had been shot four times in pitched fights with red marauders and white outlaws." Several had been marshals and deputies in the Indian Territory. "In the Indian Territory, service as a deputy-marshal meant capacity to fight stand-up battles with the gangs of outlaws."

The ages of the troopers varied. "The men in the ranks were mostly young, yet some were past their first youth," Roosevelt said. "These had taken part in the killing of the great buffalo herds, and had fought Indians when the tribes were still on the warpath. The younger ones, too, had led rough lives; and the lines in their faces told of many a hardship endured, and many a danger silently faced with grim, unconscious philosophy." Some had been to the East, and a few even across the ocean. "Others had been born and bred in the West, and had never seen a larger town than Santa Fe or a bigger body of water than the Pecos in flood." Several followed the Western habit of adopting nicknames: Cherokee Bill, Happy Jack, Smoky Moore, Rattlesnake Pete.

The regiment included four clergymen. A much larger number still needed saving. "Some were professional gamblers," Roosevelt wrote. "Some were men whose lives in the past had not been free from the taint of those fierce kinds of crime into which the lawless spirits who dwell on the borderland between civilization and savagery so readily drift."

The regiment included Texas Rangers. "Of course, these rangers needed no teaching," Roosevelt said. "They were already trained to obey and to take responsibility. They were splendid shots, horsemen and trailers. They were accustomed to living in the open, to enduring great fatigue and hardship, and to encountering all kinds of danger."

Benjamin Franklin Daniels had been marshal of Dodge City after that town supplanted Abilene as the destination of choice for Texas cattle drives and became a byword for frontier hijinks. "In the course of his rather lurid functions as a peace officer, he had lost half of one ear—'bitten off,' it was explained to me," Roosevelt said. "Naturally, he viewed the dangers of battle with philosophic calm."

A bronco-buster from Oklahoma named McGinty shared the cowboy's distaste for doing anything afoot. He never walked a hundred yards if he could possibly ride. "When McGinty was reproved for his absolute inability to keep step on the drill-ground, he responded that he was pretty sure he could keep step on horse-back," Roosevelt recounted.

The most striking members of the regiment were the Indi-ans. Primarily from the Indian Territory, they were Cherokees, Chickasaws, Choctaws, Creeks and a handful of others. "Only a few were of pure blood," Roosevelt observed. "The others shaded off until they were absolutely indistinguishable from their white comrades—with whom, it may be mentioned, they all lived on terms of complete equality." One of the full-blooded Indians was a Pawnee named Pollock—"one of the gamest and best soldiers in the regiment." Roosevelt reflected on Pollock and on American relations with the Indians in remarking, "He had been educated, like most of the other Indians, at one of those admirable Indian schools which have added so much to the total of the small credit account with which the White race balances the very unpleasant debit account of its dealings with the Red." Pollock was taciturn, but he had a good hand for writing, and when not fighting, he served as the regimental clerk. Roosevelt discovered, at the front in Cuba, that he possessed a wry sense of humor. "As he was sit-ting in the Adjutant's tent working over the returns, there turned up a trooper from the First"—Regiment—"who had been acting as barber. Eyeing him with immovable face, Pollock asked, in a guttural voice, 'Do you cut hair?' The man answered, 'Yes'; and Pollock continued, 'Then you'd better cut mine,' muttering, in an explanatory soliloquy, 'Don't want to wear my hair like a wild In-dian when I'm in civilized warfare.'"

Another impressive Indian was a Cherokee named Holder-man. "He was an excellent soldier," Roosevelt said. "He was a half-breed, and came of soldier stock on both sides and through both races. He explained to me once why he had come to the war: that it was because his people had always fought when there was a war, and he could not feel happy to stay at home when the flag was go-ing into battle."

The Indians were the best riders in a regiment of first-rate horsemen. Roosevelt recalled the finest of the bunch. "He was mounted on an exceedingly bad bronco, which would bolt out of the ranks at drill. He broke it of this habit by the simple expedient of giving it two tremendous twists, first to one side and then to the other, as it bolted, with the result that, invariably, at the second bound its legs crossed and over it went with a smash, the rider taking the somersault with unmoved equanimity."

ROOSEVELT'S ROAD TO CUBA RAN THROUGH SAN ANTONIO, where his regiment gathered and trained. His admiration for the volunteers, and his lack of military experience, caused him to blur the line between officers and men. One successful drill session inspired him to give a congratulatory order: "The men can go in and drink all the beer they want, which I will pay for!" The men cheered their lieutenant colonel and all headed for the saloon. Roosevelt was delighted with himself until Leonard Wood pointed out that drinking with the enlisted men was not conducive to military discipline. Roosevelt reddened under the reprimand before blurting out, "Sir, I consider myself the damnedest ass within ten miles of this camp! Good night, sir!"

Roosevelt soon got his role straight, but the men never lost their rambunctiousness. When their training was completed and the regiment prepared to leave for Tampa and then Cuba, San Antonio threw a celebration. The gala concluded with a concert ending in martial tunes, which the conductor bolstered by the firing of cannons. Members of the regiment had been drinking at the celebration, and their discernment was impaired. A few of them mistook the musical cannons for enemy fire upon the conductor and orchestra. "Help him out, boys!" one shouted, pulling his pistols and leaping onto the stage. Others joined him and began blazing away. The flabbergasted audience dove to the ground. The confusion intensified when the bullets shot out the lights, and darkness enveloped the scene. But the unseen enemy failed to return the troopers' fire, and things settled down. The conductor, a German immigrant, remarked the next day, "I was in the Franco-Prussian

War and saw some hot times, but I was about as uneasy last night as I ever was in battle."

From San Antonio the regiment traveled by train to Tampa. Already the eyes of America were on them. The pens of journalists scribbled profiles of the "Rough Riders," as headline writers dubbed them. Never had such a picturesque unit entered battle under the American flag. Cowboys and Indians in the same unit, fighting together? The very notion tantalized, even as it assuaged the guilt Americans felt at their country's mistreatment of the Indians. The Indians in the regiment, apparently, weren't holding a grudge, for they had volunteered to fight on behalf of the government that had seized their lands and waged war on them.

Roosevelt ensured ample coverage of the Rough Riders. He had learned the art of public relations on the police board in New York, where he had invited reporters to join him on midnight prowls through the tenderloin districts. He continued to cultivate the newsmen, who found him good for a quote or a tidbit about the regiment. Lest they miss something of interest, Roosevelt contracted to write a series of articles for *Scribner's* magazine about the Rough Riders and their exploits.

THE FIGHTING UNFOLDED DIFFERENTLY THAN ROOSEVELT expected. At Tampa, army transports were too few for all the regiments and all their gear. Roosevelt, desperate not to be deprived of his testing under fire, jawboned the regiment's way onto one of the transports, but the horses of all save the officers had to be left behind. The result was a cavalry regiment that went to war on foot. The Rough Riders became rough walkers. McGinty and the other cowboys suffered, but soldiered on.

The regiment performed gallantly in its two engagements with the enemy. "Yesterday we struck the Spaniards and had a brisk fight for 2½ hours before we drove them out of their position," Roosevelt reported after the first. "We lost a dozen men killed or mortally wounded, and sixty severely or slightly wounded. One man was killed as he stood beside a tree with me. Another bullet went through a tree behind which I stood and filled my eyes with bark." Roosevelt led the men in a series of charges. "The last charge I led on the left using a rifle I took from a wounded man," he said. "The fire was very hot at one or two points where the men around me went down like ninepins."

The second engagement was the crucial one. The San Juan Heights guarded the port of Santiago, and the Americans sought to drive out the Spanish fleet anchored there. The Rough Riders were assigned the task of taking Kettle Hill, part of the heights. Richard Harding Davis, a journalist who became a Roosevelt friend and enthusiast, described the lieutenant colonel as he led the assault on the Spanish lines. "Roosevelt, mounted high on horseback, charging the rifle-pits at a gallop and quite alone, made you feel that you would like to cheer," Davis wrote. "He wore on his sombrero a blue polka-dot handkerchief, à la Havelock"—a British hero of the Afghan War—"which, as he advanced, floated out straight behind his head like a guidon."

The Spanish fire, directed down from the heights, was intense and lethal. "The Mauser bullets drove in sheets through the trees and the tall jungle grass, making a peculiar whirring or rustling sound," Roosevelt recalled. "Some of the bullets seemed to pop in the air, so that we thought they were explosive; and, indeed, many of those which were coated with brass did explode, in the sense that the brass coat was ripped off, making a thin plate of hard metal with a jagged edge, which inflicted a ghastly wound."

The wounds were many. The Americans carried the day at San Juan, but more than a thousand—from all the regiments—were killed or wounded. Yet Roosevelt couldn't have been happier. He had been in the thickest of the fighting and hadn't flinched. Men had been killed to his left and right, and he hadn't slowed his forward pace. His men had followed him without question. "The man in command must take all the risks which he asks his men to take if he is going to get the best work out of them," he explained knowingly to a friend back home. "On the day of the big fight I had to ask my men to do a deed that European military writers consider utterly impossible of performance, that is, to attack over open ground unshaken infantry armed with the best modern repeating rifles behind a formidable system of entrenchments. The only way to get them to do it in the way it had to be done was to lead them myself."

Roosevelt would never forget the thrill of the battle or lose the glow of the victory. Decades later he declared, "San Juan was the great day of my life."

51

WEST TAKES EAST

T HE WAR MADE ROOSEVELT A HERO. THE NATION HAD never seen his like. Eastern born and Harvard educated, but an adoptive son of the West, he mingled as easily with cowboys and Indians as with Ivy Leaguers—a few of whom slipped into the ranks of the Rough Riders.

The war also made America an empire, with a western frontier thousands of miles beyond the coast of California and Oregon. Early in the war American naval forces captured Manila, the capital of the Philippines, another Spanish colony. The treaty that ended the war transferred the Philippines to the United States. The treaty provoked a debate about the meaning of the American experiment in self-government: Could a democracy become an empire without losing its soul? A vocal minority said no, but a ratifying majority in the Senate said yes, with many describing American expansion into the Pacific as being as inevitable and beneficent as American expansion across the Great Plains and Rocky Mountains had been.

Amid the debate Roosevelt converted his hero's reputation into the currency of elective politics. Thomas Platt, the boss of the New York state Republican party, was looking for a fresh face, since Platt's current protégé, the Republican governor, had become embroiled in corruption egregious even by the dubious standards of the late Gilded Age. Platt decided that Roosevelt was just the man to replace him. Roosevelt was popular enough to win votes yet young and green enough to require—and presumably follow—advice once elected.

Chauncey Depew, a Platt adviser and Republican stalwart, was delighted at the idea of a Roosevelt nomination. Depew had to defend the party against the charges of corruption, and Roosevelt would make his life much easier. Depew imagined a Democratic heckler raising the graft issue. "If Colonel Roosevelt is nominated," Depew told Platt, "I can say to the heckler with indignation and enthusiasm: 'I am mighty glad you asked that question. We have nominated for governor a man who has demonstrated in public office and on the battlefield that he is a fighter for the right, and always victorious. If he is selected, you know and we all know from his demonstrated characteristics, courage and ability, that every thief will be caught and punished, and every dollar that can be found restored to the public treasury.' Then I will follow the colonel leading his Rough Riders up San Juan Hill and ask the band to play the 'Star-Spangled Banner.'"

This was about how things happened. Roosevelt easily won the Republican nomination, and then carried the general election, albeit by a slimmer margin than Platt expected.

Perhaps the boss thought the close contest would render Roosevelt more pliable than a landslide might have. If he did, he was quite mistaken. Roosevelt made clear from his first day in office that the voters had elected *him*, not Platt. On small issues at first, then larger ones, he declined and then openly refused to do Platt's bidding.

Platt cursed himself for not having seen this coming. He began plotting how to rid himself of this ungrateful wretch.

Fate showed the way. William McKinley's vice-president had died in office. The party would name a replacement candidate at the national convention in 1900. Platt decided that the replacement should be Roosevelt. Roosevelt remained popular among the voting public; he would add luster to the national ticket. And he would be McKinley's problem rather than Platt's.

Mark Hanna, McKinley's close friend and chief adviser, yielded nothing to Platt in political chicanery. Hanna understood exactly what Platt intended in promoting Roosevelt for the vice-presidency. Just like Platt, Hanna considered Roosevelt a loose cannon. But in those days, presidents and their advisers had far less control over the nomination of vice-presidential candidates than would be the norm by the late twentieth century. Hanna tried to foil Platt's ploy. He grew worried as his efforts failed, then apoplectic as the Roosevelt nomination became unstoppable. A visitor to Hanna's suite at the convention observed that he seemed upset, and he asked what was the matter. "Matter!" shouted Hanna. "Matter! Why, everybody's gone crazy! What is the matter with all of *you*? Here is this convention going headlong for Roosevelt for vice president. Don't any of you realize that there's only one life between that madman and the presidency?"

ANOTHER STROKE OF FATE—ANOTHER DEATH—CONFIRMED Hanna's fears. The ticket of McKinley and Roosevelt won handily, and Roosevelt took up his post as vice-president. This might have augured the end of his political career, for the vice-presidency had a reputation as the office where ambition went to die. But an anarchist rescued Roosevelt by shooting McKinley, six months into the president's second term. Roosevelt raced to the president's bedside, in Buffalo, New York. The doctors stabilized McKinley, then declared him out of danger.

Roosevelt, not wishing to appear to be hovering, left Buffalo. He took his family to the Adirondacks, where he tackled Mount Marcy, the highest peak in the area. He was just starting down from the summit when a message runner found him. McKinley had suddenly relapsed. The vice-president must return to Buffalo as quickly as possible.

Roosevelt commandeered a wagon to take him to the nearest railroad. By the time he got there, the president had died, as

Roosevelt was informed at the station. He continued the journey to Buffalo, reflecting on his unlikely path to the highest office in the land.

Mark Hanna, considering the same subject, cursed again. "That damned cowboy is president of the United States," he said.

52

CASHING IN

Six months later Owen Wister dedicated a novel to Roosevelt. "Some of these pages you have seen, some you have praised, one stands new-written because you blamed it," Wister wrote. "And all, my dear critic, beg leave to remind you of their author's changeless admiration."

Wister was an Easterner by birth, like Roosevelt; a Harvard man, like Roosevelt, whom he had met there; and a visitor to the West who, like Roosevelt, had become enchanted by the land and its inhabitants. The novel was *The Virginian: A Horseman of the Plains*; its title character was the archetype of what Roosevelt and Wister—and much of America by this time—imagined the Western cowboy to be: the strong, silent, brave, honest knight of the frontier. Wister's narrator encounters the Virginian, who goes by no other name, on arrival in Medicine Bow, Wyoming. "Lounging there at ease against the wall was a slim young giant, more beautiful than pictures. His broad, soft hat was pushed back; a loose-knotted, dull-scarlet handkerchief sagged from his throat; and one casual thumb was hooked in the cartridge-belt that slanted across his hips. He had plainly come many miles from somewhere across the vast horizon, as the dust upon him showed. His boots were white with it. His overalls were gray with it. The weather-beaten bloom of his face shone through it duskily, as the ripe peaches look upon their trees in a dry season. But no dinginess of travel or shabbiness of attire could tarnish the splendor that radiated from his youth and strength."

Wister wrote of things he had personally seen and experienced, yet he realized that what he described was now history. "Any narrative which presents faithfully a day and a generation is of necessity historical; and this one presents Wyoming between 1874 and 1890," he explained in the preface. "Had you left New York or San Francisco at ten o'clock this morning, by noon the day after tomorrow you could step out at Cheyenne. There you would stand at the heart of the world that is the subject of my picture, yet you would look around you in vain for the reality. It is a vanished world. No journeys, save those which memory can take, will bring it to you now. The mountains are there, far and shining, and the sunlight, and the infinite earth, and the air that seems forever the true fountain of youth—but where is the buffalo, and the wild antelope, and where the horseman with his pasturing thousands? So like its old self does the sage-brush seem when revisited, that you wait for the horseman to appear. But he will never come again. He rides in the historic yesterday."

Wister had composed the novel in stages; chapters had been published in magazines as he wrote. There he had employed the present tense. He could do so no longer. "Verbs like 'is' and 'have' now read 'was' and 'had,'" he explained. "Time has flowed faster than my ink."

Where had it gone? "What is become of the horseman, the cowpuncher, the last romantic figure upon our soil? For he *was* romantic. Whatever he did, he did with his might. The bread that he earned was earned hard, the wages he squandered were squandered hard—half a year's pay sometimes gone in a night—'blown in,' as he expressed it, or 'blowed in,' to be perfectly accurate." Wister suggested—hoped, anyway—that the type lived on in the American soul. "He will be here among us always, invisible, waiting his chance to live and play as he would like. His wild kind has been among us always, since the beginning: a young man with his temptations, a hero without wings."

Cowboys and the West had previously been subjects for pulp fiction; *The Virginian* was the first Western novel that could have been called literature. It was an instant hit, running through many printings, and in due course it inspired multiple film adaptations.

Andy Adams's *The Log of a Cowboy*, which appeared a year after Wister's book, tapped into the same nostalgia for life on the range. Subtitled "A Narrative of the Old Trail Days," the novel was easily mistaken for a memoir. It was based on Adams's experience driving cattle on the Western Trail from Texas to Montana, and it was dedicated to "the Cowmen and boys" of that earlier time.

Adams's account is straightforward and stoic—like the model cowboy—but at the end he allows his narrator a moment of wistfulness. The crew is about to deliver the herd to its Montana destination. "Another day's easy travel brought us to within a mile of the railroad terminus; but it also brought us to one of the hardest experiences of our trip, for each of us knew, as we unsaddled our horses, that we were doing it for the last time. Although we were in the best of spirits over the successful conclusion of the drive; although we were glad to be free from herd duty and looked forward eagerly to the journey home"—by train—"there was still a feeling of regret in our hearts which we could not dispel. In the days of my boyhood I have shed tears when a favorite horse was sold from our little ranch on the San Antonio, and have frequently witnessed Mexican children unable to hide their grief when need of bread had compelled the sale of some favorite horse to a passing drover. But at no time in my life, before or since, have I felt so keenly the parting between man and horse as I did that September evening in Montana."

Adams understood that the horse was what made the cowboy, and gave the cowboy much of his appeal. This parting between cowboy and horse signaled the end of an era. Adams's narrator closes by speaking as if from years later, and as if speaking for all the cowboys on that drive, or any other, about their horses. "Their bones may be bleaching in some coulee by now," he says of the horses, "but the men who knew them then can never forget them or the part they played in that long drive."

FREDERIC REMINGTON LIKEWISE RODE THE WAVE OF NOSTAL-gia for a vanishing West. Remington was another Ivy Leaguer, from Yale, and he first made a splash as an illustrator for *Harper's Weekly*, covering the army's chase for Geronimo. His black-and-white images for publication gave way to watercolors and oils, and finally to sculpture. His subjects were cowboys and Indians and soldiers, typically on horseback; his work conveyed the drama of life on the last frontier. He connected with Roosevelt when *The Century Magazine* hired him to illustrate a serialized version of a book Roosevelt was writing on life in the West. The two became friends, sharing their fascination with the West and each admiring in the other what he couldn't see in himself: Roosevelt the artistry of Remington, Remington the energy of Roosevelt.

Remington covered the Spanish-American War; his *Charge of the Rough Riders at San Juan Hill* captured Roosevelt in full gallop as his regiment stormed the heights. At war's end the Rough Riders pooled resources to purchase a copy of Remington's bronze sculpture *The Broncho Buster* for their valiant leader. Roosevelt was deeply moved. "No gift could have been so appropriate," he told the men. "It comes from you who shared the hardships of the campaign with me, who gave me a piece of your hardtack when I had none, and who shared with me your blankets when I had none to lie upon." He paused. "This is something I shall hand down to my children, and I shall value it more than I do the weapons I carried through the campaign." For Roosevelt, this was saying a lot.

Americans at large appreciated Remington's work almost as much as Roosevelt did. His work was in constant demand by magazine publishers and the general public; *Harper's* called him the busiest artist in America. He preferred painting soldiers but realized the money was in cowboys. "Cowboys are cash with me," he said.

53

JOHN MUIR'S LAST STAND

R OOSEVELT WOULDN'T HAVE BEEN MUCH OF A POLITICIAN
if he hadn't hitched his White House agenda to the nostalgia for the West. Roosevelt was the first Western president in
the sense of being the first to have spent significant time in the
West and to take a serious interest in issues peculiar to the West.
His first annual message, delivered less than three months after
the death of McKinley, proposed an ambitious program for the
conservation and wise use of Western resources. At a time when
federal policy still favored the transfer of public lands to the private
sector, at low prices or gratis, Roosevelt advocated creating large
national forest reserves. These tracts would be withdrawn from
sale and administered by the federal government for the benefit of
all the people of the United States, not for private or local interests. The idea was hugely controversial. As Roosevelt had learned
from the Marquis de Morès in Dakota, powerful men and groups
had long treated the public domain as theirs to exploit for private
profit. The state governments were against him, too, for they considered federal lands within their borders to be theirs, in a moral
sense, if not a legal one.

Roosevelt reminded his critics that the West had been acquired
by the national government—by treaty and war from the Indians, by purchase from France, by war and purchase from Mexico,
by diplomacy with Britain. The Western states had been created

by the national government. The Western lands still in the public domain belonged to the people of the United States. It was only proper that the Western lands be administered for their owners.

Roosevelt parried criticism that he wanted to make a park out of the entire West. Far from it, he said. He intended to put the national forests to use, but to a more sustainable use than that to which they were being put at present. "Forest protection is not an end of itself," he said. "The preservation of our forests is an imperative business necessity. We have come to see clearly that whatever destroys the forest, except to make way for agriculture, threatens our well being."

Roosevelt added the development of Western water resources to his list of national priorities. He had read John Wesley Powell's report on the arid region and taken its message to heart. "In the arid region it is water, not land, which measures production," Roosevelt said. "The western half of the United States would sustain a population greater than that of our whole country today if the waters that now run to waste were saved and used for irrigation." The creation and maintenance of national forests, which held water and released it slowly, would be a start on the water problem. But more was required, and the federal government was the appropriate agent. "Great storage works are necessary to equalize the flow of streams and to save the flood waters. Their construction has been conclusively shown to be an undertaking too vast for private effort. Nor can it be best accomplished by the individual states acting alone. Far-reaching interstate problems are involved; and the resources of single states would often be inadequate. It is properly a national function." And the whole nation would benefit. A more productive West would send its bounty east; a more populous West would increase demand for the produce of the rest of the country.

Congress heeded Roosevelt's call, and six months later he signed the Newlands Act, named for the bill's sponsor in the House of Representatives, Francis Newlands of Nevada. The act put the federal government, for the first time, directly into the business of developing the natural resources of the West. In particular, it provided for the construction of the dams and irrigation systems John Powell had declared essential to the settlement and development of the West.

The Newlands law and follow-up legislation made the desert bloom; it also made possible the eventual building of large cities— Phoenix, Las Vegas—where none could have existed before. One of the dams on the Colorado River created a reservoir named Lake Powell.

JOHN MUIR DIDN'T LIKE DAMS. HE PREFERRED NATURE AS God made it. And he spent his last days battling dam-builders who had the audacity to approach his beloved Yosemite.

Theodore Roosevelt admired Muir almost as much as he admired Powell, with Muir falling short only for never having served in the military. Roosevelt learned that one of the perquisites of the presidency was the ability to get people to do things for him they wouldn't have done on their own. He had long wished to visit Yosemite, and he could think of no better guide than Muir. "I do not want anyone with me but you," he wrote to Muir, "and I want to drop politics absolutely for four days, and just be out in the open with you."

Muir by now was the acknowledged high priest of the High Sierra, and he received similar requests all the time. He knew Roosevelt, by reputation, as a loud, opinionated warmonger—hardly the sort Muir liked to camp with. But Roosevelt *was* the president, and he could be useful in the cause of wilderness protection. "I might be able to do some forest good in talking freely around the campfire," Muir wrote to a friend. The arrangements were made.

Roosevelt loved every minute of the outing. "John Muir met me with a couple of packers and two mules to carry our tent, bedding, and food for a three days' trip," he wrote afterward. "The first night was clear, and we lay down in the darkening aisles of the great Sequoia grove. The majestic trunks, beautiful in color and

Theodore Roosevelt and John Muir. These two did more to preserve the natural West than any others.

in symmetry, rose round us like the pillars of a mightier cathedral than ever was conceived even by the fervor of the Middle Ages. Hermit thrushes sang beautifully in the evening, and again, with a burst of wonderful music, at dawn." Roosevelt was surprised and quietly pleased to discover that he knew more about birds than Muir did. Muir loved trees and flowers and cliffs and mountains, not birds. "The only birds he noticed or cared for were some that were very conspicuous, such as the water-ousels—always particular favorites of mine too."

Roosevelt didn't exactly drop politics on the trip. Photographers trailed him, and a shot of Roosevelt and Muir standing at

Hetch Hetchy Valley. Not long after this photograph was taken, the valley was inundated.

the brink of Glacier Point, thousands of feet above the floor of Yosemite Valley, served the purposes of both. Roosevelt burnished his naturalist credentials, while Muir made friends with the most powerful man in America. Ever after, Roosevelt addressed Muir as "Oom John": his Dutch uncle.

Muir appreciated much of what Roosevelt accomplished in protecting the wild places of America. Working with Congress, the president set aside huge tracts of the West as national forests. He created five national parks, including Crater Lake, near the spot where Captain Jack was hanged. He made national monuments of the Grand Canyon, the Muir Woods of California, and more than a dozen other especially scenic locales in the West.

Yet when the dam-builders eyed Yosemite, Muir rebelled. In 1906 a devastating earthquake and fire leveled large parts of San Francisco. As the city began to rebuild, it sought to secure a water supply for future growth. Civil engineers and hydrologists recommended a reservoir in the Hetch Hetchy Valley, in a corner of Yosemite National Park. Gifford Pinchot, the man Roosevelt had made the nation's chief forester, endorsed the proposal and recommended it to Congress.

Muir opposed the Hetch Hetchy project with all his might. It was an atrocious sellout of nature to the interests of commerce. "These temple destroyers, devotees of raging commercialism, seem to have a perfect contempt for Nature, and, instead of lifting their eyes to the God of the mountains, lift them to the Almighty Dollar," he wrote. Muir shook his head in wonder and dismay. "Dam Hetch Hetchy! As well dam for water-tanks the people's cathedrals and churches, for no holier temple has ever been consecrated by the heart of man."

Muir lost this battle. Congress voted in 1913 to approve the project. Muir died the following year, before the rising waters reached the temple door.

THE LONG, LONG TRAIL

B Y THEN THE WEST OF MUIR'S YOUTH, AND OF ROOSEVELT'S, was a memory. The West still existed as a geographic zone, of course. The Great Plains still formed its eastern boundary, the Pacific its western. The Rockies and the Sierra Nevada were as tall as ever, the sky over the basin between the ranges as stingy as ever with moisture. The Missouri, Columbia and Colorado rivers still ran toward the sea.

But things had changed. The Great Plains were dotted with farms, including the bonanza spreads of Dakota and the debt-ridden parcels of Kansas and Nebraska. Railroads crossed the mountains, making the journey from St. Louis to San Francisco pleasant and swift. Dams were beginning to modify the aridity of the Great Basin and would soon restrain the flow of even the most powerful rivers of the West.

Something more essential had changed, too. The earlier West had been a zone of conflict; from the explosion of the *Tonquin* to the campaigns of U.S. soldiers against Crazy Horse, Quanah Parker, Captain Jack and Joseph, violence and armed conflict had characterized the American West. This hardly made the West unique in world history. Conflict has always marked the borderlands where peoples and cultures abut, and especially where one group has intruded on another. The Greeks fought their way across Asia Minor under Alexander; the sword of Caesar brought Gaul under the dominion of Rome; Spanish conquistadores, rather than Spanish friars, enforced Iberia's will in the Americas; the Comanches dominated the southern plains, and the Sioux the northern, by killing or intimidating rival tribes.

But in the United States, by the nineteenth century such regular conflict was unique to the West. America's earlier frontier had once been as violent: the "dark and bloody ground" of Kentucky saw more mayhem per square mile than any part of the trans-Mississippi West. Yet nearly all the tribes of the East had been destroyed or removed within a generation after independence. The conflict in the later West lasted longer, primarily because the region was so much larger. And while the organized violence continued, it was a defining characteristic of the West. When the violence ended, most brutally and definitively in the massacre at Wounded Knee, the West, in its historical sense, was no more.

THE WEST DISAPPEARED IN AN EMOTIONAL, OR PERHAPS sociological, sense as well. In American history the West had always represented opportunity; the West was the peculiar repository of American dreams. The dream of El Dorado had originated with the Spanish conquistadores, but it persisted deep into the American period of the West. The forty-niners were obvious descendants of Coronado; the cattle speculators of Dakota and the land-rushers of Oklahoma slightly less obvious. But material fortunes weren't the only inspiration for Western dreams. Thomas Jefferson dreamed of an easy water route from the Missouri to the Pacific. Marcus and Narcissa Whitman dreamed of Christian salvation for their Cayuse hosts. Brigham Young dreamed of a Mormon refuge beyond the reach of a gentile government.

The West had no monopoly on American dreaming. The entire American experiment in democracy was founded on a dream that ordinary people could govern themselves. And every immigrant to America came chasing a dream. But Western dreams were often larger, because the West was larger, and because for a long time it was largely unknown. In the American mind, the West was not so much a place as a condition; it was the blank spot on the map upon which grand dreams were projected.

Inevitably, the blank spot was filled in, by the very efforts of those seeking to attain their dreams. Some did attain them, at least in part. Many argonauts struck it rich in California. Many emigrants to Oregon were delighted at how their long journey ended. Theodore Roosevelt didn't become a cattle king, but he became president, which was no small consolation.

More commonly, though, the reality fell short—often far short—of the dreams. The explosion of the *Tonquin* blasted John Jacob Astor's dream of an American fur empire. The Whitmans died seeking their harvest of souls. The argonauts who ended up laboring long hours in the underground mines asked why they had ever come west. The cowboys who found themselves working the year around, at the beck of a cost-counting boss, wondered what had become of their freedom.

As the West passed from dream to reality, it became more like the East, until nothing significant distinguished the one from the other. A twentieth-century Horace Greeley might have sent his young protégé to Wall Street or Washington as readily as to the West.

Yet a residue remained. The gambling spirit of the gold rush found its echo in the venture capitalism of Silicon Valley. Hollywood was built by maverick filmmakers fleeing the constraints of Eastern cartels, much as American Texas was built by malcontents fleeing the constraints of debt and marriage. Dude ranches in Wyoming and Montana attracted cowboy wannabes in the twenty-first century in the same way working ranches in Dakota attracted dudes like Teddy Roosevelt in the nineteenth.

ROOSEVELT DIED IN 1919. THE MOST FAMOUS IMAGE THAT marked his passing was a sketch called "The Long, Long Trail," which showed him in cowboy gear riding a spectral horse into a Western sky. Other figures from the earlier West had gone before. Joe Meek died in 1875, amused that having begun life in Washington County, Virginia, he was ending it in Washington County, Oregon. John Wesley Powell died in 1902, months after passage of the Newlands Act. Nez Perce Joseph died in 1904 on the Colville reservation of Washington state, still exiled from his beloved Wallowa Valley. Quanah Parker had crossed the cultural gap between his father's people and his mother's, and become a wealthy rancher; he died in 1911 in Oklahoma.

Black Elk outlasted them all. The Lakota visionary, witness to so much of his people's history, and to the history of the West, never forgot what he saw at Wounded Knee, and what it meant. "A people's dream died there," he said many years later. "It was a beautiful dream." Black Elk lived to the age of eighty-six, and died in 1950.

ACKNOWLEDGMENTS

THE AUTHOR WOULD LIKE TO THANK DAN GERSTLE AND Lara Heimert of Basic Books for suggesting this project. And Kris Puopolo and Bill Thomas of Doubleday for letting me pursue it. As always, my colleagues at the University of Texas at Austin have been most helpful in sharing their knowledge. My students have been patient as I have tested my ideas on them. The Monday mafia—Greg Curtis, Stephen Harrigan, and Lawrence Wright— have set a high bar for literary excellence and a low bar for humor. Both are appreciated.

A book like this would be impossible without a great deal of previous work by hundreds of historians, archivists and librarians. To all of them I am deeply indebted.

NOTES

PROLOGUE

xi "It was bitterly cold . . . nearly undrinkable": Roosevelt to Alice Lee Roosevelt, Sept. 8, 1883, Theodore Roosevelt Center at Dickinson State University, https://www.theodorerooseveltcenter .org. This account of Roosevelt's Dakota experience draws on H. W. Brands, *TR: The Last Romantic* (1997).

xii "I am now feeling very well": Roosevelt to Alice Lee Roosevelt, Sept. 17, 1883, Theodore Roosevelt Center.

xiii "I have been three weeks": Brands, *TR*, 189.

xiv "In the latter part of March": Brands, *TR*, 208.

CHAPTER 1: THE RIVER AT THE HEART OF AMERICA

3 America's West entered human history: An accessible introduction to life in the Americas before European contact in the late fifteenth century is Charles C. Mann, *1491: New Revelations of the Americas Before Columbus* (2005).

6 "I would rather": Edmund S. Morgan, *Benjamin Franklin* (2002), 288.

CHAPTER 2: THE CORPS OF DISCOVERY

11 "The object of your mission . . . on your decease": Jefferson to Lewis, June 20, 1803, Thomas Jefferson Papers, Library of Congress, American Memory, http://memory.loc.gov. In this and other documents from the period, idiosyncrasies of spelling and punctuation have been normalized and abbreviations spelled out.

14   "Captain Lewis and myself": Entries for Aug. 2 and 3, 1804, in *The Journals of the Lewis and Clark Expedition*, edited by Gary E. Moulton, https://lewisandclarkjournals.unl.edu. This is the most authoritative version of the journals of the Corps of Discovery. Stephen E. Ambrose's *Undaunted Courage: Meriwether Lewis, Thomas Jefferson, and the Opening of the American West* (1996) is an enthusiastically told account of the Lewis and Clark journey informed by the author's reprise of the trek.

14   "Sergeant Floyd": Entries for Aug. 19 and 20, 1804, *Journals of Lewis and Clark*.

15   "The man who went back": Entries for Aug. 5, 7 and 18, 1804, *Journals of Lewis and Clark*.

16   "On that nation": Jefferson to Lewis, Jan. 22, 1804, Jefferson Papers, Library of Congress.

16   "We prepared some clothes": Clark entries for Sept. 24 and 25, 1804; Gass entry for Sept. 25, 1804, *Journals of Lewis and Clark*.

17   "These are the vilest miscreants": Clark, "Estimate of the Eastern Indians," undated, *Journals of Lewis and Clark*.

19   "We shewed but little sign": Clark entry for Sept. 27, 1804, *Journals of Lewis and Clark*.

CHAPTER 3: WEST BY NORTHWEST

21   "Two shots were fired": Gass and Ordway entries, Jan. 1, 1805, *Journals of Lewis and Clark*.

21   "I ordered my black servant": Clark entry for Jan. 1, 1865, *Journals of Lewis and Clark*.

23   "All the party in high spirits": Clark entry for Mar. 30, 1805 (mislabeled as Mar. 31), *Journals of Lewis and Clark*.

23   "It may be observed generally": Gass entry for Apr. 5, 1805, *Journals of Lewis and Clark*.

23   "I observed the extraordinary dexterity": Clark entry for Mar. 29, 1805 (mislabeled as Mar. 30), *Journals of Lewis and Clark*.

CHAPTER 4: TO THE PACIFIC

25   "Our vessels consisted": Lewis entry for Apr. 7, 1805, *Journals of Lewis and Clark*.

26   "We are informed": Lewis report to Jefferson, "A Summary View of the Rivers and Creeks Which Discharge Themselves into the

Missouri," undated (winter 1804–1805), *Journals of Lewis and Clark.*

27   "This morning I walked": Lewis entry for Apr. 27, 1805, *Journals of Lewis and Clark.*

27   "On arriving to the summit": Lewis entry for May 26, 1805, *Journals of Lewis and Clark.*

28   "I had proceeded": Lewis entry for June 13, 1805, *Journals of Lewis and Clark.*

30   "The Indian woman recognized": Lewis entry for Aug. 8, 1805, *Journals of Lewis and Clark.*

30   "Both parties now advanced": Lewis entry for Aug. 13, 1805, *Journals of Lewis and Clark.*

31   "I have been wet": Clark entry for Sept. 16, 1805, *Journals of Lewis and Clark.*

32   "I ascended a high cliff": Clark entry for Oct. 19, 1805, *Journals of Lewis and Clark.*

33   "The country on both sides of the river": Gass entry for Oct. 23, 1805, *Journals of Lewis and Clark.*

34   "The natives are very troublesome": Ordway entry for Oct. 22, 1805, *Journals of Lewis and Clark.*

34   "Great joy in camp": Clark entry for Nov. 7, 1805, *Journals of Lewis and Clark.* This passage in the journal was edited, for publication, to read, "Ocean in view! O! the joy!" The edited version is the more widely quoted one. See *Original Journals of the Lewis and Clark Expedition, 1804–1806,* edited by Reuben Gold Thwaites (1905), 3:207.

35   "By land from the U. States": Clark entry for Dec. 3, 1805, *Journals of Lewis and Clark.*

CHAPTER 5: ASTORIA

40   "I received, my dear sir": Jefferson to Lewis, Oct. 20, 1806, Jefferson Papers, Library of Congress.

43   He was sketching a plan: The present account of the Astor project follows Washington Irving, *Astoria* (1836), an authorized history of the enterprise. A recent account of the American fur trade is Eric Jay Dolan, *Fur, Fortune, and Empire: The Epic History of the Fur Trade in America* (2011).

45   "I am sent off": Irving, *Astoria*, 1:82–83.

46   "Indian ragamuffins": Irving, *Astoria*, 2:98.

CHAPTER 6: COMCOMLY'S DISMAY

51   At one point one of the partners: Irving, *Astoria*, 2:124–125.

CHAPTER 7: THE WHITE-HEADED EAGLE

55   The latter had deep roots: The classic history of the Hudson's Bay Company is Donald McKay, *The Honourable Company: A History of the Hudson's Bay Company* (1936).

58   "From what I had seen": John McLoughlin statement, undated, in *Transactions of the Eighth Annual Reunion of the Oregon Pioneer Association for 1880* (1881), 46.

60   *William and Ann*: Frances Fuller Victor, *The River of the West: Life and Adventure in the Rocky Mountains and Oregon, Embracing Events in the Life-time of a Mountain-man and Pioneer, with the Early History of the North-western Slope* (1871), 29–30. This indispensable and delightful book is both a history of Oregon and the fur trade and an as-told-to memoir of Joseph Meek. It is the source for the Meek tales below, which are probably no more embellished than the stories in most memoirs. Mrs. Victor was sympathetic but not gullible.

61   "It is of no use": Hubert Howe Bancroft, *History of the Northwest Coast* (1884), 2:451–452.

62   "I divulged my plan to none": McLoughlin statement, *Transactions 1880*, 48.

CHAPTER 8: MOUNTAIN MAN

63   "They did not grieve": Victor, *River of the West*, 41.

CHAPTER 9: COLTER'S RUN

71   "Sublette came round": Victor, *River of the West*, 70–71.
72   "I have been told": Victor, *River of the West*, 76–77.
73   "Go! Go away!": Thomas James, *Three Years Among the Indians and Mexicans*, edited by Walter B. Douglas (1916), 58–64.

CHAPTER 10: *URSUS HORRIBILIS*

76   "It *is* old Joe": Victor, *River of the West*, 77, 86–87.

80   "I have held my hands": Victor, *River of the West*, 120, 122, 146.

CHAPTER 11: MOSES AUSTIN'S DYING WISH

89   "We saw many signs of gold": *The Journey of Alvar Nunez Cabeza de Vaca*, edited by Ad. F. Bandelier (1905), 166.

90   "Tell dear Stephen": *The Austin Papers*, edited by Eugene C. Barker, 3 vols. (1924–1927), 1:409–410. The best biography of Stephen F. Austin, which includes a full account of Moses Austin's Texas project, is Gregg Cantrell, *Stephen F. Austin: Empresario of Texas* (2016 ed.). Background material for this section comes from H. W. Brands, *Lone Star Nation* (2004).

91   "The first 4 miles": "Journal of Stephen F. Austin on His First Trip to Texas, 1821," *Texas Historical Association Quarterly* 7 (1904): 288–296.

92   "Fifty Comanches": *Austin Papers*, 1:487, 1:631.

CHAPTER 12: TEXAS WILL BE LOST

94   "I have just had the pleasure": W. B. Dewees, *Letters from an Early Settler of Texas* (1852), 39–44.

97   "On the eastern bank . . . reserved for Mexican settlers": Manuel de Mier y Terán, *Texas by Terán: The Diary Kept by General Manuel de Mier y Terán on His 1828 Inspection of Texas*, edited by Jack Jackson (2000), 32–39, 45–46, 53–58, 74–79, 97–98, 144–155, 178–179, 217–218.

CHAPTER 13: RUIN AND REDEMPTION

103   "If any wretch": Marquis James, *The Raven: The Life Story of Sam Houston* (1929), 84. The best of the recent biographies of Houston is James L. Haley, *Sam Houston* (2002).

103   "About one o'clock": Haley, *Sam Houston*, 59–60.

104   "I have this moment heard": H. W. Brands, *Andrew Jackson* (2005), 426.

105   "It has been communicated": Brands, *Lone Star Nation*, 196–197.

105   "nineteen twentieths": Brands, *Andrew Jackson*, 517–518.

106   "The primary product": Andrew J. Torget, *Seeds of Empire: Cotton, Slavery, and the Transformation of the Texas Borderland, 1800–1850* (2015), 86–87.

CHAPTER 14: VICTORY OR DEATH

108   "It was our Lexington": Noah Smithwick, *The Evolution of a State, or Recollections of Old Texas Days* (1900), 101.

108   "We, therefore": Texas Declaration of Independence, Mar. 2, 1836, Texas State Library and Archives Commission, https://tsl .texas.gov.

110   "To the People of Texas": Travis letter from the Alamo, Feb. 24, 1836, *Papers of the Texas Revolution*, edited by John H. Jenkins, 10 vols. (1973), 4:423.

111   "The moon was up": José Enrique de la Peña, *With Santa Anna in Texas: A Personal Narrative of the Revolution*, translated and edited by Carmen Perry (1975), 46–51.

113   "Among them was one of great stature": De la Peña, *With Santa Anna*, 53.

113   "I told the people": William C. Davis, *Three Roads to the Alamo: The Lives and Fortunes of David Crockett, James Bowie, and William Barret Travis* (1998), 413.

114   "Santa Anna answered": De la Peña, *With Santa Anna*, 53. De la Peña's account of Crockett's capture and execution has been challenged, most vigorously by Texans who refuse to believe that Crockett or any of the other defenders of the Alamo would have let themselves be taken alive.

CHAPTER 15: BLOODY PALM SUNDAY

116   "I have but three citizens": *Papers of the Texas Revolution*, 4:454.

116   "The immediate advance": *The Writings of Sam Houston*, edited by Amelia W. Williams and Eugene C. Barker, 8 vols. (1938–1943), 1:365.

116   "The country around us": Herman Ehrenberg, *With Milam and Fannin: Adventures of a German Boy in Texas' Revolution*, translated by Charlotte Churchill (1935), 169–170.

117   "Grey clouds hung": Ehrenberg, *With Milam and Fannin*, 198–207.

CHAPTER 16: LAYING THERE YET

119   "I am firmly convinced": Carlos E. Castañeda, ed., *The Mexican Side of the Texas Revolution* (1928), 65–66.

120 "The first law of nature . . . trudged along": Creed Taylor, as told to James T. DeShields, *Tall Men with Long Rifles* (1971 ed.), 117–123.

122 "Sir: The enemy are laughing": *Writings of Sam Houston*, 1:412n.

123 "Remember the Alamo!" and the rest of the account of the Battle of San Jacinto: Brands, *Lone Star Nation*, 450–455.

CHAPTER 17: THE FOUR WISE MEN

131 "Immediately after we landed": *Christian Advocate and Journal and Zion's Herald*, Mar. 1, 1833.

135 "The weather was very warm": Samuel Parker, *Journal of an Exploring Tour Beyond the Rocky Mountains* (1846 ed.), 46.

136 "A man by the name": Parker, *Journal*, 46–47.

137 "Learning that this Indian": Will Bagley, *South Pass* (2014), 39.

137 "The passage through these mountains": Parker, *Journal*, 76–77.

138 "The Doctor pursued the operation": Parker, *Journal*, 80–82.

CHAPTER 18: FEMALES WANTED

140 "Is there a place": Clifford M. Drury, *Marcus and Narcissa Whitman and the Opening of Old Oregon* (2005 ed.), 1:102–104.

142 "Our expenses here": Drury, *Marcus and Narcissa Whitman*, 1:183.

143 "We will pass through this city": W. H. Gray, *A History of Oregon, 1792–1849, Drawn from Personal Observation and Authentic Information* (1870), 121–128.

145 "Among these veteran Rocky Mountain hunters": Gray, *History of Oregon*, 121–128.

146 "She was the most beautiful": Victor, *River of the West*, 176.

146 "The father seemed": Gray, *History of Oregon*, 127–128.

147 "Dearest Mother": Narcissa Whitman letter, no day given, July 1836, in *First White Women over the Rockies: Diaries, Letters, and Biographical Sketches of the Six Women of the Oregon Mission Who Made the Overland Journey in 1836 and 1838*, edited by Clifford Merrill Drury (1963), 1:73–77. This collection will be cited as *Diaries and Letters*.

148 "The whole tribe are exceedingly anxious": Narcissa Whitman diary, Aug. 1836, *Diaries and Letters*, 1:79–80.

149 "We were so swarmed": Narcissa Whitman diary, Aug. 1836, *Diaries and Letters*, 1:80–85.

149   "Before noon we began to descend": Narcissa Whitman diary, Aug. 1836, *Diaries and Letters*, 1:87–91.

CHAPTER 19: TRAPPED OUT

152   "Come . . . we are done with this life": Victor, *River of the West*, 264–265.

CHAPTER 20: WAIILATPU

158   "She is a large, healthy and strong child": Narcissa Whitman letter to sister, Mar. 23, 1839, *Transactions of the Annual Reunion of the Oregon Pioneer Association for 1891*, 117.

159   "Last Sabbath, blooming in health": Narcissa Whitman letter to Mrs. H. K. W. Perkins, June 25, 1839, *Transactions 1891*, 123–125.

160   "The greatest trial": Narcissa Whitman letter to Clarissa Prentiss, May 2, 1840, *Transactions 1891*, 133–135.

161   "These men are all firm believers": Narcissa Whitman letter to Jane Prentiss, Feb. 2, 1842, *Transactions 1891*, 140–143.

CHAPTER 21: FOR GOD AND COUNTRY

165   "We were most agreeably surprised": *New York Daily Tribune*, Mar. 29, 1843, in *Oregon Historical Quarterly* 4 (1903): 168–169.

165   "Go get some decent clothes": Drury, *Marcus and Narcissa Whitman*, 2:51.

166   "My Dear Husband": Narcissa Whitman letter to Marcus Whitman, Oct. 4 and after, 1842, *Transactions 1891*, 163.

167   "Probably there was more": Narcissa Whitman letter to her parents, Feb. 7, 1843, *Transactions 1891*, 172.

CHAPTER 22: THE WAY WEST

170   "There was a bill": Peter H. Burnett, *Recollections and Opinions of an Old Pioneer* (1880), 97–99. John D. Unruh Jr., *The Plains Across: The Overland Emigrants and the Trans-Mississippi West, 1840–1860* (1979), puts the migration to Oregon in context.

172   "They appear very willing": Marcus Whitman letter to Edward Prentiss, May 27, 1843, *Transactions 1891*, 177–178.

172 "It is four o'clock A.M. . . . . of blushing maidens": Jesse Applegate, "A Day with the Cow Column in 1843," *Oregon Historical Quarterly* 1 (1900): 372–383.
178 "He was a tall, trim": Burnett, *Recollections*, 102–103, 113–114.
180 "Up to this point": Burnett, *Recollections*, 116–118.
181 "This noble tree . . . end of our journey": Burnett, *Recollections*, 124–127.

CHAPTER 23: THE BUSINESS OF THE TRAIL

184 "The health of Mrs. Thornton": J. Quinn Thornton, *Oregon and California in 1848* (1849), 1:13–15, 1:21–26.
186 "The early part of the day": Thornton, *Oregon and California*, 1:36–37, 1:66, 1:142–143.
189 "Applegate affirmed": Thornton, *Oregon and California*, 1:161–162, 1:167–168.
190 "Water and grass good": Thornton, *Oregon and California*, 1:161–162, 1:167–168, 1:178–179, 1:184.
194 "She did not complain in words": Thornton, *Oregon and California*, 1:192, 1:198, 1:200, 1:213, 1:222–235.

CHAPTER 24: DESPERATE FURY

198 "In the fall of 1847": Catherine Sager Pringle recollections, "Across the Plains in 1844," c. 1860, available at PBS, Archives of the West, https://www.pbs.org/weta/thewest/resources/archives/two/sager1.htm.
198 "It was most distressing": Frances Fuller Victor, *The Early Indian Wars of Oregon* (1894), 98.
199 The story that did the most damage: Drury, *Marcus and Narcissa Whitman*, 2:236–237; J. B. A. Brouillet, *Authentic Account of the Murder of Dr. Whitman and Other Missionaries by the Cayuse Indians of Oregon in 1847* (1869 ed.), 35–36.
200 "The night was dark": Drury, *Marcus and Narcissa Whitman*, 2:244.
200 "He examined the patients": Catherine Sager Pringle recollections.
201 "The kitchen was full of Indians": Catherine Sager Pringle recollections.
205 "They were placed in a row": Catherine Sager Pringle recollections.
206 "The bodies, or pieces of them": Drury, *Marcus and Narcissa Whitman*, 2:251–255. This is the most careful and accurate account of the massacre.

207   "With hearts filled with fright": Catherine Sager Pringle recollections.

CHAPTER 25: AMBASSADOR FROM OREGON

213   "The Quickest Trip Yet": Victor, *River of the West*, 439.
214   "That claim is by the right": John O'Sullivan, "The True Title," *New York Morning News*, Dec. 27, 1845, quoted in Andrew Menard, *Sight Unseen: How Frémont's First Expedition Changed the American Landscape* (2012), xx.
215   "In the depth of winter": Victor, *River of the West*, 455–456.
216   "Yes, indeed": Victor, *River of the West*, 457–458.

CHAPTER 26: THE SECRET OF THE SIERRA NEVADA

225   "I picked up one or two pieces": Rodman Paul, ed., *The California Gold Discovery: Sources, Documents, Accounts and Memoirs Relating to the Discovery of Gold at Sutter's Mill* (1966), 118. General background for this section comes from H. W. Brands, *The Age of Gold: The California Gold Rush and the New American Dream* (2002).
226   "I declared this to be gold": Paul, ed., *California Gold Discovery*, 129.
227   "Damn that flag!" James A. Scherer, *The First Forty-Niner, and the Story of the Golden Tea-Caddy* (1925), 12.
228   "Gold! Gold!": Hubert Howe Bancroft, *History of California* (1888), 6:56.
228   "A frenzy seized my soul": Bancroft, *History of California*, 6:56.

CHAPTER 27: GOLD MOUNTAIN

230   "We have received": *New York Herald*, Sept. 15, 1848.
230   "Were I a New Yorker": *New York Herald*, Sept. 17, 1848.
231   "The accounts of the abundance": Polk annual message, Dec. 5, 1848, Papers of the Presidents, American Presidency Project, www.presidency.ucsb.edu.
233   "A more revolting": Kearny, quoted in George R. Stewart, *Ordeal by Hunger: The Story of the Donner Party* (1960 ed.), 276.
235   "The gold is in fine bright scales": *The Sherman Letters: Correspondence Between General and Senator Sherman from 1837 to 1891*, edited by Rachel Sherman Thorndike (1894), 45.

236 "The cradle is a very simple": Vicente Pérez Rosales, *California Adventure*, translated from the original *Recuerdos del Pasado* by Edwin S. Morby and Arturo Torres-Rioseco (1947), 51–52.

239 "With a perpendicular column": *Sacramento Weekly Union*, July 22, 1854, quoted in Rodman W. Paul, *California Gold: The Beginning of Mining in the Far West* (1947), 154–155.

239 "We descended their shaft": *Hutchings' Illustrated California Magazine* 2 (1857–1858): 147–149.

CHAPTER 28: CRIME AND PUNISHMENT

243 "In the immense crowds": Sarah Royce, *A Frontier Lady: Recollections of the Gold Rush and Early California*, edited by Ralph Henry Gabriel (1932), 109.

243 "No place in the world": Frank Soulé, John H. Gihon and James Nisbet, *The Annals of San Francisco* (1855), 645–666.

244 "Go West!": Horace Greeley to R. L. Sanderson, Nov. 15, 1871, Gilder Lehrman Institute for American History, https://www.gilderlehrman.org.

244 "Denison's Exchange": Bayard Taylor, *Eldorado, or, Adventures in the Path of Empire* (1850), 118–119.

246 "I put into this": Brands, *Age of Gold*, 255.

246 "I may have slept": Roger W. Lotchkin, *San Francisco, 1846–1856: From Hamlet to City* (1974), 175.

248 "It will be asked": Brands, *Age of Gold*, 261.

250 "The voyage from Sydney": Soulé et al., *Annals of San Francisco*, 565.

251 "We are determined": Soulé et al., *Annals of San Francisco*, 569.

252 "I believe the man had a fair and impartial trial": Soulé et al., *Annals of San Francisco*, 572–581.

CHAPTER 29: THE SPIRIT OF '87

254 "As Congress has failed": *Report of the Debates in the Convention of California on the Formation of the State Constitution, in September and October, 1849*, edited by J. Ross Browne (1850), 3.

255 "In a country where every white man": Allan Nevins, *Frémont: The West's Greatest Adventurer* (1928), 2:438.

255 "They are idle": *Report of Debates*, 137–141.

CHAPTER 30: TO BE DECENTLY POOR

258 "When we join our fortunes": Alan Rosenus, *General M. G. Vallejo and the Advent of the Americans* (1995), 90–91.

259 "All is lost": Madie Brown Emparan, *The Vallejos of California* (1968), 43.

259 "The bandits from Australia": Brands, *Age of Gold*, 321.

260 "I think I will know": Rosenus, *General Vallejo*, 230.

261 "For some time back": Frank F. Latta, *Joaquín Murrieta and His Horse Gangs* (1980), 36.

262 "When shot at": James F. Varley, *The Legend of Joaquín Murrieta: California's Gold Rush Bandit* (1995), 49–50.

262 "I have been engaged": John Boessenecker, *Gold Dust and Gunsmoke: Tales of Gold Rush Outlaws, Gunfighters, Lawmen, and Vigilantes* (1999), 91.

263 "He says he will take": Latta, *Joaquín Murrieta*, 474–479.

CHAPTER 31: WHERE CAN WE GO?

265 "The system they employed": Pérez Rosales, *California Adventure*, 44.

266 "insatiated search for revenge": *Daily Alta California*, May 30, 1850.

267 "The white man, to whom time is money": Peter Burnett message, Jan. 7, 1851, *Journals of the Legislature of the State of California: Senate* (1851), 15.

267 In hundreds of incidents: Benjamin Madley, *An American Genocide: The United States and the California Indian Catastrophe, 1846–1873* (2016). This is the most thorough—and harrowing—account of the killing. See especially the appendices.

267 "The savages were in the way": Bancroft, *History of California*, 7:474.

268 "He is a man of about 28 years": *The Mariposa Indian War, 1850–1851: Diaries of Robert Eccleston. The California Gold Rush, Yosemite, and the High Sierra* (1957), 106–107.

269 "Savage said to them": Lafayatte Houghton Bunnell, *Discovery of the Yosemite and the Indian War of 1851 Which Led to That Event* (1892), 11–12.

270 "From his long acquaintance": Bunnell, *Discovery of Yosemite*, 20–23.

272 "Burnt over 5000 bushels": *Mariposa Indian War*, 49, 67–68.

272   *"Kill me"*: Bunnell, *Discovery of Yosemite*, 172–173.

273   "We are afraid": Bunnell, *Discovery of Yosemite*, 33.

273   "Where can we now go": Bunnell, *Discovery of Yosemite*, 231.

CHAPTER 32: STEPHEN DOUGLAS'S BRAINSTORM

279   "Here, before God": Evan Carton, *Patriotic Treason: John Brown and the Soul of America* (2006), 82. Or Brown might have spoken a less dramatic version: "I pledge myself, with God's help, that I will devote my life to increasing hostility to slavery." Ibid. The former quotation was the one that became etched in American memory.

281   "Bleeding Kansas": David Potter, *The Impending Crisis, 1848–1861* (1976), 220; *New York Times*, May 30, 1856.

281   The image was misleading: See Dale E. Watts, "How Bloody Was Bleeding Kansas?" *Kansas History* (Summer 1995): 116–129.

CHAPTER 33: NORTH, SOUTH, WEST

283   Lincoln made the grand tour: The most thorough telling is Ralph Campanella, *Lincoln in New Orleans: The 1828–1831 Flatboat Voyages and Their Place in History* (2010).

284   Harpers Ferry: See Tony Horwitz, *Midnight Rising: John Brown and the Raid That Sparked the Civil War* (2011).

CHAPTER 34: FREE SOIL

289   "We cannot but feel": Junction Union excerpted in *The Big Blue Union*, Marysville, Kansas, Dec. 27, 1862.

CHAPTER 35: HELL ON WHEELS

291   construction of the Pacific railway: The best sources are David Haward Bain, *Empire Express: Building the First Transcontinental Railroad* (1999); Stephen E. Ambrose, *Nothing Like It in the World: The Men Who Built the Transcontinental Railroad, 1863–1869* (2000); Maury Klein, *Union Pacific: Birth of a Railroad, 1862–1893* (1987); and Richard White, *Railroaded: The Transcontinentals and the Making of Modern America* (2011).

292   "Four or five of the Irishmen": George T. Clark, *Leland Stanford* (1931), 213–214.

292 "Did they not build": Bain, *Empire Express*, 221.

292 "Those mountains over there": Ambrose, *Nothing Like It in the World*, 117.

293 Ropes anchored at the top of the cliff: Ambrose, *Nothing Like It in the World*, 156–157.

293 "Without them it would be impossible": Bain, *Empire Express*, 220.

293 "They really began to suffer": Bain, *Empire Express*, 362.

295 "We've got to clean the damn Indians out": Ambrose, *Nothing Like It in the World*, 223.

296 "Unless some relief": Bain, *Empire Express*, 351.

298 "Many an honest John": Ambrose, *Nothing Like It in the World*, 235–236.

299 "We send you greeting . . . our highest ambition": Clark, *Leland Stanford*, 244.

299 "Make it cheap . . . for acceptance": Bain, *Empire Express*, 447.

300 "We are cribbed in . . . not travel over too fast": J. D. B. Stillman, "The Last Tie," *Overland Monthly*, July 1869, 79–80.

301 "Durant is so strange": Bain, *Empire Express*, 651.

301 "THE LAST RAIL IS LAID": Klein, *Union Pacific*, 226.

CHAPTER 36: SAINTS AND SINNERS

304 "The cause of our exile": Leonard J. Arrington, *Brigham Young: American Moses* (1985), 128.

304 "We owe the United States nothing": *Niles National Register*, Nov. 22, 1845.

306 Perpetual Emigrating Fund: Also called the Perpetual Emigration Fund. On the fund, and for the fullest account of the handcart emigration, see David Roberts, *Devil's Gate: Brigham Young and the Great Mormon Handcart Tragedy* (2008).

307 "Take good hickory": Will Bagley, "'One Long Funeral March': A Revisionist's View of the Mormon Handcart Disasters," *Journal of Mormon History*, Dec. 2009, 58–71.

309 "There were 30 children": Roberts, *Devil's Gate*, 103–104.

309 "And thus has been": Bagley, "'One Long Funeral March,'" 76.

309 "They expect to get cold": Bagley, "'One Long Funeral March,'" 76–84, 89, 92, 111.

313 "those twin relics": Republican party platform, June 18, 1856, Papers of the Presidents.

313 "despotism of Brigham Young": Arrington, *Brigham Young*, 230.

314   "If the government dare": Juanita Brooks, *The Mountain Meadows Massacre* (1991 ed.), 138–139.
314   The decision to massacre the emigrants: The best recent account is Ronald W. Walker, Richard E. Turley Jr., and Glen M. Leonard, *Massacre at Mountain Meadows* (2008).

CHAPTER 37: ONCE WE WERE HAPPY

317   "I am a Lakota": *Black Elk Speaks: Being the Life Story of a Holy Man of the Oglala Sioux*, as told through John G. Neihardt (Flaming Arrow) by Nicholas Black Elk (2000 ed.), 6–9. This edition addresses the controversy surrounding Black Elk's famous memoir, including matters of translation and interpretation. Similar questions touch most memoirs. The present author judges the book no less reliable than many of those.
319   The biggest game included mammoths: A recent argument for climate change as the principal cause of the mammoth extinction is Eske Willerslev, John Davison, Mari Moora, Martin Zobel, Eric Coissac, Mary E. Edwards, Eline D. Lorenzen, et al., "Fifty Thousand Years of Arctic Vegetation and Megafaunal Diet," *Nature* 506 (Feb. 6, 2014): 47–51. The case for human causation is in Lewis J. Bartlett, David R. Williams, Graham W. Prescott, Andrew Balmford, Rhys E. Green, Anders Eriksson, Paul J. Valdes, Joy S. Singarayer, and Andrea Manica, "Robustness Despite Uncertainty: Regional Climate Data Reveal the Dominant Role of Humans in Explaining Global Extinctions of Late Quaternary Megafauna," *Ecography* 39, no. 2 (2015): 152–161.
319   Whether hunting or changing climate: On the extinction of American horses (and mammoths), see Andrew R. Solow, David L. Roberts, and Karen M. Robbirt, "On the Pleistocene Extinctions of Alaskan Mammoths and Horses," *Proceedings of the National Academy of Sciences of the United States of America* 103, no. 19 (May 9, 2006): 7351–7353.
320   The first horses acquired: On the spread of horses, Francis Haines, "Where Did the Plains Indians Get Their Horses?" *American Anthropologist*, n.s., 40, no. 1 (Jan.–Mar. 1938): 112–117.
320   "If you have horses": Colin G. Calloway, *One Vast Winter Count: The Native American West Before Lewis and Clark* (2003), 307.
322   "The Sioux tribes are those who hunt most": Richard White, "The Winning of the West: The Expansion of the Western Sioux in

the Eighteenth and Nineteenth Centuries," *Journal of American History* 65 (1978): 322.

322   the Sioux population quintupled: White, "Winning of the West," 329–330.

322   "The day is not far off": *Annual Report of the Commissioner of Indian Affairs, 1837–1838* (1838), 69.

323   "These lands once belonged": Mike Sajna, *Crazy Horse: The Life Behind the Legend* (2000), 77.

323   "What shall I do": Dee Brown, *Bury My Heart at Wounded Knee: An Indian History of the American West* (1970), 79.

323   "Kill all the Indians": Brown, *Bury My Heart*, 83, 90.

324   "I saw five squaws": Brown, *Bury My Heart*, 89–90.

324   "I did not see a body": Brown, *Bury My Heart*, 89–90.

325   "The white men have crowded": Brown, *Bury My Heart*, 130.

325   "A single company of regulars": Sajna, *Crazy Horse*, 196.

326   "One morning the crier": *Black Elk Speaks*, 40–45.

CHAPTER 38: THERE WOULD BE NO SOLDIERS LEFT

329   "pure beggars and poor devils": Lloyd Lewis, *Sherman: Fighting Prophet* (1993 ed.), 596.

330   "We must act": Bain, *Empire Express*, 311–312.

330   "If you don't choose": Henry M. Stanley, *My Early Travels and Adventures in America and Asia* (1895), 1:210–211.

331   "Go ahead in your own way": Stephen Ambrose, *Crazy Horse and Custer: The Parallel Lives of Two American Warriors* (1975), 281.

331   "The only good Indians": Paul Andrew Hutton, *Phil Sheridan and His Army* (1999 ed.), 180. Sheridan later denied having made the statement.

332   "I looked and saw . . . under the mother *sheo*'s": *Black Elk Speaks*, 18–29.

333   "When he went into a fight": *Black Elk Speaks*, 65–66.

334   "abominable compact": Sajna, *Crazy Horse*, 251.

335   "STRUCK IT AT LAST": Donald Jackson, *Custer's Gold: The United States Cavalry Expedition of 1874* (1972 ed.), 89.

337   "If anything happens . . . and got his scalp": *Black Elk Speaks*, 82–85.

339   "Hoka hey," the war chief cried: Ambrose, *Crazy Horse and Custer*, 401.

340   "We could not see much . . . into his forehead": *Black Elk Speaks*, 95–96.

CHAPTER 39: ADOBE WALLS

341   "I regard Custer's massacre": *New York Herald*, Sept. 2, 1876.

342   "anyone who wants to fight me" Ernest Wallace and E. Adamson Hoebel, *The Comanches: Lords of the South Plains* (1952), 4.

342   "He makes but an awkward figure": Wallace and Hoebel, *The Comanches*, 47–49.

342   Quanah Parker: The most gripping account of Quanah Parker is S. C. Gwynne, *Empire of the Summer Moon: Quanah Parker and the Rise and Fall of the Comanches, the Most Powerful Indian Tribe in American History* (2010). Another good one is Bill Neely, *The Last Comanche Chief: The Life and Times of Quanah Parker* (1995). On the Comanches generally, see T. R. Fehrenbach, *Comanches: The Destruction of a People* (1974), and Thomas W. Kavanagh, *Comanche Political History: An Ethnohistorical Perspective, 1706–1875* (1996).

343   "When I told them": Seth Hathaway, "The Adventures of a Buffalo Hunter," *Frontier Times*, Dec. 1931, reprinted in Randolph B. Campbell, ed., *Texas History Documents* (1997), 2:8–12.

346   "Nothing of interest occurred": Hathaway, "Adventures of a Buffalo Hunter."

348   The buffalo had been under pressure: The best account is Andrew C. Isenberg, *The Destruction of the Bison: An Environmental History, 1750–1920* (2000). But see also Dan Flores, "Bison Ecology and Bison Diplomacy: The Southern Plains from 1800 to 1850," *Journal of American History* 73, no. 2 (Sept. 1991): 465–485.

348   "Those white men can't shoot you": Wilbur Sturtevant Nye, *Bad Medicine and Good: Tales of the Kiowas* (1962), 179.

348   "We charged pretty fast": Brown, *Bury My Heart*, 266.

349   "It was each man for himself . . . of their medicine": Hathaway, "Adventures of a Buffalo Hunter."

351   "The buffalo hunters were too much": W. S. Nye, *Carbine and Lance: The Story of Old Fort Sill* (1969 ed.), 191.

351   "All the boys went out": Hathaway, "Adventures of a Buffalo Hunter."

CHAPTER 40: LOST RIVER

354   "General, we can make peace quick": Jeff C. Riddle, *The Indian History of the Modoc War* (1914), 64–67. This memoir draws on Jeff Riddle's memories, those of his mother and father, and some

official documents. Whether the conversations he quotes verbatim, forty years after the fact, are precisely accurate is open to question. But no more so than is the case with many memoirs. And they doubtless capture the essence of what was said.

357   "I for one": Riddle, *Indian History of the Modoc War*, 69–72.

358   "Do not go": A. B. Meacham, *Wigwam and War-Path* (1875), 467–470.

359   "If you kill all these soldiers . . . The soldiers are coming": Riddle, *Indian History of the Modoc War*, 90–97; Meacham, *Wigwam and War-Path*, 482–500.

361   "All the Modocs are involved": *Eyewitnesses to the Indian Wars, 1865–1890: The Army and the Indian*, edited by Peter Cozzens (2005), 113; Perry D. Jamieson, *Crossing the Deadly Ground: United States Army Tactics, 1865–1899* (1994), 32.

CHAPTER 41: THE PRIDE OF YOUNG JOSEPH

362   "The Nez Percé comes into history": *New York Times*, Oct. 15, 1877.

363   "There was no stain": Joseph, "An Indian's Views of Indian Affairs," *North American Review* 128, no. 269 (Apr. 1879): 415–429.

365   "They stole a great many horses": Joseph, "An Indian's Views of Indian Affairs."

367   "Why do you sit here": Joseph, "An Indian's Views of Indian Affairs."

369   "It is cold": Elliott West, *The Last Indian War: The Nez Perce Story* (2011), 282–292. This book, the most thorough account of the Nez Perce war and its context, raises questions about the verbatim authenticity of the surrender speech. But the gist of Joseph's remarks is certainly accurate, and this version was the one that was repeated in newspapers all around the country. The most recent account of the Nez Perce war is Daniel J. Sharfstein, *Thunder in the Mountains: Chief Joseph, Oliver Otis Howard, and the Nez Perce War* (2017).

CHAPTER 42: ABILENE

373   No image in American history: An intriguing explanation of the power of the cowboy image is in Larry McMurtry, "Take My Saddle from the Wall," *Harper's Magazine*, Sept. 1, 1968.

375 "In short, it was to establish . . . toward completion": Joseph G. McCoy, *Historic Sketches of the Cattle Trade of the West and Southwest* (1874), 40–51.

378 "The ordinary trail-herd . . . over the prairie": "The Old Cattle Trails," in *Prose and Poetry of the Live Stock Industry of the United States* (1904), 1:532–534.

382 "Corn bread, mast-fed bacon . . . and death": McCoy, *Historic Sketches*, 10–13, 138.

383 The most famous of all the gunfights: Paula Mitchell Marks, *And Die in the West: The Story of the O.K. Corral Gunfight* (1989). On the nature and incidence of gunfights, an encyclopedist of the form has concluded, perhaps ruefully, "If showdown duels were the only legitimate gunfights, this would be a very short book." Bill O'Neal, *Encyclopedia of Western Gunfighters* (1979), 3.

384 "At frontier towns where are centered . . . and tenderest memory": McCoy, *Historic Sketches*, 120–121, 138–141.

CHAPTER 43: HARD LESSON

388 "Dear Brother": James S. Brisbin, *The Beef Bonanza, or How to Get Rich on the Plains* (1881), 59–70.

389 "Sixteenth Street": Ernest Staples Osgood, *The Day of the Cattleman* (1929), 96.

391 "Cowboys don't have as soft a time": Osgood, *Day of the Cattleman*, 229.

CHAPTER 44: INTO THE GREAT UNKNOWN

395 "Long ago, there was a great": *Report of J. W. Powell: Exploration of the Colorado River of the West* (1875), 7. The classic account of the life and feats of Powell is Wallace Stegner, *Beyond the Hundredth Meridian: John Wesley Powell and the Second Opening of the West* (1954). More recent is Donald Worster, *A River Running West: The Life of John Wesley Powell* (2001).

396 "The good people of Green River City": *Report of J. W. Powell*, 8–25.

401 "We start up a gulch": *Report of J. W. Powell*, 33–34.

402 "We pass through a region": *Report of J. W. Powell*, 46, 58, 76–100.

408 "We glide rapidly along the foot": *Report of J. W. Powell*, 100–102.

CHAPTER 45: THE ARID REGION

412   "The redemption": J. W. Powell, *Report on the Lands of the Arid Region* (1879 ed.), vii–31.

413   "The landscapes of the Santa Clara Valley . . . the magnificent dome-head": John Muir, *The Yosemite* (1912), 4, 8–9, 21–22, 65–66, 77–78, 87, 131–132.

417   "public use, resort, and recreation": Act of June 30, 1864 (13 Stat., 325).

418   "The intelligent American": "The Wonders of the West II—More About the Yellowstone," *Scribners' Monthly*, Feb. 1872, 388–396.

418   "The entire area": Remarks by Congressman Dunnell on H.R. 764, in *Preliminary Report of the United States Geological Survey of Montana and Portions of Adjacent Territories*, by F. V. Hayden (1872), 163–164.

419   "It is important to do something": Jay Cooke, in Richard A. Bartlett, *Nature's Yellowstone* (1989 ed.), 207–208.

419   "The effect of this measure . . . in the world": Aubrey L. Haines, *Yellowstone National Park: Its Exploration and Establishment* (1974), 127–128.

CHAPTER 46: MORE LIKE US

422   Geronimo, the last of the holdouts: Robert M. Utley tells the Geronimo story in *Geronimo* (2012).

423   "We destroyed everything": Recollection by Jacob Wilks, in Frank N. Schubert, *Voices of the Buffalo Soldiers* (2003), 42.

423   "The officers say": Frances M. A. Roe, *Army Letters from an Officer's Wife, 1871–1888* (1981 ed.), 65.

423   "This is the best arranged . . . to enlist": "The Comanches and the Peace Policy," *The Nation*, Oct. 30, 1873. An alternative, or complementary, explanation for the label "buffalo soldiers" is given by William H. Leckie, who contends that it connoted respect—the same kind of respect the Plains Indians felt for the buffalo. *The Buffalo Soldiers: A Narrative of the Negro Cavalry in the West* (1967), 26.

424   "I immediately attacked": Stance to B. M. Custer, May 26, 1870, in Schubert, *Voices of the Buffalo Soldiers*, 36–37.

425   "domestic dependent nations": Cherokee Nation v. Georgia, 30 U.S. (5 Peters) 1 (1831).

425   "If they remain": Jackson's annual message, Dec. 8, 1829, Papers of the Presidents.

426   Dawes Severalty Act: Janet A. McDonnell, *The Dispossession of the American Indian, 1887–1934* (1991), 1–18; Stuart Banner, *How the Indians Lost Their Land: Law and Power on the Frontier* (2005), 257–290.

427   "The preparations for the settlement . . . have just begun": William Willard Howard, "The Rush to Oklahoma," *Harper's Weekly*, May 18, 1889.

CHAPTER 47: IT GREW VERY COLD

433   "I was frightened": *Black Elk Speaks*, 108.

434   "There were more people . . . dance with them": *Black Elk Speaks*, 178–183.

436   "They would not stop . . . to run away": *Black Elk Speaks*, 191–201.

CHAPTER 48: LESS CORN AND MORE HELL

440   "Stand at Cumberland Gap": Frederick Jackson Turner, "The Significance of Frontier in American History," in Turner, *The Frontier in American History* (1921), 12, 37–38.

442   "The hot winds burned up": *The Populist Mind*, edited by Norman Pollack (1967), 34–35.

443   "Take a man": *The Populist Mind*, 3–4.

444   "Wall Street owns the country": John D. Hicks, *The Populist Revolt: A History of the Farmers' Alliance and the People's Party* (1931), 160.

445   "What's the matter with Kansas?": William Allen White, "What's the Matter with Kansas?" in *The Autobiography of William Allen White* (1946), 280–283.

447   "Having behind us": William Jennings Bryan, *Selections*, edited by Ray Ginger (1967), 46.

CHAPTER 49: BONANZA

448   "When the river crosses": William Allen White, "The Business of a Wheat Farm," *Scribner's Magazine*, Nov. 1897, 531–548.

CHAPTER 50: ROUGH RIDING

456   "Have you and Theodore": Brands, *TR*, 327.

456   "He had served in General Miles's . . . unmoved equanimity": Theodore Roosevelt, *The Rough Riders* (1899), 7–31.

460   "The men can go in . . . ever was in battle": Brands, *TR*, 342–343.

461   "Yesterday we struck . . . like a guidon": Brands, *TR*, 349, 356.

462   "The Mauser bullets": Roosevelt, *Rough Riders*, 120.

462   "The man in command . . . great day of my life": Brands, *TR*, 357.

CHAPTER 51: WEST TAKES EAST

465   "If Colonel Roosevelt is nominated": Brands, *TR*, 364, 397.

467   "That damned cowboy": H. H. Kohlsaat, *From McKinley to Harding: Personal Recollections of Our Presidents* (1923), 101.

CHAPTER 52: CASHING IN

468   "Some of these pages . . . hero without wings": Owen Wister, *The Virginian: A Horseman of the Plains* (1902), vi–ix, 4.

470   "the Cowmen and boys": Andy Adams, *The Log of a Cowboy: A Narrative of the Old Trail Days* (1903), dedication page, 381–382.

471   "No gift": Roosevelt, *Rough Riders*, 318, 320.

471   *Harper's* called him . . . "Cowboys are cash with me": Peggy and Harold Samuels, *Remington: The Complete Prints* (1990), 33.

CHAPTER 53: JOHN MUIR'S LAST STAND

473   "Forest protection": Roosevelt, annual message, Dec. 3, 1901, Papers of the Presidents.

474   "I do not want anyone": Linnie Marsh Wolfe, *Son of the Wilderness: The Life of John Muir* (2003 ed.), 290.

474   "John Muir met me": Theodore Roosevelt, *An Autobiography* (1913), 347–349.

476   "These temple destroyers": Muir, *The Yosemite*, 261–262.

CHAPTER 54: THE LONG, LONG TRAIL

481   "A people's dream died there": *Black Elk Speaks*, 207.

INDEX

H. W. Brands holds the Jack S. Blanton Sr. Chair in History at the University of Texas at Austin. A *New York Times* bestselling author, he was a finalist for the Pulitzer Prize in biography for *The First American* and *Traitor to His Class*. He lives in Austin, Texas.

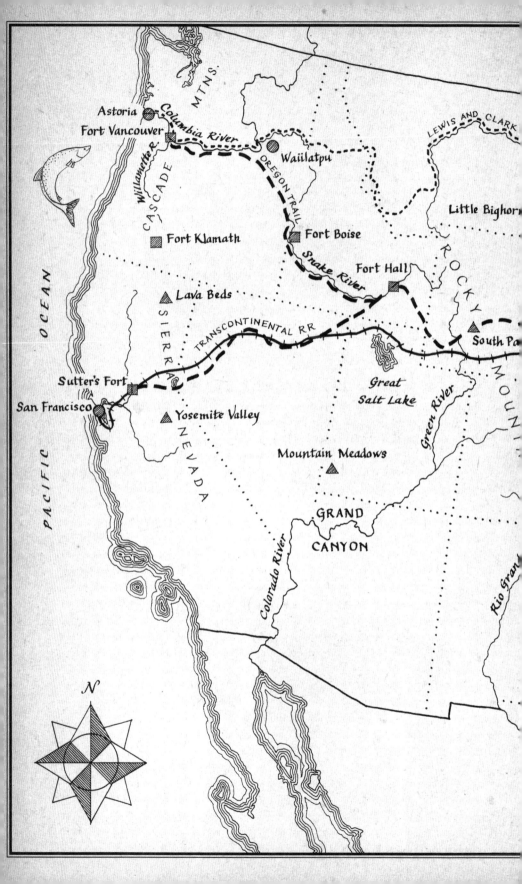

Astoria
Fort Vancouver
Columbia River
CASCADE MTNS.
Willamette R.
OREGON TRAIL
Waiilatpu
LEWIS AND CLARK
Little Bighorn
Fort Klamath
Fort Boise
Fort Hall
Snake River
ROCKY
Lava Beds
SIERRA
TRANSCONTINENTAL RR
South Pa
Sutter's Fort
Great
Salt Lake
Green River
MOUNTI
San Francisco
NEVADA
Yosemite Valley
PACIFIC
OCEAN
Mountain Meadows
GRAND
Colorado River
CANYON
Rio Gran
N